M000247494

FORMS OF NATIONHOOD

RICHARD HELGERSON

FORMS OF NATIONHOOD

The Elizabethan Writing

of England

THE UNIVERSITY OF CHICAGO PRESS

Chicago and London

The University of Chicago Press, Chicago 60637
The University of Chicago Press, Ltd., London
© 1992 by The University of Chicago
All rights reserved. Published 1992
Paperback edition 1994
Printed in the United States of America

00 99 98 97 96 95 94   5 4 3 2

ISBN (cloth): 0–226–32633–0
ISBN (paper): 0–226–32634–9

This publication has been supported by a grant from the National
Endowment for the Humanities, an independent federal agency.

"Barbarous Tongues" in chapter 1 was originally published in a
different form in *The Historical Renaissance,* edited by Heather Dubrow
and Richard Strier (Chicago: University of Chicago Press, 1988).

Library of Congress Cataloging-in-Publication Data

Helgerson, Richard.
  Forms of nationhood: The Elizabethan writing of England / Richard
Helgerson.
    p. cm.
  Includes bibliographical references and index.
  1. English literature—Early modern, 1500–1700—History and
criticism. 2. Politics and literature—England—History—16th
century. 3. Literature and society—England—History—16th century.
4. National characteristics, English, in literature. 5. Great
Britain—History—Elizabeth, 1558–1603. 6. England—
Civilization—16th century. 7. Nationalism in literature.
8. England in literature. I. Title.
PR428.P6H44   1992
820.9′358′09031—dc20   91–28847
                                                           CIP

⊗ The paper used in this publication meets the minimum requirements
of the American National Standard for Information Sciences—Permanence
of Paper for Printed Library Materials, ANSI Z39.48–1984.

For Jessica

Contents

Acknowledgments ix

Note on the Text xi

Introduction: The Kingdom of Our Own Language 1

1 Two Versions of Gothic 19
Barbarous Tongues 25
The Politics of Chivalric Romance 40
A Miltonic Revision 59

2 Writing the Law 63
Plans for an English *Corpus Juris* 73
Reporting the Unwritten Law 78
The Form of Coke's *Institutes* 88
Uncouth Learning and Professional Pride 101

3 The Land Speaks 105
Maps and the Signs of Authority 108
From Court to Country 125
The Ideology of Place and Particularity 131
The Muse on Progress 139
Chorography and Whiggery 146

4 The Voyages of a Nation 149
Class, Nation, and Camões 155
Commodity and Vent 163
Merchants, Gentlemen, and Their Genres 171
Spain's Tyrannical Ambition 181
Posthumous Writings and Rewritings 187

5 Staging Exclusion 193
Popular Revolt 204
Carnival and Clowns 215
Losing the Common Touch 228
Purged from Barbarism 240

6 Apocalyptics and Apologetics 247
Antichrist and the Suffering Elect 254
Defending the Ecclesiastical Polity 269
In the Body of the Beast 283

Afterword: Engendering the Nation-State 295

Notes 303

Index 351

Acknowledgments

My chief debt, acknowledged more particularly in the notes, is to the men and women who have preceded me in the half-dozen fields explored by this book. Scholarship is always a collaborative undertaking, but, as a newcomer to several of these fields, I am more than usually aware of my dependence on my predecessors.

I have many personal debts as well. My colleagues at Santa Barbara—Lee Bliss, Paddy Fumerton, Don Guss, Alan Liu, Michael O'Connell, Mark Rose, and Garrett Stewart—have been willing and helpful readers. The book has also benefited from the advice and encouragement of colleagues elsewhere: Jackson Cope, Heather Dubrow, Ned Duval, Stephen Greenblatt, Kent Hieatt, Fritz Levy, Mac Pigman, Len Tennenhouse, and Don Wayne; from the suggestions of its official press readers: Christopher Hill, Leah Marcus, and Steven Mullaney; from the comments of audiences at the various universities and conferences where bits of it have been given as talks; and from the support of my principal partner in conversation, Marie-Christine Helgerson.

The Guggenheim Foundation, the Huntington Library, the University of California, Santa Barbara, and the California Institute of Technology have supplied valuable material assistance. The editors of the *Modern Language Quarterly, Representations,* and *The Yearbook of English Studies* have allowed me to reprint material they first published in a different form. Permission to reproduce figures 2, 3, 7, 9, and 11 has been granted by the British Library. The National Portrait Gallery, London, has permitted me to reproduce figure 4. All the other illustrations are reproduced with the kind allowance of the Huntington Library, San Marino, California.

Note on the Text

Except when quoting from Spenser's verse, where archaism has authorial warrant, I regularize spelling and (less systematically) punctuation in all quotations. This is true of quotations from both older and more recent works. Thus a twentieth-century British scholar who wrote "honour" will find himself saying "honor" in this book. I also silently expand abbreviations and translate most material from foreign languages.

I supply a full bibliographic identification the first time a work is cited in each chapter. Subsequent references are kept as brief as possible, often only to page numbers for modern books and signature (or, in the case of Coke's *First Institute,* leaf) numbers for sixteenth- and seventeenth-century books. In the notes, titles appear as spelled on the work cited with the result that the title of a work may look different in the text than it does in the note.

Dates inserted parenthetically into the text sometimes appear more precise than they are. For works published shortly following their composition, I usually give the date of the first printed edition. For works that have never been printed or that were not printed until some considerable time after they were written, I give a conjectural date of composition. And for plays, I give the date under which the play is listed in the *Annals of English Drama, 975–1700,* edited by Alfred Harbage, S. Schoenbaum, and S. S. Wagonheim, 3rd ed. (London: Routledge, 1989). I leave the early seventeenth-century county chorographies, most of which long remained in manuscript and whose composition often cannot be fixed even in a particular decade, undated. Where an exact date matters to my argument, I try to establish it.

Introduction

THE KINGDOM OF OUR OWN LANGUAGE

Spenser's *Faerie Queene.*
Coke's *Institutes of the Laws of England.*
Camden's *Britannia.*
Speed's *Theater of the Empire of Great Britain.*
Drayton's *Poly-Olbion.*
Hakluyt's *Principal Navigations of the English Nation.*
Shakespeare's English history plays.
Hooker's *Laws of Ecclesiastical Polity.*
These texts belong to different fields. But they also belong together. All were written by men born within a few years of one another, from 1551 to 1564. All take England—its land, its people, its institutions, and its history—as their subject. All are massive in size and scope. And, with the exception of Speed's *Theater* and Drayton's *Poly-Olbion,* all have had a major influence on some large area of English life. Never before or since have so many works of such magnitude and such long-lasting effect been devoted to England by the members of a single generation. Nor was this generation's contribution to the writing of England limited to the work of these eight men. Many others— Sidney, Lyly, Daniel, Warner, Peele, Bacon, Cowell, Finch, Greville, Hayward, Norden, Raleigh, Chapman, Marlowe, Sandys, and Andrewes come quickly to mind—participated in what retrospectively looks like a concerted generational project.[1]

This project is my subject. I was directed to it by a sentence from a letter Spenser wrote Gabriel Harvey in 1580. "Why a God's name," Spenser exclaimed, "may not we, as else the Greeks, have the kingdom of our own language?"[2] I had been working for some time on the authorial self-presentation of Spenser, Sidney, and the other young poets of their generation and had been struck by their evident anxiety and uncertainty.[3] These were the men who got English poetry going again after nearly two centuries of only sporadic accomplishment. Yet

1

the roles they assumed—the roles of lover, prodigal, and shepherd—
revealed a tension between their literary undertaking and the claims of
the state to whose service both their humanist upbringing and the
exigencies of the "new monarchy" had directed them. One way of
dealing with this tension, the way characteristically adopted by the
courtly amateurs, was to enclose and depreciate their own poetic accomplishment, to label their poems as the outbreak of licentious
youth, something they would gladly renounce in favor of more worthy employment, if only worthier employment could be had. Another
way of dealing with the tension, the way taken by poets of laureate
ambition, such as Spenser, Daniel, and Drayton, was to make poetry
itself serve, if not the state, then the nation. In chivalric romance,
historical narrative, and topographical description, these poets sought
to articulate a national community whose existence and eminence
would then justify their desire to become its literary spokesmen. What
Spenser's sentence reveals is both the difficulty of even that more
dutiful enterprise and the sense of need to which it responded.

Consider for a start those last six words, "the kingdom of our own
language." They carry us from an essentially dynastic conception of
communal identity ("the kingdom") to an assertion of what we recognize as one of the bases of postdynastic nationalism ("our own
language"). A kingdom whose boundaries are determined by the language of its inhabitants is no longer a kingdom in the purely dynastic
sense, but neither, so long as it goes on identifying itself with the
person of a hereditary monarch, is it quite a nation. Which is the poet
to represent? Nor are possible competitors for representational attention exhausted by the extremes of "kingdom" and "language," for
between them comes that first-person plural "our" with its suggestion
of shared participation and possession. King, people, and language.
Which, if any, is to be given priority? From this formulation it is
impossible to tell. But even a small acquaintance with the history of
England in the next century or so will remind us that conflict was to
develop along precisely the lines suggested by those few words: between royal prerogative, subjects' rights, and the cultural system.[4]

For the conflict to get started, we do not even have to leave
Spenser's sentence. No sooner are those last six words reinserted into
their original context than they lose their evenhanded representational
character and are captured by a purpose that upsets the delicate dy-
namic equilibrium that had been so neatly, though precariously,
achieved. In Spenser's impatient question, "the kingdom" does not,
after all, initiate the semiautonomous noun phrase we have been re-

garding, a stable syntactic and conceptual entity to which further qualification (as, for example, "the *glorious* kingdom of our own language") might be added. No, rather it belongs with the verb *have*. Spenser wants to "have the kingdom" of his own language. He wants to exercise sovereignty over English, wants to make it do what he wants it to do. Of the triangularly balanced forces that weigh against one another in "the kingdom of our own language," Spenser selects one and gives it priority. "Our" makes a claim to omnipotence that reduces "kingdom" to the role of action and "language" to that of object. But this is no longer a communal "our" standing indifferently for all speakers of English. As Spenser makes his bid to become the absolute lawgiver for English poetry, his first-person plural pushes in the direction of a royal "we," an expanded and empowered "I."[5] With the individual writer as a fourth corner, the triangle of king, people, and language breaks into a square. And not even this enlarged structure remains stable or static. Instead of an ideal representation, Spenser's sentence provides a dramatic expression of ambition, cultural envy, and frustration. The Greeks had the kingdom of their own language. Why, Spenser asks, can't we? Why must we be consigned to perpetual subjection and inferiority? This pressure, this tension, this conflict of aspiration and insecurity, brings us close to the crisis from which both Elizabethan poetry and the larger project of English self-representation emerged, close to the desperately hopeful sense that, were England to rival the greatness of Greece and Rome, something decisive needed to be done.

And what was that something? To have the kingdom of their own language. To govern the very linguistic system, and perhaps more generally the whole cultural system, by which their own identity and their own consciousness were constituted. To remake it, and presumably themselves as well, according to some ideal pattern. An extraordinary ambition! But as extraordinary as it is, that ambition is no more extraordinary than the historical circumstances that prompted it. For Spenser to feel he had to have the kingdom of his own language and for that feeling to be as widely shared as it was in his generation, a very considerable distance must already have been traveled. A half century earlier the sufficiency or insufficiency of the English language and of English cultural institutions generally would not have mattered so much.[6] To men born in the 1550s and 1560s, things English came to matter with a special intensity both because England itself mattered more than it had and because other sources of identity and cultural authority mattered less.

The large political shape of this change is well known. "We are
familiar," G. R. Elton wrote some forty years ago, "with the notion
that the sixteenth century saw the creation of the modern sovereign
state: the duality of state and church was destroyed by the victory of
the state, the crown triumphed over its rivals, parliamentary statute
triumphed over the abstract law of Christendom, and a self-contained
national unit came to be, not the tacitly accepted necessity it had been
for some time, but the consciously desired goal."[7] Elton points to the
1530s as the crucial moment of change. In that decade parliament
declared England "an empire," severed the ties that bound the English church to the church of Rome, and established the king as
"supreme head" of both church and state. And in that decade, if Elton
is right, a "revolution in government" transformed the essentially
household rule of what was still thought of as the king's estate into a
genuinely national administration. During the next half century, as
these changes were being variously resisted and reaffirmed, there was
a growing and widespread anxiety, very like what we encounter in
Spenser's brief exclamation, concerning England's cultural identity.
Sovereignty of this new sort put a greater burden on a specifically
national sense of self than any existing evidence of national accomplishment could easily sustain. England was now calling itself an empire. Where were the signs of imperial stature?

Spenser's own *Shepheardes Calender* and *Faerie Queene* supplied
part of the answer. Here at last was an English poet to rival Virgil,
English poems that could be set by the *Eclogues* and the *Aeneid*. But
England needed more than a Virgilian poet: King Henry and his royal
servants had made a revolution; their Elizabethan successors were left
to make sense of the result. This was a task not just for one poet, but
for a whole generation of writers. The list of texts with which I began
is strong evidence that the younger Elizabethans, those men who
grew up under the Elizabethan settlement, accepted the task as a
generation. This does not mean that they were all working in collaboration with one another, though in many individual areas they did
collaborate. Nor does it mean that they agreed about much more than
that England needed to be written in large, comprehensive, and foun-
dational works and that they were the ones to do the writing. But even
so limited an agreement is significant. It reveals the outline of a shared
generational location.[8]

In the six chapters that make up the body of this book, I examine
the younger Elizabethans' response to the demands and opportunities
afforded by their generational location. Each chapter enters a different

field and focuses on a different text or group of texts. The first chapter concerns poetry and is divided into two parts, one on the prosodic form of all Elizabethan verse and the other on the generic form of the most ambitious single Elizabethan poem, Spenser's *Faerie Queene.* Law is the subject of the second chapter; its principal texts are Coke's *Reports* and *Institutes.* In the third chapter I take up the broad and seemingly heterogeneous category of cartographic and chorographic description and look particularly at Camden's *Britannia,* Speed's *Theater,* Drayton's *Poly-Olbion,* and a slightly earlier book that informed all three: Christopher Saxton's atlas of England and Wales. Hakluyt's *Voyages* is the central text in the fourth chapter, which deals with England's overseas expansion and the relation of that expansion to national self-representation. The last two chapters are about a new institution and a newly reconstituted one: the theater and the church. Shakespeare's English history plays provide the main text for chapter five; Hooker's *Laws of Ecclesiastical Polity* does the same for chapter six. Though the six chapters are together meant to achieve a cumulative effect that none would have alone, they are essentially separate ventures. Part, in fact, of their cumulative effect should be a sense of that separateness. By date of birth, the men whose books I am studying belonged to the same generation. And by social and economic status, they had enough in common to respond to that similarity in birthdate in roughly comparable ways. But as poets, lawyers, chorographers, propagandists for overseas expansion, playwrights, and churchmen, they also belonged to different discursive communities and, as a result, wrote England differently.

The boundaries between such communities were erected and reinforced as a function of the Elizabethan writing of England. In observing them, we attend to the pluralist communal base of the early modern nation-state, its resistance to the hegemony of either the crown or any other interest. But unexpected similarities nevertheless link the divided communities, suggesting that the walls between them were less solid than they sometimes seem. To illustrate these similarities, my six chapters are arrayed in pairs. The first two chapters show the cultural dialectic made available (indeed, made inescapable) by Renaissance humanism, the dialectic between antiquity and the middle ages, at work in both poetry and the law. From this temporal concern with England's relation to one or another of two possible pasts, the next chapters turn to England's identity in space, its appearance on the map, whether the map of England itself in chapter three or the map of the world in chapter four. It is no accident that both Camden's

Britannia and Hakluyt's *Voyages* were prompted by correspondence with the great Flemish mapmaker Abraham Ortelius. A common cartographic impulse underlay both. And, finally, in chapters five and six issues concerning the narrative construction of national identity, and particularly the relation of narrative to social hierarchy, emerge in theater and church. Shakespeare and Hooker may not much resemble one another, but the writing of England both opposed was in many respects the same.

Crossing boundaries, as well as observing them, has been part of the methodological undertaking of this book. Two of its six chapters, the first and the fifth, are concerned with texts that normally belong to my home discipline of literary history. But the other chapters take me into territories inhabited by historians of other sorts: legal, cartographic, economic, and ecclesiastical. I cannot pretend to rival these experts, on whose work I am heavily dependent, at their own business. But I do regard texts that belong more properly to them from a perspective that is usually not theirs. As a literary historian, I am more preoccupied with form than are other kinds of historians. I assume— an assumption that is tested throughout the book—that discursive forms matter, that they have a meaning and effect that can sometimes complement but that can also contradict the manifest content of any particular work. Forms in this view are as much agents as they are structures. They make things happen. Given my sense of the importance of forms, of their part in constituting the nation, I attend as closely to them as I do to the texts that embody them. Instead of describing the book as concerned with a set of texts, one could as accurately describe it as concerned with a set of forms: rime and chivalric romance in the first chapter, the law report and institute in the second, chorography in the third, the voyage (as a discursive form) in the fourth, the national history play in the fifth, and the apology in the sixth. But these two concerns, the formal and the textual, are not really separable. Form and text are the *langue* and *parole*, the enabling system and the concrete realization, of a single interdependent whole. Without texts, forms are unknowable; without forms, texts are unproducible.

Even a quick glance over the following pages will, however, show that, so far, my introductory list of texts and forms is seriously incomplete. Chapter six considers not only apology and Hooker's *Laws* but also apocalyptic discourse and a book published at about the time the younger Elizabethans were born, Foxe's *Acts and Monuments*. National history plays from the Henslowe companies figure in chapter five alongside Shakespeare's, and in chapter three chronicle competes for attention with chorography. Other chapters go still further afield. Tasso's *Gerusalemme Liberata* is discussed at some length in chapter one; Justinian's *Corpus Juris Civilis* is a constant point of reference in chapter two; and in chapter four Camões's *Lusiads* gets a whole section to itself. What is all this doing here? Its inclusion is the result of another methodological assumption. My literary training may have made me a formalist, but I have tried, even when looking at literary texts, to be a historical formalist. I do not suppose, as literary critics often have, that certain forms have an intrinsic or universal meaning, an ineradicable aesthetic appeal. On the contrary, I assume that meanings and aesthetic affinities are historically established and historically maintained. They arise from the quite specific relations in which particular texts and forms are enmeshed at some particular time and place. If a chivalric romance meant something different, functioned to construct a different social and political order, in England in the 1590s than it had done in Italy in the 1510s or in France in the 1170s, it was because there had been changes in the material conditions of its production and reception and also—and this is the point I want to emphasize here—because the discursive forms it opposed had changed. The meaning of chivalric romance in the 1590s was determined by a new opposition to epic, and *Gerusalemme Liberata* was the poem that made that new opposition and its ideological import apparent. I thus read Spenser in relation to Tasso, chivalric romance in relation to epic. And though the nature of the relation changes from chapter to chapter, in each a historically specific play of differences is central to my argument.

Like chivalric romance, every form I discuss depended for its meaning and its effect on its difference from some openly or latently competing form. Rime opposed quantitative verse; common-law reports opposed Roman-law institutes; chorographical description opposed chronicle history; voyage, like chivalric romance (though to a quite different end), opposed epic; Shakespeare's kind of English history play opposed Henslowe's; and apologetic discourse opposed apocalyptic. I do not pretend that one binary opposition, an opposition that could often result in co-option, exhausts the meaning of any of these kinds. Each entered into signifying relations in many directions. But I do claim that the particular differences I attend to were active and meaningful for at least some important contemporary audience and that they usually remained active for decades and sometimes for centuries. As evidence of the continuing effect of these texts, these forms, and these differences, I also cite (usually in a concluding section) material from later periods as well. So, with texts brought in from earlier times or foreign places to reveal a synchronic system of differences and post-sixteenth-century texts brought in to show that system's extension in time, I have ended by putting the Elizabethan texts with which I began in a much broader, more heterogeneous company.

In choosing the title *Forms of Nationhood,* I was thinking of the many discursive kinds embodied in the fat books younger Elizabethans wrote about England. But I was also thinking of the different social and political orderings those books imagined and helped bring into existence. "Nought shall make us rue, / If England to itself do rest but true." These lines from the end of Shakespeare's *King John* suppose, as does most nationalist discourse, a stable and unified national self to which English men and women can remain true. But the England Shakespeare and his contemporaries represented was as various as their representations of it. Not even its name remained fixed. Following the lead of King James, John Speed called the entity he described the "Empire of Great Britain." Camden adopted rather the ancient Roman name and wrote of "Britannia." Spenser's England was alternatively "Britayne land" and "Faery lond"; Warner's was "Albion"; and Drayton's, "Poly-Olbion." Nor was the national territory designated by these names any more stable. For many Englishmen, "England"—or whatever they called it—included Wales. Did it also include Ireland and Scotland? For some it did; for others it didn't. And such uncertainty concerning name and territory points back to the still more pervasive uncertainties I teased out of Spenser's phrase, "the kingdom of our own language." Was the nation—itself a problematic though widely used term—to be identified with the king, with the people (or some subdivision of the people), or with the cultural system as figured in language, law, religion, history, economy, and social order? Which of these or what combination of them was to define and control the state? In every chapter such questions arise, and in every chapter formal differences are discovered to have been the carriers of specifically political meaning.

I was no doubt predisposed to make this discovery. I share, after all, the expectation common among literary critics of my generation that issues of power are likely to be involved in any human exchange. But I had not expected the evidence to be quite so clear, nor could I have foreseen the particular connections of discursive form and political meaning I found, connections that sometimes seem as arbitrary as those linking phonetic signifiers to the concepts they conventionally stand for. Nothing about the acoustically or visually perceptible characteristics of the two prosodic forms I discuss in the first chapter would have led me to expect that royal absolutism would be associated with one and a government limited by rights established under the common law with the other, but such an association was in fact made and came in time to feel natural: altogether unarbitrary. Other connections, particularly those concerning the literary texts I already knew, were no less surprising. I didn't expect Spenser's apparent devotion to the queen to be qualified in quite the way a reading of his poem in the light of Tasso's insisted that it be; I didn't anticipate that *Poly-Olbion*'s strongest generic and political affiliations would be not with other literary works but with the atlases and chorographies of Saxton, Camden, and Speed; and I neither expected nor wanted to make the argument concerning Shakespeare that the Henslowe plays obliged me to make. Indeed, I had planned to say the opposite and still feel upended by the evidence. With Coke, Hakluyt, and Hooker, I had less chance for surprise because my expectations were less precise. But, again, when I placed them in relation to a historically signifying other—Coke to Justinian (and to Bacon), Hakluyt to Camões, and Hooker to Foxe—the political shapes their books give the nation snapped clear in ways I could not have predicted.

And there was another surprise. Though the forms of nationhood imagined by these various texts are many, the political issues that engage them can, in a gross and not quite exclusive way, be reduced to just two. One concerns the monarch and monarchic power. The other involves the inclusion or exclusion of various social groups from privileged participation in the national community and its representations. Influential work in my own field—work that passes under the general rubric of "the new historicism"—has recently put such emphasis on the ideological power of the royal court that Elizabeth and James have come almost to seem the "authors" of Elizabethan and Jacobean literature.[9] The early modern writing of England supplies much evidence to support this view, but it supplies still more to contradict it. The monarch was unquestionably the single most powerful unifying force in the English state. Without the long history of monarchic consolidation, dating back even before the Norman conquest, there would have been no England.[10] And the decisive events of the 1530s, reaffirmed under Elizabeth in the 1560s, made the monarch's position still stronger. The intense national self-consciousness of the younger Elizabethans arose under the aegis of Tudor absolutism. Not surprisingly, their work shows this influence. In one way or another, the queen or king figures significantly in nearly everything they wrote about England. But in most of that writing some other interest or cultural formation—the nobility, the law, the land, the economy, the common people, the church—rivals the monarch as the fundamental source of national identity. In seeking to establish their own authority and the authority of the different groups they represented, the younger Elizabethans were often guilty of an involuntary (and sometimes not so involuntary) lèse-majesté. They pushed claims that subverted the absolute claim of the crown. In their books—and more particularly in the discursive forms assumed by those books—we thus find traces of the difficult and, in England at least, never quite complete passage from dynasty to nation.

The other main issue concerns class. Who counts as a member of the nation? Who gets represented? This issue overlaps extensively with the question of kingship. The conflict between epic and chivalric romance turns, for example, on the tension between the new monarchy and its values and the remnants of the feudal nobility and its set of values. In similar fashion, antagonism between court interests and landowning, country interests was at stake in the development of chorography. But though claims to a share in power are always at work, the representation of class is nevertheless worth considering as an issue in its own right, particularly since modern accounts of what was going on in this regard differ so strikingly. Ernest Gellner, writing of nations and nationalism, links national state formation to an increase in social mobility and a lowering of class barriers.[11] Industrial society, Gellner argues, requires the open and relatively homogeneous labor market provided by the nation-state. And what is now effect was once cause. The national order industrialism requires, itself fostered industrialism. Nationalism and industrialism are thus mutually constitutive, and both depend on at least some lessening of social difference. Yet Peter Burke in a study of popular culture in early modern Europe has observed a movement in precisely the opposite direction.[12] Far from becoming more like their economic inferiors, the upper classes withdrew from participation in a culture which had once also been theirs. Accepting Burke's lead, one might argue that if modern nationalism, the nationalism that has proved such a potent and disruptive force throughout the world since the late eighteenth century, has characteristically based itself on the recovery (or the invention) of a "national" folk and on a reduction in the depth of class divisions (though not in the intensity of class struggle), early modern national self-representation went the other way.[13] It based its claim to cultural legitimacy on removing itself from popular culture, on aligning itself with standards of order and civility that transcended national boundaries but enforced boundaries of class. Having the kingdom of one's own language, as Spenser aspired to do, meant being less like the people and more like the aristocratic cultures of Greco-Roman antiquity and of modern Italy, France, and Spain.

How are we to reconcile these differences? I do not think they can be reconciled, certainly not on the basis of evidence I examine in this book. Both Gellner's inclusion and Burke's exclusion go on actively in the Elizabethan writing of England. England's overseas expansion depended on the participation of merchants, so mercantile interests were included. The social elevation of the London theater depended on separation from the base commoners who originally made up a large part of the theater's audience, so commoners were excluded. Apocalyptic was radically inclusive. Ordinary craftsmen and laborers, even women, had a significant part in it. Apologetic was fundamentally exclusive. It reasserted order and hierarchy. Where the formal oppositions that underlie chapters one, two, and three pit royal absolutism against some rival force, those underlying chapters four, five, and six all concern matters of exclusion or inclusion. One discursive form works to broaden the national community; its competitor works to narrow it. In the bright light of retrospection, both inclusion and exclusion can be seen to have had their function in the making of the modern nation-state. The association of inclusion with mercantile expansion and Protestant reform and of exclusion with high culture and a hierarchical state church fits familiar notions about the rise of nation-based capitalism and nation-based sovereignty. But the Elizabethans did not produce their books in the bright light of retrospection. Their efforts were more opportunistic and more uncertain. They did not know where either they or history were going. But they did have a firm grasp on the interests they served, and they sensed that identifying those interests with the nation and the nation with those interests would satisfy several needs at once.

The discursive forms of nationhood and the nation's political forms were mutually self-constituting. Each made the other. Something of this reciprocal process can be seen in the sixteenth-century development of chronicle history. Chronicle was the Ur-genre of national self-representation. More than any other discursive form, chronicle gave Tudor Englishmen a sense of their national identity. Every one of the younger Elizabethans I discuss drew on chronicle. They imitated it, borrowed from it, reacted against it, and rewrote it. But chronicle itself did not remain static. In response to changes in the political order of England, it too changed. According to the report of F. J. Levy, "the late medieval chronicle may be seen as a compilation, loosely organized, whose author had no firm grasp of the essential differences between past and present, who thought of the events of a hundred years before his own time as occurring in a context identical to the world in which he himself lived." By the end of the sixteenth century both this structure and this attitude had changed. The sense of anachronism had sharpened and so had the organizational focus. "Because society was important, and because society was identified with the state, history writing was centered on the personality of the monarch, and this meant that the rather formless narrative of the medieval chroniclers was hammered into a new, more organized, form."[14] The "politic" history of the younger Elizabethans themselves, of Bacon, Camden, Hayward, and Daniel, goes furthest in this direction, but even the sprawling chronicles of Hall, Grafton, Holinshed, and Stow show signs of a more coherent organization.[15] Chronicle history got more sharply focused because the state was more sharply focused. Where before, a chronicler had indiscriminately accumulated a record of everything that had happened in some vaguely defined region, he now had a quite specific story to tell, the story of the state and its "improvement [in] sovereignty."[16] But as the focus sharpened, chronicle, like monarchy, became more obviously contestable. Indeed, the two were contested together, not by a return to the miscellaneous gathering of scattered happenings characteristic of medieval chronicle, but by the invention or adoption of other discursive forms to represent the newly consolidated national state, forms that directed attention away from the royal center of power and toward the nobility, the law, the land, the economy, the church, and the citizens and saints who were the victims of monarchic rule.

At one pole in the reciprocal process by which England was written is the nation—or rather, if we are to recognize the most obvious tension within that pole, the kingdom/nation. At another pole, also fissured, is the text/form. The kingdom/nation authorizes—indeed, authors—the text/form. And the reverse is also true. The text/form authorizes and authors the kingdom/nation. But even this clumsily comprehensive formulation is incomplete, for it ignores the human agents by whom and for whom the authorizing and the authoring take place. It ignores Spenser, Coke, Camden, Speed, Drayton, Hakluyt, Shakespeare, Hooker, and the various discursive communities to which they belonged. The Elizabethan writing of England was, as my reading of Spenser's sentence has already suggested, a four-way process. The kingdom/nation, the text/form, the individual writer, and the discursive community each depended for its identity and its very existence on the others. I have spoken of forms as both agent and structure. The same could be said of any of the other three. We think more easily of people as agents and of the things they make or imagine as structures. But people themselves, whether individually or in groups, are made and imagined. Their identity—*our* identity—is a structure, a cultural construct. And those more obvious constructs, texts and nations, are also agents, making things happen in the world of men and women and the face-to-face groups of which men and women are part. In this four-way exchange there is no unique point of origin, no single originating agent. Instead, points of origin and originating agents are many. Texts, nations, individual authors, particular discursive communities—all are both produced and productive, productive of that by which they are produced.

Tracing the pathways through which this generative energy flowed will be the work of individual chapters. Here I want to say something of the two poles I have not so far discussed: the individual authors and the particular discursive communities. In addition to a common generational location, the men who wrote England shared an unusual social, economic, and psychic mobility. They were what students of more recent nationalist movements have called "transitional men," men uprooted by education and ambition from familiar associations and local structures, men who were free—and compelled by their freedom—to imagine a new identity based on the kingdom or nation.[17] Spenser, whose father was a journeyman clothmaker and who attended Merchant-Tailors School as a "poor boy" and Pembroke Hall, Cambridge, as a "sizar" (another name for a poor boy), went on to become a colonial official and gentleman leaseholder in Ireland. Grammar school and university education also served to lift Camden, Hooker, and Hakluyt from modest beginnings to positions of considerable prominence—Camden as Clarenceux king-at-arms, Hooker as master of the Temple, and Hakluyt as the absentee beneficiary of a substantial living. Though neither Shakespeare, the son of a Stratford glover, nor Speed, the son of a London clothmaker, attended university, they too were socially and economically mobile. With the proceeds from his London theater career, Shakespeare bought his father a coat of arms and bought himself the second largest house in Stratford, and Speed used his skill as a mapmaker to win freedom from the "daily employments" of the "manual trade" to which he was brought up.[18] Only Coke, whose father owned a manor in Norfolk, came of distinctly gentle lineage, but he too rose—as solicitor general, attorney general, chief justice of the Court of Common Pleas, chief justice of the Court of King's Bench, privy councillor, and leading member of parliament—to a position far above his origins. And even Drayton, who achieved no comparable success, showed in his restless movement from patron to patron and from literary project to literary project the same "transitional" character in another guise.[19] "My verse," wrote Drayton, "is the true image of my mind, / Ever in motion, still desiring change."[20] A desire for change infected all these men, even when they asserted most loudly their attachment to stability.

The self-presentational pressure in Drayton's lines, the claim that his verse is the true image of his mind, was also widely shared. Mobility put a heavy burden on identity. Getting the nation to bear some of that burden seemed a fair turnaround. Drayton's poem ends, "My muse is rightly of the English strain, / That cannot long one fashion entertain." Drayton mocks both himself and the English for their lack of any single fixed identity. Yet in this self-mockery there is also pride. Drayton's very mobility, his ready adaptability, is presented as quintessentially English. England is a field of change where foreign modes are put on and taken off with vertiginous speed. Drayton was not thinking of Spenser's letter to Harvey when he wrote this poem, but he might as well have been. To be like the Greeks, to have the kingdom of one's own language, to base one's identity and the identity of one's country on a project of imitative self-transformation is precisely to adopt "the English strain," as Drayton defines it. Self and nation are here caught in a mutually self-constituting process, just as text and nation were. Indeed, it is about texts and their form that both Drayton and Spenser are writing. Text, self, and nation are "true images" of one another. And all three are "ever in motion, still desiring change."

But selves do not usually identify with either text or nation directly or alone. The younger Elizabethans may have been partially uprooted from traditional associations of locality, family, and guild, but they did nevertheless enter into a wide variety of new or newly reformed discursive communities, and it was often on behalf of those communities that they represented England. In Spenser's correspondence with Harvey, we get an intimation of at least three such communities, each of which had an eventual effect on the form of *The Faerie Queene:* the royal court, the aristocratic patronage network centered on the earl of

Leicester, and the Areopagus, the circle of poets and young men of learning that included Spenser, Sidney, Dyer, Greville, Harvey, and, by extension, the other aspiring English writers of their generation. The communal location of the others is no less marked and no less a part of the work they produced. Coke wrote as a common lawyer, a denizen of the Inns of Court and Westminster Hall, and Hooker as a clergyman of the church of England, the protégé of bishops and archbishops and academic churchmen. Two communities with extensively overlapping interests, the merchant-adventurers of London and the colonizing west-country gentlemen led by Raleigh, determined the shape of Hakluyt's *Principal Navigations,* while Camden's *Britannia* was itself responsible for the founding of the Society of Antiquaries, to which Camden and Speed belonged and with whose members Drayton was closely associated. As for Shakespeare, he was one of the two or three most successful participants in the new London public theaters. None of these men was born to the community or communities on whose behalf he wrote. Most could not have been. The communities either did not exist or existed in very different form when they were born. But, as a result of their work, those communities have continued to flourish for centuries as integral parts of a broader national community. Hooker is remembered as the patron saint of Anglicanism, Coke as the oracle of English common law, Camden as the founder of English chorographic and antiquarian study, Hakluyt as the prophet of English overseas expansion, Shakespeare as the principal author of England's national theater, and Spenser as the English poets' poet. If, as I have said, there are no unique points of origin and no single originating agents, these men and their books have nevertheless been made to stand for the beginning of half a dozen different discursive communities and, more broadly, for the beginning of the English nation-state.

"For the Elizabethans," as Roy Strong has remarked, "all history led up to them. For the Stuarts all roads finally led back to Elizabeth."[21] The reign of Elizabeth, and, more particularly, the image of that reign in the work of the men who came of age midway through it, has continued to function as a focal point of English national self-understanding well beyond the century of the Stuarts. Telling evidence of this backward look comes from the second great period of English national and imperial self-assertion, the reign of Queen Victoria. Beginning in 1838, the year after Victoria came to the throne, learned societies were founded in each of the fields covered by the six chapters of this book—poetry, law, antiquarian study, overseas travel, theater, and church—and each of these societies named itself for a noted Elizabethan progenitor. Four took names from my list of principal writers of England: the Camden Society, the Shakespeare Society, the Hakluyt Society, and the Spenser Society. The other two chose an older and a younger contemporary. The society for the publication of the works of the early writers of the reformed church was named for Elizabeth's first archbishop of Canterbury, Matthew Parker, and the society for the publication of materials relating to the history of English law for John Selden, a friend and collaborator of Camden, Drayton, and Coke.[22] To be a member, not so much of one of these organized societies, but of the larger and more amorphous discursive communities from which they arose was to have let one's sense of oneself be in some measure shaped by the formal patterns and the ideological entailments of Spenser's chivalric romance, Coke's reports and institutes, Camden's chorographic description, Hakluyt's collection of voyages, Shakespeare's national history plays, or Hooker's ecclesiastical apology. These are the paradigmatic figures, their books the paradigmatic texts, of a range of discursive practices that have exerted an influence that has reached far beyond the actual readership of the particular books themselves, an influence that now extends to parts of the world the Elizabethans never heard of.

This book was written at the edge of their geographical awareness, on the Pacific coast of North America, a region first visited by Englishmen during the reign of Queen Elizabeth. While I was at work on it, the discovery of a barnacle-encrusted cannon in the Santa Barbara surf provoked a debate about whether or not Drake had wintered in a tidal estuary a few hundred yards from the campus where I teach. From this perspective, Spenser's phrase, "the kingdom of our own language," gets still another twist. Drake claimed the land he visited for Queen Elizabeth and called it New Albion. It is now part of the United States. When an American says "the kingdom of our own language," he has a simultaneous sense of belonging and of estrangement. The language is ours, but the kingdom isn't. England is the kingdom of the English language. America is one of that language's many provinces. To have the kingdom of our own language in this outlying republic has often meant to speak or at least to write some acceptable facsimile of the king's English. And when the speaker or writer is, as most Americans are, of non-English background, the sense of estrangement is doubled. There is, however, nothing new about this, nothing specific to our immigrant, American situation. Self-estrangement was already the fundamental condition of national self-representation in Elizabeth's England. If we think of the Elizabethans as early modern and of ourselves as not quite postmodern, it is in large part because the linked discourses of estrangement and nationhood still connect us.

That cannon on the Santa Barbara beach turned out not to be Drake's, but much that is genuinely Elizabethan has been brought to the American shore. Until well into the nineteenth century, one could become a lawyer in the United States simply by studying Coke's *First Institute*.[23] American Episcopalians continue to attach special importance to Hooker's *Laws*. There are American Spenser and Shakespeare societies, and Hakluyt is still regarded as having told something of our story as well as England's. And if Camden, Speed, and Drayton are not much read here, the chorographic project they initiated has had many American imitators. But the more significant influence of the Elizabethans in America and elsewhere is not tied quite so narrowly to any particular following their books have enjoyed or may still enjoy. Rather the generation of younger Elizabethans has together provided an experiential and structural model of national self-writing, an example of what it can be like to have the kingdom of one's own language.

I began my teaching career in West Africa just a few years after the countries of that region gained their independence from England and France. As I have studied the Elizabethan writing of England, I have often been reminded of postcolonial Africa. Both Europe's imperial expansion and the nationalist ideology that fostered expansion—an ideology that later contributed to the overthrow of the empires expansion produced—got started in the sixteenth century, and both were articulated in the various European discourses of nationhood. In constructing nations of their own, the Africans have written themselves from within a discursive field that first took shape in England, France, Spain, Portugal, and Holland some four hundred years ago.[24] And, once again, education, cultural mobility, and the bureaucratic demands of the state have pointed them toward this task. Like those younger Elizabethans, removed from their artisanal backgrounds, schooled in the alien values of Greco-Roman antiquity, and directed to the service of the newly consolidated monarchic state, the Africans began with self-alienation. They were taken from their village homes, given a European education, and prepared for subaltern positions in a colonial administration they have since taken over and turned to the ends of a numerous array of national states. It should be no surprise that in their frustration, envy, and ambition they often sound so much like Spenser. They don't have to read Spenser to echo him. Their situation is at once strikingly like his and the distant product of his.

The discursive structures within which we all—Africans, Americans, Europeans, and everyone else—now live and work, the division of the world into a system of at least nominally sovereign nation-states and the division of the nation into such substructures as literature, law, history, geography, economics, and religion, came from the sixteenth century. As Debora Shuger has recently written, "With the advent of modernity the borders between both conceptual and national territories were redrawn as solid rather than dotted lines."[25] This book was conceived according to the dictates of those solid lines, but also in opposition to them. Its focus on England respects national boundaries, and its division into chapters on poetry, law, chorography, overseas expansion, theater, and church accords with disciplinary boundaries that, despite significant shifts, have persisted from the sixteenth century to the twentieth. This organizational scheme testifies to the strength of those divisions and, by replicating them, cannot help but reinforce them. Yet in directing attention to the boundaries as having been drawn at a certain historical moment to meet the psychic needs and to satisfy the material interests of certain individuals and groups, I hope to demystify them. For reasons that are both academic and political, I have crossed lines that just a few years ago firmly marked off the disciplinary territory in which I was trained. I have studied law books and maps and travel writings and ecclesiastical polemics with the same attention as poems and plays. Crossing lines is not, however, the same as denying their existence. Indeed, my own crossings have served rather to point out the ideological function of the lines than to pretend they aren't there. Still, if we cross the established lines often enough, and if we imagine others that intersect them at various odd angles, there is a chance we can create a freer, more permeable world, a world of dotted instead of solid lines. That, as I understand it, is what a truly postcolonial, postnational, postmodern age would mean. In writing England, the younger Elizabethans also wrote us. To study that writing is to expose one root of our own identity. But it is also to open the possibility of another project like theirs, another attempt in another world to remake our individual and collective selves by once again having the kingdom of our own language.

1

TWO VERSIONS OF GOTHIC

"TWO GREAT PRINCIPLES DIVIDE THE WORLD AND
contend for the mastery," wrote Lord Acton in 1859, "antiquity and
the middle ages. These are the two civilizations that have preceded us,
the two elements of which ours is composed. All political as well as
religious questions reduce themselves practically to this. This is the
great dualism that runs through our society."[1] The language of these
few sentences is so nearly our own that one could easily mistake them
for something written in the 1990s. Yet "the great dualism" Acton
describes is no longer ours. We still borrow from antiquity or the
middle ages—the Kennedy "Camelot" of the 1960s is one recent
example—but we no longer represent our borrowings from one as a
reaction against the other. Nor are those borrowings particularly frequent or conspicuous. The accumulated weight of cultural change has
squeezed all but the last drops of life from this system. But when
Acton wrote, at a time close enough to sound like the present, it was
still hardy. The English nineteenth century experienced both a Greek
and a chivalric revival, adopted classical and Gothic architectural styles
for its major public and private buildings, aligned its art, literature,
religion, philosophy, and even its politics with ancient and medieval
models.[2] And not only were numerous bits of the ancient and medieval past appropriated and reused in the quite foreign setting of newly
industrialized Britain, but antiquity and the middle ages supplied the
two sides of a comprehensive binary opposition, a "great dualism," in
terms of which Victorian Englishmen represented themselves, their
institutions, and their moment in history. When Acton saw himself as
the heir of romantic medievalism, saw his century as a period in revolt
against Renaissance and eighteenth-century classicism, saw representative government as medieval and its absolutist opponent as classical,
saw classical education as an antidote to an excessively "one-sided
partiality" to the middle ages, he drew on a dialectic of ancient and
medieval that had persisted as one of the constitutive elements in
European self-understanding and self-representation from the Italian
Renaissance of the fifteenth century up to his own time and that
continued to function well into the early twentieth century. And because these were centuries of national consolidation and imperial ex-

21

pansion, the articulation of those large movements depended inevitably on the resources of that dialectic.

The rhetoric of nationhood is a rhetoric of uniformity and wholeness. The unified self of the Englishman or Frenchman, the Italian or German, is founded on the political and cultural unity of the nation to which each belongs. The denial of nationhood is experienced as a denial of integrated selfhood. Yet at the historic root of national self-articulation we find intractable doubleness and self-alienation. Both are there in Spenser's "Why a God's name may not we, as else the Greeks, have the kingdom of our own language," and they are there still in Acton's "great dualism." Put most abstractly, to be is to mean, and meaning depends on difference. Writing of ethnicity in general, Emile Benveniste has remarked that "every name of an ethnic character, in ancient times, was differentiating and oppositional. There was present in the name which a people assumed the intention, manifest or not, of distinguishing itself from the neighboring peoples. . . . Hence the ethnic group often constituted an antithetical duality with the opposed ethnic group."[3] Even here one finds an element of self-alienation. Meaning arises not from some central core of identity but rather at a margin of difference. Self-definition comes from the not-self, from the alien other. But in the discourses of nationhood, such alienation cuts still deeper. To constitute itself as a nation-state, a political or cultural community must distinguish itself not only from its neighbors but also from its former self or selves. This is obvious in the case of more recent national movements in the Americas, Africa, and Asia. The very national idea, though it may claim some local basis, is borrowed, and so are the discursive forms in which the nation enunciates itself. But something of the same sort was already true of the prototypical nation-states of early modern Europe. These seemingly "natural" nations did not just happen; they were made, and their making required a period of self-alienation. Prompted by the cultural breaks of Renaissance and Reformation, sixteenth-century national self-articulation began with a sense of national barbarism, with a recognition of the self as the despised other, and then moved to repair that damaged self-image with the aid of forms taken from a past that was now understood as both different from the present and internally divided.

By semiotic necessity, but also by a quite specific set of historical operations, the assertion of national unity arose from cultural division. Adapting the American national motto (itself borrowed from Rome in a century of "enlightened" classicism), we might label this process *e duobus unum*. Out of the divided legacy of antiquity and the middle ages—a division produced deliberately by Italian humanists of the fifteenth century as a lever for change—the new unity of the nation-state was understood and made known. In the minds of many who claimed to speak for them, the modern nations of Europe had, for all their differences from both antiquity and the middle ages, to be represented as either ancient or medieval, either Greek or Goth. The authority of the spokesmen themselves, indeed their very identity, was felt to derive from the identity and authority of the cultural pole to which they attached themselves and their country. Over the half millennium that this binary system was in place, the meaning of its two principal terms did not, however, stay fixed. Ancient and medieval functioned rather as floating signifiers, terms that remained opposed to one another though their specific referents repeatedly changed. Erasmus's ancients were not Acton's. Nineteenth-century parliamentary Gothic was not sixteenth-century humanist. And even at any one moment, there could be profound differences concerning not only which term to prefer but the very significance of each. Rome could stand simultaneously for empire and republic; the middle ages, for monarchy and popular resistance to it. But unlike the dialectical opposition between antiquity and the middle ages, differences of this sort often went unperceived, one group developing an understanding of classical and medieval that suited its own interests and practices without noticing that its ancients and its Goths bore little likeness to those of some neighboring group. In this sense, the actual American motto is more accurate: *e pluribus unum*. Out of many individual binary differences the apparent, but only apparent, unity of the nation-state was created.

In this chapter and the next I will be looking at three particular instances of the ancient-medieval dialectic and its function in the ideological construction of the early modern English nation. Two of these, the two versions of Gothic that are the subject of this chapter, concern poetry. The third, which I discuss in the following chapter, concerns law. Having a distinctly national poetry and a distinctly national legal system was then thought, as it is still thought today, to be fundamental to a nation's cultural sovereignty. But neither poetry nor law could be conceived apart from the forms in which each had been embodied elsewhere. Certain rules of verse, certain poetic genres, certain discursive orderings of the law taken either from Greco-Roman antiquity or the middle ages provided the recognized models of civility and barbarity against which English writings were inevitably measured. Picking the civilized model and imitating it would seem to have been the obvious course for both poets and lawyers, and many recommended precisely that. But this was a course fraught with difficulty and danger. Even supposing that the structure of the English language and the structure of the English sociopolitical system permitted such imitation—something that was far from obvious—it inescapably involved an extraordinary degree of national self-alienation and, as we will see, a no less extraordinary degree of personal political self-abnegation, both of which risked destroying the very individual and communal autonomy that a discourse of nationhood had seemed otherwise to promise. As a consequence, writers in both poetry and the law were drawn between alternatives that seemed equally unappealing and equally necessary.

The reason for accumulating three separate examples is that together they reveal disjunctions and connections that would otherwise be invisible. The first of the two literary versions of Gothic surprisingly anticipates constitutional arguments that get more fully developed in the writing of English law. The issues of discursive form, though not of course the forms themselves, engaged in these two quite different areas and the ideological implications of those issues are also surprisingly similar. But no less surprising are the ideological dissimilarities between the two specifically literary versions of Gothic that I juxtapose in this chapter, particularly since the poet most fully implicated in both, Edmund Spenser, is the same. Because the institutional identity of English poetry was notably weak when Spenser began writing in the 1570s, poetry was obliged to draw its authority from other better established and more prestigious institutions and activities: from the court, from the law, and from the literatures of other countries. And because those more powerfully institutionalized domains had differently constituted the fundamental ancient-medieval opposition, English poetry found itself in the position of offering incongruous and even contradictory representations of itself and the nation. Those incongruities and contradictions did not, however, lead, as they would in a logical proof, to a *reductio ad absurdum* in which the whole enterprise was shown up as irretrievably flawed. On the contrary, English poetry owed something of the strength it achieved in this generation to its very ideological diversity, to the fact that it situated itself politically in several ways at once. Poetry thus became a scene of contention, one of the high places that various interests with a stake in the development of an English national culture thought worth commanding. How this happened is the particular concern of this chapter.

Barbarous Tongues

Let's begin with the sentence that got me started on this project, Spenser's pressing question: "Why a God's name may not we, as else the Greeks, have the kingdom of our own language?"[4] Here, by the indirection of adamant denial, Spenser points to a first version of the Gothic. Unlike the Goths, the Greeks had the kingdom of their own language. Now Spenser wants to do something of the same sort with and to English. This, as I remarked earlier, represents an extraordinary ambition on Spenser's part, no less than an attempt to remake the very cultural matrix in which his own identity had been formed, to separate himself from himself to become a self-dominating other. Such ambition was central to the early modern writing of England. Yet, for most readers, its edge will be blunted, its momentous significance reduced to antiquarian peculiarity, as we finally step back to take in more of the surrounding context. "I like your late English hexameters so exceedingly well," Spenser writes to Harvey,

> that I also inure my pen sometime in that kind, which I find indeed, as I have heard you often defend in word, neither so hard, nor so harsh, that it will easily and fairly yield itself to our mother tongue. For the only or chiefest hardness, which seemeth, is in the accent, which sometime gapeth and, as it were, yawneth ill-favoredly, coming short of that it should, and sometime exceeding the measure of the number, as in *carpenter,* the middle syllable being used short in speech, when it shall be read long in verse, seemeth like a lame gosling that draweth one leg after her. . . . But it is to be won with custom, and rough words must be subdued with use. For why a God's name may not we, as else the Greeks, have the kingdom of our own language and measure our accents by the sound, reserving the quantity to the verse? (10.16)

So *that* is what Spenser was talking about: the comically misguided effort to base English prosody on the rules of ancient quantitative meters. How can anything said in such a context be taken seriously?

Yet Spenser himself seems to have been quite serious about it. The greater part of both his published letters to Harvey is given over to detailed and enthusiastic discussion of this project. He assures Harvey that he is "of late more in love with my English versifying than with riming" (10.6), gives several brief examples of his work in this reformed mode, promises to send a more substantial "token" of "what and how well therein I am able to do" (10.17), and names as fellow partisans not only Harvey himself but also Sidney and Dyer. That Harvey and Dyer should have been mistaken in this way causes us no concern. Nor are we much bothered at finding elsewhere in these letters and in other documents the names of Drant, Preston, and Still, of Stanyhurst, Puttenham, and Webbe associated with the quantitative movement. Even Greville and Campion are figures small enough to have erred thus greatly without provoking much alarm. But Sidney and Spenser! If, as most commentators since the end of the sixteenth century have agreed, modern English literature got its first solid foundation in the second half of Elizabeth's reign, these two men have the best claim to being its founders. A project that concerned them deeply just at the moment when their careers were beginning and their most significant works were being written is perhaps less negligible than we are sometimes inclined to think.

To a student of English literary history, the correspondence between Spenser and Harvey comes heavy with the promise of things shortly to be known. When the first of Spenser's letters was written toward the end of 1579, *The Shepheardes Calender* was as yet unpublished. Indeed, the question of whether to publish at all is among the issues he most worriedly discusses. In these letters, too, we find the earliest reference to *The Faerie Queene,* mentioned along with Spenser's *Slomber,* his *Dying Pellicane,* his nine comedies, and a whole collection of other works that, like these, have disappeared leaving no other trace behind. What if their fate had been shared by *The Shepheardes Calender* and *The Faerie Queene?* How different the course of our literature would have been! The future that to us is known as a secure past, so familiar that it seems inevitable, was in those years no less laden with uncertainty than with promise. Harvey, who, like Spenser, then stood on the threshold of what appeared a likely, even brilliant, career and whose ambition was, if anything, still greater than Spenser's, went on to a series of failures and public humiliations that have made him a near joke to posterity, saved from total ridicule by little more than his association with Spenser.

A similar fate has, of course, overtaken the quantitative movement. It now seems no less foolish than Harvey, no less futile than the *Dying Pellicane.* Success has a way of making failure look silly. But what if success needs failure as the guarantor of its own identity, the comic (yet still fearful) double that tells what success is not but might have been, tells of the historical abyss into which all ambition threatens to fall? The works that were finally not written, the vocational ambition that was not rewarded, the verse form that was not adopted stand to their successful counterparts as the sounds and meanings that we don't make or intend stand to those that we do. They enable by their absence and difference the production and reception of an intelligible message. But that intelligibility depends too on some more generally accepted standard of meaning.

For Spenser and Harvey it was, of course, not yet clear which of their many projects would succeed and which would fail—indeed, not clear that any would surely succeed or fail—but the weight of approval in their letters is invariably determined by the humanist preference for the classical over the medieval. Harvey shows this when he praises Spenser's Apollonian "nine English comedies" at the expense of his Hobgoblinish *Faerie Queene*. The meaning of each is defined not only by its difference from the other but also by its likeness to one or the other of an authoritative, fixed, and prejudged pair. In a similar but more elaborate way, the two correspondents define themselves in terms of their differences, Spenser playing giddy Petrarchan love poet to Harvey's wise counselor and learned scholar, "our age's great Cato." Again the medieval bows to the ancient.[5] So, to quote Harvey, "our new famous enterprise for the exchanging of barbarous and balductum rimes with artificial verses" (10.463) derives both intelligibility and authority from a play of differences made natural by assimilation to the great classical-medieval divide. Only in contrast to the ancient artifice of quantitative verse can rime be seen as inescapably crude and trashy.

These meanings and these valuations have not held. In the more than four centuries since the letters between Harvey and Spenser were published, *The Faerie Queene*, Spenser's poetic identity, and English riming verse have entered into many new systems of difference, altering their meanings as they prospered, while the nine comedies, Harvey's reputation for wisdom, and the dream of English verse in quantitative meters have dropped almost completely from memory, to be recalled only with amusement and wonder. But those changes could hardly have been accomplished without some alteration in the way the basic terms of reference were understood.

The first hint of that change—and it is only a hint—comes from an unlikely source, from Harvey himself. Though Harvey was the earlier and keener partisan of the quantitative movement, he thought that on the crucial matter of having the kingdom of their own language Spenser had gone too far.

> In good sooth and by the faith I bear to the Muses, you shall never have my subscription or consent (though you should charge me with the authority of five hundred Master Drants) to make your *carpenter,* our

carpĕnter, an inch longer or bigger than God and his English people have made him. Is there no other policy to pull down riming and set up versifying but you must needs correct *magnificat* and against all order of law and in despite of custom forcibly usurp and tyrannize upon a quiet company of words that so far beyond the memory of man have so peaceably enjoyed their several privileges and liberties without any disturbance or the least controlment? (10.473–74)

Where Spenser had used the language of sovereign power eager to subdue rough words and have the kingdom of them, Harvey responds in terms made familiar by centuries of resistance to royal encroachment, terms that would become still more familiar in the first half of the next century. He accuses Spenser of usurpation and tyranny, locates authority not in the king but in "God and his English people," proclaims the value of custom and the order of law, supports the peaceful enjoyment of immemorial privileges and liberties. Against Spenser's version of the absolutist cultural politics of antiquity, he sets, without quite calling it that, a Gothic, common-law tradition. If quantitative verse means correcting *magnificat,* Harvey opposes it.[6] His is, of course, a local response to a very particular provocation. He never develops its implications. Indeed, his arguments elsewhere contradict them. But the intervention is nevertheless significant. For here Spenser and Harvey together discover, almost inadvertently it would seem, an oppositional politics of national literary self-representation, a politics that would later become far more open and explicit. And in doing so, they suggest one way of reversing the hierarchy of values that had prompted them to try quantitative verse in the first place.

For those involved in the quantitative movement, the most influential expression of that hierarchy came from a book of their fathers' generation, a book that had great currency in the crucial decade of the younger Elizabethans' coming of age, a book that in many ways shaped their nonliterary, as well as their literary, behavior. That book is Roger Ascham's *Schoolmaster* (1570). Written by the queen's tutor, dedicated to her principal secretary, prompted by a discussion that involved a number of the most prominent officeholders in the realm, and based on the ideas of leading English and continental humanists of the first half of the sixteenth century, *The Schoolmaster* spoke with the unmistakable voice of cultural authority. A young man, who, like Spenser or Harvey, aspired to occupy a position of such authority himself and who knew that his success would depend in large part on the approbation of those publicly identified with Ascham's book, could hardly have ignored its recommendations. Spenser and Harvey clearly did not ignore them. On the contrary, they each refer specifically to Ascham and his views. In him they recognize the first begetter of the quantitative movement to which they both subscribe.

But Ascham did not only "exhort the goodly wits of England" to "give themselves" to the task of "making perfect . . . this point of learning in our English tongue."[7] He also linked his particular exhortation to the more general choice of cultures that is a defining characteristic of English self-understanding from the sixteenth century through the nineteenth. "Now," he wrote, "when men know the difference and have examples both of the best and of the worst, surely to follow rather the Goths in riming than the Greeks in true versifying were even to eat acorns with swine when we may freely eat wheat bread amongst men" (p. 145). Knowledge of historical difference is what, for Ascham, distinguished his moment from all previous moments in English history. And such knowledge brings with it the possibility of choice. Ascham thus presents that active model of self-fashioning to which Spenser, in seeking to have the kingdom of his own language, fits himself—a model based on choice and imitation. What Ascham most despises is the passive acceptance of "time and custom," eating acorns with swine. What he most admires is the "forward diligence," as he calls it, of those who choose to eat wheat bread amongst men, those who make themselves over in the likeness of a pattern of civility superior to what mere barbarous custom affords.

The deliberate fashioning of oneself and of others is what *The Schoolmaster* is all about. A schoolmaster is, after all, a professional molder of selves, and Ascham is particularly concerned with the process by which such molding is accomplished. He does, however, recognize the importance of natural differences. Many pages of the first half of his book, the section on "the bringing-up of youth," are given over to a detailed discussion of differing temperaments and their effect on learning. But Ascham's purpose is to upset expectation, to argue that hard wits make better pupils than quick ones. In going against the grain, a schoolmaster can make his most lasting impression. Translated to the cultural realm, this argument would seem to suggest that the very resistance of English speech and perhaps English institutions as well to the classical pattern might be evidence of their long-term aptness. Like hard wits, they are "hard to receive but sure to keep" (p. 24). Before Virgil and Horace corrected it, Latin, Ascham tells us, was as rude and barbarous as English. And though he does not himself make this point, many others claimed that Homer had similarly reformed Greek. This is what Spenser has in mind when he talks of the

Greeks having had the kingdom of their own language. And given the way the Elizabethans pronounced the classical languages, particularly Latin, it must have seemed to them that the ancients' wielding of authority over their tongues was as much an act of arbitrary will as would be their own imposition of quantitative rules on English.[8] What, after all, distinguishes wheat bread from acorns but the planting, the harvesting, the threshing, the grinding, the sifting, and the baking? Acorns are barbarous and natural—barbarous *because* natural. They are fit food for Goths and for swine. To eat wheat bread is to give a sign of one's superiority over nature, a sign of one's power to make, ultimately to make oneself. "Follow[ing] the Greeks in true versifying" provides another sign of the same distinctly human power.

Power and its institutional embodiment are as central to the Spenser-Harvey correspondence as they were to *The Schoolmaster.* Spenser's two letters are dated from Westminster and from Leicester House, and they speak mysteriously of "his excellent lordship" and, no less mysteriously, "of my late being with her majesty" (10.5 and 6). Ascham's project of English self-making was conceived in just such a setting, near the center of power, and Spenser lets us know that the project is being carried on there by this new generation. The quantitative movement chooses for itself the language appropriate to this setting and to its own absolutist ambition, the language of power. Its two leading advocates, Sidney and Dyer, have, Spenser tells us, "proclaimed in their Areopagus a general surceasing and silence of bold rimers and also of the very best too, instead whereof they have, by authority of their whole senate, prescribed certain laws and rules of quantities of English syllables for English verse" (10.6). No one has known quite what to make of the Areopagus. Was it a formal society, an informal group of friends, or merely a name jokingly created by Spenser in this letter for some still less structured association? Without more evidence, we will never know. But it is clear that the word is Greek and the action peremptory.[9] In both respects it conforms to Ascham's model of self-fashioning.

Ascham's influence did not limit itself to Spenser, Harvey, Sidney, and Dyer. Nor, though the active involvement of these men was short-lived, did interest in English quantitative meter stop with them. In 1582 Richard Stanyhurst, quoting from the Spenser-Harvey correspondence and claiming to have taken it upon himself "to execute some part of Master Ascham his will," brought out his hexameter translation of the first four books of the *Aeneid.* Four years later, William Webbe, again with specific reference to both the Spenser-

Harvey correspondence and Ascham, made the reformation of prosody the principal desideratum of his *Discourse of English Poetry* (1586). George Puttenham in his *Art of English Poesy* (1589) was a less ardent partisan of what he called "Greek and Latin feet"—in fact, he began as an opponent—but he too ended by advocating their adoption and he supplied six chapters of detailed discussion.[10] The publication in the next few years of much highly accomplished English rime, among it *Astrophel and Stella* and the first books of *The Faerie Queene*, seems to have temporarily stilled the call for a new prosody, but in 1599 the anonymous author of the *Preservation of Henry VII* attempted to reignite the issue and Thomas Campion took it up with greater skill and greater vehemence in 1602. And through all these years poems in quantitative verse continued to be written, not only by these self-acknowledged advocates, but also by many others, including the countess of Pembroke, Fulke Greville, Abraham Fraunce, Robert Greene, Thomas Lodge, and even the Marprelate combatants.

A few bits of this verse still make good reading. Others have become, as Nashe said of Stanyhurst's lumbering hexameters, "famously absurd."[11] Most have been quietly forgotten. But if we measure success in other terms, this very active movement can be considered extraordinarily successful. It succeeded, though not quite single-handedly, in putting English poetry high on the list of projects to be completed in the course of England's self-making. It, furthermore, succeeded in directing attention to technical questions of prosody that would have to be answered were English poetry itself to succeed. (It thus makes sense that Sidney and Spenser, the two main contributors to the development of that poetry and particularly to its metrical development, were also deeply involved in the quantitative movement.) And it succeeded in serving as a principal focal point for the discussion of national self-fashioning itself. This last is, of course, my main concern here. The rivalry between quantitative meter and rime was caught up in a much larger rivalry between two ways of being—between active self-making on the human-Greek-wheat-bread model and passive acceptance of time and custom on the swine-Goth-acorn model. Now, of course, put in this Aschamite way, it was not hard to make a choice. And for some time English poets, like Spenser and Sidney, sided with Ascham or at least made no frontal attack on his values, even though they might in practice go against his particular precepts regarding prosody. But, as Harvey's response to Spenser has already suggested, there were other values that could be attributed to even his terms, crushingly unequivocal though he meant them to be, and other terms that could equally alter the polarity he sought to establish.

Take, for example, the opposition between wheat bread and acorns. Nearly sixty years after the publication of *The Schoolmaster*, Ben Jonson can still use it with just Ascham's meaning. "Say that thou pourest 'hem wheat," he writes in the angry "Ode to Himself" that was prompted by the theatrical failure of his *New Inn* in 1629,

> And they would acorns eat:
> 'Twere simple fury still thyself to waste
> On such as have no taste,
> To offer them a surfeit of pure bread,
> Whose appetites are dead.
> No, give them grains their fill,
> Husks, draff to drink and swill.
> If they love lees and leave the lusty wine,
> Envy them not; their palate's with the swine.[12]

Not only is "pure bread" firmly identified with Jonson's classical (though not, of course, quantitative) art, but in the poem's concluding stanza that art is further associated with the absolute power of the king, with "the acts of Charles his reign." Here then the cluster of linked terms that so impressed Spenser, Harvey, and their contemporaries recurs. But difference marks this recurrence, for in 1629 both Jonson and his king were on the defensive. Just a year earlier parliament had faced Charles with a petition of right that defended the privileges and liberties of Englishmen against royal usurpation in much the way that Harvey had defended the "privileges and liberties" of English words against Spenser's attempted tyranny. And, of course, Jonson had been pushed from the chair of wit. In such circumstances, neither the king nor his poet could speak with Ascham's settled authority.

The half century that separates Ascham and Jonson had granted even the lowly acorn more favorable associations. It reminds Don Quixote, as it must have reminded many Elizabethans, of the Golden Age, a distant time of innocence and perfection that found its modern expression in poetic depictions of shepherds and goatherds. Acorns may also have been linked in the minds of some Elizabethans to the *siliquae porcorum,* the swine's food envied by the prodigal in Saint Luke's Gospel.[13] Prodigal son fiction and pastoral poetry were two of the literary kinds most favored by Spenser's generation, each of which figures a testing and often a revision of the midcentury humanist values most fully expressed by Ascham. Representing themselves as prodigals or as shepherds (and sometimes as both at once), Spenser, Sidney, and many other younger Elizabethans rebelled against paternal admonition and paternal expectation, sought a refuge from which they might examine their relation to a system of authority that at once provided only the narrowest definition of fit employment (one that excluded riming along with much else) and then denied them access to even such limited employment when they dutifully sought it.[14]

In begging Harvey to play Cato and to dissuade him from the folly of love, Spenser casts himself in precisely this prodigal role (a role he plays again as Colin Clout in *The Shepheardes Calender*) and seeks redemption. His efforts at quantitative verse are meant to signal this salutary turn. But, if his aim was promotion in the courtly world of power, he need not have bothered. The cultural instability that could make even the barbarous acorn a sign of pristine innocence or of a fortunate fall was affecting the whole constellation of values represented by Ascham. Though Ascham located his humanist *Schoolmaster* at court, an actual humanist who tried to exhibit his schoolmasterly attainments in that region would have been in for a rude shock. At court, not the lover dedicated to pleasure and driven by passion but rather the upright Cato with his stiff hexameters and classical learning was in need of reform, for the court wanted elegant entertainment, not grave counsel or pedantic display. G. K. Hunter has argued this point at length in the well-known opening chapter of his book on John Lyly, and the two parts of Lyly's own *Euphues* (1578 and 1580) furnish a diagrammatic example of an actual Elizabethan's discovery of its truth.[15] The first part, heavily and quite obviously influenced by Ascham, affirms the humanist lesson by taking a quick-witted young man from "Athens" to courtly "Naples" where unhappy experience teaches him to embrace the precepts he had rebelliously neglected. The second part, *Euphues and His England,* reverses that lesson. It celebrates love, exposes the inadequacy of classical learning, and advertises the skills of courtship. It sets, moreover, England against Greece so that a representative of the latter ends by singing the praises of the former. Instead of making England over in the image of Greece, as Ascham himself, the Aschamite Spenser of the Harvey correspondence, and the equally Aschamite Lyly of the *Anatomy of Wit* all seemed intent on doing, the author of *Euphues and His England* wants us to laugh at the foolish Greek for not becoming wholly English.[16] Such laughter is precisely what greeted the unreformed Harvey when he brought his graceless learning to court.

It would, of course, also turn itself on the quantitative movement.

We already sense something of this transmutation of values in Puttenham's juxtaposition of the two sorts of poetry. "Now passing from these courtly trifles," he says at the conclusion of his discussion of various sorts of artful riming stanzas, "let us talk of our scholastical toys, that is of the grammatical versifying of the Greeks and Latins and see whether it might be reduced into our English art or no."[17] Already quantitative verse, whose great claim to authority resided in its presumed association with imperial power, finds itself banished from court and forced to content itself with the schoolhouse. And though Puttenham thinks such verse can be naturalized in English, he does not wish that it "be generally applauded at to the discredit of our forefathers' manner of vulgar poesy or to the alteration or peradventure total destruction of the same." The possibility of English verse in quantitative meter furnishes rather another, by now almost superfluous, bit of evidence that an "art of English poesy" is not a ridiculous misnomer. In his *Defense of Poesy* (1580), Sidney, who just a year or two earlier had been proclaiming reform and promulgating new laws, is equally cool, and he too gives more credit for eloquence to "smally learned courtiers" than to official "professors of learning."[18] In the course of very few years from the late 1570s to the early 1580s, humanist learning and courtly advancement have come to a parting of the ways. English rime follows the lead of the court, while quantitative verse is left to take the path that leads away from power. In these circumstances, the charge of barbarousness loses its force. If acorns are being consumed at court, they are by that very fact made courteous and civil.

The adoption of riming verse by the court and by courtiers, or at least the close association of one with the other, thus obscured for a while the issue that had been so clear in Ascham. In the interim a vast amount of highly accomplished riming verse was written and published—the most impressive and influential examples of it written by those two former partisans of the quantitative movement, Sidney and Spenser. But if their achievement went a long way toward making the earlier controversy moot, it did not erase that controversy. Under the aegis of pastoralism, Petrarchan prodigality, and chivalric romance, none of which Ascham would have approved, rime prospered, first at court and then in the literate community generally. But the particular terms of Ascham's argument remained unanswered—indeed, unaddressed.

The undiminished cultural prestige of classical antiquity, particularly when combined in the late 1590s with the much diminished prestige of the royal court, made this a perilous situation. On what foundation of authority could English rime depend? Was the mere fact of Sidney's and Spenser's accomplishment enough to turn what even they had thought barbarous into a mark of civility? How could the taint of cultural inferiority be removed from rime in the face of its undoubted medieval origin? How for that matter, could that taint be removed from the identity of England itself, since its language seemed irradicably bound to a barbarous and "inartificial" mode of literary expression? Though Sidney and Spenser had written much and written well, they had failed in their attempt to have the kingdom of their own language. What significance was to be attributed to that failure? Was the original project misguided, or had they simply given up too easily and too soon? Or, more worrisome, was English nature unalterably resistant to the nurture of civility? "You taught me art," the pupil nation might say to the master races of antiquity, "and my profit on't is I know how to rime."

To my knowledge, no Englishman was willing to speak of himself and his countrymen as cultural Calibans, a vile race deservedly confined to their island rock. But they did suspect that others saw them this way, and sometimes their suspicion found galling confirmation. On a trip to Italy early in the 1590s, Samuel Daniel heard the poet Guarini

> oft embase the virtues of the North,
> Saying our coasts were with no measures graced,
> Nor barbarous tongues could any verse bring forth.[19]

Just a few years later Daniel put a similar charge in the mouth of the worldly-wise Philocosmus, the antagonist of his poetry-loving spokesman, Musophilus.

> Is this the walk of all your wide renown,
>   This little point, this scarce discerned isle,
>   Thrust from the world, with whom our speech unknown
> Made never any traffic of our style?
>   And is this all where all this care is shown,
>   T'enchant your fame to last so long a while?
>   And for that happier tongues have won so much,
>   Think you to make your barbarous language such?
> Poor narrow limits for so mighty pains.[20]

Nor could the accomplishment of the greater Elizabethans silence doubts like these.

How many thousands never heard the name
Of Sidney or of Spenser or their books?
And yet brave fellows. . . . (p. 81)

Undoubtedly the grounds for a defense of English riming poetry were far more solid than they had been twenty years earlier when Sidney and Spenser began their literary careers. But that defense had still to be made. As it happens, it was Daniel himself who made it—though not until he had been provoked by Thomas Campion's renewal in 1602, the last year of the old queen's reign, of the campaign for English verse based on the ancient model.

In dedicating his *Observations in the Art of English Poesy* to Lord Buckhurst, Burghley's successor as lord treasurer and one of the small inner circle of privy councillors who dominated affairs in Elizabeth's declining years, Campion not only attempted to associate his views with a representative of royal power. He also evoked that early Elizabethan moment, before the arrival on the literary scene of either Sidney or Spenser, when humanist values were exercising their strongest attraction. Forty years before receiving the dedication of Campion's *Observations,* Baron Buckhurst, then Thomas Sackville, had collaborated with Thomas Norton on *Gorboduc,* the most nearly regular of English tragedies. It is to the clearly articulated clash of cultures characteristic of that moment that Campion returns. Once again rime is stigmatized as "vulgar and inartificial" and quantitative meter praised as the "true form of versifying."[21] And once again the humanist story of European cultural development, the story of monkish decline and classical revival, is rehearsed.

In his *Defense of Rime* (1603), Daniel flatly denies the assumptions that governed this story, boldly rejecting the whole set of historical premises on which the quantitative movement had depended. Though he was no less deeply bothered than Ascham or Campion by the charge that England was a barbarous nation, Daniel's response to that charge is the opposite of theirs. Where they sought to rip out barbarous custom and impose in its place the civility of Greece and Rome, he celebrates the cultural accomplishments of the barbarians themselves. "All our understandings are not," he says, "to be built by the square of Greece and Italy. . . . The Goths, Vandals, and Longobards, whose coming down like an inundation overwhelmed, as they say, all the glory of learning in Europe, have yet left us their law and customs . . . which well considered with their other courses of government may serve to clear them from this imputation of ignorance. . . . Let us go no further but look upon the wonderful architecture of this state of England and see whether they were deformed times that could give it such a form" (pp. 139–40 and 145).

But Daniel not only dismisses the historical basis of the Ascham-Campion argument, he also rejects its humanist and absolutist model of self-making. Far from wishing to "have the kingdom of our own language," Daniel accepts and delights in a form of verse that, as he puts it a few years later in a poem prefaced to his *Certain Small Works* (1607),

> Confirmed by no edict of power doth rest
> But only underneath the regency
> Of use and fashion. (p. 5)

He evokes the language of royal power only to deny its relevance, to depose the monarchic (or Areopagite) pronouncer of edicts. At the origin of English rime is not the act of a primal lawgiver or a sovereign maker but rather the immemorial workings of custom and nature, "custom that is before all law, nature that is above all art" (p. 131). Like Harvey, who in responding a quarter of a century earlier to Spenser's attempt to bend *carpenter* to his will had defined Spenser's act as tyrannous usurpation and had defended the privileges and liberties of English words, Daniel couches his argument in specifically legal and political terms. For both Harvey and Daniel, as for their opponents, the form of English verse was as much a political as an aesthetic matter. Indeed, they could understand the aesthetic only as a subset of the political. The distribution of syllables in a line of verse inevitably figured the distribution of power in the state. Innovation in either carried with it the threat (or the promise) of disruption in the other.

In the *Defense of Rime,* political innovation seems to worry Daniel still more than the changes in verse form that Campion was suggesting. And well it might. Only a few months before the book was published a reign that had lasted longer than Daniel's life had finally ended and a new monarch, a foreigner, had assumed power. It is to this event that Daniel attributes the augmentation and publication of his treatise, which he claims to have first written a short while earlier as a private letter. "The times," he says, "promise a more regard to the present condition of our writings, in the respect of our sovereign's happy inclination this way, whereby we are rather to expect an encouragement to go on with what we do than that any innovation should check us with a shew of what it would do in another kind" (p. 127). By that "happy inclination," Daniel may have been thinking not only of James's more general reputation for learning but also of his specific support for rime in his *Short Treatise of Scottish Poesy* (1584). If, however, James's "prentice" view of poetry was comforting, his views on government may not have been, at least not to one who had attended to them carefully. Thus Daniel's emphasis on the danger of innovation, on "the plain tract . . . beaten by custom and the time" (p. 147), on laws which have "ever been used amongst us time out of mind" (p. 150) responds directly to concerns aroused by the accession of a king who claimed ancestral conquest as the ultimate sanction of his authority, a king who thought his will should be law. In opposing "the unjust authority of the law-giver" Campion (p. 149), Daniel also implicitly opposes any comparably tyrannous act on the part of the new sovereign. England's verse is Gothic, and so is the English state. To alter either, even according to a plan borrowed from classical antiquity, would be to do "wrong to the honor of the dead, wrong to the fame of the living, and wrong to England" (p. 153). "Here I stand forth," he declares, "only to make good the place we have thus taken up" (p. 155).

That Daniel was quite consciously taking his stand in the face of the new king is further suggested by the company in which the *Defense of Rime* first appeared. It was printed (and quickly reprinted) as the last work in a small volume that began with "A Panegyric Congratulatory to the King's Most Excellent Majesty." The concerns of this poem are precisely those of the *Defense,* though it prudently assumes that the king, unlike Campion, will be in full agreement. "We shall continue," says Daniel, speaking out of this far from proven assumption,

> and remain all one,
> In law, in justice, and in magistrate;
> Thou wilt not alter the foundation
> Thy ancestors have laid of this estate,
> Nor grieve thy land with innovation,
> Nor take from us more than thou wilt collate;
> Knowing that course is best to be observed,
> Whereby a state hath longest been preserved.[22]

From a situation (the situation that produced Spenser's letters to Harvey) in which authority was thought to reside in innovation, in institutions as yet unfounded and which thus depend for their very existence on the exercise of sovereign will, we arrive at one in which even the sovereign's will is made subject to institutions that are said to date back to "time out of mind." Reversing the humanist call for action, Daniel denies that any action is wanted. In neither poetry nor politics does England need to make itself. It needs only to recognize, value, and use the self it already has.

More than a decade before they argued over rime, Daniel and Campion had been publicly linked. Both published their first poems as addenda to Thomas Newman's edition of *Astrophel and Stella* (1591). Campion's five poems are all experimental in form; two are in quantitative meter. Daniel's twenty-three are all Petrarchan sonnets. Both sets owe an obvious debt to Sidney: Campion's to the experimental verses of the *Arcadia;* Daniel's to *Astrophel and Stella* itself. Between them they divide the Sidneian legacy and reveal the rift within it and within the larger literary and cultural project to which it belonged. Campion follows the "Greek" line; Daniel, the "Gothic." What this collection of poems makes clear, and what Daniel so marvelously obscures in his *Defense of Rime,* is that neither was particularly English. Rime itself had been borrowed from the French little more than two centuries earlier, and the form that rime most often took, the form of the fourteen-line sonnet that Campion attacks and Daniel practices, was a still more recent acquisition. To identify immemorial custom with the sonnet was to invent history.

This was the final and most decisive triumph of the quantitative movement: to make an import scarcely older than itself appear native and natural. Translated into the terms of the confrontation between Goth and Greek, French and Italian poetic form came to stand for the customary and the unmade, for the purely English. Sidney and Spenser had succeeded in having the kingdom of their own language *because* of the failure of their quantitative experiments, had succeeded so thoroughly that they made it appear their language had had the kingdom of them. To this accomplishment Daniel's *Defense* adds the finishing touch. By asserting continuity and calling this renaissance medieval, Daniel makes their work the sign of a community whose authority can both enable other poets, like Daniel himself, and repel the encroachment of royal invaders who might try to do to English law what Campion wanted to do to English verse. Like many later nationalist movements, this early one established its legitimacy through the invention of tradition, the invention, in this case, of a Gothic past to which some of its most recent cultural innovations might be attributed.[23]

Not all Daniel's readers would have accepted the shift in value promoted by his *Defense,* a shift from Greek to Goth, from active self-making to passive acceptance of time and custom. Ben Jonson, whom we have noticed defending his own art in terms that could easily have been borrowed from Ascham, told Drummond that "he had written a discourse of poesy both against Campion and Daniel, especially this last," and late in his life he talked of reviving the quantitative experiment.[24] Nor was Jonson's classicism an isolated phenomenon. He shared it with his literary generation—a generation that defined itself in opposition to the practices of Sidney and Spenser—and, in a more general way, with his monarch. James may have defended rime, but he did not otherwise much favor the Gothic. In his royal self-presentation, the new king affected, as Daniel feared he might, a Roman manner.[25] But by 1603 the Gothic had taken too firm a hold to be easily dislodged. As a result, a cultural divide that could be seen in opposed styles of architecture and in opposed legal systems, as well as in differing modes of pageantry and poetry, opened between court and country. When Jonson, who appreciated the power of the values he sometimes disdained, set Gothic Penshurst against its newer neoclassical rivals, against buildings adorned with touchstone and marble, polished pillars and roofs of gold, he employed precisely the system of differences we saw at work in the quantitative controversy, an opposition between deliberate making ("their lords have built") and an acceptance of what time and custom have already made ("but thy lord dwells").[26] And when in the parliament of 1628 the great common lawyer Sir Edward Coke struggled on behalf of the "immemorial rights" of Englishmen in opposition to Stuart absolutism, an absolutism that yearned for Roman civil law as eagerly as Ascham had yearned for Roman measures, these were still the terms he used, terms that had been shared by humanists, poets, architects, lawyers, and kings for over fifty years.[27]

The Politics of Chivalric Romance

Spenser died long before the open break between court and country. He died even before the exchange between Campion and Daniel. And his only direct contribution to the quantitative debate had been made twenty years before his death. But his name came to be associated with a far more obvious attachment to the Gothic, a far more conspicuous neglect of the Greek, than his abandonment of quantitative verse and his adoption of rime would justify. In 1715, in response to an increasing clamor of hostile comment on the fabulous knight-errantry of *The Faerie Queene* and the poem's lack of a strongly unified design, John Hughes ascribed these objectionable traits to "the remains of the old Gothic chivalry" that was "not quite abolished" in Spenser's time. To compare Spenser's poem "with the models of antiquity would," he argued, "be like drawing a parallel between the Roman and the Gothic architecture."[28] This Gothic characterization of Spenser's poem stuck. Nearly fifty years later, Richard Hurd took it up in his famous *Letters on Chivalry and Romance* (1762), proclaiming that "under this idea of a Gothic, not classical poem, *The Faerie Queene* is to be read and criticized."[29] From then on, so long as such distinctions continued to matter, *The Faerie Queene* stood as an example of an unclassical, "Gothic" mode of apprehension and expression.

Now, this clearly is a very different version of the Gothic from the one intuited by Harvey and defended by Daniel. Instead of a legal and constitutional Gothic, a Gothic associated with the immemorial customs and privileges of England and the English people, Spenser's poem represents a Gothic of chivalry and romance. Knights-errant, not lawyers, are its characteristic figures, and its dominant literary concern is rather the narrative design of large, heroic poems than the prosodic stuff of all poetry. Where Daniel's version of Gothic is popular, in the sense that it represents the communal will of the people, Spenser's is aristocratic and individualistic. In the place of peaceful resistance to royal encroachment and innovation, it glorifies knightly combat. Yet both are understood in opposition to the classical—and, in particular, in opposition to the classical art of poetry. As riming verse violates the ancient rules of quantity, so chivalric romance violates the laws of unity and verisimilitude. The humanist charge of barbarism could thus be directed—and was directed—at either. Only with the aid of some nonhumanist standard, a medieval or Gothic standard, could either be defended.

In the case of rime, that defense came, as we have seen, quite early. Its essential elements, though not the specifically medieval designation, already emerge in Harvey's rebuke of Spenser, and its full expression comes just two decades later in Daniel's *Defense of Rime*. In the case of chivalric romance, the wait for a defense is much longer—more than a century. But it took almost that long to mount a concerted attack. Not until the Restoration did readers in any considerable numbers begin objecting to Spenser's Gothic failings, to his "blindly rambling on marvelous adventures," to his "antic tales" for a "barbarous age," to "the wild fairies" that "blasted his design." Only then did critics discover how "by not following those [classical] rules," Spenser "fell so very short of the ancients."[30]

Does this delay mean that neither Spenser nor his first readers noticed the Gothic character of his poem? Many may not have. Like Virgil, Spenser had progressed from pastoral to epic, and in his epic, as in his pastoral, he had borrowed heavily from his Roman predecessor. On the strength of these bits of classical imitation, he was widely hailed as an English Virgil. Given England's acute need for such a poet, few were inclined to deny that he had appeared. There were, however, scattered murmurs of discontent. Sidney, writing of *The Shepheardes Calender*, objected to Spenser's "old rustic language . . . since neither Theocritus in Greek, Virgil in Latin, nor Sannazaro in Italian did affect it."[31] It must have been obvious that a similar charge could be directed at *The Faerie Queene*. More to the point, Daniel, who in the 1590s was a far more "correct" poet than his later defense of the Gothic would suggest, anticipated neoclassical complaints when he blamed Spenser for writing of "feigned paladins" instead of true English heroes like Bourchier, Talbot, Nevile, and Willoughby.[32] And in his own heroic poem, the *Civil Wars* (1609), Daniel adhered to the supposedly classical virtues of unity and historicity far more strictly than Spenser had done. But for a first negative reaction to *The Faerie Queene*, it is not necessary to wait even for the poem's publication. In 1580, ten years before the initial installment appeared in print, Gabriel Harvey told Spenser (and anyone else who chose to read their published correspondence) that *The Faerie Queene* could not compete with the young poet's presumably more classical "nine comedies." As far as Harvey was concerned, Spenser had let "Hobgoblin run away with the garland from Apollo" (10.472).

These are just hints. None can compare in neoclassical rigor to the strictures of Dryden, Rymer, Addison, Blackmore, Dennis, or Cobb. Nor do they show anything of the developed theory of opposing cultures to be found in Hughes and Hurd—or, for that matter, in Daniel's *Defense of Rime*. But they do suggest that even in the last decades of the sixteenth century, it was possible for an Englishman to notice that Spenser's poem was less uniformly classical than its borrowings from Virgil would seem to promise. The grounds for such a judgment were firmly in place. If one chose to follow the lead of the early English humanists, it would, indeed, have been possible to have been considerably more severe. Ascham, writing under the influence of such authorities as More, Erasmus, and Vives, had condemned romances of chivalry for their "open manslaughter and bold bawdry." "In our forefathers' time," he wrote with marked insistence on the medieval origin of romance,

> when papistry as a standing pool covered and overflowed all England, few books were read in our tongue, saving certain books of chivalry, as they said, for pastime and pleasure, which, as some say, were made in monasteries by idle monks and wanton canons; as one for example, *Morte*

Darthur . . . in which book those be counted the noblest knights that do kill most men without any quarrel and commit foulest adulteries by subtlest shifts. . . . What toys the daily reading of such a book may work in the will of a young gentleman or a young maid that both liveth wealthily and idly, wise men can judge and honest men do pity. (pp. 68–69)

Set against a charge like this—and it would be easy to produce others of the same sort—Spenser's claim that "the general end" of his Arthurian romance "is to fashion a gentleman or noble person in virtuous and gentle discipline" takes on a tone of defiance.[33] Spenser does, of course, hedge his defiance with allegory. But still a chivalric romance, however moralized, would hardly have pleased Ascham or his fellow humanists.

Though he does not specifically mention Spenser, Ben Jonson may imply such disapproval in the verses he wrote in 1610 for *Prince Henry's Barriers*. Ostensibly designed to celebrate the revived chivalric spirit associated with King James's eldest son, the text turns chivalry against itself. Instead of trying to shape Henry in the chivalric mold, Jonson has Merlin advise the prince *not* to imitate

> the deeds
> Of antique knights, to catch their fellows' steeds,
> Or ladies' palfreys rescue from the force
> Of a fell giant, or some score unhorse.

"These," he continues, "were bold stories of our Arthur's"—he could have said "our Elizabeth's"—"age,"

> But here are other acts; another stage
> And scene appears; it is not since as then:
> No giants, dwarfs or monsters here, but men.
> His arts must be to govern and give laws
> To peace no less than arms.[34]

Humanism of this sort is not only antichivalric but antimilitaristic and even antiaristocratic. It ascribes honor, as Jonson himself goes on to do, not to valor in war but to such unheroic activities as trade, farming, and the manufacture of cloth. In the place of daring knights, it strives to fashion competent governors and obedient, productive citizens.[35]

All this may seem remote from the formal literary concerns of Spenser's Restoration and eighteenth-century critics. Yet such a radical shift of values is never far from a humanism that, unlike chivalric romance, was born not in the great feudal kingdoms of France and England but in commercial Italy, a humanism that was brought to

northern Europe by a Dutch burgher whose *miles christianus* bears
little likeness to a knight of the Round Table and that was propagated
in England by a London lawyer whose ideal Utopians take pride in
violating every article of the chivalric code.[36] For such men, rejecting
the middle ages did not only mean tidying up the forms of poetry. It
meant replacing one polity, one form of government, one governing
class, and one economic organization with another. The immediate
political concerns of More and Erasmus were certainly not identical to
those of Ascham, nor were Ascham's identical to Jonson's. From the
1510s to the 1560s to the 1610s, enormous changes occurred that
altered the particular significance of propositions that superficially
resemble one another. But at all three moments, and during the century that connected them, the humanist revival of classical antiquity
involved a decisive break with the fundamental structures of authority
by which both the state and the individual had been constituted and
maintained. One version of that break is represented by the attempt to
supplant rime with quantitative verse. The rejection of chivalry and its
literary manifestation in romance represents another.

The specifically literary debate does not, as we have noticed,
emerge in any very open way in England until the latter part of the
seventeenth century, nearly one hundred years after the publication of
The Faerie Queene. But in Italy that debate had been underway since
the 1540s, and it came to a head in the early 1580s, just as Spenser
was reshaping and extending his own chivalric romance. The poem
that prompted this Italian debate and remained central to it was,
moreover, Spenser's own chief model, Ariosto's *Orlando Furioso*
(1516–32). It is impossible to say how much, if any, of this controversy Spenser knew when he began work on *The Faerie Queene*. Many
of the most important contributions to it, including those of Gian
Giorgio Trissino, Giraldi Cinthio, Giovanni Battista Pigna, and Antonio Minturno, had by then been in print for more than a decade. And
so had Bernardo Tasso's *Amadigi* (1560), with a preface by Lodovico
Dolce summarizing the major points at issue. There is, however, no
proof that Spenser had read or even heard of any of these. But to get
a sense of the argument and its relevance to his own poem he would
not have had to read them. It was enough that he read, as we know
from his many borrowings that he did, the great poem that arose from
the conflict, Torquato Tasso's *Gerusalemme Liberata* (1581).[37]
Gerusalemme Liberata not only "trimmed," as Bishop Hurd was to
say of it, "between the Gothic and the classic" (p. 56), it also made the
conflict between the two central to its thematic import. Reading

Gerusalemme Liberata, Spenser would have been forced to acknowledge the limits of his own accommodation with the classical. He would have seen, as with Tasso's help we can still see, the "Gothic" character of his poetics *and* of his politics.

Gerusalemme Liberata is founded on a conflict that goes far beyond the obvious struggle between Christians and pagans for the possession of Jerusalem. Within the Christian camp itself and within the narrative structure of the poem, the opposed values of epic and romance vie for mastery. Epic finds its prime representative in Goffredo, the divinely chosen ruler of the Christian forces. Romance, as fits its multiplicity of motive and action, has many champions—most prominent among them Eustatio, Tancredi, and Rinaldo. Only Goffredo is single-mindedly devoted to the communal cause which has brought the crusaders to Jerusalem. The others contribute to that communal cause. Indeed, its success depends on their participation. But each is at some point led astray by other motives and by other desires—by love, honor, or the romantic quest for adventure.

One episode of many will have to serve to illustrate the strongly political terms in which Tasso presents the opposition between his epic and his romance heroes. In Book 5, Rinaldo slays Gernando, another of the Christian nobles, in a fight over honor and precedence. Despite the plea of Tancredi, who recalls Rinaldo's "worth and courage" and "that princely house and race of his," Goffredo resolves to punish the offender. "If high and low," he answers,

> Of sovereign power alike should feel the stroke,
> Then, Tancred, ill you counsel us, I trow;
> If lords should know no law, as erst you spoke,
> How vile and base our empire were, you know;
> If none but slaves and peasants bear the yoke,
> > Weak is the scepter, and the power is small,
> > That such provisos bring annexed withal.[38]

"Sovereign power," "law," "empire," and "scepter"—these are the dominant terms of Goffredo's discourse of rule. As the commander of the crusading forces besieging Jerusalem, he governs neither a single nation nor a fixed territory. But he is a royal absolutist nonetheless. His power was "freely given" him by God, and he refuses to see it diminished. "Since you are all in like subjection brought, / Both high and low," he tells Tancredi, "obey and be content" (5.38). It is precisely such obedience that Rinaldo denies. Indeed, he refuses even to submit to trial.

> Let them in fetters plead their cause, quoth he,
> That are base peasants, born of servile strain;
> I was free born, I live and will die free. (5.42)

For Rinaldo, the freeborn nobleman, submission to the law is a sign of servile subjection. The state and its claims must give way before the higher claim of honor and lineage. And that higher claim is indissolubly linked to the behavior characteristic of romance. Having defied the law, Rinaldo rides off in search of "hard adventures": "*alone* against the pagan would he fight" (5.52). If sovereign power is the mark of Goffredo, solitary adventure is that of Rinaldo.

Tasso leaves no doubt concerning the official allegiance of his poem. It supports Goffredo. Where Goffredo's inspiration is divine, the moving forces on the other side are demonic. Satan, acting most often through such pagan women as Clorinda, Erminia, and the enchantress Armida, seduces the Christian champions and leads them into romance. Their recovery not only permits the final liberation of Jerusalem, but marks a decisive victory of unity over multiplicity, of historic verisimilitude over the marvelous, of antiquity over the middle ages—and, one must add, of the modern absolutist state over its feudal predecessor. "The old chivalric code is," as one recent critic has remarked, "denied and overwhelmed in an epic world that reorganizes itself according to a new custom, a world where for the concept of 'ventura' (the medieval 'aventure') is substituted that of 'service,' where the role of 'knight errant' is suppressed for that of 'soldier' to a collective cause."[39]

That Tasso's epic allegiance is only official, that his poem betrays a "secret solidarity" with the feudal, romantic ideology that it ostensibly rejects, has been a commonplace of criticism almost since the poem was issued. But if *Gerusalemme Liberata* does not make the choice easy, it does make it clear. Here epic stands not only for a supposedly superior literary form but for a whole system of values in which politics has a prominent part. In late sixteenth-century Italy, those values were associated with the reinvigorated universalism of the Counter-Reformation church. Elsewhere they would find expression in the absolutist regimes of sixteenth-century Spain and seventeenth-century France. It was in France particularly that critics, though favorably impressed with the unity of Tasso's "fable," refused to forgive "the mixture of the Gothic manner in his work."[40] That mixture and its undoubted imaginative appeal called in question the commitment to absolute authority—aesthetic authority, religious authority, and polit-

ical authority—on which neoclassicism was founded. Goffredo's obedient assertion of sovereign power had its counterpart in Tasso's acceptance of the classical rules of unity and verisimilitude. Both serve
and express what Mervyn James (with particular reference to England) has called "the dominant theme of . . . sixteenth-century political aspiration": "the desire and pursuit of the whole."[41] But the
individual aristocratic prowess of Tancredi and Rinaldo, their resistance to royal justice, their solitary feats at arms, their erring loves,
belong rather to the freer world of Ariostan romance, a world in which
the ruler is a marginal figure and his imperial project of negligible
importance. If Tasso's poem was to satisfy the increasingly repressive
and intolerant standards of seventeenth-century neoclassical judgment, that world of romance had not merely to be bounded by the
epic but wholly replaced by it.

Tasso himself anticipated this need. Tormented by the thought of
his own sinful errancy, he rewrote his poem, transforming the still
half-romantic *Gerusalemme Liberata* into the fiercely correct
Gerusalemme Conquistata (1593). He cut Armida, Rinaldo, Erminia,
and the Ariostan episodes associated with them; he chastened his
language, eliminated marvels, increased the number of battles, stayed
closer to history, and succeeded in alienating his readers almost as
completely as the classicizing Gian Giorgio Trissino had done with his
significantly titled *Italia Liberata dai Goti* (1547–48). But long before making this radically destructive attack on the Gothic elements in
his poem, Tasso had responded to similar doubts with a remarkable
postpublication addition. As early as 1581, the same year as the first
complete edition of *Gerusalemme Liberata,* the poem began appearing with a self-protective statement of authorial intention, "The Allegory of the Poem."[42] According to Tasso's allegorical interpretation,
civic happiness, represented by the capture of Jerusalem, is the goal,
and Goffredo, who stands for the understanding of the politic man, is
the hero. Solitary enterprise can, from this point of view, only be
condemned. Thus, as Tasso puts it, "love, which maketh Tancredi and
the other worthies dote and disjoin them from Godfrey, and the disdain which enticeth Rinaldo from the enterprise do signify the conflict
and rebellion which the concupiscent and ireful powers"—that is, the
love and war of the feudal nobility—"do make with the reasonable"—
with the newly rationalized and absolute power of the state.[43] If the
civic enterprise is to succeed, these errant powers must be subjected to
their natural master, as, to use Tasso's simile, the hand is subject to the
head. Thus, however much the values associated with the civil life may

be qualified in *Gerusalemme Liberata* by an affective preference for
romance, Tasso insists that, whether one thinks of politics or of poetics, the public side rather than the private, the side of the divinely
appointed ruler rather than that of the errant knight, must predomi-
nate. In this, form and content are at one. The strongly unified epic
must, Tasso clearly feels, be a poem of public life, a poem in which
unity of purpose and unity of rule are the guarantors of neoclassical
conformity.

All this *The Faerie Queene* lacks. Its principal ruler, the Faery Queen
herself, never appears in the poem and exercises only the loosest and
most intermittent control over its action—or, rather, over its actions,
for there are many. Redcross, Guyon, Scudamore, Artegall, and
Calidore are said to have been assigned their quests by the Faery
Queen, but she does not oversee their progress in anything like the
way Goffredo oversees the taking of Jerusalem. Nor are the quests
themselves parts of a unified enterprise—unless it be on the allegorical
level where magnanimity and glory are said to be central. But in one's
experience of the poem, such conceptual unity plays little part, if any.
Indeed, what readers of *The Faerie Queene* experience is, in this regard,
not unlike what they would experience in reading Boiardo or Ariosto:
they encounter a large and varied collection of more or less independent adventures that serve no common end. That, in effect, is what is
meant by chivalric romance, what Bishop Hurd and the Italian critics
of the sixteenth century meant by the Gothic. As a Gothic poem, *The
Faerie Queene,* unlike *Gerusalemme Liberata,* allows no place for the
representation of a powerfully centralized and absolutist governmental
order. It acknowledges and celebrates a sovereign lady, but it grants a
high degree of autonomy to individual knights and their separate pursuits, represents power as relatively isolated and dispersed.

In his letter to Raleigh, a letter clearly based on Tasso's "Allegory"
and that presents a reading of *The Faerie Queene* informed by acquaintance with Tasso's poem, Spenser acknowledges the limited
place *The Faerie Queene* occupies in the epic tradition. Like Tasso, he
argues that that tradition has been divided between the representation
of private and public virtues and remarks that Tasso himself dissevered
these qualities, distributing them between two different figures—the
"virtues of a private man, colored in his Rinaldo," those of a political
man "in his Goffredo." *The Faerie Queene,* or at least that part of it
which he had so far written, belongs, Spenser says, entirely to
Rinaldo's side, to the private side. Indeed, not only the three books he
here presents, but the next nine (only three of which he actually

wrote) will be similarly confined. Together these twelve books are to portray "in Arthur, before he was king, the image of a brave knight, perfected in the twelve private moral virtues . . . which, if I find to be well accepted," he says, "I may be perhaps encouraged to frame the other part of politic virtues in his person after that he came to be king" (1.167–68). Spenser does not refuse the politic in favor of the private, the king in favor of the "brave knight," but he does put the kingly and the politic off to a time that, given the length of the poem, could be expected never to arrive. A similar split and a similar exclusion mark his representation of Elizabeth. As "most royal queen or empress," she is figured by the Faery Queen, who, as we have noticed, never enters the poem. Belphoebe, who does enter it, stands rather for the queen's private person as "a most virtuous and beautiful lady." Again the private side dominates, and the political is kept waiting for some unreachable narrative prolongation. But that exclusionary deferral is itself an inescapably political act.

Spenser's division of public and private has a long history, going back at least to Aristotle's separate treatment of politics and ethics. And its history as a device for describing the Homeric poems and their various successors is scarcely less long. James Nohrnberg lists some fifteen instances from a period covering two millennia—from the ancient Greek allegorists down through Servius and Macrobius to Landino, Scaliger, and Chapman. Nor is Nohrnberg content to stop with this Western, Greco-Roman line. "The Indo-European division of the gods, founder-figures, and castes into a kingly or priestly function (Mitra) and a warrior function (Varuna)" also claims relevance. And even this is too narrow a frame for this capacious tradition. "There seems," writes Nohrnberg, "to be no reason to restrict this [divided] characterization of heroism to Indo-European culture."[44] The effect of such wonderfully expansive scholarship is to naturalize and universalize the formal order of Spenser's poem. Freed from all particular location in time or space, the poem resides in triumph with the immortal archetypes. Though Spenser had heard of neither Jung nor Frye, his own evocation of "all the antique poets historical" aims at a similar elevation. It does something like what E. K. said the antique diction of *The Shepheardes Calender* would do: it brings "auctority to the verse" (9.8). But in Spenser a self-protective motive lurks just beneath the surface, a motive he acknowledges in explaining why he has picked Arthur as his hero. "I chose the history of King Arthur as most fit for the excellency of his person, being made famous by many men's former works, and also furthest from the danger of envy and suspicion of present time" (1.167). The present is dangerous and can be approached, if at all, only by the indirection of a pretended universality.

But no poetic form is universal. None can escape the particularity of time and ideology—certainly not chivalric romance. The early English humanists' open opposition to chivalry and chivalric romance, the debate over Ariosto's *Orlando Furioso,* and, most tellingly, the sharp conflict between sympathy and doctrine within *Gerusalemme Liberata* all point to the controversial nature of the genre in which Spenser chose to write his major poem. The militant aristocratic autonomy figured by the knight-errant was potentially upsetting to reborn classicism, to civic humanism, to bourgeois commercialism, to royal absolutism, and even (as in *Gerusalemme Liberata*) to the new strategic military collectivism.[45] Humanist critics and scholars, merchants, ministers of state, and soldiers might thus all find themselves at odds with the chivalric knight. But if chivalry and its representative forms and figures could be highly controversial, they were also powerfully supported by the festive and poetic practices of the Elizabethan court. As Bishop Hurd pointed out, "tilts and tournaments were in vogue; the *Arcadia* and *The Faerie Queene* were written" (pp. 116–17).

The Elizabethan vogue for tilts and tournaments is one of the best known and most intensely studied aspects of that "romantic" age. From the 1570s through the end of Elizabeth's reign, the queen's Accession Day was regularly celebrated with lavish tournaments, and additional tournaments marked other significant court occasions. Indeed, it would not overstrain the evidence to claim that in the last two and a half decades of the sixteenth century the language of chivalry became the primary language of Elizabethan public display, outdistancing even the biblical and classical motifs that had been more prominent earlier. Courtiers became knights, and their queen became a lady of romance.[46] But to recognize the extraordinary importance of the Elizabethan chivalric revival and its part in bringing *The Faerie Queene* into existence is not to dispel the air of potential controversy that, from other sources (including Tasso), we might have supposed to be gathering about Spenser's poem. Elizabethan chivalric display was itself a practice intended to deal with conflict, a way of simultaneously releasing and containing pressures that might otherwise threaten the delicate equilibrium of the Elizabethan state. "Through its conventions of feudal loyalty and romantic devotion, Elizabethan chivalry confirmed," as Richard McCoy has observed, "Tudor sovereignty." But it also gave vent to aristocratic aggression and competition. It thus represented, in McCoy's words, "a precariously incompatible, sometimes contradictory combination of purposes. . . . It allowed a kind of compromise between conflicting interests of the crown and her aristocratic courtiers as well as a mediation of factional and personal conflicts among the courtly ranks."[47]

In a remarkable study of the earl of Essex, McCoy has himself provided an illustration of these conflicting interests and their expression in chivalric display.[48] During the last years of Elizabeth's reign, Essex was not only the queen's most prominent courtier and the most renowned of her generals, he was also the most conspicuous challenger at the many tournaments designed to celebrate her rule. And he carried his taste for knightly combat even onto the battlefield. At least twice, once before the walls of Lisbon and once again outside Rouen, he challenged his foes to meet him in single combat for the honor of their mistresses. Earlier in the French campaign, "a bold and pointless dash across enemy territory . . . into the allied camp of Henri IV" had earned Essex an official rebuke. "You . . . shall understand," wrote the lords of the privy council, "that her majesty findeth no good success of this your voyage thither . . . yet your leaving the army without any head or marshal, and none else but a sergeant major. Her majesty doth greatly dislike such an enterprise, which she accounteth an undutiful act of yours." More seriously "undutiful acts" were later to cost Essex first his liberty and then his life. But before that fatal revolt, tension was already apparent in his performances in the tiltyard. McCoy cites the 1590 Accession Day tilt in which Essex, who had recently offended the queen by marrying Sir Philip Sidney's widow, appeared "Yclad in mighty arms of mourners' hue" in honor of Sidney "whose successor he / In love and arms had ever vowed to be." Equally annoying was his part in the 1595 tilt where his attempt to dramatize the conflict between self-love and obligation provoked the queen's angry departure. "If she had thought there had been so much said of her," she was reported to have remarked, "she would not have been there that night." The queen was not adverse to attention. But certain scriptings of her part, Essex's obviously among them, could prove objectionable—as Francis Bacon recognized when he warned Essex against confronting the queen with the "dangerous image" of "martial greatness."

Celebrated by Spenser as "Great Englands glory and the Worlds wide wonder, / Faire branch of Honor, flower of Chevalrie, / That fillest England with thy triumphs fame,"[49] Essex stood—and died—for the martial and aristocratic values that were essential to chivalric romance. In this stance, he and Tasso's Rinaldo have much in common. Each is torn between a private code of honor based on a combination of noble lineage and individual military accomplishment and the public duty any subject owes his sovereign. And each has been seen as central to the last of a particular medieval "kind"—Rinaldo the enabling figure of the last Italian chivalric romance and Essex the leader of the last English "honor revolt."[50] Indeed, for each the end closes in before his individual story is quite finished. In the final books of *Gerusalemme Liberata*, Rinaldo is reintegrated into the poem's epic design, becoming once again a dutiful soldier in Goffredo's army. And Essex, who through his trial had maintained a posture of defiant steadfastness, collapsed before his execution into abject penance, violating "almost with deliberation . . . all the canons of honor."[51] The canons of honor and the canons of romance were rapidly succumbing—as they do succumb in the experience of both Rinaldo and Essex—to a new, more powerfully statist conception of moral obligation, a conception that found support in the unity and verisimilitude of classical literary form. Seen this way, Aristotle's rules (which were really Minturno's and Scaliger's) appear as the literary equivalent of Mervyn James's "desire and pursuit of the whole." The "political culture" of late Tudor England was, in James's words, one "whose stress [fell] exclusively on the creation and watchful maintenance of wholeness: i.e., on the effective incorporation of the individual into the body of the realm, under its head the queen" (p. 460). Change a word or two and this description would equally fit *Gerusalemme Liberata* and the Counter-Reformation literary culture that produced it. In both the political and the literary cultures of sixteenth-century Europe, wholeness was emerging as a dominant value.

In its Virgilian intimations, its attempts at unity, and its celebration of Elizabeth, *The Faerie Queene* participates in this cult and these cultures of wholeness. But in its adherence to chivalric romance, it remains with the errant Rinaldo and the insubordinate Essex on the Gothic side of the great sixteenth-century cultural divide. Spenser came to know the danger of such errancy and insubordination. In Book 5 of *The Faerie Queene,* an incautious poet, who has spoken ill of Queen Mercilla, is found nailed by his tongue to a post. And since Mercilla's court is the poem's nearest representation of Elizabeth's, the warning is particularly telling. Nor is this the only sign of danger. A sense of peril hangs over the whole of the 1596 installment. Book 4, the first of the newly published books, begins with an acknowledgment that Spenser's own work has found disfavor in high places:

> The rugged forehead that with grave foresight
> Welds kingdomes causes, and affaires of state,
> My looser rimes (I wote) doth sharply wite,
> For praising love, as I have done of late.

And Book 6, the last of the new books, ends with the Blatant Beast of envy and detraction threatening Spenser's "homely verse," which, as he again admits, has already been brought "into a mighty Peres displeasure."

That "mighty peer," the possessor of the "rugged forehead" of Book 4, is universally identified as William Cecil, Lord Burghley, the lord treasurer of England and the queen's principal counselor.[52] Educated at Cambridge in a college dominated by Ascham and his humanist friends, Burghley was no partisan of the Elizabethan chivalric revival. Nor did he much approve those most prominently identified with it. Essex was, for example, at odds with Burghley and with Burghley's son and political heir, Robert Cecil, throughout his public career. Referring to Burghley and Essex, the French ambassador wrote, "there was always great jealousy between them in everything, one against the other, and a man who was of the lord treasurer's party was sure to be among the enemies of the earl."[53] And in this antagonistic relationship, Essex was only taking the place of his political mentor and Spenser's one-time patron, the earl of Leicester. Spenser himself advertises this Leicester-Essex succession and his own relation to it. Catching sight of Leicester House in the course of his "Prothalamion," he recalls that it was here

> Where oft I gayned giftes and goodly grace
> Of that great Lord, which therein wont to dwell
> Whose want too well now feeles my freendles case.

"Yet therein now," he continues, "doth lodge a noble Peer," the earl of Essex, whose praises he goes on to sing in words I have already quoted. From 1579, when he dated a letter to Harvey from Leicester House, to 1596, when he celebrated Essex as "Great Englands glory," Spenser's strongest associations were with the party that opposed Lord Burghley. No wonder Burghley disapproved of his poetry.

"Spenser [was] the poetic spokesman *par excellence* of militant Protestant chivalry."[54] This statement by Roy Strong and Jan van Dorsten in their book on Leicester's Netherlands expedition sums up a widely held view. What I have been arguing is that the Gothic form of *The Faerie Queene* does more than this. In addition to supporting the militant, interventionist policy of the Leicester-Essex faction, Spenser's image of chivalric multiplicity also represents a form of political organization in which the private initiative and private *virtù* (to use a familiar Italian word that includes both *virtue* and *strength*) of individual aristocratic champions plays an exceptionally large part. Whether consciously or unconsciously, Spenser makes his poem the implicit advocate of a partially refeudalized English polity. The literary authority of Ariosto might at first have naturalized and thus concealed this political orientation, even from Spenser himself. Ariosto's could, after all, be considered simply the accepted way of writing a long heroic poem in the sixteenth century, whatever your politics. But with the publication of *Gerusalemme Liberata,* in which the debate over Ariosto found at once literary and political expression, the mask of Ariostan legitimacy would have slipped badly. Setting Tasso's poem next to Spenser's, anyone could see, as I think Spenser himself saw, how powerful and how powerfully significant his variance from the epic and its statist ideology really was. Faced with this recognition, he may indeed have felt sufficiently uncomfortable to make some effort to unify and to "Virgilize" *The Faerie Queene,* as many critics think he did sometime between 1580 and 1590. But that effort could not alter the poem's fundamentally multiple and chivalric character. Whatever those qualities had "said," they went on saying—saying perhaps more forcefully for the very acknowledgment that they were not all that might be said. Like Tasso's, Spenser's is a poem divided against itself, but in it the balance comes down more firmly on the Gothic side.

The chivalric character of *The Faerie Queene* is so pervasive that it is almost invisible to any but the most superficial regard. And because literary critics are taught to eschew superficiality, it does not figure in most recent accounts of the poem.[55] In this the eighteenth-century critics had the advantage. They were not yet much given to our kinds of close reading, or at least they labored under no institutional constraint requiring them to turn their close readings into published monographs. But they were still deeply involved, as we no longer are, in the Renaissance conflict between classical and medieval forms, and they knew that in terms of that conflict *The Faerie Queene* was a very troubling poem, a poem that in various ways resisted the ordering, unifying, and rationalizing tendencies of the previous two centuries. When Hughes or Hurd call *The Faerie Queene* "Gothic" or when Thomas Warton charges, as he did in his *Observations on the Faerie Queene* (1754), that "Spenser made an unfortunate choice and discovered little judgment in adopting Ariosto for his example, rather than

Tasso," they recognize this resistance and reveal that to them it still mattered.[56] This recognition may, as we have noticed, go back as far as Harvey's accusation of Hobgoblinishness, and it continued to be repeated with increasing critical and historical elaboration so long as the dialectic of Greek and Goth remained central to England's self-understanding and self-representation.

But if the mere (and massive) fact of romance design and chivalric action was enough to make a powerful ideological statement, it is nevertheless true that many individual passages of *The Faerie Queene* reveal the ambivalence concerning absolute royal power that underlies the poem's representation of aristocratic autonomy. *The Faerie Queene* is, as many recent critics have insisted, a poem of praise, an important contribution to the cult of Elizabeth.[57] But that praise is variously qualified. Not only is the Faery Queen herself kept out of sight on the poem's furthest periphery, but those figures of royal power that do enter the poem—all dangerously recognizable likenesses of Queen Elizabeth—inspire more apprehension than allegiance.

This is obviously the case of the "mayden Queene" Lucifera in Book 1 and her royal look-alike Philotime in Book 2.[58] Both represent a demonic perversion of majesty, one that threatens those knights that approach the seat of power with dishonorable subjection. But even the "gratious" Mercilla, who, like Lucifera and Philotime, is first seen "Upon a throne of gold full bright and sheene, / Adorned all with gemmes of endlesse price" (5.9.27), presides over a court that knows nothing of the chivalric honor Spenser's poem is bent on celebrating. The bright armor of Arthur and Artegall "did . . . much amaze" the clamorous mob of petitioners that filled Mercilla's hall "For never saw they there the like array, / Ne ever was the name of warre there spoken" (5.9.24). And when, later in the episode, two sons of Belge come seeking aid for their oppressed mother, "none of all those knights" belonging to Mercilla's court is willing to undertake the enterprise "for cowheard feare." So it is the stranger knight Arthur, here figuring Leicester, who

> stepped forth with courage bold and great,
> Admyr'd of all the rest in presence there,
> And humbly gan that mightie Queene entreat,
> To graunt him that adventure for his former feat. (5.10.15)

Mercilla "gladly" grants his request, but both the initiative and the subsequent action are his doing, not hers. If Lucifera and Philotime represent a perversion of honor, Mercilla's court betrays a passive

56   *Chapter One*

neglect of it—though to say so in any less veiled way than Spenser does would be to risk the fate of the tongue-nailed poet Bonfont/Malfont.

In Book 2, Mammon tells Guyon that from his royal daughter Philotime alone "Honour and dignitie . . . derived are" (2.7.48). In his proem to Book 6, Spenser says something very similar of and to his own "most dreaded Soveraine": "from you all goodly vertues well / Into the rest, which round about you ring" (6.proem.7). This monarchic claim to a monopoly on honor, dignity, and virtue is precisely what marked the shift from a feudal to an absolutist regime.[59] Spenser's description of Elizabeth as the unique fount of virtue contributes to this shift, but his parodic ascription of similar authority to Philotime resists it. And in the context of Book 6, the book of courtesy, even the positive assertion is so qualified that monarchic authority seems to be in competition (sometimes losing competition) with other, more private sources of validation. The book begins "Of Court it seems, men Courtesie doe call," but its narrative finds its prime representatives of courtesy far from court, in the woods and countryside. Indeed, one of the most attractive of those representatives, the old shepherd Melibee, berates the "roiall court" as a place of vanity, delusion, and idle hopes. And at the allegorical center of the book, in the scene on Mt. Acidale, the poet puts his own love in the privileged place hitherto reserved for the queen.[60] He apologizes for the substitution, but he makes it all the same. Such displacements are anticipated earlier in the poem when the queen herself, in her "private" guise as Belphoebe, is removed from the court and made to speak against it.

> Who so in pompe of proud estate (quoth she)
>   Does swim, and bathes himselfe in courtly blis,
>   Does waste his dayes in darke obscuritee,
>   And in oblivion ever buried is. (2.3.40)

And, significantly, it is in this private role that she values "deedes of armes and prowesse martiall" most highly. "All vertue merits praise," she says, "but such the most of all" (2.3.37). Where Mercilla presides over a "cowheard" court (the class slur in Spenser's spelling is surely no accident) and where even the Faery Queen recalls the heroic Artegall before his "reforming" work is thoroughly complete, Belphoebe herself bears, if not the instruments of war, at least those of the warlike chase. Divided from her royal power, in her private body, the queen appears as a martial figure, a fit exemplar of Spenser's heroic creed. But enthroned in her public body, she misleads, deflects, frustrates, or simply fails to nourish chivalric valor.[61] It is thus appropriate that Spenser should have chosen to represent the deeds of Arthur as "a brave knight . . . *before* he was king" rather than his achievements *as* king. Kingship in the modern "politic" and absolutist sense is inimical to knightly, aristocratic virtue.

But if *The Faerie Queene* expresses much ambivalence concerning the strongly centralized monarchic order that was to a large degree the very enabling condition of its existence, it entertains no similar doubts concerning the aristocratic myth of natural, inborn superiority. Virtuous plowmen, "salvages," and shepherd lasses regularly turn out to be the foundling offspring of nobles and kings, while base-born upstarts are just as regularly betrayed by their pride, insolence, and cowardice. Unlike those humanists who favored virtue over lineage and who argued that the state might recognize virtue with the reward of noble title (as Elizabeth did for William Cecil), Spenser refuses to envisage the separation of blood and virtue.[62] "Shame is to adorne," he charges, with the "brave badges" of arms and knighthood one "basely borne" (6.6.36), but

> O what easie thing is to descry
> The gentle bloud, how ever it be wrapt
> In sad misfortunes foule disformity. (6.5.1)

What then are we to make of his claim that "the general end . . . of all the book is to fashion a gentleman or noble person in virtuous and gentle discipline"? This, it must be insisted, is fashioning of a quite limited sort. Spenser does not mean to make gentlemen of what he calls "cowheard villains." That, he supposes, would be impossible.[63] His aim is rather to perfect the well-born in the discipline appropriate to their class. And central to that discipline, as Spenser teaches it, is an aristocratic independence that would make a Leicester or an Essex a dangerous figure in the Tudor-Cecil state—as a similar romantic and chivalric discipline and a similar insistence on the prerogatives of blood make Rinaldo a disruptive figure in the regime governed by Goffredo. The difference between Spenser and Tasso is that Spenser endorses claims of birth that Tasso admires but ends by reducing to obedience.

That reduction was essential to the making of the modern state and it was powerfully underway in Tudor England. New men and the service of a new monarchy were, as we have noticed, turning the state into the unique fount of honor. Without such changes, *The Faerie Queene* would have been quite literally inconceivable. Yet, as much as it is the product of a new monarchic centralism, *The Faerie Queene*

resists that centripetal force. It represents an uneasy and unacknowl-
edged compromise between a monarch who gives both the poem and
the nation whatever unity and identity either has and individual aristocratic knights whose adventures are the glory and the safety of the
nation. Private virtue, "*ethice*" in the term of the letter to Raleigh, is
made the sole instrument of public action. Instead of a princely
Goffredo at the head of a highly organized and complexly equipped
army, solitary knights embody England's Protestant destiny in *The
Faerie Queene,* destroy the enervating Bowre of Blis, overcome the
enemies of Belge and Irenae, and capture the Blatant Beast. In a letter
to Sir Philip Sidney, Sidney's political guide, the Burgundian humanist
Hubert Languet, warned his pupil against independent action on behalf of the Belgian states. "It is not your business, nor any private
person's, to pass judgment on a question of this kind; it belongs to the
magistrate, I mean by magistrate the prince, who, whenever a question of the sort is to be determined, calls to his council those whom
he believes to be just men and wise. You and your fellows, I mean men
of noble birth, consider that nothing brings you more honor than
wholesale slaughter; and you are generally guilty of the greatest injustice, for if you kill a man against whom you have no lawful cause of
war, you are killing an innocent person."[64] In their principal quests,
Spenser's knights are not guilty of such injustice. Their actions are
licensed by the magistrate. But they do enjoy an autonomy that such
Elizabethan generals as Leicester and Essex exercised only with peril
and reproach. Though tempered by statist ideology, the chivalric form
of *The Faerie Queene* strengthens the association that Languet, like
earlier humanists, blames, the association of aristocratic honor with
"wholesale slaughter"—an association that, as Languet realizes, men-
aces the monarch's authority as the sole dispenser of justice.

In standing against neoclassical order and verisimilitude, Spenser's
Gothic image of England stands against the rationalizing tendencies
of the modern state. This oppositional stance is the constant preoccupation of his various proems. In each he sets what he calls "antiquity,"
a time that belongs rather to the idealizing historical imagination than
to any particular period but whose most prominent features are romantic and chivalric, against the present—with the unfailing proviso
that his dread sovereign mistress be understood as exempt from all
blame. Indeed, antiquity and the queen are repeatedly presented as
the twin sources of his poem. But clearly there is a tension between
them, a struggle in Spenser's effort to fit "antique praises unto present
persons" (3.proem.3). That tension and that struggle were not, how-

ever, his alone. They belonged equally to the militant Protestant faction with which, through most of his career, he was associated—to Leicester, to Sidney, to Essex, and to the many lesser figures who supported them. Bridled by a parsimonious queen and a cautious minister, the members of this faction found themselves, like Tasso's Rinaldo, repeatedly torn between private honor and public duty. By enforcing the claims of duty, both civic humanism and Aristotelian neoclassicism worked to restrict and ultimately deny the aristocratic cult of honor. Spenser's chivalric romance pulls the other way. It enlarges the sphere of honor and identifies private virtue with public obligation. *The Faerie Queene* represents a nation of indistinct boundaries and uncertain political organization, at once British and Faery, but it leaves no doubt concerning the value of lineage and heroic endeavor.[65] For all its claims to some larger truth, claims that generations of critics have expanded and elaborated, Spenser's poem thus serves a quite particular and partisan ideology, a Gothic ideology of renascent aristocratic power.

A Miltonic Revision

To use the term *Gothic* with reference only to chivalric romance is, however, to forget that other version, the one used to defend rime against its Greco-Roman rival. Nothing in Harvey or Daniel's constitutional and common-law Gothic makes it the particular site of aristocratic dominance. On the contrary, in Harvey's image of a "quiet company of words" or in Daniel's evocation of immemorial "custom," we hear rather the voice of the commons. What unites the two is a shared resistance to the totalizing encroachment of a royal authority on which both nevertheless depend. By writing the crown into one or the other of these two versions of Gothic, as Spenser does by calling his poem *The Faerie Queene* or as Daniel does by coupling his *Defense of Rime* with a panegyric on James, poets could erect something of their own representation of that now comfortably familiar English notion of the "king-in-parliament"—what Sir John Fortescue a century earlier had called a *dominium politicum et regale* and had opposed to the imperial Roman *dominium regale*.[66] Once again, whether the argument took the part of the lords, as it did in Spenser, or of the commons, as in Daniel, the opposing form was classical. But now with the increased power of the new monarchy and the increased prestige of reborn antiquity, the threat was much greater than it had been in Fortescue's time, so great that poets were sometimes inclined to think that their only hope lay in classical form and royal patronage. Nor, for all the Gothic qualification in their work, do either Spenser or Daniel renounce that classical and monarchic path. Both *The Faerie Queene* and the *Defense of Rime* address the ruler and seek royal support and both attempt to rival the cultural accomplishment of Greece and Rome. But they nevertheless find in a largely fictional English medieval tradition a space of cultural and political resistance.

It may thus seem surprising that Spenser and Daniel's greatest successor in the English poetic tradition, a man whose opposition to the king led him into open rebellion, should have rejected both their versions of Gothic. But that is precisely what happened. Introducing *Paradise Lost* (1674), John Milton identified rime as "the invention of a barbarous age to set off wretched matter and lame meter," and in the poem itself he scorned chivalric romance. Rime had, he conceded, been "graced . . . by the use of some famous modern poets, carried away by custom," but it was nevertheless "a fault avoided by the learned ancients" and one that should be avoided still. In producing his own poem without rime, Milton was presenting an example for emulation, "the first in English, of ancient liberty recovered to heroic poem from the troublesome and modern bondage of riming."[67] As for chivalric romance, its "chief maistry" had, he mockingly charged, been

>   to dissect
> With long and tedious havoc fabled knights
> In battles feigned. . . .
> The skill of artifice or office mean,
> Not that which justly gives heroic name
> To person or to poem. (9.29–41)

And here too he had his own substitute, though in this case one equally neglected by the ancients: "the better fortitude / Of patience and heroic martyrdom."

Milton did not compose in quantitative meter, but he did describe his "measure" as "English heroic verse" and likened it to "that of Homer in Greek and of Virgil in Latin." It thus presented itself as the English equivalent of the ancient heroic meter, and Milton himself emerged in the position the humanist advocates of quantitative verse regularly assigned to Homer and Virgil, the position to which Sidney and Spenser, in the days of their quantitative experiments, aspired. He took the place of the imperial lawgiver for his nation's heroic poetry. His choice of generic forms reveals a similar bias. Though he competes as fiercely with the ancient epic poets as he does with medieval and Renaissance romancers, he nevertheless models his poem on the classical epic, strictly observing the laws of unity and historical verisimilitude laid down by the Italian Aristotelians. Indeed, he goes beyond them and beyond the poetic exemplar of the position they advocated, the Tasso of the Goffredo side of *Gerusalemme Liberata,* to redefine heroism in a way more suited to the antimilitaristic humanism of More and Erasmus. The "better fortitude" he sings is a quality realized in moral choice rather than in battle. But he does not, for all that, abandon the absolutist ambition of the neoclassical epic. He simply transfers that authority from the monarch to God and, more significantly, to the individual moral agent. As he wrote in *Eikonoklastes* (1649), they in whom "true religion, piety, justice, prudence, temperance, fortitude, and the contempt of avarice and ambition . . . dwell eminently need not kings to make them happy but are architects of their own happiness and whether to themselves or others are not less than kings."[68]

Inasmuch as he appears in his poem as a figure of "patience and heroic martyrdom," Milton himself assumes this kingly role. He does the same in calling his attack on King Charles's book *Eikonoklastes,* for *eikonoklastes* was, he recalls, "the famous surname of many Greek emperors" (3.343). And, of course, his prosodic lawgiving once again elevates him, at least implicitly, to a similarly regal eminence. In *Paradise Lost* and in Milton's later career generally, the poet moves into the place formerly reserved for the ruler, appropriating as he does so the ancient forms that once stood for imperial power.[69] From this vantage point, the self-protective uses of the Gothic practiced by Daniel and Spenser seem unnecessary. Instead of defending against royal usurpation by associating poetry with the immemorial rights and customs of the English people or with the chivalric ethos of the feudal nobility, Milton himself does the usurping. The revolution for which he struggled failed, but he claims victory even in defeat. Nor is this solely a personal triumph. It is rather an example to the English nation of an inner freedom from which political freedom can arise—not, to be sure, an anarchic freedom but freedom found in obedience to a thoroughly rational and God-centered state. In Milton, epic form and heroic meter are as much the vehicles of a statist ideology as they were for any Aristotelian theorist or neoclassical poet of the sixteenth century.

The confidence with which Milton expresses his imperial design depends on the prior accomplishment of Spenser and Daniel. Their Gothic versions of England and of English poetry, different as they are from one another, established a cultural space that Milton and the many English poets after him, whether neoclassicist or medievalizing and romantic, could then occupy. That space was variously defined. But to the extent that it was the space of a distinctly English poetry, it continued to serve the interests of a national state, as Spenser and Daniel had served a national monarch. In this way both Goth and Greek were adapted to a nationalist discourse. The differences between them and between the ways in which each was used by various groups and interests nevertheless continued to matter. Daniel's constitutional Gothic, Spenser's chivalric Gothic, and Milton's republican Greek each made a claim to legitimacy both on the part of the poet and on the part of a particular social formation—whether legal and parliamentary, militant and aristocratic, or independent and middle class—with which the poet and his work were associated. The Renaissance invention of an ancient-medieval dichotomy provided each of these poets and each of these groups, as it did many other poets and groups over the next several centuries, with a rich but fluid set of terms, terms in which present fears and ambitions could be invested with the authority and distinction of the past.

2

WRITING THE LAW

THE
FIRST PART
OF THE Institvtes
OF THE LAWES OF
England.
OR,
A COMMENTARIE
vpon Littleton, not
the name of a Lawyer onely,
but of the Law it felfe.

MARTIAL.
Quid te vana iuuant miferæ ludibria Cartæ ?
Hæc lege, quod poſſis dicere iure meum eſt.
CICERO.
Maior hæreditas venis vnicuiq, noſtrum à Jure, &
Legibus, quàm à Parentibus.
Hæc ego grandæuus poſui tibi candide Lector.
Authore EDW: COKE *Milite.*

The ſecond Edition, corrected ; With an Alphabe-
ticall Table thereunto added.

LONDON,
Printed by the Aſſignes of *Iohn More*
Eſquire ; and are to be ſold by
Richard More in S. *Dun-*
ſtans Churchyard.

Anno 1629.

SOME THIRTY YEARS BEFORE ROGER ASCHAM
attacked English rime, another humanist made a similar attack on
English law. "Who is so blind," Thomas Starkey wrote in his *Dialogue
between Pole and Lupset* (1529–32), "that seeth not the great shame
to our nation, the great infamy and rot that remaineth in us, to be
governed by the laws given to us of such a barbarous nation as the
Normans be?" Again English practice is condemned as medieval and
barbarous. And again the solution is radical extirpation and replacement. "All," writes Starkey, "by . . . one remedy should be amended
and correct, if we might induce the heads of our country to admit the
same: that is, to receive the civil law of the Romans, the which is now
the common law almost of all Christian nations."[1] As Roman verse
would repair the barbarism of English poetry, so Roman law will cure
the infamy and rot of English law.

Since the twelfth century, Roman civil law, the body of law that in
late antiquity was instituted, digested, and codified by order of the
Emperor Justinian, had been "received" as the common law of most
parts of Europe. Roman law was taught in the universities and gradually came to be practiced in the courts. Though some early English
jurists, Bracton most notable among them, studied this newly recovered Roman law and brought Roman ideas to the discussion of English law, England resisted the reception. Neither the procedure nor
the substance of English law bore the Roman stamp. Its leading
spokesmen were not university professors but serjeants-at-law; its
prime source was not a written text but unwritten precedent; its language was not Latin but law French. In all these respects, English law
seemed from Starkey's humanist perspective repellently uncouth: "full
of much controversy," "of small authority," lacking all "stable
ground." Clearly, this whole farrago of "barbarous customs and ordinance" would best be "wiped away" and replaced with that "which we
call the very civil law . . . the most ancient and noble monument of the
Romans' prudence and policy" (p. 175).

Starkey's advice was not followed. Indeed, it may not have been
heard. Unlike Ascham's *Schoolmaster*, the *Dialogue between Pole and
Lupset* was not published until the nineteenth century and seems even

65

in manuscript never to have reached its intended recipient, King Henry VIII.[2] All the same, in our own century, the few paragraphs Starkey devoted to the need for legal reform have been much cited. A celebrated legal historian, F. W. Maitland, is responsible for this attention. In 1901, in his famous Rede Lecture, *English Law and the Renaissance,* Maitland presented Starkey's views as evidence of a serious threat to the continuity of English law. In the second quarter of the sixteenth century, the common law of England was, according to Maitland, experiencing a crisis that made a reception of the sort Starkey recommended a distinct possibility. The institutional machinery for it was in place. Newly endowed professorships of civil law at both Oxford and Cambridge were there to train the necessary legal practitioners, while existing courts, like Star Chamber, Chancery, and Requests, could have served as a scene for a decisive expansion of their activity, as similar courts had already done in the German and Scottish receptions. There were, moreover, indications that the life of the common law was, as Maitland put it, "by no means lusty."[3] The yearbooks, which for centuries had provided an account of current Westminster practice, ceased publication in 1535; in 1547 "divers students of the common laws" appealed formally to the privy council, claiming that the old laws were being set aside in favor of the "law civil"; and a decade later one observer reported that King's Bench and Common Pleas, the principal courts of the common law, had so little business that the lawyers just stood and "looked about them" (p. 82). The menace was of course averted. The common law regained its former vigor, and no reception occurred. But the fear (or the hope) of its occurrence was not wholly groundless.

Or so Maitland claimed. In the more than nine decades since he wrote, that claim has been subjected to much scrutiny and much criticism, criticism so severe as to have been characterized as successful demolition. Starkey, say the critics, was an unrepresentative figure out of touch with the English legal community, and he may, in any case, not have meant what he seemed to be saying. Yearbook-style reporting continued unabated in manuscript. Common-law business experienced no significant decline, and there was no great increase in civilian practice. The continuity of English law was, in short, never threatened.[4]

Sweeping as this rejection would seem to be (and not all the critics would agree with all its points), it nevertheless shares with Maitland's original thesis a powerful set of assumptions. English law and the course of English legal history are fundamentally unlike their counterparts elsewhere in Europe. Germany, Scotland, France, Italy, Spain, Portugal, and Holland all received Roman civil law. England didn't. England's law is homegrown, continuous, insular, and unique. Law elsewhere is borrowed, shared, historically broken. In their legal institutions, foreigners are thus doubly foreign: foreign to themselves as well as to the English. No wonder that even on the continent few writers in Maitland's time could be found willing to give "a hearty good word for the reception" (p. 8). It had meant their own national undoing. Thus, whether one agrees with Maitland that the English themselves barely escaped a similarly disastrous self-alienation or with his critics that the threat was never particularly great, a happy celebration of English difference seems well justified.

Maitland himself cogently defined the ideological basis of this widespread agreement. "We have all of us," he remarked, "been nationalists of late. Cosmopolitanism can afford to await its turn" (p. 8). Perhaps that turn has now arrived. In what must be the most radically unsettling reassessment of Maitland's thesis, J. H. Baker has recently argued that medieval law did not survive in sixteenth-century England and that there was no reception, as such, on the continent.[5] Maitland's initial question—how and why did England resist the reception that overwhelmed the rest of Europe?—was based on a misunderstanding of both the English and the continental situation. England did not resist and the continent did not succumb, at least not to a formal reception. Instead, both underwent much the same process of fundamental change. "In point of detail the English story could not be more different from continental legal history. But in the shift of emphasis from *doctrine* (or common learning) to *jurisprudence* (or judge-made law) the similarity is striking" (p. 59). Both English and continental lawyers paid far more attention to decided cases, particularly to cases decided in the newly strengthened central courts, at the end of the century than they did at its beginning, and both paid less attention to common reason and erudition. The vaunted difference of English law from law on the continent is thus less profound than it is usually made to seem. Not only do both systems have a history marked by significant discontinuity, they have, if we believe Baker, much the same history.

In discussions of Maitland's thesis, Baker's cosmopolitanism stands out as extraordinarily rare. But anticipations of it can easily be found elsewhere in the development of English legal scholarship. In the 1610s, precisely at a time when claims of the uniqueness and antiquity of English law were being pressed with particular intensity, the lawyer and antiquary John Selden argued that the differences had been much exaggerated. Like Baker, Selden denied that the continent had experienced anything like a full reception. Contrary to the usual English assumption that "the supreme and governing law of every other Christian state (saving England and Ireland) . . . [is] the old Roman imperial law of Justinian," he insisted that "no nation in the world is governed by [that law]." "Doubtless," he continued, "custom hath made some parts of the imperials to be received for law in all places where they have been studied, as even in England also," but that only means that they have become part of the local law. England is thus not unique in its uniqueness. "Every Christian state hath its own common laws, as this kingdom hath."[6] Nor can the English boast of the greater antiquity or more perfect continuity of their law. "All laws in general are equally ancient. All were grounded upon nature, and no nation was that out of it took not their grounds; and nature being the same in all, the beginning of all laws must be the same." Though this last does not much resemble Baker's argument, it does have a similar effect. It minimizes difference and suggests that English and continental law have equivalent, if not identical, histories.

Why then, if a "cosmopolitan" account of English legal history has been available for nearly as long as a "nationalist" one, does Baker's rejection of Maitland seem so novel, novel even with respect to Baker's own previous work, since just a few years earlier he had concluded another examination of Maitland's thesis with the "nationalist" opinion that "parallels with the continent seem to be neither close nor instructive"?[7] Is it simply that the differences are obvious and inescapable, while the likenesses are deep and difficult to ferret out? To some extent this is surely the case. The various civil law systems of continental Europe have more in common with one another than any of them has with the English legal system, and that shared similarity is in large part owing to a greater dependence on the authority of Roman civil law. In this sense, the continental reception and the English failure to undergo such a reception are historical realities that cannot be denied. But those realities can themselves function to mask ideological engagements. That Baker has moved toward a "cosmopolitan" understanding of English legal history at a time when England itself has been moving toward greater participation in the European Community is no more surprising than Selden's move in the opposite direction when legal cosmopolitanism appeared a threat to the parliamentary interest he supported.[8] The most carefully researched and disinterested legal history is, like any other history, strongly inclined to tell the story its author and the audience for which he writes want to hear.[9] And for a very long time the favored story has been one of essential difference.

The telling of that differentiating story seems to have begun late in the fourteenth century with John Wycliffe's *De Officio Regis* (1379), and it was strongly seconded a century later by Sir John Fortescue in his *De Laudibus Legum Angliae* (1470), where the political implications of legal difference are made explicit.[10] In a passage to which I alluded at the end of the last chapter, Fortescue distinguished between what he called the *dominium politicum et regale* characteristic of England and the continental (particularly French) *dominium regale*. Where in England the king had no power to change the laws without gaining the assent of the whole realm represented in parliament, the French monarch's will was absolute. Empowered by the Justinianic maxim *Quod principi placuit legis habet vigorem* ("What has pleased the prince has the force of law"), civil law kings might easily degenerate into tyranny. English common law provided a barrier against such degeneration and thus served to maintain the liberty of the subject. Seen this way, England's legal difference seemed a proper cause for rejoicing, a legitimate source of national pride.

And so it was to remain, by most accounts, for centuries—indeed so it is still today. But difference can as easily cause anxiety as pride. We have already encountered one notable instance of such anxiety in Spenser's lament: "Why a God's name may not we, as else the Greeks, have the kingdom of our own language?" For Spenser, England's difference was a mark of inferiority, a sign of insufficient civility. Some such fear troubles even Fortescue's *De Laudibus*. It was, after all, the "glorious fame" of Roman law and the possibility that an English prince beguiled by that fame might wish to impose Roman law on his people that made Fortescue's defense of English law necessary. And with the spread of humanist ideas in the next century that need increased. Starkey's complaint and his proposal may have had no influence whatsoever. But they are nevertheless symptoms of a crisis no less significant than the one Maitland identified. Even if Maitland's critics are right that English law was in no danger of being replaced by Roman law, English law *was* in danger of being replaced by a "Romanized" version of itself. Indeed, that is what happened. England did not receive Roman law. But it did receive a Roman idea of the law, or rather a Roman idea of the form in which the law should present itself.

Starkey argues for this lesser reception as well as for the greater. If England is not to receive Roman law, it should at the very least "use the same remedy that Justinian did in the law of the Romans." It should gather the law and cause it "to be written . . . in our mother tongue, or else put into the Latin" (p. 174). A few years later, Richard Morison, who had been at Oxford and Padua with Starkey and who, like Starkey, had entered the service of Thomas Cromwell, presented the king with a *Discourse Touching the Reformation of the Laws of England* (1535) in which he proposed "to attempt if the common laws of this your realm that now be unwritten might be written; that now be dispersed and uncertain might be gathered together and made certain; that now be in no tongue might be reduced into the Latin tongue."[11] And Morison too takes as his model for this reforming enterprise the work of Justinian. "This thing, though it be hard, as all noble things be, yet is it not impossible. The laws which now we call civil, before the Emperor Justinian's time were as much dispersed and as far out of order as ours be" (pp. 440–41). What the Romans did the English can and should do. They should write the law, produce an English equivalent of the *Corpus Juris Civilis.* Not only would such a book remedy the law's confusion and uncertainty, it would stand as a mark of civility, a mark of England's freedom from barbarism.

Neither Starkey nor Morison ever produced such a book. Morison tried but with little success. Starkey did not even try. Nor did anyone else of their generation. They identified a need but were unable to satisfy it. In this they resemble Ascham, who called for a classicizing reform of English verse but failed to accomplish that reform himself. Spenser, Sidney, and their contemporaries responded to Ascham's call, struggled to provide England with the missing quantitative meter, and ended by producing an art of English poetry equivalent to, though distinct from, the ancient art, one that justified itself in Daniel's *Defense of Rime* by association with English law. In the law itself, there could, however, be no comparable answer to Starkey's call, no completion of Morison's aborted project, for the obvious reason that the work of Starkey and Morison, unlike Ascham's *Schoolmaster,* remained unknown. Younger men, men of precisely the age of Sidney and Spenser, did nevertheless manage to reconceive the "Romanizing" project that had preoccupied their Henrician predecessors, and they brought it to a conclusion that was both as successful and as far removed from the original ambition as was the Elizabethan erection of barbarous rime into a distinguished "native" art of poetry.

The most conspicuous of these younger men was then and still remains Sir Edward Coke. Born in 1552, the same year as Spenser, Coke provided in his *Reports* (1600–1615), his *Book of Entries* (1614), and his *Institutes* (1628–44) something of a *Corpus Juris* for England. To identify Coke as the chief "Romanizer" of English common law may, however, seem little short of absurd. No less likely candidate for such a distinction seems imaginable than this man whose mind, in the memorable phrase of J. G. A. Pocock, "was as nearly insular as a human being's could be."[12] Yet I would contend that Coke's very insularity, his myopic insistence on the uninterrupted Englishness of English law, was the product of a constant sense of legal and national difference, a persistent awareness of a rival system of law against which English law had to defend and define itself. Coke was insular not by ignorance but by ideological necessity. His insularity was part of a self-presentational strategy. Furthermore, neither that insularity nor the cosmopolitan awareness that underlay and enabled it were his alone, though in him both reached extraordinary proportions and led to no less extraordinary results. Both were shared by his generation, the generation of lawyers and legal scholars born between the midcentury and the mid-1560s. Coke's massive legal writings were just one manifestation of a common, age-based project, a project that began to emerge in the last years of Elizabeth, was powerfully shaped by the conflicts of James's reign, and produced its most enduring monument, Coke's own *Institutes,* only after Charles had become king.

Though there are real differences between English law and the law practiced elsewhere in Europe and real similarities between the history of English law and the histories of those other legal systems, neither the nationalist nor the cosmopolitan position is simply a matter of getting the facts right. Each is ideologically motivated, and each depends on the other (even if only as a signifying absence) to be a position at all. So in the sixteenth and early seventeenth centuries, the project, anticipated by Starkey and Morison and realized by Coke and his generation, of writing English law derived both its inspiration and its cogency from its Roman and continental rival. Nor was the rivalry only between domestic law and a foreign counterpart, for the civil law had its schools, its professors, its practitioners, and its courts in England. In law, as in other areas, national consolidation had a double face. It turned inward to find out and eliminate those practices and those institutions that failed to reflect back its own unitary image, and it turned outward to declare its defining difference—*and* to assure itself that such difference was not so different that it would be taken as a sign of backwardness or barbarity. And what I here express in this abstract personification, this figure of a nationalist Janus, was for Coke and his contemporaries a matter of immediate and lived experience.

Their own individual interest and identity, the interest and identity of the professional community (or communities) to which they belonged, the interest and identity of the nation they were helping (for whatever reason) to construct depended on the meanings they succeeded in attaching to their activities. And those meanings depended in turn on the play of differences in a system of signifying relations—a *langue,* as a Saussurian might say, to enable their *paroles.*

What then did it mean in Coke's generation to write the law? This question has no simple answer. There was a general agreement that such writing was needed and an equally general understanding that it must in some way be related to Justinian's writing of Roman law. In this agreement and understanding, Starkey and Morison shared. But the particular situation of the Elizabethans differed considerably from that of Starkey and Morison, and individual Elizabethans were differently situated from one another.[13] From these differences in situation came differences in their sense of how the writing should be carried out and whose interests should be served by it. Differences in training and practice between common lawyers and civilians, jurisdictional conflicts between common-law courts, civil-law courts, and courts of equity, questions of royal prerogative and parliamentary privilege, more particular issues like the proposed union of Scotland and England, personal antagonisms and ambitions: all these served to divide Coke and his legal contemporaries from one another and to make their writing of the law a counter in their personal, political, and professional disputes. Nor did the struggle end with the death of this generation and the posthumous publication in the 1640s of the final three volumes of Coke's *Institutes.* Controversy continued for centuries as the products of their joint undertaking were variously appropriated, annotated, emulated, revised, criticized, or replaced by their English and American successors.

In the discussion that follows, I will not often be able to look forward to these subsequent developments. Nor will I have much chance to look across the Channel at the similar projects that were going on there. But some awareness of later and distant events is necessary if we are not to construe the meaning of the Elizabethan enterprise too narrowly. For that enterprise reaches back through the early sixteenth-century humanists to late antiquity and beyond and forward even to our own day, and it has many parallels in the other emerging nation-states of early modern Europe. To give equal attention to this broad range of related activities would be to miss the specificity of the Elizabethan experience. But to neglect the broader range would result in a no less serious distortion. It would be to mistake the dialect of sixteenth- and early seventeenth-century legal discourse in England for a self-enclosed and self-sufficient language. The accent and inflections of Coke's project, even some of its essential vocabulary and syntax, may have belonged to him and his generation alone, but its deep structure made it part of a language spoken wherever national self-representation and the Roman legal tradition converged.

Plans for an English *Corpus Juris*

Members of the same generation do not necessarily like each other. Nor do they always agree. Edward Coke's most persistent antagonist was a lawyer just nine years his junior: Francis Bacon. Rivals in the 1590s for the post of solicitor general, for the attorney-generalship, and for the hand of Lady Hatton (all of which Coke got), their mutual scorn flared up in an Exchequer proceeding in 1601. As Bacon told the story to Robert Cecil, Coke "kindled" at an apparently slighting motion Bacon had made. "Mr. Bacon," Coke is supposed to have said, "if you have any tooth against me, pluck it out, for it will do you more hurt than all the teeth in your head will do you good." Bacon answered coldly: "Mr. Attorney, I respect you. I fear you not. And the less you speak of your own greatness, the more I will think of it." The exchange continued in much the same vein, Coke declining "to stand upon terms of greatness" toward Bacon, who, he said, was "less than little, less than the least," and Bacon insisting that Coke "not depress me so far, for I have been your better, and may be again, when it please the queen." At this Coke spoke, as Bacon put it, "neither I nor himself could tell what, as if he had been born attorney general; and in the end bade me not meddle with the queen's business, but with mine own."[14]

Anger, animosity, and injured pride are not all that finds expression here, though they are obvious enough. The exchange also foreshadows an ideological break that would soon separate the two men, if it hadn't already. For Bacon, all status depended on the queen. The son of a man the queen had appointed lord keeper, he had once been Coke's better. With Coke as attorney general, that ranking was reversed but might change again "when it please the queen." Coke, on the other hand, is made to speak as if he thought his greatness his own, "as if he had been born attorney general."

Bacon no doubt misrepresents Coke, who could on occasion show a keen awareness of his dependence on royal favor. And, in writing to the queen's principal secretary, Bacon may also have had reason to misrepresent himself. But seen in the light of the continuing relation between the two men, Bacon's dramatic rendering of their confrontation seems prophetically true. Over the course of the next two decades, he and Coke would repeatedly differ in situations where royal prerogative and the common law—in Coke's view, the subject's most precious birthright—were in conflict. In 1613, as King James's solicitor general and with the express intent of weakening Coke and recovering "that strength to the king's prerogative which it hath had in times past and which is due unto it" (11.381), Bacon got Coke transferred from the Court of Common Pleas to the less crucial Court of King's Bench. In the next few years, with Bacon now attorney general, he and Coke clashed over Peacham's Case, the Case of Commendams, and the Case *De Rege Inconsulto*, all of which pitted the king's prerogative against judicial freedom. Then in 1616, as a result of these conflicts, Bacon succeeded in having Coke removed from the privy council and dismissed as chief justice. From this triumph, Bacon's fortunes continued to rise, as he assumed in turn the posts of lord keeper and lord chancellor, until in 1621 a strong common-law parliament, led by Edward Coke, found Bacon guilty of accepting bribes and impeached him.

Which is ultimately superior, the king or the law? Whatever else was at stake in these various confrontations, this was a question that ran through all of them. In their actions and institutional commitments, Bacon and Coke consistently took opposite sides. Bacon favored the king; Coke, the law. Yet with regard to that great project of writing the law, the project which produced as its most significant accomplishments Coke's *Reports* and *Institutes,* even these antagonists agreed. If Coke wrote English law in such a way as to answer the objections that humanists like Starkey had directed at it, Bacon foresaw and defined that need. From 1593, when in his first reported parliamentary speech he called for an abridgment of the laws and statutes of the realm, to the 1620s, when he included an "Example of a Treatise on Universal Justice" in his *De Augmentis Scientiarum* (1623), Bacon made the writing of the law the single most important and most prominently reiterated element in his program for civic reform.[15] Like Starkey, he considered the uncertainty of English law its greatest defect and, again like Starkey, he presented Justinian's redaction of Roman law as the exemplary remedy for such a failing. He never attacks English law for its barbarousness. By the 1590s such outright condemnation was no longer possible, particularly for a common lawyer like Bacon. Nor does he urge a reception of Roman law. That too had passed beyond the verge of even hypothetical possibility. But he does recommend "a general amendment of the state of [the] laws" and a reduction of them "to more brevity and certainty" (7.316) that in all but the smallest details adheres to the Justinianic program.

What that program stood for in Bacon's mind was first a certain formal order and then a certain conception of authority. Following Justinian's *Corpus Juris,* Bacon recommended that the two main bodies of English law, common law and statute law, be separately reduced and recompiled, for "this," he says, "was the plan followed by Trebonianus"—Justinian's chief assistant—"in the *Digest* and *Code*" (5.100). He then urged that this "heroic" (10.336) two-part work be surrounded with a set of auxiliary books: "institutions; a treatise *de regulis juris;* and a better book *de verborum significationibus,* or terms of the law" (13.70). Like the *Digest* and *Code,* each of these has its counterpart in Justinian's *Corpus Juris.* The *Institutes* is one of the four major parts of the *Corpus,* while *De Verborum Significatione* and *De Regulis Juris* are the two last titles in the *Digest.* In describing what such books should be like, Bacon obviously had these Roman models in mind. Institutes, to take only the example most relevant to our consideration of Coke, should, he advised, "be arranged in a clear and perspicuous order," should "run through the whole private law," and should not "touch . . . the public law" (5.105), all characteristics of Justinian's *Institutes.*[16] But form was not the only thing Bacon derived from his Roman model. He also drew on that model for a conception of authority and its appropriate expression. From first to last, Bacon imagined the writing (or rewriting) of the law as belonging essentially to the monarch.[17] The formal order he seeks derives from monarchic authority. As Justinian "wrote" Roman law, so Elizabeth or James should "write" the law of England. Unless an English monarch would play Justinian, Bacon could not be the English Tribonian he clearly aspired to be. Without a royal author the law could not be written. No other source of authority was imaginable.

This combination of formal adherence to the pattern of the *Corpus Juris* and an association of the writing of the law with monarchic (or imperial) power recurs with some regularity in the Bacon-Coke generation. In 1613, Henry Finch, a collaborator of Bacon's on a commission whose charge was to reduce "concurrent statutes . . . to one clear and uniform law" (13.71), published a book of his own that W. S. Holdsworth has called "the most complete and best institutional book before Blackstone."[18] This book, Finch's *Nomotechnia* (1613), later Englished as *Law, or a Discourse Thereof* (1627), began

with a dedication to King James, based its organizational scheme on
Justinian's *Institutes,* and devoted a portion of every chapter to what
one historian has called an "obsequious" consideration of the relevant
function of royal prerogative.[19] Still more obviously devoted both to
Justinian and to the king was John Cowell, whose law dictionary, *The
Interpreter* (1607), stirred up a storm of parliamentary opposition by
its uncompromising advocacy of royal absolutism and whose *Institutes
of English Law* (1605) follows the order of Justinian's *Institutes* chapter by chapter.[20] Others—William Fulbecke, Lodowick Lloyd, Sir
John Hayward, and Sir John Dodderidge—while they did not go as
far as Bacon, Finch, or Cowell in the project of writing English law
according to the Roman pattern did nevertheless argue that the two
systems were amenable to such reduction to a common order. And
when they were not asserting the similarity of the two laws, English
lawyers of this generation agonized over the differences between
them. In 1588, Abraham Fraunce could, for example, worry about the
familiar charge that "the civil law . . . is both in itself more constant
and philosophical [than the common law] and also by Justinian more
methodically . . . put down."[21] Two decades later, Sir Thomas Ridley
gave new point to such worry with his highly laudatory *View of the
Civil and Ecclesiastical Law* (1607). King James's open admiration for
this *View* moved Coke "from thence to prophesy the decay of the
common law."[22] No one of this generation, including Ridley, called
for the kind of reception Starkey had proposed in the 1530s. But their
work as a whole testifies to a pervasive insecurity regarding the stability and authority of English law and an equally pervasive sense that the
appropriate remedy was to write that law in accordance with the
Roman model. To that extent they were all partisans of an English
reception.

But could even so limited a reception be undertaken without sub-
stantive alteration? Wouldn't the very nature of both English law and
the English state be affected? "The common law of England is," as
Bacon several times notes, "no text law, but the substance of it consisteth in the series and succession of judicial acts from time to time
which have been set down in the books we term yearbooks or reports"
(12.85). He does not wish to alter this fundamental character. That
would, he says, be "to cast the law into a new mold"—a "perilous
innovation" (13.67). But whatever he may claim to the contrary,
wouldn't that be the result of his reform? In England, the chief example of text law was statute, law enacted by the king-in-parliament. If,
as he intends, Bacon's proposed registering and recompiling of the

common law is itself accomplished by the same king-in-parliament, won't its product be statute law? The chief foreign example of text law, Roman civil law, was made text law through just such a process of registration and recompilation. "Justinian the emperor," wrote Bacon, "by commissions directed to divers persons learned in the laws, reduced the Roman laws from vastness of volume and a labyrinth of uncertainties unto that course of the civil law which is now in use" (13.66). This is how Justinian became the Roman lawgiver, how Elizabeth or James might become an English lawgiver.

Bacon continues to differentiate between *lex scripta* and *lex non scripta*, between "text law" and "customs well registered," but in the light of his project the difference is increasingly hard to see. When customs are registered at the king's behest, they become text law and the king becomes their author. In his *True Law of Free Monarchies* (1598), King James based his own claim to absolute sovereignty on just such an act of royal authorship: "kings were the authors and makers of the laws, and not the laws of the king."[23] Whether the law is authored by a conquering monarch, as James here imagines, or reauthored, as Bacon recommends, by a king who has inherited his crown by due descent, the effect is much the same. Absolute royal prerogative is expressed and confirmed. And the loser is always the judge. Instead of those "judicial acts," which Bacon identified as the source of English common law, royal acts now make the law. "Leave not the law to the pleasure of the judge," James told parliament in 1607, "but let your laws be looked into"—by which he clearly intended just such an "amending and polishing" as Bacon had been urging on him, "for," as James said, "I desire not the abolishing of the laws, but only the cleaning and sweeping off the rust of them" (p. 293).

Always there, lurking about the edge of consciousness, was the menacing stigma of barbarism. Set against all others, Finch claimed, English law holds its head as high "as cypresses among the pliant shrubs" ("quantum lenta solent inter viburna cupressi"). To any sixteenth-century grammar school boy, these words would have had a special resonance. They are taken from Virgil's *Eclogues*, where they celebrate the superiority of Rome.[24] Rome's erstwhile eminence, Finch seems to be saying, is now England's. But then comes the familiar complaint. "Among the innumerable men trained in this august discipline [of English law], no one has yet arisen to supply an excellence of method to match its excellence of matter." The law lies "damaged" and "fragmented" in "a more than Anaxagorean confusion." Describing English law as an "ancient palace that hitherto hath been accounted (howsoever substantial) yet but dark and melancholy" and announcing his own project of "gaining some comfortable lights and prospects toward the beautifying of this ancient palace," Cowell expresses a similar view.[25] Gothic buildings are dark and melancholy. Light and prospect belong to the newer classicizing architecture. Both Finch and Cowell bring us once again to the verge of a reception. What is "damaged," "fragmented," "dark," and "melancholy" in English law is uniquely its own and must be sacrificed. When legal reform has done its reordering and opened its neoclassical "lights and prospects," the remaining substance will be essentially Roman. In all but detail, the *Corpus Juris Communis Anglicani* Bacon, Finch, and Cowell envision will be indistinguishable from Justinian's *Corpus Juris Civilis*. And the consequences of that likeness will be more than aesthetic. To imitate the self-presentational form of Roman law is not only to escape barbarism; it is also to adopt something like the imperial order of the Roman state. That is the program Bacon and Cowell were urging, one in which Finch's *Nomotechnia* and Cowell's *Institutes* participate.

But for all the importance of Bacon's various programmatic statements, of Finch and Cowell's institutional writings, of the lesser contributions of Fraunce, Fulbecke, Dodderidge, and the rest, theirs were not, even in their own generation, the works that made it possible for Englishmen to feel that their law had been written in an authoritatively satisfying way. That role fell rather to the work of Bacon's great rival, Sir Edward Coke, a man who ignored Finch, called Cowell "Doctor Cowheel," and stood firmly against the absolutist conception of royal prerogative that seemed to Bacon, Finch, Cowell, and the others an intrinsic part of their project. If Ridley's *View* with its detailed and eulogistic description of the *Corpus Juris,* if Cowell's books and Bacon's schemes seemed threats to the common law and particularly to that preeminence that Coke felt the law should exercise over even the king's prerogative, then those threats would have to be answered in something like their own terms: by a writing of the law. This is what Coke did. But he did it in a way that altered the fundamental understanding of what such writing meant, by writing against writing.

Reporting the Unwritten Law

Late in his life, Coke made a catalog of his extensive library. Among the books he listed were Bacon's *Instauratio Magna,* Fulbecke's *Par-*

allels, Cowell's *Interpreter,* Ridley's *View,* and no less than eight different editions of various parts of the *Corpus Juris.* He did not list either Finch's *Nomotechnia* or Cowell's *Institutiones,* but a copy of the former survives with his other books at Holkham House and the latter is quoted in the catalog itself.[26] Passing from books on the laws of England to those on the civil law, Coke recalls Cowell's assertion of the similarity between the two systems: "Dr. Cowell in his *Institutions of the Laws of England* . . . saith that 'the principles of both . . . are the same, the definitions and divisions of things are the same, the rules plainly agree, the statutes are similar; they differ only in idiom and method.'"[27] Clearly Coke had been attending to what his contemporaries were writing and thinking. But, as one might expect, he did not approve of everything he saw. On the title page of Bacon's *Instauratio Magna,* he wrote, "It deserveth not to be read in schools, / But to be fraughted in the ship of fools," to which he added in Latin: "You purpose to reconstruct the teaching of wise men of old. Reconstruct first our laws and justice."[28]

Bacon's judgment of Coke was more generous. "Had it not been for Sir Edward Coke's *Reports,*" he wrote James in 1616, "the law by this time had been almost like a ship without ballast." But a few pages later he uses the same image for "the treatise *de regulis juris*" on which he was himself engaged. "I hold it of all other things the most important to the health, as I may term it, and good institutions of any laws. It is indeed like the ballast of a ship, to keep all upright and stable." And not many lines go by before the implicit comparison is made explicit. "I do assure your majesty, I am in good hope that when Sir Edward Coke's *Reports* and my *Rules and Decisions* shall come to posterity, there will be (whatsoever is now thought) question who was the greater lawyer" (13.65 and 70).[29] In Bacon's cosmopolitan philosophizing, Coke saw only folly. For Coke, Bacon stood outside the legal pale. His *Instauratio Magna* contributed nothing to the restoration of English law. Bacon himself drew the line differently. Both he and Coke are within it. They compete in the common enterprise of ballasting the ship of English law. But underlying the difference in their judgment of one another was a shared sense of need. They agreed that "to reconstruct our laws and justice"—"instaurare leges justiciamque"—was a task of great urgency.

Bacon identified Coke's *Reports* as part of this undertaking. That Coke also saw his *Reports* this way puts a distance between those reports and all previous books of the same sort. When Coke began publishing reports in 1600, the shelf to which they would naturally be added contained some fifteen printed volumes: nine volumes of collected yearbooks, the abridgments of Fitzherbert and Brooke in three volumes, two volumes of Plowden's reports, and one volume of reports left by Sir James Dyer. In addition, many lawyers would have had a few volumes of manuscript reports (Coke had at least sixteen), whether of their own composition or copied from the work of others.[30] But in all this material, nothing would have presented itself as a response to the humanist critique of English law. Rather than defending the law, these books were its unreflective products. Yearbooks, abridgments, and reports supplied a record, a more reliable record than that provided by memory and oral transmission, of what had happened in court, what pleadings had been used, and what decisions had been reached. But they said nothing of the relation of English law to other legal systems, nor did they address any but an immediate and professional audience.

Coke's work as a reporter began in this narrow tradition. From 1572, when at the age of twenty he entered the Middle Temple, he regularly attended court proceedings in Westminster Hall. And from 1581, he kept a careful record of the many cases he observed. Assembled in seven fat notebooks (the first alone filled 900 octavo leaves), these manuscript reports were a principal source of Coke's vast legal erudition.[31] As such, they performed to an extraordinary degree the quite ordinary function of such literature. They helped make the reporter himself a more able lawyer. But by 1600, when he published his first volume of reports, Coke began to have a new idea of what they could do. No longer were reports merely a convenient aid to memory. They now had a polemical purpose as well. They provided a defense and illustration of the English legal system itself, a defense against precisely those threats represented by the humanist interest in Roman law.

The recourse to print was itself a sign of this change. Prior to Coke's, only Plowden's reports had been printed in their author's lifetime, and Plowden felt compelled to apologize for the innovation. He allowed it only to prevent a pirated and defective edition. Coke too expressed some reluctance about committing his work to print, but he did so in a preface that was otherwise devoted to the importance of writing. Without written and published yearbooks, "the opinions, censures, and judgments" of past judges would have been "long sithence wasted and worn away with the worm of oblivion," and with them the certainty of the law itself would have been lost. "For," he continued, "I have often observed that for want of a true and certain report, the case that hath been adjudged standing upon the rack of many running reports (especially of such as understood not the state of the question) hath been so diversely drawn out as many times the true parts of the case have been disordered and disjointed and most commonly the right reason and rule of the judges utterly mistaken."[32] Coke objected not only to the fallibility of "slippery memory" but also to the anonymity and vagary of the common-law manuscript culture, to what he called "wandering and masterless reports." Fixed in print and authored by the queen's attorney general, his work was meant to remedy this defect.

In this first preface, Coke made no direct reference to any competing legal system. Nor did he insist on the particularity of English law. But from the opening sentences of his second preface of 1602, the vigorous defense of English law against all rivals became his constant theme. "Of all laws," he insisted, the common laws of England "are most equal and most certain, of greatest antiquity and least delay, and most beneficial and easy to be observed." Had he simply taken the standard humanist complaints and reversed them, Coke could hardly have produced a more blindly partisan claim. Equality, certainty, antiquity, efficiency, and accessibility were the very qualities others attributed to the written law of Rome, qualities they found sadly lacking in England's unwritten law. Coke denied all that. Though he admitted that the Romans may "justly . . . boast of their civil laws," he argued that even they recognized the superiority of English law. Had they not thought it superior, they would have changed it during the centuries when they occupied ancient Britain. But this they didn't do, for the law now practiced in England is the same that Brutus brought from Troy a millennium before the Roman invasion.

Even among Coke's contemporaries, this fantastic historical claim was widely rejected. "Hyperbolical praise," Hayward called it, praise of a sort "now out of season, as never suitable but with artless times."[33] Less artless notions were widely available. Many agreed with Starkey that English law descended from the Normans. Others attributed its essential features to the Saxons. And still others, Hayward among them, thought it of mixed origin, mingling Roman, Saxon, Danish, and Norman elements. But Coke's assertion, though he argued for it at length in subsequent prefaces, was less a matter of historical truth than of polemical necessity. One way to escape the charge of medieval barbarism was to claim an origin well before the arrival of the barbarians, an origin that reached back to "time out of mind." Nor was this merely a matter of establishing the superiority of

English law through its superiority of age. The immemorial character of that law also made it proof against royal encroachment.

Already in his second preface, written and published while Elizabeth was still queen, Coke praised "the ancient law of England" for its independence from monarchic will. Against English government by law, he set "the tyranny of other nations wherein powerful will and pleasure stands for law and reason. . . . In other kingdoms the laws seem to govern, but the judges had rather misconster law and do injustice than displease the king's humor" (2.¶iv^v–v). With James's arrival on the throne of England, the threat to the law's independence became more immediate, and Coke's warnings became proportionally more precise. The preface to his fourth volume of reports, the first published under James, is a sermon against legal innovation. The correcting of old laws is dangerous; the making of new ones, more dangerous still. Even the digesting and expounding of the law has its perils. Two particular events prompted Coke's concern. One was a conversation with the new king in which James complained of the uncertainty of English law. The other was a royal command that the penal statutes be abridged and digested. Coke warmly applauds the king's initiative in both instances, but he hedges his applause with such reminders and such qualifications that James might well have doubted his sincerity. His description of the king's complaints leads to this quotation from Bracton: "The king is under no man, but only God and the law, for the law makes the king. Therefore let the king attribute that to the law which from the law he hath received, to wit, power and dominion. For where will and not law doth sway, there is no king" (4.Bv). And his discussion of the command ends in a series of potentially disabling cautions. "Certain statutes concerning the administration of justice . . . are," Coke writes, "so woven into the common law . . . as it will be no small danger to alter or change them." And as for bringing the common law itself "into a better method," he doubts "much of the fruit of that labor" (4.Biii^v).

This last set of objections speaks directly to the project of writing English law on which not only James but also Bacon, Finch, Cowell, and many others were already engaged. Undertaken "in the high court of parliament" and limited to penal statutes ("with such caution as is beforesaid"), such writing, Coke is willing to acknowledge, would be "an honorable, profitable, and commendable work for the whole commonwealth" (4.Biii^v). But then it immediately reminds him—the lack of any transition is striking—of another project, one far more closely in keeping with the true spirit of English law and far better calculated to answer the complaints that have been directed at it: his own. "This fourth part of my *Reports*," he writes,

> doth concern the true sense and exposition of the laws in divers and many cases never adjudged or resolved before, which for that they may in my opinion tend to the general quiet and benefit of many, the only end (God knoweth) of the edition of them, I thought it a part of my great duty that I owe to the commonwealth not to keep them private, but being withal both encouraged and in a manner thereunto enforced to publish and communicate them to all, wherein my comfort and contentation is great, both in respect of your singular and favorable approbation of my former labors, as for that I (knowing my own weakness) have one great advantage of many famous and excellent men that have taken upon them the great and painful labor of writing. For they to give their works the more authority and credit have much used the figure *prosopopeia* in feigning divers princes and others of high authority, excellent wisdom, profound learning, and long experience to speak such sentences, rules, and conclusions as they intended and desired for the common good to have obeyed and observed. . . . But I without figure or feigning do report and publish the very true resolutions, sentences, and judgments of the reverend judges and sages of the law themselves. (4.Biii^v–iv)

Coming immediately after Coke's discussion of the king's intended redaction of the penal laws, this passage inevitably suggests a relationship—perhaps a rivalry—between the two projects. Both involve writing the law; both are meant to secure "the general quiet and benefit of many"; both claim to serve the commonwealth. But the two differ in ways that make one a bulwark of the law, the other a threat to it.

So long as the common law was left untouched, Coke did not oppose a redigesting of the penal statutes. But he was clearly worried that reform would not stop there. For more than a decade, Bacon had been proposing that all English law, common law as well as statute law, be brought "into a better method." In James, England now had a king who was reacting favorably to such suggestions, a king who had already ordered that the work be begun, a king who showed neither sympathy for nor understanding of the judge-centered law that for Coke was the very mark of the English nation. Such a menace could not be left without a response. Indeed, the shape of a response had already emerged. If James and Bacon thought the law needed writing, Coke had his own way of writing it. Instead of digests, abridgments, and methodical rearrangements, he presented reports. "For," he said, "I hold him not discrete that will *sectari rivulos* when he may *petere fontes*"—"that will follow rivulets when he may seek out sources" (4.Biii^v). An abridgment leads away from the law; a report reveals its very source. "The reporting of particular cases or examples is," he insists in one of his later prefaces, "the most perspicuous course of teaching the right rule and reason of the law, for so did almighty God himself when he delivered by Moses his judicial laws. . . . And the glossographers, to illustrate the rule of the civil law, do often reduce the rule into a case" (6.¶vi). Not even Coke can resist the temptation to draw authority from the civil law, but he does so to legitimate a quite un-Roman literary mode.

And why should his avoidance of *prosopopeia* be a matter for such ardent self-congratulation? Perhaps because *prosopopeia* is the figure adopted in the most famous of all legal abridgments, Justinian's *Institutes*—"which," as Coke elsewhere remarks, "Justinian assumeth to himself, although it were composed by others" (8.diii^v). Coke was as eager not to make the king speak the law as Justinian, Tribonian, and such English followers of theirs as James and Bacon were to make him its speaker. *Rex est lex loquens.* Against this Roman maxim favored by James and his supporters and represented by the literary fiction of Justinian's *Institutes,* Coke and his *Reports* reply, *Judex est lex loquens.*[34] The law speaks not through the king but through "the very true resolutions, sentences, and judgments of the reverend judges and sages of the law themselves, who for their authority, wisdom, learning, and experience are to be honored, reverenced, and believed" (4.Biv). Coke does not deny that English law is the king's. But it is the king's only as the kingdom is his, by due and lawful inheritance; it is not his to make or to alter.

What most provoked Coke's royalist opponents was not the omission of a kingly speaker from his *Reports.* The genre did not, after all, invite such an intrusion. What bothered them was rather the inescapable presence of another voice, that of Sir Edward Coke himself. "Let not the judges . . . meddle with the reports," wrote Bacon in the *De Augmentis,* "lest from being too fond of their own opinions, and relying on their own authority, they exceed the province of a reporter" (5.104), and in an earlier memorandum he left no doubt what judge he had in mind. "Great judges," he told the king, "are unfit persons to be reporters, for they have either too little leisure or too much authority, as may appear by [the reports of Dyer and Coke], whereof that of my Lord Dyer is but a kind of notebook, and those of my Lord Coke's hold too much *de proprio*" (12.86). But it was Bacon's elder collaborator, the lord chancellor Thomas Egerton, who reacted with greatest outrage to Coke's *de proprio*. "That your lordship is *lex loquens*," he scribbled angrily on a draft of his "Observations upon the Lord Coke's *Reports*," "out of whose mouth like oracles proceed laws to posterity, that as you are Lycurgus in prescribing laws for the commonwealth, so you will be a means in protecting literature for their necessary use; that as you are *a lato* in counseling for the good of all, so you will be a Hercules in defending that which is for the good of all."[35] In Egerton's view, Coke had not merely exceeded the province of a reporter, he had usurped the place of the king. He, not James, is the *lex loquens* in his *Reports,* the English Lycurgus and Hercules.

The individual reports, in which Coke offends, according to Egerton, by "scattering or sowing his own conceits almost in every case" (p. 297), provide one scene for this usurpation. But another is furnished by the often expansive prefaces that from 1600 to 1615 head all eleven volumes. These prefaces were as much a departure from generic precedent as was Coke's deliberate resort to print. Unlike the prefaces that introduce the earlier reports of Plowden and Dyer, these constitute a running defense of England's native legal system, an extended occasional and polemical discussion of the nature, sources, and proper acquisition of the common law. And here, still more obviously than in the reports themselves, Coke speaks in his own person and out of his own authority. He lists the law's essential features and asserts their immemorial history; he describes the ancient and modern books of the common law; he discovers the law's hidden coherence and warns against alteration; he praises not only the law itself but all its institutions, texts, and practitioners;[36] he dismisses the testimony of chronicle history and the authority in legal matters generally of anyone but common lawyers; he defines the constitutional relationships of the king, parliament, and the law; he claims primacy in jurisdiction for the common law and its courts over all other law and all other courts; and he insists repeatedly on the importance of true reports. So wide-ranging and so influential were these prefaces, that it would not be too much to say that in them Coke transformed a largely unreflective cultural practice into an ideological weapon. If he did not quite invent English law, he did invest it with a new polemical meaning. And in doing so, he won for himself in sober fact a position not unlike the one Egerton sarcastically attributed to him. He came to be known as the supreme oracle of English law.

The English-speaking world divides the study of legal history between two distinguishable scholarly communities. In one are those trained as lawyers and affiliated with schools of law; in the other, those

trained as historians and located in departments of history. Coke's
Reports have been differently appropriated by each. The law-school
scholars have concentrated on the substance of the reported cases and
on the mode of their reporting; the mainline historians have been
more interested in the prefaces and the constitutional ideas they express. Each emphasis has its blindspot. Where the lawyers regard
Coke's prefaces as a charming but largely negligible adjunct to the real
legal stuff of his *Reports,* the historians treat his ideas as though they
had no textual embodiment at all.[37] From neither point of view can
one appreciate the representational force of Coke's amphibious literary form. The law-French cases address a purely professional audience
and insert themselves into a textual sequence that stretches from the
yearbooks, through the printed reports of Plowden and Dyer, down
to the court reports of our own time. The prefaces, printed in both
Latin and English but not in law French, speak to a broader English
and even continental readership and belong rather in the company of
books like Fortescue's *De Laudibus,* Christopher St. Germain's *Doctor
and Student* (1530), or Sir Thomas Smith's *De Republica Anglorum*
(1565). Coke's great accomplishment was to bring the two together,
to make the characteristic court-centered form of English legal literature the vehicle for a description and defense of English law. The
special authority of each was thus made to support the other. Here, on
the one hand, were the sages of the law, advocates and judges, debat-
ing and deciding the great leading cases—467 of them in all—that had
been heard in the various English courts for a period of some thirty-
five years. And here, on the other hand, was Sir Edward Coke, attorney general, chief justice of Common Pleas, chief justice of the King's
Bench, a man who had been in constant attendance at Westminster
Hall for those thirty-five years and more, introducing the law and
explaining its special place in the life of England's commonwealth.
These were working books, books that every common lawyer needed
to own and consult. But they were also ideal figurations of the legal
community and the nation—books that told not only how the law
functioned and what the courts had decided but also what England
was and what part lawyers had in the making of its identity.

This potent combination of polemical preface and reported proceedings found a highly significant imitator just as the last of Coke's
eleven volumes was appearing. In 1615, Sir John Davies, the king's
attorney general for Ireland, published his *Irish Reports* with a lengthy
"preface dedicatory" addressed to the lord chancellor. Coke's prefaces
were never dedicatory. He deliberately avoided any reliance on pa-

tronage. The authority of his books derives from the law alone—and from their author's special relationship to it. And had Coke dedicated one of his books, it would certainly not have been to Thomas Egerton. But despite Davies's participation in a social and political circuit that by 1615 was openly hostile to Coke, his book draws on the energy released by Coke's coupling of prefaces and reports, and it makes still more explicit the meaning of that literary exploit.

In Davies's account, reports are so intrinsic to the common law, to the English *jus non scriptum,* that one could hardly survive without the other. Thus, though no reports remain from the twelfth or thirteenth centuries, Davies assumes that they must once have existed, for Glanville and Bracton "affirm that the law of England was *jus non scriptum* in their times."[38] "Reports are but comments or interpretations upon the text of the common law, which text was never originally written, but hath ever been preserved in the memory of men, though no man's memory can reach to the original thereof" (sig. *1^{v}–2). Reports put in writing what is always and forever unwritten. They are a form of writing that denies the supremacy of the written, that forbids access to an identifiable origin or author, whether king, parliament, or judge. The unwritten law that reports represent is "connatural to the nation," made by the English people "out of their own wisdom and experience . . . not begging or borrowing the form of a commonwealth either from Rome or from Greece as all the other nations of Europe have done" (sig. *2^{v}). Of all systems of law, it is "the most perfect and most excellent and without comparison the best to make and preserve a commonwealth . . . far more apt and agreeable than the civil or canon law or any other written law in the world besides, howsoever some of our own countrymen, who are *cives in aliena republica et hospites in sua,* may perhaps affirm the contrary" (sig. *2–2^{v}).

Davies thus joins Coke in giving the lie to Starkey and all his humanist descendants. What the humanists read as a sign of England's barbaric inferiority is in fact the mark of its constitutional superiority. But this answer depends for its credibility on a written text, the reports to which it is attached. If the common law of England truly has "more certainty in the rules and maxims, more coherence in the parts thereof, [and] more harmony of reason in it" (sig. *2^{v}) than does any other human law, the evidence is to be found in the proceedings of its courts as recorded in texts such as these. In Coke's *Reports* and in Davies's, the writing that Starkey, Morison, Bacon, Finch, Cowell, and the others demanded is accomplished. But it is a writing against writing, a writing in defense of the unwritten, a writing that opposes any institute, digest, or code, one that opposes even the written laws of England itself, "namely our statutes or acts of parliament" (sig. *2). It is, furthermore, a writing that in English and Latin prefaces addresses those unlearned in the law only to tell them of that which they cannot understand, the impenetrably written/unwritten law-French reports that fill the greater part of the volume they hold in their hands. As such, this writing preserves the special prerogative of the professional community in whose collective memory the unwritten law resides, making that community "connatural," as Davies says of the law itself, "to the nation."

The Form of Coke's *Institutes*

In the preface to his second volume of *Reports*, Coke praised Elizabeth for never interfering with the law. "Bless God for Queen Elizabeth," he wrote, "whose continual charge to her justices . . . is that for no commandment under the great or privy seal, writs or letters, common right be disturbed or delayed and, if any such commandment (upon untrue surmises) should come, that the justices of her laws should not therefore cease to do right in any point" (2.¶v). King James failed to exercise the same restraint. In 1616, he sent order by Francis Bacon, then his attorney general, to the twelve common-law judges that they should halt proceedings in what has since come to be known as the Case of Commendams. Before taking any further action, they were to consult with the king himself. Under Coke's leadership, the judges refused. Their oath of office forbad them, they said, to respect such an order. They were then summoned before the king and coerced into submission. Eleven acquiesced. Only Coke resisted. Asked how he would respond to a future royal directive, he answered, "When the time shall come, I shall do that which will become a judge."[39]

This answer did not please the king. Within a month Coke was suspended from the privy council, forbidden to ride circuit, and ordered to revise his *Reports*, "wherein, as his majesty is informed, be many extravagant and exorbitant opinions set down and published for positive and good law." Behind this last demand stood a detailed and highly critical set of "observations" on Coke's *Reports* written by Lord Chancellor Egerton. These charged that Coke had "purposely labored to derogate much from the rights of the church and the dignity of churchmen and to disesteem and weaken the power of the king in the ancient use of his prerogative, to traduce or else to cut short the jurisdiction of all other courts but of that court wherein he himself doth sit, and in the cases of [the] subject sometimes to report them otherwise than they were adjudged."[40] Coke's own opinion of his work was quite different. After several months, he announced that he could find in all eleven volumes only five trivial errors, none of which touched any of the great issues that were exercising the king, the chancellor, and the attorney general.[41] This last act of defiance brought swift retribution. "For certain causes now moving us," the king commanded, "we will that you shall be no longer chief justice."

Coke never again sat on the bench of an English court of law. Nor did he publish any further reports.[42] He did not, however, abandon all hope of royal preferment. Instead, in one of the ugliest episodes of his life, he reingratiated himself with the king by forcing his daughter to marry Sir John Villiers, the elder brother of the king's new favorite, the earl of Buckingham. As a result, Coke was returned to the privy council, where he proved sufficiently amenable to be chosen for a parliamentary seat under royal control. But once in parliament, he caused the crown no less annoyance than he had as a judge. Indeed, so objectionable was his behavior in the parliament of 1621 that he was dismissed from the council and briefly imprisoned on a charge of treason. He returned to parliament in 1624 and supported the policies of Prince Charles and Buckingham. But in 1625, in Charles's first parliament, he renewed the attack, and in the parliament of 1628, at the age of seventy-six, he took a leading part in promoting the petition of right. "Shall I," he demanded early in the debate leading to the petition, "be made a tenant-at-will for my liberties, having property in my own house but not liberty in my person? There is no such tenure in all Littleton! . . . It is a maxim, *the common law hath admeasured the king's prerogative,* that in no case it can prejudice the inheritance of the subjects. It is against law that men should be committed and no cause shown. I would not speak this, but that I hope my gracious king will hear of it. Yet it is not I, Edward Coke, that speaks it but the records that speak it."[43]

As his parliamentary colleagues would have known, no man could say with greater authority than Coke what was or was not in Littleton. At just about the time that he made this speech, his own massive commentary on Littleton's *Tenures,* the first part of his *Institutes of the Laws of England* (1628), appeared in print. After a lapse of thirteen years, the years that had passed since the publication of his last volume of *Reports,* Coke thus returned to the job of writing English law. But the form of this new writing was significantly unlike that of his *Reports*. By its title this work proclaimed its affinity with Justinian's writing of Roman law. Here, as if in belated recognition of the need defined by Starkey, Morison, Bacon, Finch, and Cowell, was a comprehensive introduction to the common law of England—not merely a collection of cases, nor even the kind of general defense found in the earlier prefaces, but a genuine institutional work. Even the four-part organization, which Coke announces, though only the first part was immediately available, might be taken as alluding to the four books of Justinian's *Institutes*. But in every other way the two are strikingly unlike. If Coke, whom Selden in this same year called the "great *monarcha juris,*" wrote institutes of the laws of England, as the emperor Justinian had written institutes of Roman law, he did so in the name of principles like those embodied in his *Reports* and his parliamentary speeches, principles inimical to royal lawgiving. And for that purpose he invented an institutional method so foreign to that of Justinian and his legion of followers that it has often seemed no method at all.

Systematic organization—what Bacon called "clear and perspicuous order" (5.105)—is the mark of Justinian's *Institutes*. Following the example of the second-century *Institutes* of Gaius, Justinian (or rather his law-writing commissioners, Tribonian, Theophilus, and Dorotheus) divided the law into three large categories: the law of persons, the law of things, and the law of actions. This division was itself highly significant. But underlying and preceding it was another still more fundamental division, one that Bacon notices when he says that an institutional work should "run through the whole private law" but should not "touch . . . the public law" (5.105). With the exception of a brief final chapter on criminal trials, public law has no place in Justinian's *Institutes*. The imperial state is responsible for the book's existence. Its every word is said to proceed "from the emperor's lips." But from within the book the constitutional order of the state, though pervasively present, is invisible. In this organizational scheme power flows only one way. The public creates and sustains the private. The private has no effect on the public. Here the "maxim" Coke produced for the parliament of 1628—"the common law hath admeasured the king's prerogative"—would be unthinkable. Not only is there no common law, but such law as there is provides no access to the imperial prerogative. From the perspective of Justinian's *Institutes,* the emperor's prerogative remains immeasurable for the simple reason that it is kept almost completely out of sight. And the glimpses one does get of it—the prefatory announcement that the *Institutes* themselves have been composed "with our authority and at our instigation" and the famous declaration in the second chapter that "what has pleased the prince has the force of law"—hardly invite further question.[44] By dividing the public from the private and making only the latter the subject of the basic introductory book by which Roman lawyers were initiated into their profession, Justinian defines the proper sphere of their activity. They are to concern themselves with "the well-being of individuals," as that well-being has been established by imperial rule. They are not to interfere with "the organization of the Roman state."

The publication and reception of Coke's *Institutes* would seem to have been governed by a similar division. The work as a whole was written in four parts, three of which—the second part "containing the exposition of many ancient and other statutes," the third part "concerning high treason and other pleas of the crown and criminal causes," and the fourth part "concerning the jurisdiction of the courts"—deal in obvious and important ways with public law. In these volumes, Coke addresses issues that have no equivalent in Justinian's *Institutes,* such matters as the ancient liberties of Englishmen, the laws protecting the person and power of the king, the function of the various English courts, beginning with the high court of parliament. But none of these volumes was printed in Coke's lifetime, and none has been reprinted as often or read as intensively as part 1, the commentary on Littleton, the one part that does limit itself to private law. Royal intervention was responsible for the delayed appearance of the last three volumes. Hearing that Coke was about to "set forth" a book in 1631, King Charles ordered that it be suppressed. "The king fears," wrote Lord Holland to Secretary Dorchester, "somewhat may be to the prejudice of his prerogative, for [Coke] is held too great an oracle amongst the people, and they may be misled by anything that carries such an authority as all things that he either speaks or writes."[45] And a few days before Coke's death in 1634 the king had the dying oracle's manuscripts seized. Seven years later parliament arranged for their release and publication.[46] But even after parts 2, 3, and 4 appeared, they failed to attain the professional centrality of *Coke on Littleton.* While they each had seven editions, *Coke on Littleton* went through at least nineteen, plus numerous synopses, abridgments, and rearrangements. Whether by royal allowance or professional choice, the first part was the only one that truly functioned as an institutional work. For two and a half centuries, it alone, unaccompanied by the other three parts, provided both English and American lawyers with a basic introduction to the common law.

The frame of Coke's *First Institute* was provided by Littleton's *Tenures* (1482), a work that on its own account had already been compared to Justinian's *Institutes*. In a passage Coke twice quotes, William Camden said that "the students of the common law are no less beholding" to Littleton's *Tenures* "than the civilians to Justinian's *Institutes*."[47] Like Justinian's book, Littleton's is perspicuously ordered, confined to private law, and free from learned citation. It presents just one part of the law, the part that dominated the practice of most lawyers, clearly and on its own authority. But these apparent similarities conceal large and significant differences. Justinian's *Institutes* draws its authority from an emperor whose word is law. Littleton has only his own authority as a judge, a judge who here speaks not from the bench but privately to his son, for whose instruction his book was written. Justinian's *Institutes* is the law. Littleton's *Tenures* (and eventually Coke's commentary with it) came to be regarded as law, but it refuses to make such a claim itself. "And know, my son," Littleton writes in the epilogue to his book, "that I would not have thee believe that all which I have said in these books is law, for I will not presume to take this upon me."[48] For Littleton, as for Coke after him, the law itself is always elsewhere. Nor is this the only difference between the English book and the Roman. The order and coverage of Littleton's *Tenures* are strikingly unlike those of Justinian's *Institutes*. Instead of Justinian's division into persons, things, and actions, Littleton divides his book into estates in land, tenures and services, and other legal characteristics of landed estates. Littleton's attention is thus confined almost entirely to land law, to real property, a subject that in Justinian has no independent identity—as persons, things, and actions have none in Littleton.

If Littleton's *Tenures* was regarded merely as a treatise on medieval land law, its narrowness of focus would be of no great consequence. But when it was made, as Coke and the legal profession made it, the foundation for an English institute, for the book that would introduce Englishmen to the legal order under which they lived, then the consequences of its peculiar limitations were significant indeed. Consider the difference between a book that begins, as Justinian's does, by defining law and justice in broad and abstract terms and one whose opening words are: "Tenant in fee simple is he which hath lands or tenements to hold to him and his heirs forever" (1.1a). In Littleton, abstract justice is never mentioned and persons, Justinian's next subject, emerge only as tenants, whether in fee simple, fee tail, or dower, for life or years, at will or by copy. No wonder learned foreigners thought the book barbarous.[49] But out of its hard and narrow rules of tenancy, Coke constructed a defense of English liberties against the encroachment of royal absolutism. "Shall I have estate in my land and be tenant-at-will for my liberty? Littleton never discovered that!"[50] In a statement like this, ownership of landed property—and in Coke's account tenancy takes a long step toward outright ownership—becomes the basis for and a type of the liberty of the subject. And Littleton's *Tenures*, the book that tells all about such ownership, becomes a notable work of *public* law, one capable of measuring, as Coke put it, the king's prerogative.

Simply by reprinting Littleton's *Tenures* under the new title of *The First Part of the Institutes of the Laws of England*, Coke made an important statement. He said to any who would advocate court-sponsored legal reform, as Bacon, Cowell, and James had done, that English law had already been written and that its writing, far from being an expression of royal power, demonstrated the limits of that power. But Coke was unwilling to leave it at that. In addition to reprinting and translating Littleton's *Tenures*, he commented on it at extraordinary length. *Coke on Littleton* is set forth in three parallel columns, one for Littleton's original law French, one for Coke's English translation, and one for Coke's commentary (fig. 1). But most often the commentary, though printed in smaller type, runs past the other two, spilling around the bottom of the other columns to fill many extra lines and even many extra pages. Nor is the commentary Coke's only addition. Down the margins, so thickly crowded on many pages as to constitute an independent fourth column, are references to a wide variety of sources. Together, this commentary and these references not only greatly augment the length of Littleton's *Tenures*. They change its ideological character and the experience of reading it.

In his *Irish Reports*, Sir John Davies had made the lack of any significant commentary on Littleton a sign of the certainty of English law. Mocking the civil law for its "gloss upon gloss and book upon book," Davies pointed to the English difference. "Of the professors of

<hr>

Overleaf

1. Facing pages from Coke's *First Institute* (1628). Littleton's text in law French is in large black letter; Coke's translation is in roman and his commentary in small black letter; references are in italics in the margin. Huntington Library.

* 40. ¶ 27.

Littleton fo. 50. b.
42. E. 3. 5. 28. E. 3. 395.
20. H. 6. 28.

ued before, and shall bee often hereafter. Nihil quod est inconveniens est licitum. And the Law that is the perfection of reason cannot suffer any thing that is inconuenient.

It is better saith the Law to suffer a mischiefe (that is particular to one) then an inconuenience that may preiudice many. See more of this after in this chapter.

Note the reason of this diuersitie betweene Frankalmoigne and Frankmarriage standeth vpon a maine Maxime of Law, that there is no land, that is not holden by some seruice spirituall or temporall, and therefore the Donee in Frankmariage shall doe Fealty, for otherwise hee should doe to his Lord no seruice at all, and yet it is Frankmariage, because the Law createth the seruice of fealty for necessity of reason, and auoyding of an inconuenience. But tenant in Frankalmoigne doth spirituall and diuine seruice which is within the said Maxime and therefore the Law wil not cohort him to doe any temporall seruice. See the next Section,

¶ *Et enconter reason.* And this is another strong argument in Law. Nihil quod est contra rationem est licitum. For reason is the life of the Law, nay the Common Law it selfe is nothing else but reason, which is to be vnderstood of an artificiall perfection of reason gotten by long studie, obseruation and experience and not of euery mans naturall reason, for nemo nascitur artifex. This legall reason est summa ratio. And therefore if all the reason that is dispersed into so many seuerall heads were vnited into one, yet could hee not make

ses heires deuant le quart degree passe, &c. il semble que cy: Car il nest pas semble quant a cel entent a tenant en frankalmoigne, pur ceo que tenant en frankalmoigne ferra, p cause de sa tenure, diuine seruice pur son Sñr come deuant est dit, & ceo il est charge a fait p la ley del saint esglise, & pur ceo il est excuse & discharge de fealtie, mes tenant en frankemariage ne ferra pur son tenure tiel seruice, & sil ne ferra fealtie, donq̃ il ne ferra a son Seignior ascun mañer de seruice, ne spiritual ne temporal, le quel serroit inconuenient & encount reason que home serra Tenant Destate denheritance, a vn auter & vncore l̃ sñr auera nul maner de seruice de luy, & issint il semble que il ferra fealtie a son sñr deuant le quart degree passe. Et quãt il ad fait fealty il ad fait touts ses seruices.

nor or his heires before the fourth degree be past, &c. it seemeth that he shall, for he is not like as to this purpose to tenant in frankalmoigne, for tenant in frankalmoigne by reason of his tenure shall doe diuine seruice for his Lord, (as is said before) and this hee is charged to doe by the Law of holy Church, and therefore he is excused and discharged of fealty, but tenant in frankmariage shall not doe for his tenure such seruice, and if he doth not fealty, he shall not doe any manner of seruice to his Lord neither spiritual nor temporall, which would be inconuenient, and against reason, that a man shall be tenant of an estate of inheritance to another, and yet the Lord shall haue no manner of seruice of him. And so it seemes he shall doe fealtie to his Lord before the fourth degree be past. And when hee hath done fealtie, he hath done all his seruices.

such a Law as the Law of England is, because by many succession of ages it hath beene fined and refined by an infinite number of graue and learned men, and by long experience grown to such a perfection for the gouernment of this Realme, as the old rule may be iustly verified of it Neminem oportet esse sapientiorem legibus : No man (out of his owne priuate reason) ought to be wiser than the Law, which is the perfection of reason.

Se&ct.

Sect. 139.

SETT si vn Abbe tient de son Sur en frankalm. et Labbe et le couent south lour common seale alien mesmes les tenements a vn seculer home en fee simple, en ceo cas le seculer home ferra fealtie a l' Seignior, put ceo que il ne poit tener de son Sur en frankalmoigne. Car si le seignior ne doit auer de luy fealty, donque il auera nul manner d' seruice que serroit inconuenient, ou il est Sur, & le tenement est tenus de luy.

And if an Abbot holdeth of his Lord in frankalmoign, and the Abbot and Couent vnder their common seale alien the same tenements to a secular man in fee simple. In this case the secular man shall doe fealtie to the Lord, because hee cannot hold of his Lord in frankalmoigne, for if the Lord should not haue fealty of him hee should haue no manner of seruice which should bee inconuenient where he is Lord, and the tenements be holden of him.

This case is worthy of great obseruation for hereby it appeareth, that albeit the Alienors held not by fealty nor any other terrene seruice but only by spirituall seruices and those incertaine, yet the alienees shall hold by the certaine seruice of fealty (and of this opinion is Littleton in our bookes agreeable with former Authoritie) for the Law createth a new temporall seruice out of the Land to be done by the Alienee wherewith the Abbot was not formerly charged for the auoyding of an inconuenience, viz. that the Feoffee should doe no manner of seruice, and consequently the land should bee holden of no man, wherein it is to bee remembred that (as hath been said before) all the lands and tenements in England in the hands of any subiect are holden of some Lord or other, and that euery tenant must doe some kinde of seruice. And that all Lands and Tenements are holden either me-

31.E.3. Cessauit 22.
33.H.6.67. 21.E.4.11.
lib.9.fo.123.
Anth. Lowes case.

diatly or immediatly of the King, for originally all lands and tenements were deriued from the Crowne. And it is to be obserued that when the Law createth any new tenure, it is the lowest, (viz. Tenure in Socage) and with the least seruice that can be done, and neerest to the freedome of the former seruice, as in this case a Tenure in Socage by fealty only is created by the Law, which is the lowest and least seruice the Law can create, because fealty is incident to euery tenure except Tenure in Frankalmoigne, for if it should Create any other seruice it must create fealty also. And the Law according to equitie and Iustice giueth this fealtie to the Lord of whom the land was before holden in Frankalmoigne. And lastly that the Law so abhorreth an inconuenience, as it Createth out of the Land a new seruice for auoyding thereof. It appeareth by our bookes that a Seigniory in Frankalmoigne may bee granted ouer, and consequently the Tenant shall hold of the Grantee by fealty only, and therefore Britton said well, that no seruice could be demanded of a Tenant in Frankalmoigne tant come les terres remaine en les maynes les feoffees.

Lib.9.fo.123.in Anth. Lowes case.
42.Ass. Pl.6.
Britton 164.b.

Sect. 140.

Item si home graunta a cel iour a vn Abbe, ou a vn Prior terres ou tenements en frankalmoigne, ceux prolx (frakalmoigne) sont

Also if a man grant at this day to an Abbot or to a Prior, lands or tenements in Frankalmoigne, these words (frakalmoigne) are voide, for it is or-

Bb 2

Ordeine per lesta- tute. Here it appeareth by the authoritie of Littleton, that this is a Statute, and yet the King alone speaketh, viz. Dominus Rex in Parliamento suo, &c. ad instantiam magnatum regni sui concessit prouidit & statuit. But our law, whoever yet hath made any gloss or interpretation upon our Master Littleton, though into that little book of his he hath reduced the principal grounds of the common law with exceeding great judgment and authority and with singular method and order?"[51] Coke violated that reserve. He wrapped Littleton's spare text in a thick garb of commentary, to which subsequent English jurists—Chief Justice Hale, Lord Chancellor Nottingham, Francis Hargrave, and Charles Butler—have added still further layers. One effect of this continuing labor of commentary has been, as Davies's remark suggests it would be, to make English law more nearly resemble the text-law of the Roman tradition, particularly as that tradition appeared in the *mos italicus* of the glossators and post-glossators. Seen this way, Coke becomes an English Azo or Bartolus. His own copy of Justinian's *Institutes* with the glosses of Azo's student Franciscus Accursius—a copy that contains many marginalia in Coke's own hand—belongs to this type.[52] The resemblance would thus not have been lost on him, even if he forgot Davies. Dressed in Coke's commentary, Littleton became fit company for the glossators' Justinian Coke knew best.

But the other effect Davies predicted, the introduction of the uncertainty characteristic of the civil law, was specifically denied by Coke. In the preface to his *Second Institute,* in a passage that clearly recalls Davies, Coke distinguished between his commentaries and those of the civilians. "Upon the text of the civil law," he wrote, "there be so many glosses and interpretations and again upon those so many commentaries, and all these written by doctors of equal degree and authority, and therein so many diversities of opinions, as they do rather increase than resolve doubts and incertainties." So far Coke agreed with Davies. But his own commentaries, though similar in appearance, were not liable to the same charge. "The difference then between those glosses and commentaries and this which we publish is that their glosses and commentaries are written by doctors, which be advocates, and so in a manner private interpretations, and our expositions or commentaries . . . are the resolutions of judges in courts of justice in judicial courses of proceeding, either related and reported in our books or extant in judicial records or in both, and therefore being collected together shall (as we conceive) produce certainty, the mother and nurse of repose and quietness" (2.A6ᵛ). From Starkey on, certainty was the great desideratum, the mark of civility over barbarism. In claiming that his commentaries attain that certainty, while those of the civilians do not, Coke responds in a particularly pointed way to the humanist critique. The unwritten law of England, the law of the judges and the courts, is not less civilized than the imperial law of Rome. It is more civilized—more civilized because more certain.

Coke's departure from the civilians was, however, also a departure from Littleton. As J. H. Baker has remarked, "Littleton relied on reason and common learning, and disdained to cite precedents."[53] Coke cited them in such profusion and at such length that his *Institutes* seem at times almost a continuation of his *Reports*. The *doctrine* (to use Baker's term) which supplied Littleton's authority, as it supplied the authority of the medieval civilians, was thus replaced by *jurisprudence,* by law decided in court. In this process, the law became less writable even as it was written. For all his modest disclaimers, Littleton set down the law as he understood it to be. The law for him was a purely synchronic system. It existed only in the present. Where it came from, whether or how it had changed, what cases it may or may not have been applied to—these were matters of no concern to him. A book, whose systematically ordered sentences were all equally present, could thus readily contain the law.[54] Coke's thickly layered work says something quite different. In it, Littleton himself becomes a figure of the past. The law dates back to time out of mind, but it has been revealed in many cases, many statutes, and many books, of which Littleton's is only one. Commenting on Littleton's first paragraph—a commentary that fills nearly eighteen tightly printed folio pages— Coke ranges from *Domesday Book, Magna Carta,* Bracton, Britton, and Fleta to his own *Reports*. He cites dozens of cases and a still more numerous array of statutes. From this perspective, the law seems rather a diachronic practice than a synchronic system. Always faithful to itself, it can nevertheless not be fully apprehended in any one schematic representation.

Rivaling the praise for Coke's vast learning that echoes down the centuries are complaints about his obscurity and want of method. Lord Keeper North said that *Coke on Littleton* "is the confusion of a student and breeds more disorder in his brains than any other book"; Blackstone called it "greatly defective in method"; and Sir James Stephens thought the defect Coke's: "A more disorderly mind . . . would be impossible to find."[55] It is certain that anyone coming to Coke's *First Institutes* with expectations formed by reading Justinian or Blackstone—or even Littleton—will be bewildered and dismayed. Topic follows topic with no apparent order and often with only the smallest suggestion from Littleton's text. The single phrase "maxim in law" from a section concerning an uncle's inheriting from his nephew leads to a definition of *maxim,* a discussion of the particular maxim in

question, a list of twenty-two "fountains" from which Littleton derives "his proofs and arguments in these three books," and another list
of fifteen bodies of English law, from the *lex coronae* to "the laws of
the east, west, and middle Marches, which are now abrogated"
(1.11a–b). Juries are discussed in a chapter on rents, parliament under
tenure in burgage, the king's prerogative under socage, and *Magna
Carta* under knight's service. Some word in Littleton usually sets
Coke off on these digressions, but anticipating what chapter will
prompt what topic is virtually impossible. Who, for example, would
think of looking for a defense of ancient readings in a chapter on
releases or a discussion of justices of assize in one on continual claim?
In the *First Institutes,* as Coke published it, the only way to find these
passages and hundreds of others like them is to read straight through.
No acquaintance with Littleton will tell where in the commentary a
particular subject can be found.

Coke himself foresaw this difficulty. "I had once intended," he
wrote, "for the ease of our student, to have made a table of these
Institutes." But he decided against it. "When I consider that tables and
abridgments are most profitable to them that make them, I have left
that work to every studious reader" (1.395a).[56] Behind this apparently
offhand refusal is a theory that shapes all Coke's writing. "Reason,"
he remarked in commenting on the chapter from Littleton concerning
frankalmoign that I have reproduced in figure 1, "is the life of the law;
nay, the common law is itself nothing else but reason." But this reason
neither is nor should be immediately accessible to all. For this is not
"everyman's natural reason." It is rather "an artificial perfection of
reason, gotten by long study, observation, and experience," a quality
proper to the law and to those who have immersed themselves in it.
"If all the reason that is dispersed into so many several heads were
united into one, yet could he not make such a law as the law of England
is, because by many successions of ages it hath been fined and refined
by an infinite number of grave and learned men, and by long experience grown to such a perfection for the government of this realm as
the old rule may be justly verified of it, *Neminem opportet esse
sapientiorem legibus:* No man (out of his own private reason) ought to
be wiser than the law, which is the perfection of reason" (1.97b).

Coke's "no man" had, as Thomas Hobbes noticed, one particular
man in sight: the king.[57] Kings did not make the law—Coke's "grave
and learned men" are obviously lawyers and judges—nor are kings fit
to interpret or apply it. This, according to his own report, is what
Coke told King James to his face. Sometime early in his reign (the

precise date is unclear), in support of a claim that he might decide cases in person, James is supposed to have said that "he thought the law was founded on reason, and that he and others had reason as well as the judges." Coke's answer, an answer that he may or may not actually have given but that he certainly wanted to be thought to have given, closely resembles what he was later to write in his *Institutes*. "True it was," he claimed to have said, "that God had endowed his majesty with excellent science and great endowments of nature. But his majesty was not learned in the laws of his realm of England, and causes which concern the life or inheritance, or goods, or fortunes of his subjects. They are not to be decided by natural reason, but by the artificial reason and judgment of law, which law is an act which requires long study and experience before that a man can attain to the cognisance of it; and that law was the golden metewand and measure to try the causes of the subjects; and which protected his majesty in safety and peace." At this reply, the king was "greatly offended" and said "that then he should be under the law, which was treason to affirm." To which Coke quoted Bracton: "The king must not be under any man but only under God and the law."[58]

One way of keeping the king under the law was to preserve the distinction between natural and artificial reason, to write the law according to a method governed by the latter rather than the former. In adopting Ramistic logic for his *Nomotechnia*, Finch violated this distinction, as Justinian did in reducing Roman law to "perspicuous order." Both make the artificial reason of the law accessible to the natural reason of princes and other laymen. Coke's commentary makes no such concession. Though Coke himself points to "Littleton's arguments logically drawn *a divisione*" (1.235b) and says that lawyers should study logic, the effect of his own book is to keep whatever rational order the law may have hidden, to preserve something of the oral even in the midst of a written and printed text. Coke was enough a man of his time to admit that various branches of the law can be logically diagrammed, that individual maxims can be written, that terms can be defined and legal relations described, that cases can be cited and the reasons governing them can be set forth. But, for him, the law's fundamental coherence, its reason, resides only in the mind of the diligent and experienced *artifex*, the well-trained lawyer.

In Coke's work, this lawyerly perception of coherence takes on an almost mystical quality.[59] "The knowledge of the law is," he wrote in commenting on Littleton's chapter "Of Escuage," "like a deep well, out of which each man draweth according to the strength of his understanding. He that reacheth deepest, he seeth the amiable and admirable secrets of the law, wherein, I assure you, the sages of the law in former times . . . have had the deepest reach" (1.71a). And elsewhere he suggests that ideally the lawyer should so merge with the law that its mind and his will be one. "*Ratio est anima legis.* For then are we said to know the law when we apprehend the reason of the law, that is, when we bring the reason of the law so to our own reason that we perfectly understand it as our own; and then, and never before, we have such an excellent and inseparable property and ownership therein as we can neither lose it nor any man take it from us" (1.394b).

Property no man can take from us, a self identified with the legal order of the nation, artificial reason beyond the reach of lay understanding: these are the products of professional study as Coke presents it. But more than that, they are meant to arise in a quite specific way from the experience of his book, arise as a result of its deliberate want of method. More perspicuous orderings are merely misleading. They pretend that the whole can be perceived apart from the multiplicity of particulars that constitutes it. Coke disagrees. Though he sometimes talks of making the student's way easy and of opening the law to "any of the nobility and gentry of this realm or of any other estate or profession whatsoever," he realizes that frustration and confusion will often be the reader's first experience. "And albeit the reader shall not at any one day (do what he can) reach to the meaning of our author or of our commentaries, yet let him no way discourage himself, but proceed, for on some other day, in some other place, that doubt will be cleared" (1.¶¶4–4ᵛ). Breaking through to a larger, more complete understanding is the experience Coke promises the diligent reader.[60] But until one has taken the arduous and twisting path that leads to that summit, to what Coke calls the *summa ratio* (1.97b), one must simply accept the visionary promise on faith. Borrowing from Roman law, James talked often of the *arcana imperii*, the secrets of state, that were reserved to the king alone.[61] As Coke presents (and represents) it, the common law has its own *arcana, arcana* that would exclude the king even from the judgment seat in his own Court of Star Chamber, where an empty throne and cloth of state awaited him, and empower rather a professional community of learned lawyers. Not merely the product of a disorderly mind, Coke's lack of method was both politically motivated and politically effective. It allowed him to write the law without weakening its oppositional prerogative, allowed him to produce what was in effect a writing against the written, a writing against the Roman imperial tradition and all that it stood for.

The idea of writing the law in a book of institutes belonged to Justinian and imperial Rome. And the idea that England needed such a book came from the combined influences of Renaissance humanism and national consolidation. In succumbing to those ideas, Coke joined a movement that was strong not only in his own generation but that was to find numerous adherents throughout Europe for the next two hundred years. Thus broadly considered, his *Institutes* is a profoundly cosmopolitan work. But in abandoning Justinian's model for a scheme of his own devising, one that better represented the particularity of England and of English law, he took a distinctly nationalist stand. He made insularity the sign not of barbaric inferiority but of political freedom, and in so doing he wrote the nation, albeit from a limited polemical and professional perspective, even as he wrote the law.[62]

Uncouth Learning and Professional Pride

Two statements from another nation and a much later time suggest the power and persistence of Coke's work and the continuance of the system of differences within which its meaning was originally generated. The first comes from Thomas Jefferson, writing to James Madison in 1826.

> You will recollect that before the Revolution, *Coke Littleton* was the universal elementary book of law students, and a sounder Whig never wrote, nor of profounder learning in the orthodox doctrines of the British constitution, or in what were called English liberties. You remember also that our lawyers were then all Whigs. But when his blackletter text and uncouth but cunning learning got out of fashion, and the honied Mansfieldism of Blackstone became the student's hornbook, from that moment, that profession (the nursery of our congress) began to slide into Toryism, and nearly all the young brood of lawyers now are of that hue.[63]

The second comes from a Jeffersonian judge, George Sharswood of Philadelphia, addressing the publishers of the first American edition of *Coke on Littleton* in 1854.

> I have been much gratified by the examination of your elegant edition of *Coke upon Littleton,* with Hargrave and Butler's notes. It is highly creditable to your enterprise as a publisher. The work itself is one which cannot be too highly prized, or too earnestly recommended to the diligent study of all who wish to be well grounded in legal principles.

For myself, I agree with Mr. Butler in the opinion that "he is the best lawyer, who best understands *Coke upon Littleton.*"

My judgment is altogether in favor of the use of the book in its original form, and not as presented in Thomas's *Coke.* It may be that the original wants method; but the life and spirit of it are lost when it is hacked to pieces to be refitted together upon a new and different skeleton. Lord Coke was deeply imbued with the love of his profession, and one of the advantages derived from the study of his works is that somewhat the same spirit is insensibly transferred to his readers.[64]

Two hundred and twenty-six years after its original publication, in a country that had severed its ties with England more than seven decades before, *Coke on Littleton* was still in competition not only with Blackstone's *Commentaries* but also with a rearrangement of itself for the place of "student's hornbook."

But behind the competition with Blackstone and Thomas was the old competition with Justinian. As many scholars have noticed, Blackstone's *Commentaries* takes much of its analytic frame from Justinian. And Thomas's rearrangement of Coke, which agrees with Blackstone almost chapter for chapter, does the same.[65] The division of persons, things, and actions can clearly be discerned in both. And what doesn't come from Justinian, an overarching binary division into rights and wrongs, comes from Finch's original ordering of his *Nomotechnia.* These structural influences were variously mediated by such books as Sir Matthew Hale's *Analysis of the Law* (1713) and Thomas Wood's *New Institute of the Imperial or Civil Law* (1704) and *Institute of the Laws of England* (1720), but they nevertheless remain obvious. The perspicuous ordering that for Bacon was the mark of an institutional work thus had in the eighteenth and nineteenth centuries the same prime exemplars as when Bacon wrote. But more interesting still, the opposition between these orderly institutes and Coke's cunningly unmethodical book persisted, and the significance of that opposition remained much the same. In Jefferson's view, Coke's "uncouth" learning was the vehicle for a political position that he called "Whig" and that he opposed to the "Toryism" of Blackstone's "honied" *Commentaries.* For Sharswood, not politics (at least not explicitly) but rather professional pride was at stake. *Coke on Littleton,* unlike Thomas's rearrangement, filled lawyers with the love of their profession. And since Thomas boasted that he had retained every word of *Coke on Littleton,* the form of the original, not its content, must have produced this effect.

Intimately linked to one another in the reception of Coke's writings, even at so great a remove as nineteenth-century America, politics, professional pride, and literary form were also linked at their inception. Whether in his *Institutes* or his *Reports,* Coke associated England's "ancient constitution," a constitution that subordinated executive power to the common law, with a particular way of writing the law. In the case of the *Reports,* that association was easy and obvious. Reports, like the yearbooks before them, provided a "natural" record of the unwritten law. They remain tied by their very form to the courts and their proceedings. Institutes have a different history and a different set of formal allegiances. They belong to the *Corpus* of a written law and emanate from the emperor. In both respects they would seem antagonistic to the legal and constitutional values Coke supported. Only the sense of a severe menace directed at the common law, a menace associated with both the civil law and the monarch, could explain the production of a book like his. To preserve the common law and make it a power in the political and professional struggles that engaged him, Coke had both to write it and to write it in a form that could claim at least some affiliation with the Roman imperial model. To that extent he too was *civis in aliena republica et hospes in sua.* Such self-estrangement is endemic to national self-writing. Not even the arch-insular Coke could avoid it. But he did nevertheless so successfully attenuate his alienation and the inescapable Roman affiliation that went with it that one could set his *Institutes* not only in the line of Justinian and his progeny, including eventually Blackstone and Thomas, but also and more obviously against them. Coke made his *Institutes* bear an anti-institutional, anti-monarchic, anti-Roman ideology, an ideology that left the king, the very font of the law for the civilians, looking like a foreigner in his own country—a task no doubt made easier for Coke by the fact that King James *was* a foreigner.

Coke's defense of English law has much in common with Daniel's defense of English rime. Both respond to humanist attacks; both repel expressions of sovereign power; both celebrate immemorial custom; and both turn the Renaissance against itself. Coke's position could not, however, be claimed as still another version of Gothic, at least not as he presented it. In his view, English law was originally Trojan, and its first written form in Britain was Greek. But this historical myth was the most vulnerable part of his work and the least essential. Many of his contemporaries rejected it, and within a very few years the rejection was universal. Instead his readers took him as a kind of Goth— "uncouth," as Jefferson put it—a defender of ancient Saxon liberties, a man who said that he would "derive from the conqueror as little as [he] could" (3Inst.B1^v). Overriding and informing these particular oppositions of Trojan and Roman, Goth and Greek, Saxon and Norman, was for Coke, as for Daniel, the fundamental opposition of self and other, English and foreign. Not only was the common law "appropriated to this kingdom of England as most fit and apt for the government thereof," it had "no dependency upon any foreign law whatsoever" (2Inst.D1^v). Like rime, the common law was quintessentially English, a sign of unity snatched from the play of difference: *e duobus unum*. And as Daniel and Spenser glorified poets, so Coke glorified lawyers. They were the alchemists whose minds held the secret of this national quintessence. Individual self-assertion (still more marked in Coke than in Spenser or Daniel), communal self-assertion, and national self-assertion once again depend both on one another and on the formal characteristics of a certain body of writing. For Coke and the many English and American lawyers who have been formed by his work, reports and institutes have been more than mere generic categories. They have been ways of constituting identity, ways of being in the world.

3

THE LAND SPEAKS

IN 1579, WHILE SPENSER, SIDNEY, AND THEIR AREO-pagitican friends were struggling to have the kingdom of their own language, Englishmen made another, more immediately successful conquest. For the first time they took effective visual and conceptual possession of the physical kingdom in which they lived. And they did it without much struggle. Their accomplishment was enabled by a book published that year, one of the most significant of the many extraordinarily significant books to come from English presses in the last quarter of the sixteenth century: Christopher Saxton's great collection of county maps. There had, of course, been earlier maps of Britain.[1] But never before had England and Wales—or, for that matter, any country—been seen in such detail or with such accuracy. Here in a single volume, comparable in size, organization, and aesthetic appeal to Ortelius' revolutionary world atlas, the *Theatrum Orbis Terrarum* (1570), were thirty-five maps, a general map followed by thirty-four maps of individual counties or groups of counties, representing the little world of Elizabeth's kingdom. The book's effect was enormous. For over two hundred years—until the Ordinance Survey of 1794—nearly every printed map of England and Wales derived from Saxton.

But if the effect of Saxton's maps was large and lasting, not everyone felt it in the same way. Maps were of more immediate use to those with property and power than to those without. It is thus perhaps not surprising that this, the first detailed survey of England and Wales, was undertaken at the behest of the queen's government, for the satisfaction of its particular requirements, and, not incidentally, as an expression of its power. Power and its representation were no less deeply involved in the conquests of Renaissance cartography than in the various campaigns, Spenser's among them, to master and reform the European vernaculars—and the historical ironies generated by that involvement were as intense.

In the case of Saxton's atlas, the very success of the project produced consequences that had not been foreseen and that were certainly not desired by the royal authority that sponsored it. A bibliographic accident provides a preliminary intimation of this irony.

Bound with one of the British Library copies of Saxton is a map, printed in the eighteenth century from plates engraved in 1644, which bears the following legend: "This map was reduced from the county maps of Mr. Saxton by order of Oliver Cromwell for the use of his armies."[2] The truth is less dramatic. The map did derive from Saxton's, but it was ordered not by Cromwell but merely by a London printseller of parliamentary leaning. Armies on both sides of the civil wars used it.[3] But the real historical irony is still deeper. If Saxton's maps were never the exclusive instruments of the army that overthrew the monarchy which had first sponsored them, they did have their part in the long, slow movement of thought and action that brought the king's enemies to the field.[4] Only the early phase of that story concerns me here—the production, use, and ideological significance of Saxton's maps and the subsequent development, particularly in the generation that came of age just as those maps were first appearing, of a cartographically and chorographically shaped consciousness of national power. Without maps, as J. R. Hale has remarked, "a man could not visualize the country to which he belonged."[5] But what happened when he could visualize it, when the very possibility of doing so was still fresh and new?

Maps and the Signs of Authority

We speak of these maps as Saxton's. In this we are at one with our eighteenth-century legend writer, with seventeenth-century advertisements, catalogs, and handbooks, indeed with everyone who has ever referred to the maps all the way back to the last years of the sixteenth century, when Abraham Ortelius and John Norden, both mapmakers themselves, each acknowledged the prior accomplishments of Saxton. Since then no name but Saxton's has been associated with "his" maps. But even this unanimity has its limits. The earliest allusions put the matter differently. Raphael Holinshed in the first volume of his *Chronicles* (1577) and William Harrison in his *Description of Britain,* published with Holinshed, both refer, in virtually identical language, to "the great charges and notable enterprise of that worthy gentleman, Master Thomas Seckford, in procuring the charts of the several provinces of this realm to be set forth," and both go on to hope "that in time he will delineate this whole island so perfectly as shall be comparable or beyond any delineation heretofore made of any other region."[6]

Who was Thomas Seckford? And why should we identify *his* maps with Saxton's? A privy council pass of March 11, 1576, makes the connection inevitable. "A placard to [Christopher] Saxton, servant to Master Seckford, master of the Requests, to be assisted in all places where he shall come for the view of meet places to describe certain counties in cartes."[7] Saxton was employed by Seckford. But Holinshed and Harrison agree in associating the maps with the master, not with the man, and William Camden, in the only other published reference before Ortelius' of 1595, only partially accommodates our very different understanding. "England," he writes in the preface to the first edition of his *Britannia* (1586), "has been most accurately and laudably described in maps by the worthy gentleman Thomas Seckford, master of Requests to the queen's majesty, at his costs and by the labors of the excellent chorographer Christopher Saxton."[8] Though Camden recognizes Saxton's labor, he has Seckford doing the describing, just as Holinshed and Harrison had him delineating. The syntax of all three gives chief responsibility and chief credit to the purchaser of the labor rather than to the laborer himself, whose describing and delineating hand is called by Seckford's name.

Nor does the question of appropriate attribution stop here. If we read to the end of that privy council pass, we will discover a third candidate: "being thereunto appointed by her majesty's bill under her signet." Some six other official documents—Saxton's original commission; another privy council letter of introduction; grants of land, of reversion of office, copyright privilege, and arms—all tell the same story.[9] Though the immediate costs of Saxton's survey may have been borne by Thomas Seckford (who in 1579 was rewarded by advancement to the profitable post of surveyor of the Court of Wards and Liveries), the prime movers were the queen and her government.

What are we to conclude from this evidence? Should we adopt the practice that has governed our naming of the King James Bible and call this the Queen Elizabeth Atlas? Or are Holinshed and Harrison closer to the mark in thinking the book Seckford's? Or should we stay (as we undoubtedly will) with Saxton? These are not questions of who did what. Let us accept for the moment that the queen (or, more likely, her privy council) ordered the maps, that Seckford supplied the surveyor and paid his costs, that Saxton traveled, surveyed, and drew. Agreement about such matters does not, as we are beginning to see, solve the deeper problem of attribution—nor can that problem be solved by a study of the maps themselves, for they invite and confirm all three claims (fig. 2). Every sheet of the 1579 atlas displays the royal arms, Seckford's arms, and the inscription "Christophorus Saxton

2. Christopher Saxton's map of Somerset (1579). The royal arms are displayed under
the canopy at the top of the sheet, Thomas Seckford's arms in the lower right-hand
corner, and Saxton's name on the banner behind the compass in the lower left-hand
corner. This banner was lacking on the early sheets. British Library.

descripsit." Here the whole system—from royal authority, through
gentry patronage, to commoner craftsmanship—is set forth.

But when we look closely at the separate sheets, not in their final
form but as they were first printed from 1574 to 1578, the stasis of a
fully articulated system dissolves into story, a story very like the one
that emerged from our study of the early allusions. Only Seckford's
arms appear on all thirty-four sheets. The royal insignia make a tardy
entry, crowded into a narrow margin as an apparent afterthought, on
the second map to be printed, but from then on they are never absent.
For Saxton's name the wait is much longer—three full years, twenty-
five sheets into the series.[10] Obviously, to the maps' first producers the
identity of the surveyor was the least essential bit of information. Of

far greater significance were the patron and the monarch. But in the subsequent history of the survey Saxton gets his revenge. Later printings, whether from the original plates or from reengravings, quickly drop Seckford's arms. The royal arms stay on a little longer, though changed after 1603 from Elizabeth's to James's, but then they too vanish. By the mid-seventeenth century, when any name or identifying mark appears other than that of the new engraver or printseller, it is Saxton's. Seckford's maps and the queen's have become his.

Literary historians know the similar story that emerges from the bibliographical study of Shakespeare. The earliest quartos mention no author but say only something like "as it hath been sundry times acted by the right honorable the lord chamberlain his servants." Then for the next dozen years or so "by William Shakespeare" shares the title page with assurances of noble patronage and royal approval. But finally, Shakespeare's name, like Saxton's, is left to stand alone. In these small changes we can discern the traces of a momentous transfer of cultural authority from the patron and the royal system of government of which patronage was an integral part to the individual maker. Our sense, however strongly qualified it may sometimes be by a recognition of other sources of validation, that the ultimate legitimacy and authority of an artifact derive from the skill and integrity of the individual artificer is not, we need constantly to remind ourselves, merely a matter of fact. As I have already suggested, even when we know all the relevant facts, the real question of authority remains. And that is always a question that will be answered in terms governed by our ideological commitments, commitments so pervasive that we are hardly aware of them. Only the discovery that they have not been universally shared, that there was a time when buyers were more interested in knowing that a play was put on by the Lord Chamberlain's Men than that it was written by Shakespeare, more interested in knowing that maps were produced under the patronage of Thomas Seckford than that they were drawn by Christopher Saxton, can make us see our very different interest for the historically contingent thing that it is.[11]

In displaying the royal arms, the maps do not, however, speak only of the source of their authority—that is, of the power that through the system of patronage brought them into existence—but also of the relation of that power to the land they depict. And that second meaning would for the queen and her leading councillors undoubtedly have been the more important. Not only are these the queen's maps; this is the queen's land, her kingdom. Mere heraldic labeling has its part here. The royal and imperial arms that appear on a few (very few, as it happens) of the maps in Ortelius' *Theatrum* seem to function this way. To those who can read them, they say "England" or "France" or "Holy Roman Empire." But the prominence of this feature in Saxton's atlas, its conspicuous inclusion on every sheet, suggests that something more is being said. These maps proclaim royal sovereignty over the kingdom as a whole and over each of its provinces. As we turn the pages, we are invited to remember that Cornwall is the queen's, Hampshire the queen's, Dorset the queen's, and so on county by county. And lest one miss the point, the frontispiece bears no title, no reference to either Seckford or Saxton, but only an engraving of the queen enthroned, surmounted by her arms and an emblem of her rule, flanked by figures of cosmography and geography, underscored by verses celebrating the accomplishments of her benign reign (fig. 3). Clearly a significant contribution to the "cult of Elizabeth," Saxton's atlas provides a deliberate and insistent statement of royal claims—a statement that we can perhaps see "read" and repeated in the famous Ditchley portrait where Queen Elizabeth towers over an England drawn after the Saxton model (fig. 4).

These two objects, Saxton's atlas and the Ditchley portrait, so similar in their apparent political allegiance, nevertheless differ sharply in their effect. Where the portrait unambiguously enforces the royal cult, the atlas, however unintentionally, undermines it. The Ditchley portrait provides only one possible reading of Saxton, and not the more frequent or persistent one. Far closer to what must have been the usual reading is the Quartermaster's Map of 1644—the reengraving of Saxton that the eighteenth century attributed to the orders of Cromwell. It retains the geographical information supplied by Saxton, but clears away everything else. After all, by putting the queen *on* the map, the Ditchley artist had hidden what most people bought an atlas to see—a representation of the land itself. The needs of cartographic representation are such that, for it to be successful, information concerning such matters as royal patronage or sovereignty must be pushed to the side. While rivers and woods, towns and castles, even political boundaries appear on maps as features intrinsic to the land, explicit symbols of royal control are necessarily made to look marginal, merely decorative, and thus ultimately dispensable. There is really no way to overcome this built-in bias. The harder the mapmaker tries, the larger and more elaborate he makes the signs of sovereignty, the more out of place they seem. Reduced in size and importance, they pass easily enough as mere labels, identifying marks like the

Clemens et Regni moderatryx usta Britanni
Hac forma insigni conspicienda nitet.

Tristia dum gentes circum omnes bella fatigant,
Cæciq terrores toto grassantur in orbe:
An: Dni   pace beas longa, vera et pietate Britannos: 1579
Iustitia moderans miti sapienter habenas,
Chara domi, celebriſq foris, longævaq regni
Hic teneas, regno tandem fruitura perenni.

3. Saxton's frontispiece (1579). British Library.

place-names written elsewhere on the sheet. But expanded, as Saxton often expands them, they construct around themselves a representational space separate from and foreign to the space supposed by the map itself. They exist on another plane, in another dimension.

Our inclination when looking at maps like the Quartermaster's might be to think that, though cartographic representations are important instruments of power, vital tools in the conduct of politics, diplomacy, and war, they are themselves ideologically neutral. They serve the purposes of their user, whatever side he or she may be on. They do not themselves represent or shape those purposes. But much evidence suggests that in the decades following the publication of Saxton's atlas, when the experience of accurate maps was still unfamiliar, this was not so. The cartographic representation of England did have an ideological effect. It strengthened the sense of both local and national identity at the expense of an identity based on dynastic loyalty. "Delight[ing] to look on maps," "beautify[ing] their halls, parlors, chambers, galleries, studies, or libraries" with them, reproducing them in tapestries, book illustrations, paintings, and playing cards, alluding to them metaphorically in poems, even bringing them on stage, as Shakespeare does in *1 Henry IV* and *King Lear,* sixteenth-century Englishmen exposed themselves to the pervasive influence of an image scarcely less potent and considerably more durable than that of Elizabeth herself.[12] Maps let them see in a way never before possible the country—both county and nation—to which they belonged and at the same time showed royal authority—or at least its insignia—to be a merely ornamental adjunct to that country. Maps thus opened a conceptual gap between the land and its ruler, a gap that would eventually span battlefields.

The maps that follow Saxton's contain no overtly antimonarchical signs. It would be more than surprising if they did. But they do show—particularly those issued in the decade after James's accession to the English throne—a diminution of the place accorded the insignia of royal power and a corresponding increase in the attention paid to the land itself. Still close to Saxton are the county maps published by John Norden in his descriptions of Middlesex (1594) and Hertfordshire (1598). Norden gives the royal arms not only a place on his maps, but also a full quarto page of each of his books.[13] But in 1604 those arms fail to appear on his manuscript map of Cornwall, and they occur on only eleven of the fifty-six county maps added to Camden's *Britannia* in the edition of 1607 (fig. 5). This lack in Camden is all the more remarkable in that the originals from which his

4. The Ditchley portrait of Queen Elizabeth, attributed to Marcus Gheeraerts the Younger (1592?). National Portrait Gallery, London.

5. William Camden's map of Somerset (1607). A close copy of Saxton's map, with the royal arms replaced by an ornamental cartouche. Huntington Library.

maps were drawn do, in every case that can be checked, bear the royal arms. Apparently this feature, so prominent in Saxton's atlas, no longer mattered much to either Norden or Camden. John Speed may have cared a little more. Thirty-six of the forty-two maps of the English counties in his *Theater of the Empire of Great Britain* (1611) still display those arms, but in doing so they inflict another sort of displacement. In Speed the royal arms are usually much reduced in scale and always joined by a whole array of other features—arms of local gentry, colleges, or guilds; plans of cities and castles; scenes of battle; pictures of buildings, monuments, and local heroes—features that direct attention away from the king and toward the country (fig. 6). And what Speed does on his maps, he, Norden, and Camden all do far more extensively in the texts that accompany their maps, for their

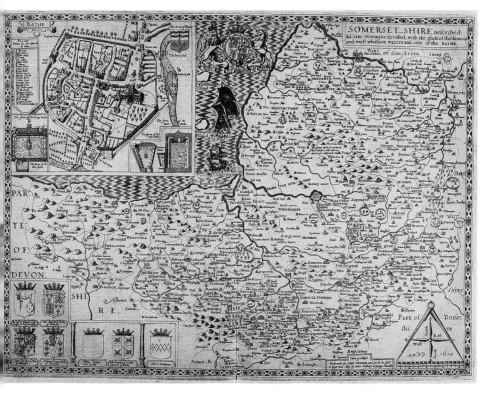

6. John Speed's map of Somerset (1611). Another copy of Saxton, this one with a map of Bath filling the upper left-hand corner. The Stuart arms appear in the upper center and the arms of local nobility in the lower left-hand corner. Huntington Library.

books are not merely atlases, as Saxton's is, but full-scale chorographic descriptions of the land and people of Britain. And such description, at least as they practiced it, left little place for the representation of royal power. The choice they made, the choice of what to study and describe, was, however little sense they may have had of its broader implications, a choice of one system of authority, one source of legitimacy, over another.

Nowhere is that choice more evident than in the eighteen maps that in 1612 illustrated the first installment of Drayton's *Poly-Olbion* (fig. 7). Here the shift in attention and ideological commitment initiated by Saxton's atlas achieved its iconographic culmination. From these maps all dynastic insignia are banished. Instead of elaborate coats of arms, we find, as Drayton puts it, "every mountain, forest,

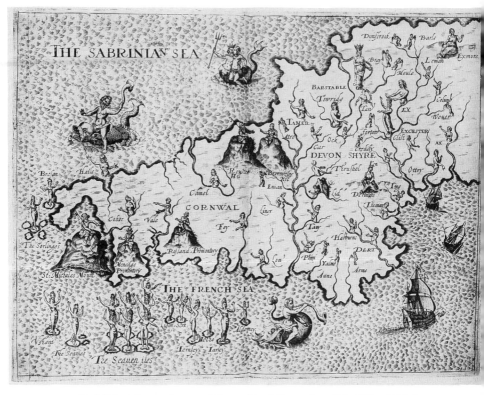

7. Michael Drayton's map of Cornwall and Devon from *Poly-Olbion* (1612).
British Library.

river, and valley, expressing in their sundry postures their loves, delights, and natural situations."[14] The map, already a lively image in
Saxton, Norden, and Speed, here comes alive in a still more immediate
way. Drayton's Britain is "peopled" by its natural and man-made land-
marks. Its streams are nymphs; its hills, shepherds; its differing regions, rival choirs. Its only crowns are worn by towns and natural sites.
And its scepter, as shown on Drayton's frontispiece, is held by the land
as a whole, by an allegorical personification of Great Britain, a
goddesslike woman dressed in a map (fig. 8). The imagery of authority, the crowns and the scepter, are still monarchical. The visual imagination knew no other way to represent power. But the monarch is
now the land, the land as Saxton and his successors had been making
it known.

8. Frontispiece to Drayton's Poly-Olbion (1612). Huntington Library.

Drayton's remarkable frontispiece is itself as much an iconographic culmination as the maps it introduces. Already Camden had
moved the map of Britain to the front of his book, and he had shown
it surmounted by an allegorical personification of Britannia (fig. 9).
Drayton combines the two images, making map and allegorical representation one. But he does more than that. He also seats his figure
in a position strongly reminiscent of that assumed by Queen Elizabeth on Saxton's frontispiece, an image that was itself already an
adaptation of the familiar icon of the Virgin Mary as queen of
heaven. As the cult of Elizabeth had replaced the cult of the Virgin,
so the cult of Britain now assumes power in its turn. From universal
Christendom, to dynastic state, to land-centered nation: this is the
historic sequence suggested by this succession of images. And the
fact that the dynastic claim was being pressed more unequivocally
than ever before just as Drayton's book appeared makes its imagery
all the more significant. That imagery not only realizes the implications of much that had gone before, making manifest the latent
meaning of books like Saxton's; it does so in the face of an absolutist
claim to ideological monopoly that would have denied the very existence of a rival source of authority to which it might legitimately
refer. Drayton quite simply pushes such claims to the side. Off at the
edge of the frontispiece, on columns flanking the sceptered figure of
Britain, he places those princes that "Time hath seen / Ambitious of
her": "Aeneas' nephew, Brut," "Laureate Caesar," the Saxon Heng-
ist, and finally the Norman William. That, Drayton seems to suggest,
is where such ambitions belong—off to the side. Marginality is the
best they can hope to achieve

Drayton's frontispiece supplies the answer to a question generated
by the intense study of British antiquity that had been going on for the
preceding half century. Put most simply: What is British history the
history of? What is the element of continuity in that history? What
holds it together? The more the antiquaries learned, the less easily
they could say that their histories told the story of a single British
people or of a single governing dynasty stretching back to Brut and his
Trojan warriors. As the imagery of both Drayton's frontispiece and
the frontispiece of Speed's *Theater* (fig. 10) suggests, quite different
peoples have occupied and ruled Great Britain. Only someone as
blindly devoted to the myth of historical identity as Sir Edward Coke
could persist in tracing English institutions back to time immemorial.[15] More characteristic of the understanding being forced on Englishmen by the accumulated results of their own historical investiga-

9. Frontispiece to Camden's Britannia (1607). British Library.

tions was Samuel Daniel's remark that the Saxon invasion, "con-
curr[ing] with the general mutation of other states of the world"
attendant on the dissolution of the Roman Empire, marked an absolute break in the institutional history of Britain.[16] And he is only a
little less insistent on the break caused by the Norman invasion, from
which he begins the main line of his narrative. What Daniel says,
Speed's frontispiece, with its Britain, Roman, Saxon, Dane, and Norman, shows.

Drayton shows it too, but he shows something else as well. In the
center of this image of historical discontinuity, he places that new
figure inspired by the work of the cartographers and chorographers,
the figure of the land itself. While his four monarchs warily eye one
another or their intended prey, this new figure gazes serenely out, a
confident source of identity and continuity. Edgy and mutually destructive male rivalry is theirs; power and plenty remain always with
her. Where they are mere artifacts of stone, "trophies," as Drayton
calls them, raised to adorn her triumphal arch, she, holding the fruits
of her bounteous womb in the position traditionally reserved for the
Madonna's divine child, is a living embodiment of nature.[17] So satisfying is this image, so whole and so right, that it makes any suggestion
of underlying ideological struggle seem forced. But that is precisely its
strength. Drayton's frontispiece presents the results of a conceptual
revolution as though nothing had happened at all.

One hears much of the Renaissance discovery of the self and much
too of the Elizabethan discovery of England.[18] In the emergence of
Saxton as sole "author" of his survey and of the land he depicts as a
figure of authority, these maps and frontispieces give evidence of both
discoveries. But that evidence suggests something further, something
anticipated by our discussion in previous chapters of poetry and the
law. Not only does the emergence of the land parallel the emergence
of the individual authorial self, the one enforces and perhaps depends
on the other. Nationalism and individualism, to use the dangerously
convenient general terms for these two tendencies, are, as I have been
arguing, deeply implicated in one another. That mutual implication
begins with the sharing of a common term of difference. Each comes
into being in dialectical opposition to royal absolutism—an absolutism that in its most extreme form would claim both parts, would claim
to be both that which is represented (the land is the body of the king)
and that which does the representing (these are the king's maps,
produced by the exercise of his power). In this view, all words and all
images are the king's.[19] Saxton's intended meaning is not far from

A BRITAINE
A ROMANE
A SAXON
BRITANNIA
A DANE
A NORMAN
THE
THEATRE
OF THE EMPIRE
OF GREAT
BRITAINE:
Presenting
AN EXACT GEOGRAPHY
of the Kingdomes of ENGLAND,
SCOTLAND, IRELAND,
and the ILES adioyning:
With
The Shires, Hundreds, Cities and
Shire-townes, within ye Kingdome
of ENGLAND, divided and
described
By
IOHN SPEED.
IMPRINTED AT LONDON
Anno
Cum Privilegio
1611
And are to be solde by Iohn Sudbury & Georg
Humble, in Popes-head alley at ye signe of ye white Horse.

10. Title page from Speed's Theater of the Empire of Great Britain (1611). Huntington Library.

this, and many passages in Elizabethan and Jacobean literature come still closer. The chorographies that follow Saxton never explicitly reject this absolutist notion. But they nevertheless edge toward a very different sense—a sense of words and images caught in a complex and mutually self-constituting exchange between individual authors, the communities to which they belong, and the land they represent. Authority in this emerging system is not centered but dispersed. Land and self are semi-independent functions of one another. Neither has the absolute autonomy claimed by the king, but neither quite collapses into the other. As our look at the maps and frontispieces has suggested, the self gives the dumb and inanimate land voice and life, in exchange for which the land grants the self an impersonal and historically transcendent authority. In this mysterious and thoroughly mystified relationship—after all, dirt and water cannot really speak and authority can never escape history—authors are enabled by the authority they confer on the land they describe. And royal power is disabled by both.

Or so one might conclude from a reading of these images. The same kind of analysis could, however, have led to a quite different conclusion. James based his claim to the English throne on conquest—the conquest of his Norman ancestor. In Drayton's array of conquering monarchs, the king would have seen that claim illustrated. Feminized, the land becomes a fitting object for male desire and appropriation. Furthermore, the title given that female personification, "Great Britain," explicitly supports a particular and highly controversial element in James's political program, his attempt to unite the kingdoms of England and Scotland as the Empire of Great Britain. Looked at this way, the potentially antimonarchical image becomes a specifically pro-Jacobean one. Both readings are possible. Both may in some vague way have been intended. But good evidence suggests that, among those most involved in the production and reception of these maps and chorographic descriptions, a reading that gave value to the land at the expense of the monarch came to dominate. Forms find their historical meaning not in some abstract configuration of lines and language but rather in the experience of particular communities. What was the experience of the men who, following Saxton, allowed images of the sort we have been regarding to occupy an important place in the shaping of their behavior and their consciousness? Who supported the production of these images? And who benefited from them?

From Court to Country

In 1598, nineteen years after the publication of Saxton's atlas, John Norden presented a copy of his description of Hertfordshire, the second part of his *Speculum Britanniae,* to Queen Elizabeth. Onto the flyleaf of the printed book he wrote by hand the following letter.

To the gracious consideration of the queen's most excellent majesty:

Right gracious sovereign, I cannot but humbly exhibit these my simple endeavors unto your highness' most princely consideration.

I was drawn unto them by honorable councillors and warranted by your royal favor.

I was promised sufficient allowance and in hope thereof only I proceeded. And by attendance on the cause and by travail in the business, I have spent above a thousand marks and five years' time.

By which, being dangerously indebted, much grieved, and my family distressed, I have no other refuge but to fly unto your majesty's never failing bounty for relief.

The right honorable lord treasurer hath thrice signified his good conceit of the work and of my deservings under his hand unto your majesty. Only your majesty's princely favor is my hope, without which I myself most miserably perish, my family in penury and the work unperformed, which, being effected, shall be profitable and a glory to this your most admired empire.

I endeavor to do your majesty service. I pray for your highness unfeignedly. Quid ego miser ultra.

Your majesty's most loyal distressed subject.

J. Norden[20]

Norden had been employed, or so he claimed two years earlier in the *Preparative to his Speculum Britanniae* (1596), "after the most painful and praiseworthy labors of Master Christopher Saxton, in the redescription of England" (sig. A5). But clearly the system of patronage that had so effectively supported Saxton was not supporting him. The financial assistance he had been promised (or thought he had been promised) had not been forthcoming, and his project was foundering badly. Though by 1598 Norden had surveyed at least five other counties, Hertfordshire was only the second to be printed, and it, despite renewed appeals to King James and his ministers, was to be the last.

Norden had tested the system. He had come to the government with a project that he thought (and that Burghley seems to have thought) of legitimate interest to it. But that interest proved evanescent. Though the many surviving documents provide no sure evidence that the royal government actively disapproved of Norden's redescription, they also provide no evidence of active approval—at least not after the early 1590s. Expectations aroused by Saxton's success were shown to be misplaced. If, as Norden fondly believed and tirelessly repeated, the redescription of Britain fulfilled a duty he felt toward his country, then duty to country and duty to king no longer quite coincided. Were the work of representing Britain to go on at all, it would have to be under other auspices and with other support.

That it did go on, and go on vigorously, is proven by the continuing augmentation, republication, and finally translation of Camden's *Britannia,* by the publication of Speed's *Theater* and Drayton's *Poly-Olbion,* and by the extensive work of such local chorographers as Richard Carew, John Stow, George Owen, Tristram Risdon, Thomas Habington, and William Burton. Here—particularly in Camden's book and in Speed's, each of which printed a number of Norden's maps—the *Speculum Britanniae* came closer to realization than it ever had in Norden's own publications. But in doing so, it took a very different road than the one of official patronage marked out by Saxton and followed, so unhappily, by Norden. In place of the royal government, a dispersed network of individuals and communities—a schoolmaster, a London tradesman, a number of lawyers and country gentlemen working at their own expense, courtiers supplying patronage unrelated to official court purposes, printers responding to commercial opportunity—ensured the continued production of chorography.

This new social figuration depended on and enabled the twin emergence we have already noticed—the emergence of the author and the land, of the self and the nation. In this regard, Camden can be seen as exemplary. Where Saxton only becomes the author of his atlas retrospectively, Camden is an author from the beginning. *Britannia* is his book. Its authority is his. The kind of accusation that was leveled at Camden, that he borrowed too heavily from Leland's notes and with too little acknowledgment, would have made no sense directed at Saxton, not because he did or did not rely on the work of others, but because he makes no claim to a specifically individual authority. But, likewise, the doubts we did have about the "true" authorship of the atlas—Saxton, Seckford, or the queen?—have no counterpart with regard to *Britannia,* unless, of course, we wish to credit Ortelius with the original book and the English chorographical community for its gradual transformation into the *Britain* that was finally translated in 1610. Camden's individual authority was supported not by the system of royal patronage but by two communities—first an international one, then an English one—communities whose interest it was to advance the claims of their most productive members.

Against Norden's plaintive letter to the queen in which the frustrations of the court-centered system speak so painfully, we may set a passage from a letter Camden wrote a fellow antiquary.

> I know not who may justly say that I was ambitious, who contented myself in Westminster School when I writ my *Britannia* and eleven years afterward, who refused a mastership of Requests offered and then had the place of king-of-arms without any suit cast upon me. I did never set sail after present preferments or desired to soar higher by others. I never made suit to any man, no, not to his majesty, but for a matter of course incident to my place, neither (God be praised) I needed, having gathered a contented sufficiency by my long labors in the school.[21]

Camden defines ambition exclusively in terms of the court system. For him ambition equals desire for promotion at court. But surely this letter and Camden's career as a whole are shaped by what we would call ambition—indeed, by an ambition of a far more audacious sort, the ambition to "soar higher" *without* the aid of others. "I . . . gathered a contented sufficiency by *my* long labors," Camden proudly insists. "*I* writ *my Britannia*." What enables such ambition, what justifies Camden in denying it the very name of ambition, is his ardent "natural affection" for his country—that and membership in a community that accepted the overriding claims of such affection. If, as Kevin Sharpe has remarked, Camden "kept aloof from politics after having obtained the post of Clarenceux king-at-arms . . . and was to show dangerous indifference to James I's wishes when he wrote his history of Elizabeth's reign," it was because he had another, independent source of pride and authority, one untainted by courtly ambition.[22]

Camden's "dangerous indifference" was, however, more than matched by the crown's passive neglect and eventual open disapproval of the attempts this new social figuration made to give itself permanent institutional form. In 1586, the year of the publication of *Britannia,* Camden and a group of friends founded a Society of Antiquaries, which came to number among its members most of the leading English chorographers.[23] For the next fifteen years, this society met regularly as a private organization, independent of any official authority, to read papers on English institutions, customs, and topography. But when in about 1602, three of its members presented a petition to Queen Elizabeth requesting formal recognition and establishment, they had no success.²⁴ And James, to whom they renewed their request, was still less sympathetic. Though the society had explicitly resolved not to "meddle with matters of state, nor of religion," the king demanded that it abandon even its private meetings.²⁵

The antiquaries were all loyal to the crown—some, like John Speed, rabidly so. None had any idea of altering the established form of government or even of diminishing the authority of the king. Yet their activities were seen as threatening. As I have been arguing, this perception was fundamentally correct. From a Norden, still fully caught up in the system of court patronage, there was little to fear. His projects could be frustrated, his energies easily diverted. But from a Camden, though the formal society he founded could be turned off with "a little mislike," there *was* something to fear. The individual autonomy of Camden himself, the communal autonomy of the group to which he belonged, the national autonomy of the land he and his fellow chorographers represented—these did menace the king's claim to absolute power. The attractive force of this new enterprise could not be ignored. Its products provoked an almost sensual response, aroused an undeniable passion—a passion that could draw a man from what otherwise would have remained his deepest allegiance.²⁶ Among those touched by the new cartographic and chorographic representations, "natural affection" for one's country ("by far the strongest affection that is," according to Camden) was pushing all other affection to the side. Affection for the monarch that had been so powerful an element in Elizabeth's success was being marginalized, just as the signs of royal authority were marginalized on maps and frontispieces.

The direction in which attachment to the land was carrying at least some Englishmen in the first decades of the seventeenth century is seen most clearly in the group that formed around the second part of Drayton's *Poly-Olbion* when it appeared in 1622. Already the first part, published in 1613, with its extensive notes by John Selden and its obvious dependence on Camden's *Britannia,* had been firmly located in the orbit of the Society of Antiquaries, many of whose members had been among Drayton's closest friends. And already the first part had expressed a keen sense of alienation from the royal court and from the literary practices associated with it. As Drayton remarks in his prefatory address "to the general reader," he found "the times since his majesty's happy coming in to fall . . . heavily upon [his] distressed fortunes," and he despaired of success "in this lunatic age . . . when verses are wholly deduced to chambers" (4.v*–vi*). He dedicated the poem to Prince Henry, whose court was then a center of opposition to the king, and in the body of the poem itself he conspicuously stopped his catalog of the English kings with Elizabeth, thus omitting all mention of James. Other poems from the *Pastorals* in 1606 to *The Shepherd's Sirena* in 1627 fill that blank with thinly veiled satire of James who, under the pastoral name of Olcon, "leaves the poor shepherd and his harmless sheep . . . to the stern wolf and deceitful fox" (2.562). "The power of kings I utterly defy," Drayton makes Fame say in the 1619 version of *Robert, Duke of Normandy,* "Nor am I awed by all their tyranny" (2.392).[27] In his own person he was never quite so bold. Yet an undertone of defiance does emerge in the poems he wrote during the years shortly before and after the publication of part 2, and that same tone characterizes the small community that rallied around the augmented *Poly-Olbion* and around Drayton himself.

Three commendatory poems head the 1622 addition to *Poly-Olbion.* Their authors, William Browne, George Wither, and John Reynolds, had been small children a quarter of a century earlier when Drayton began his great chorographical project, and they naturally regard him as a survivor from another age—an age that puts the Jacobean present to shame. "England's brave genius, raise thy head," writes Browne,

> and see,
> We have a muse in this mortality
> Of virtue yet survives. All met not death
> When we entombed our dear Elizabeth.
> Immortal Sidney, honored Colin Clout,
> Presaging what we feel, went timely out.
> Then why lives Drayton when the times refuse
> Both means to live and matter for a muse?
> Only without excuse to leave us quite,
> And tell us, durst we act, he durst to write. (2.393)

Elizabeth, Sidney, and Spenser—these were the heroic figures younger Jacobeans looked to for inspiration. Nor were they alone in this. Just a decade earlier Fulke Greville, the patron of Camden and Speed, wrote his anti-Jacobean *Life of Sidney* (1612) and in the same years Camden produced his *Annals; or the History of the Most Renowned and Victorious Princess Elizabeth, late Queen of England* (1615).[28] For Drayton's generation, to which Camden and Greville also belonged, and for the generation of Browne, Wither, and Reynolds, an intensely patriotic attachment to the land and its depiction and an equally intense nostalgia for the age of Elizabeth went hand in hand with a disdain for the Stuart monarch and his court. This is something of what it meant to be, as Drayton, Browne, and Wither each were, a Spenserian poet.[29] Ideally, such a poet would simultaneously serve, as they supposed Spenser had done, the interests of crown and country. But under James, this was no longer possible. So, forced to choose, these men took the side of the country—a country they identified with the memory of the great queen.[30]

Such partisanship had its risks. In 1621, John Selden spent some time in custody for advising parliament in a way James disapproved, which may explain why the second part of *Poly-Olbion* appeared without notes. In the same year George Wither was subjected to interrogation for breaking a royal order that prohibited discussion of state affairs. A more serious breach of the same order sent John Reynolds to jail for at least two years from 1624 to 1626. And in 1622 Drayton too worried lest he might violate the king's prohibition. "I fear, as I do stabbing, this word *state*" (3.206). But in the eyes of his admirers *Poly-Olbion* itself committed just such a violation, though in a cleverly indirect way.[31] For as they saw it, Drayton's "free-born numbers" exposed the pusillanimity of the Jacobean regime. "'Tis well," says Wither,

> thy happy judgment could devise,
> Which way a man this age might poetize,
> And not write satires. Or else so to write
> That scape thou mayst the clutches of despite. (4.395)

Wither's explanation for this remarkable immunity—"For through such woods and rivers trips thy muse, / As will or lose or drown him that pursues"—is not, as it may appear, merely an amusing conceit. The woods and rivers of England, or rather their representation, provided an ideologically secure refuge against official despite, a sanctuary whose authority could be impugned only by one willing, as the king was not, to set himself openly against the country. But not even this protective strategy could shield poets weaker and younger than Drayton himself. "Had my invention," Wither continues,

> Enabled been so brave a flight to make . . .
> Though I to no man's wrong had gone astray,
> I had been pounded on the king's highway.

By the second decade of James's reign, chorography had become a dangerously political activity. And a statement like Browne's at the start of his *Britannia's Pastorals* (1613), "Thus dear Britannia will I sing of thee," had a distinctly partisan feel, particularly when it came in a Spenserian poem and followed commendatory verses by such men as Drayton and Selden. Britannia and the British monarch, so firmly identified with one another as to be virtually interchangeable through most of Elizabeth's reign, now occupied separate and mutually hostile camps.[32]

The Ideology of Place and Particularity

From a project conceived, financed, and all but executed at court, a project that could fairly be said to have been authored by the queen and her government, we thus arrive some forty years later at one that balances its own authority and the authority of its representations *against* the authority of the crown. But what justification have we for comparing the two? How can an atlas and a lengthy poem be considered points on a single line—a line that also passes through an odd assortment of other texts, descriptive and antiquarian? Is it enough that they all represent in their different ways the same land? Part of the answer is already before us. These books belong together because they refer so often and so conspicuously to one another. They are bound by a dense net of intertextual relations. Nor are the relations only between texts. They are also between people. Though the group that supported *Poly-Olbion* in 1622 had little in common with the one that produced Saxton's atlas in 1579, the two are nevertheless linked by various intermediary social figurations, most importantly the one that formed around Camden's *Britannia* in its successive editions from 1586 to 1610.

All these seemingly disparate activities clustered under a single shared set of terms, terms that I have been using but have not yet stopped to examine. The most frequent were *survey, description,* and *chorography.* In sixteenth- and seventeenth-century usage, all the makers of these books might be called "chorographers" or "surveyors"; the work they all did was to "survey" or "describe"; and their common product, whether mapbook, prose discourse, or poem, was a "description," a "survey," or a "chorography." A fairly late example, one of the many that remained in manuscript, Tristram Risdon's *Chorographical Description or Survey of the County of Devon,* managed to crowd all three terms into one title, and all three were used with reference to each of those liminal, genre-straining figures, Saxton and Drayton.[33] Heterogeneous as they now seem to us, *Poly-Olbion* and *Britannia,* Saxton's atlas and Speed's *Theater,* Norden's *Speculi,* Harrison's *Description,* Stow's *Survey,* and the various county chorographies of Lambarde, Carew, Burton, Owen, Erdeswicke, Coker, Risdon, Westcote, Habington, and Pole could once be called by the same names because they were recognized as members of the same genre.

What features distinguish this genre? Most important, of course, is the concern with place. Though the two terms and the practices they represent inevitably contaminate one another, chorography defines itself by opposition to chronicle. It is the genre devoted to place, as chronicle is the genre devoted to time. The opposition was not, however, necessarily antagonistic. In at least one of the traditions that contributed to sixteenth-century chorography, the two kinds flourished in symbiotic union. Medieval British chronicles, from Gildas in the sixth century to Ranulf Higden in the fourteenth, typically begin with a description of place.[34] One book for the *orbis loca* is Higden's formula, and six for the *orbis gesta*. With a significant difference in scale (the "little world" of England having replaced the whole world), Harrison's *Description* has precisely this relationship to Holinshed's *Chronicles*, as Speed's *Theater* does to his *History*. Each is the topographical introduction to a chronological book. A striking number of other chorographers, including Leland, John Hooker, Stow, Drayton, and Camden, coupled the kinds in their careers, if not in any single work. Clearly these men saw no incompatibility between the two kinds. On the contrary, they understood the two as forming a necessary union. Omit either and the resulting work would, as Speed argued, be "but unperfectly laid open"—a soul without a body or a body without a soul.[35]

But it does nevertheless make some difference which of the two one chooses to emphasize. A chronicle history is, almost by definition, a story of kings. "The Succession of England's Monarchs" is the running title of Speed's *History*, and, as we turn over the pages of Hall, Holinshed, Stow, Speed, or Daniel, we find at the head of each the name of some particular king or queen. To judge from books like these, England is its monarchs. To be loyal to England is to be loyal to the monarch. The chorographers present a very different image of England. In them England is Devonshire, Stafford, and York; Stratton Hundred, Cripplegate Ward, and the Diocese of Rochester; Chiverston, Chester, and St. Michael's Mount. Loyalty to England here means loyalty to the land; to its counties, cities, towns, villages, manors, and wards; even to its uninhabited geographical features.

In the minds of most Elizabethans, the land and the monarch were no doubt as closely bound to one another as Harrison's *Description* was to Holinshed's *Chronicles*. Ubiquitous urgings of service to "king and country" testify to this mentality. But in the seventeenth century the formula occurs more and more often without mention of the monarch. Service to the country alone—with all the ambiguous meaning the word *country* then had: kingdom, nation, county, locality, countryside—was displacing service to king *and* country, just as the latter had displaced service to God and his church or service to one's liege lord regardless of country. The emergence of the country as a single, if variously significant, term for the focal point of allegiance parallels the emergence of the description, survey, or chorography as an autonomous and widely practiced genre. The new autonomous chorography turns the old pattern, represented by Higden and by Harrison-Holinshed, inside out. Particular description, often many times longer than the general description that precedes it, takes the place of the chronicle history, which itself often reappears in a much abbreviated form within the general description. Kings and their doings, when they are not simply eliminated, are marginalized. They move, as they did on Drayton's frontispiece, from the center to the periphery. What moves to the center in their place is not, however, the land as a whole, at least not most frequently, but rather the land in all its most particular divisions.

Chorographies are repositories of proper names. Saxton's wall-map of 1583 contains some four thousand of them (fig. 11). His atlas may have as many as another thousand.[36] And to these thousands, the discursive descriptions add several times as many more: ancient place-names; names of places too small to be mapped; names of particular properties, buildings, and institutions; names of families and of individual people. As the genre develops, however, the weight shifts from one end of this list to the other. Where the earlier chorographers—Lhuyd, Lambarde, and Camden—concentrated on place-names and made etymology their principal tool, the later ones prefer genealogy and the names of people. More and more, chorographies become books where county gentry can find their manors, monuments, and pedigrees copiously set forth.

The signs of the new emphasis are everywhere to be seen in the seventeenth-century county chorographies—and after Drayton and Speed there are *only* county chorographies. The national vision that had dominated the work of Leland, Lhuyd, Harrison, Lambarde, Saxton, Norden, Smith, Camden, Speed, and Drayton gives way to a narrower, more particular view quite in keeping with the particularist vocation of the genre itself. Richard Carew's *Survey of Cornwall*

(1602) already contains much information about individual landowners and their families, and his successors go considerably further in this direction. In dedicating his *Survey* to the gentlemen of Worcester, Thomas Habington simply announces that "the occasion whereupon I first undertook this work was because it was objected by one that our county contained few gentlemen of antiquity," and Thomas Westcote feels he must apologize for having failed to note "every ancient house and generous tribe."[37] "I have passed none," he says, "that I found

11. Full-size detail from Saxton's wall-map of England (1583) showing the dense array of individual place-names. British Library.

recorded, or by inquiry could learn of." Other works that are little more than undigested collections of manorial and genealogical records—Simon Archer's *Warwick*, Roger Dodsworth's *York*, Thomas Jekyll's *Essex*, William Pole's *Devon*, or Augustine Vincent's *Northampton*—nevertheless count as members of the genre. And even in a discursively articulated survey like John Coker's *Dorset*, chorographic particularism routinely produces such entries as:

> Walterston Piddell, the more ancient house of the noble family of Martins, from whom, in Edward the Third's time, it passed by an heir general to John de Gouis, and from him likewise, by the Newburghes and Marneys, to Thomas Viscount Bindon, whose second son Thomas (after Viscount Bindon) built an house there, now belonging to Sir John Strangeways.[38]

And though Coker omits genealogies as such, he does include 295 coats of arms belonging to the gentry of Dorset. In just a few decades, chorography had progressed from being an adjunct to the chronicles of kings to being a topographically ordered set of real-estate and family chronicles. The individualizing process that made Saxton and Camden autonomous authors was making the representation of places like Walterston Piddell a matter of intense concern. King James might argue that in some ultimate sense all the land was the king's. Books like Coker's show to whom it really belonged, to the Newburghes, the Marneys, the Bindons, and Sir John Strangeways.

At the root of all representation is differentiation. A place or a person can be represented only if it can be in some way distinguished from its surroundings. Proper names do much of the work of distinguishing, and it is on them that the chorographers most heavily rely. But many undertook differentiation of a more pointed sort. Reading them, we learn that "the cordage or ropes for the navy of England should be twisted and made nowhere else" but in Dorset, that there is "in all England . . . [no place] where the ground requireth greater charges" than in Devon, that the catch of pilchard is particularly abundant in Cornwall, that the common people are the "shrubbiest" in Pembroke, that Plymouth is "second to no town in England for worth every way."[39] Such marking of difference seems often to have been their chief justification for writing. As Carew puts it, where he "can say little worth the observing for any difference from . . . other shires," he passes on.[40] Its differences make Cornwall worth describing and Carew's book worth reading. Because of these differences, Cornwall has meaning. And so do the lives of Cornishmen like Carew.

Their individual identity and authority depend on their participation in a system of local differences that chorographers, Carew among them, make it their self-justifying business to describe.

Authority and the representation of place had another, more obviously political sense in the sixteenth and seventeenth centuries. Richard Carew not only represented his native county in his *Survey of Cornwall,* he also represented two of its boroughs in parliament.[41] There was a marked resemblance between the genre and the political institution. If a chorography was a representative body, so was parliament. The same anatomical metaphor—the "body of all England"— was used repeatedly for both, as it was for the land itself. As tension increased between monarch and parliament, between court and country, so too did the importance of those things in which chorographers were specialists—local difference, local identity, and local representation—until parliament came almost to seem a living chorography, a map made flesh.

In the actual chorographies, as in their parliamentary counterpart, the more overtly political aspect of topographical representation took the form of a sometimes jealous assertion of local prerogative or, when the prerogative was no longer in force, of a fond memory of former authority. Thus both William Smith and William Webb in their descriptions of Cheshire dwell at length on the privileges of a county palatine, and George Owen gives many pages to demonstrating that Pembrokeshire once enjoyed a similar status. "For you must understand," Owen insists, "that the earls of Pembroke of late time . . . were not earls only in name, as the rest of the earls of England were, but they were earls in deed," and he goes on to describe "their royal jurisdiction, power, and authority, which they more like princes than subjects had over their people of this country in times past."[42] Even the more distant independence of Wales when as Cambria it stood on equal footing with English Lhoëgr and Scots Albania, or of Kent when it held a sovereign place in the Anglo-Saxon heptarchy, or of Cornwall when "as an entire state [it] at diverse times enjoyed sundry titles of a kingdom, principality, duchy, and earldom" can be proudly recalled by a Lhuyd, a Lambarde, or a Carew.[43] None of these writers wished to restore such independence, but neither were they quite willing to be merely English. Sovereignty, they agreed, was properly invested in the present kingdom and its monarch. But the memory of a not wholly departed local autonomy remained a powerful sign of individual identity.

The relation of the land to all this is suggested by a local practice

William Lambarde describes, the Kentish custom of gavelkind. The subject first comes up in the course of Lambarde's discussion of the yeomanry which, he claims, "is no where more free and jolly than in this shire."[44] He gives three reasons for this happy state: (1) "the communality of Kent was never vanquished by the conqueror, but yielded itself by composition"; (2) "the forward in all battles belongeth to them (by a certain preeminence) in right of their manhood"; and, most important, (3) "there were never any bondmen (or villains, as the law calleth them) in Kent" (p. 7). All three are associated with the custom of gavelkind. Because of it "everyman is a freeholder and hath some part of his own to live upon." From this land-owning self-sufficiency came hardihood and resistance to conquest, which in turn secured "the continuance of their ancient usages, notwithstanding that the whole realm beside suffered alteration and change" (p. 19). Thus "they of all England . . . obtained forever their accustomed privileges" (p. 21). Local particularity, individual autonomy, accustomed privilege, and resistance to royal encroachment— these, even in the mind of so ardent a supporter of the queen as Lambarde, belonged together.

What exactly is gavelkind? It is a mode of inheritance, peculiar to Kent, whereby property passes to all male offspring (or, in the absence of male offspring, to all female offspring) equally—"give all kin," as Lambarde's pseudo-etymology has it. Whenever the custom originated, however it was maintained, and whatever its effects (all matters of concern to Lambarde), it belongs inalienably to the land—to the land as a whole and to each individual parcel. To change it is beyond the power of any owner, including the king. The custom partakes, as Lambarde puts it, of the land's very "nature," is "so inseparably knit to the land as in a manner nothing but an act of parliament can clearly dissever them" (pp. 482 and 485–86). Only, he seems to be saying, the assembled representatives of the whole land can alter a custom so firmly attached to any part of it. Individual will, be it the king's, counts for nothing. Customary usage counts for all. "And this," Lambarde insists, "is not my fantasy, but the resolution of all the justices" (p. 482).

Such local particularism and local prerogative are the very stuff of chorography. I do not by this mean to claim that many of these books describe institutional arrangements as tenaciously landbound as gavelkind. They don't. As well as being a chorographer, Lambarde was an accomplished legal scholar. He naturally sought a legal basis for Kent's distinguishing difference. But whatever the inclination of the individ-

ual chorographer, the generic nature of his undertaking obliged him
to emphasize particularity and its relation to place.

What then becomes of the nationalist impulse with which the whole
chorographic enterprise began? Does it simply subvert itself by the
momentum of its own representational methods? If we compare
Camden's *Britannia* at one end of the process and Sir William
Dugdale's *Antiquities of Warwickshire* (1656) at the other, our initial
inclination may well be to say yes. In Dugdale the eleven folio pages
Camden had devoted to Warwickshire expand to 826. Though the two
authors present similar sorts of information in similar ways, so massive
a change in scale amounts almost to a change in kind. Overwhelmed
by the particularity of Warwickshire, we risk losing sight of Britain. But
that risk is considerably less severe than it might seem. The particular-
ities, after all, constantly remind us of the whole of which they are part
and from which they take meaning, even if only by difference. Nationalism is what ultimately justifies a project as particular as Dugdale's.
And the nation, unlike the dynasty, is in turn strengthened by its very
receptiveness to such individual and communal autonomy. The dialectic of general and particular that is built into the structure of a chorography in the end constitutes the nation it represents.

Between a Camden or a Dugdale and the nation stands the genre.
It is the counterpart of those other institutional bodies, including
parliament, that support the body of the state and the body of the self.
It recruits new authors and defines the object they describe, even as it
is itself written and defined by the authors and the object. Chorography, still more than most such institutions, assumes the form of a
self-consciously intended project. In the first contribution to the kind,
Lambarde expressed the wish "that someone in each shire would make
the enterprise for his own country to the end that by joining our pens
and conferring our labors . . . we might at the last by the union of
many parts and papers compact one whole and perfect body and book
of our English topography," and Dugdale repeats the call eighty years
later.[45] In the nineteenth and on into the twentieth century the Victoria History of the English Counties was still responding to this call
and still representing the country in terms of place and particularity.
But by the nineteenth century the ideological import of this representational mode had been fully absorbed, had indeed proved triumphant. Three hundred years earlier, chorographies pictured an entity
that, as a basis of authority, hardly existed, an entity that had remained
subordinate to the dynastic regime whose power defined its limits.
Conquest and inheritance had created the kingdom of England, as, in

the lifetime of most of our chorographers, inheritance created the empire of Great Britain. But however its political boundaries were set, the land did nevertheless emerge in Elizabethan and Jacobean chorographies as a primary source of national identity—emerged by means of a process both dependent on and responsible for the emergence of chorography itself as an autonomous genre.

The Muse on Progress

I began this chapter with an allusion to Spenser and Sidney not only because, as a literary historian, I felt more comfortable taking off from my home base. The institutionalization of English poetry, its establishment as a communal enterprise that could justify by its own internal dynamism the efforts of its practitioners, finds, as I have been suggesting, a counterpart in the development of English chorography. Both begin in close alliance with the court, which provides not only patronage and protection but also an image of power—an image that both poetry and chorography represent and, in representing, emulate. But from emulation springs difference, alienation, finally even opposition, until both representational modes emerge as sources of cultural authority that, in a period of political tension, will rival the authority of the crown. The two developments occur simultaneously, center on the same generation. Sidney, Spenser, Camden, and Speed were born within three years of one another, came of age together in the relatively tranquil period of institutional consolidation midway through Elizabeth's reign, felt alike the influence of both Ascham and Saxton. The task of articulating an England that for the first time could be "seen" was theirs jointly by birth. It remained, however, for someone a decade younger than they, someone close enough to them in age to share their generational location and the duty that came with it, but far enough to know them and their work when he began his own, to try putting the two kinds together, to write a chorography that is also a poem. That, of course, is what Drayton does in his *Poly-Olbion*.

Poly-Olbion differs from most chorographies in lacking an introductory section specifically reserved for general description. Instead, it begins immediately with a particular description of "the Cornish and Devonian grounds" of southwest England and proceeds from there, region by region, until it ends thirty songs later in the far northern counties of Westmorland and Cumberland. Drayton does not, however, neglect general description or the chronicle matter that occupied such a large place in most general descriptions. Rather he folds such information into his particular descriptions, making the various places themselves recite England's chronicle history. Already in the first song the river Dent tells of Brut's conquest of Albion, and in other songs the rivers, hills, and woods of England and Wales tell of the various dynasties that since Brut have ruled Britain. Yet for all Drayton's efforts to find and assert continuity, the picture that emerges from his recension of chronicle history is very like the one we earlier noticed on his frontispiece—a picture of discontinuity and mutual hostility. Looking at such a picture one sees the image of many nations, all ultimately foreign to the land they have occupied. One does not see the single nation, the integrated and cohesive body, that would justify Drayton's literary project or the more general representational project of his generation.

Perhaps the most interesting thing about *Poly-Olbion*'s chronicle material is that it is contained within a chorography. However strong Drayton's commitment to the kind of providential dynastic history favored by Holinshed and his fellow "compilers," he nevertheless chose a generic form that puts the main emphasis elsewhere. He took as his model Camden, not Holinshed, let the shape and order of his poem be determined by the divisions of an atlas, not by the steps of a pedigree. Not king, but country dominates his vision. Before Brut came, the land was there awaiting him. Through all the dynastic changes that have occurred since, the land has kept its integrity. Various streams and woods and mountains have become partisan supporters of the different peoples that have lived near them. The rivers of Wales recount the conquests of Arthur and the English rivers answer with the glorious deeds of the Saxons. But these differences and the many others that have no dependence on human history—differences between hills and valleys, between forests and fields, between marshlands and drylands—are parts of an animating *discordia concors,* a dialectic of the particular and the general, characteristic of chorography. In the poem, as on its frontispiece, the one unified body is the body of the land.[46]

Drayton is a Spenserian poet; *Poly-Olbion,* his *Faerie Queene.* But there is a significant difference between a poem like *The Faerie Queene,* whose every quest is said to originate at and lead back to a single central court, and one that contains no court; between a poem whose every book claims to represent the actual queen of England and one that never mentions the reigning monarch. As we noticed in an earlier chapter, Spenser, in his attachment to "Gothic" values and a "Gothic" representational mode, already figured a displacement and dispersal of authority, an anti-"Greek" deconstruction of sovereign will. In Drayton this process goes much further, so far that its product can retrospectively obscure the boldness of Spenser's own anti-monarchic departures, making Spenser's neofeudal poem look absolutist by contrast.

Multiplicity figures in the very title of *Poly-Olbion,* and the representation of multiplicity is Drayton's highest aesthetic goal. As Drayton says in his invocation to Nature, he aspires to suit his "varying vein" to the character of "the varying earth." In keeping with this attachment to multiplicity, *Poly-Olbion* contains not one but many claims to sovereignty. The Dert, the Parret, the Severn, the Lug, the Thames, the Trent, the Humber, and the Teis, Dean Forest, Malvern Hill, the Vale of Evsham, and the Isle of Man are all called king or queen. But none exercises effective rule beyond a narrow region, and such rule as they do achieve inspires in Drayton images that reveal his antipathy to royal centralism. When, for example, the Ex, after having gathered the tribute of many smaller streams, empties into the queenly Dert, Drayton is reminded of

> some unthrifty youth, depending on the court,
> To win an idle name, that keeps a needless port;
> And raising his old rent, exacts his farmers sore
> The landlord to enrich, the tenants wondrous poor,
> Who, having lent him theirs, he then consumes his own,
> That with most vain expense upon the prince is thrown,
> So these, the lesser brooks, unto the greater pay. (4.14–15)

Monarchy impoverishes the land. Such anticourtly satire is, of course, common in Elizabethan, as in Jacobean, poetry. Spenser, as we have seen, is full of it. But in Drayton, the satire finds no antidote, is countered by no positive image of the monarch or of monarchic rule. Instead, positive value is invested in an implicitly antimonarchic image, an image of the headless (or, better, the many-headed) body of the land.

When Spenser thinks of rivers flowing into one another, he too thinks of the courtly center of power, but differently. "So from the Ocean all rivers spring," he says to his "most dreaded Soveraine" in the proem to Book 6,

> And tribute backe repay as to their King.
> Right so from you all goodly virtues well
> Into the rest, which round about you ring. (6.proem.7)[47]

The more elaborate prosopopoeic renderings of rivers and their merging, those *epithalamia fluviorum* in which both Spenser and Drayton excel, make still more apparent the ideological difference suggested by these brief images. To Spenser's marriage of the Thames and the Medway (4.11.8–53) all the watery folk of the world, from King Neptune to the humblest fountain nymph, come in strict hierarchical procession. This is a royal wedding. Thames, on whose bank stands "famous Troynovant" where "her kingdomes throne is chiefly resiant" (4.11.28), is the king of all English and Irish rivers and receives as his due the attendance of all.

> Ne none disdained low to him to lout:
> No not the stately Severne grudg'd at all,
> Ne storming Humber, though he looked stout;
> But both him honor'd as their principall,
> And let their swelling waters low before him fall. (4.11.30)

In *Poly-Olbion,* Severn is herself a queen; Humber, a king. Neither pays obeisance to King Thames, nor does either attend any fête outside his or her own region. When the Thames's parents, Tame and Isis, wed in Drayton's poem, only their actual tributaries and the contiguous natural sites, the Chitern Hills, the Vales of Alesbury and White Horse, and the forests of Whichwood and Bernwood, join in the celebration, a celebration that in comparison to Spenser's is a very homely affair. Clearly Drayton was far less susceptible than was even Spenser, despite Spenser's neofeudal predilections, to the humbling and exalting thrill of absolutism. His image of authority, an image determined by the genre in which he chose to write, is at once more dispersed and less personal.

Though Spenser's river marriage seems to have begun as an autonomous poem, the *Epithalamion Thamesis,* and though it draws heavily on Harrison's *Description* and Camden's *Britannia,* it can never have been truly chorographical. It violates the very premise of chorography, fidelity to the natural disposition of the land. In Spenser, sovereign will—the will of King Thames and the will of the poet—assembles rivers whose waters would otherwise meet only in the great oceanic annihilation of fluvial identity, in that ultimate sovereign body, where all individual bodies are lost. *The Faerie Queene* thus presents an image of royal and artistic power exercised in defiance of the very geographical differences that it seems intent on celebrating. Such tension cannot be found in Drayton's poem. His rivers stay in their beds. They attend only the marriages to which the course of nature and the representational conventions of chorographic description invite them. Like a king, the Spenserian mythopoeic artist creates another nature, gathers the Ganges, the Tagus, and the Thames in a single imagined space as easily as he gathers their names in a single sentence.[48] Drayton denies himself this power. He does mention widely separated rivers, but he only mentions them.[49] If a map won't bring them together, neither will he.

Poly-Olbion locates itself, as I have said, at the crossing of two representational modes, at the intersection of two communities. It is both poem and chorographical description. As chorography, it must respect the actual disposition of the land. It can only meet the Severn, the Thames, or the Humber in the parts of the country where they actually flow. But as poem, it can make them speak. It animates the land and gives it voice.

These two functions—the perambulatory and the inspirational—meet in the figure of Drayton's Muse, the one "character" who is present throughout the poem. From Lambarde on, all but a very few chorographers arranged their descriptions by order of topographical proximity, and in most the movement from one place to another—the "perambulation," as Lambarde calls it—was figured as a journey accomplished by the chorographer himself. "Now will I, by God's assistance," says Camden, as he makes the transition from general to particular description, "make my perambulation through the provinces or shires of Britain," and Carew at precisely the same point in his *Survey of Cornwall* says, "In my particular view, I will make easy journeys from place to place as they lie in my way."[50] And as the different descriptions proceed, repeated turns of phrase ("Following the tract of Edgehill, it leads me to Tisoe" . . . "Now I thought I might have left Chumleigh, but I am staid at Stone Castle" . . . "I think it's time to take boat and pass to the other shore") keep both the voyage and the voyager before us.[51] Nor is the chorographical traveler a mere passive observer of what most readily presents itself to his eyes. Rather he actively seeks out information that will make the land known. "Writing I could see none," says Simon Erdeswicke of an elaborate Staffordshire tomb, "nor any other matter whereby I might discern whose it was, until, seeking something narrowly, I found under the arch of the monument . . . "[52] What Erdeswicke finds under that arch is in some sense himself, for he, like the other chorographers, is exploring his own native land, the land on whose identity his is founded. The chorographic project is a project in self-description—and, indeed, in self-making. Thus the prominent inclusion of the chorographer himself (and often of the reader, who is presumed to be traveling with the chorographer) is not a mere expository device. It is, on the contrary, essential to the meaning, to the cultural import, of chorography as genre.

In the figure of his Muse, Drayton both expands this role and significantly alters it. As his favorite epithet for her insists, his Muse is as "industrious" as any chorographer, and she is more prominently featured than any. To take as an example the activity specified by just one typical argument, the one that introduces his fourth song, she "brings" rivers down, "sings" Merlin's birth, "makes" to Pembroke, "sees" Milford, "tells" the islands, "visits" Saint David's cell, "sports" along the shores, and "prepares" the ensuing song (4.97). She bears, moreover, a remarkable likeness to Drayton himself. Both are English, both natives of Warwickshire, both recipients of the Astons' generous patronage. And often their voices so mingle and merge as to be utterly indistinguishable. A speech that begins "What help shall I invoke" can end, "Thus scarcely said the Muse" (4.1–2). Who was speaking? He or she? It seems hardly to matter.

Yet it does matter that Drayton should have felt the need to project himself into such a figure, for she represents that intermediary body— call it genre, community, or representational mode—that stands between the individual writer and the land he describes. Drayton several times renames the Muse "Invention." She is the finding out, the institutionalized power of subject making, on which both he and, in the fiction of his poem, the land depend for inspiration. The Medway, the Tyne, Holland Fen, and the Devil's Ditch call on the Muse just as the poet does, mingle their voices with hers in precisely the same way. In *Poly-Olbion*, poet, Muse, and land are represented in the very mutually enabling relation to one another that we earlier observed between Saxton, cartography, and England or between Camden, chorography, and Britain. Because of the Muse and the privileged access she gives him to the land, Drayton can set his authority above even that of the king, for

> not the greatest king, should he his treasure rain,
> The muses sacred gifts can possibly obtain;
> No, were he monarch of the universal earth,
> Except that gift from heaven be breathed into his birth. (4.421)

The poet is not a king, but he, like the cartographer and the chorographer, has a power and represents a power that kings might well envy. Remember that it was Saxton's name, not the royal arms, that endured on his maps; Camden's brand of patriotic independence, not James's absolutism, that governed England's self-image for the next three and a half centuries.

One critic has noticed a likeness between the Muse's peregrination through England and Wales and a royal progress. "The forms of entertainment the Muse receives resemble," she writes, "those enjoyed, or endured, by Elizabeth and James on their progresses: long orations everywhere, often setting forth the merits and history of the place visited; debates and disputations; musical entertainments; elaborate festivals."[53] Whatever royal authority accrues to the Muse by virtue of this likeness is, however, shared by the poet. Though Drayton does not often use the term *progress,* when he does use it, it can apply as easily to either.[54] The displacement of the monarch works in favor of both the individual authorial self and the enabling community to which he belongs. But it depends on the authority of the impersonal third figure that both serve, the figure of the land itself. Together the poet and the Muse go on progress, but the function of their progress is to provide the occasion and the inspiration for the land's self-expression.

In its almost exclusive emphasis on the land's revelation of itself, the chorographic progress of *Poly-Olbion* differs strikingly from the royal progresses of either Elizabeth or James. However much these monarchs were obliged to hear of local history and topography (and James, at least, heard as little as he could), their primary aim was rather to make their own power manifest. They traveled more to be seen than to see. They were set, as both several times remarked, high on a stage "in the sight and view of all the world."[55] Their authority depended on its visibility, depended on making itself known in a real-life theater of power. But here too chorography invades the royal domain, usurps the stage, puts its image of the land in the place of the monarch. What we see when we open *The Theater of the Empire of Great Britain*—or, for that matter, any other chorographical book—is not the king but the country. The function of such books is precisely to make the land visible, to set it before us in such a way that we will know both its greatness and its particularity, a particularity in which its primary viewers, the landowning gentry of England and Wales, had their part.

Poly-Olbion combines the visual and the verbal, the cartographic, the chorographic, the iconographic, and the poetic. Aesthetically, inasmuch as aesthetics can be distinguished from ideology, the combination may not be altogether successful. A fifteen-thousand-line descriptive poem in pedestrian hexameters is enough to sate the heartiest literary appetite. In its own time, whether for this reason or because, as Drayton himself charged, court-influenced readers were disinclined to "see the rarities and history of [their] own country delivered by a true native muse" (4.v*), *Poly-Olbion* probably reached a far smaller audience than did Saxton's atlas, Camden's *Britannia,* or Speed's *Theater.* But Drayton's book does, nevertheless, express more openly than any of the others the new social and political values that were the unintended product of chorographic description. In the poem itself, in the notes and commendatory verses that accompany it, in its frontispiece and cartographic illustrations, Drayton and his collaborators make known both their antipathy to Stuart absolutism and their allegiance to a rival source of authority—a source of authority that legitimates that antipathy and enables them as individual authors and as members of several overlapping communities. In *Poly-Olbion,* the poet, the Muse, and the land at last assume the monarchic role toward which their counterparts in more than a dozen chorographic descriptions had been unconsciously moving. No wonder the poem, whatever its aesthetic qualities, was not much liked at court.

Chorography and Whiggery

The material I have been considering in this chapter prompts a question: Is there a natural and inevitable antagonism between mapping and chorographical description on the one hand and royal absolutism on the other? Are maps and descriptions of place (say, tour guides) always Whiggish in their ideological effect, always implicit advocates of parliamentary supremacy? To claim so much would be hazardous and probably untrue. In seventeenth-century France—the France most notably of Henri IV and Louis XIV—maps seem to have functioned in untroubled support of a strongly centralized monarchic regime.[56] But elsewhere there are signs of conflict. In the Low Countries mapmaking and the widespread use of maps went hand in hand with a nascent bourgeois republicanism.[57] And in Philip II's Spain, Pedro de Esquival's great cartographic survey of the Iberian peninsula was kept in manuscript, locked in the Escorial as "a secret of state."[58] These examples suggest (and of course for them to be more than merely suggestive they would have to be developed in much greater detail) that the English experience cannot simply be taken as the type of what happened in Europe generally. But neither can that experience be dismissed as irrelevant to what happened elsewhere. At the very least, it should help us to remember an obvious though easily forgotten point, that wherever maps and chorographic descriptions were used and whatever the consequences of their use, they could never be ideologically neutral, could never be mere tools, whether of monarchic centralism or of any other organization of power.[59] They inevitably entered into systems of relation with other representational practices and, in doing so, altered the meaning and the authority of all the others.

Saxton, Camden, Norden, Speed, Drayton, and the many county chorographers, however faithfully they may have gathered and repeated the "facts" of England's history and geography, had an inescapable part in creating the cultural entity they pretended only to represent. And in creating that entity, they also brought into being, as I have been arguing, the authority that underwrote their own discourse. They thus made themselves. They are the prototypes of what might be called the *novus homo chorographicus*—new chorographical man—whose voice can be heard in Camden's claim that he was moved to publish *Britannia* by "the love of my country which compriseth all love in it," in Speed's offering of his *Theater* "upon the alter of love to my country," or in Stow's statement that describing London "is a duty that I willingly owe to my native mother and country and an office that of right I hold myself bound in love to bestow upon the politic body and members of the same."[60] Love and country, this is their common theme. A century earlier such expressions would have been nearly incomprehensible. A decade or two later they could have served as rallying cries for a political faction that opposed the court and called itself the "country."[61] By then—that is, by the 1620s—the publication of chorography had become an overtly political act. But, if my reading of these texts is right, it was always a political act, though its politics were not always what its sponsors or even what its authors thought them to be.

4

THE VOYAGES OF A NATION

THE

PRINCIPAL NAVI-
GATIONS, VOYAGES,
TRAFFIQVES AND DISCOVE-
ries of the *English Nation*, made by Sea or ouer-
land , to the remote and fartheſt diſtant quarters of the
Earth, at any time within the compaſſe of theſe 1600. yeres:
Diuided into three ſeuerall Volumes, according to the
poſitions of the Regions , whereunto they
were directed.

The firſt Volume containeth the worthy Diſcoueries,
&c. of the *Engliſh* toward the North and Northeaſt by Sea, as of
Lapland,Scrikfinia, Corelia, the Baie of *S.Nicolas*, the Iſles of *Colgoieue,Vaigatz*,
and *Noua Zembla*, toward the great Riuer *Ob*, with the mighty Empire of *Ruſſia*,
the *Caſpian* Sea, *Georgia, Armenia, Media, Perſia, Boghar* in *Baſtria*,
and diuers kingdomes of *Tartaria*:

Together with many notable monuments and teſtimonies
of the ancient forren trades, and of the warrelike and other
ſhipping of this Realme of *England* in former ages.

VVhereunto is annexed a briefe Commentary of the true ſtate of Iſland,
and of the Northren Seas and lands ſituate that way : As alſo the
memorable defeat of the *Spaniſh* huge *Armada*, Anno 1588.

¶ The ſecond Volume comprehendeth the principall
Nauigations, Voyages, Traffiques, and diſcoueries of the *Engliſh*
Nation made by Sea or ouer-land, to the South and South-eaſt
parts of the World, as well within as without the Streight of
Gibraltar, at any time within the compaſſe of theſe 1600.
yeres: Diuided into two ſeuerall parts, &c.

¶By R I C H A R D H A K L V Y T Preacher, and ſometime Student of Chriſt-Church in Oxford.

¶ Imprinted at London by *George Biſhop,*
Ralph Newberie, and *Robert Barker.*
A N N O 1599.

WITH FEW EXCEPTIONS, CHOROGRAPHIES ARE narratives. They tell the story of a voyage through the territory they describe. But they are weak narratives. The voyages they recount have no immediacy. The chorographic traveler never encounters bad weather, impassible roads, or poor fare. His trip is rather an expository device (though an expository device laden with ideological signifi- cance) than a historical event. In this, chorographies differ from an- other, still more prevalent and more ideologically significant six- teenth-century geographical kind, the overseas voyage. These are the books that acquainted Europeans with the discoveries of Columbus, Vespucci, da Gama, Magellan, and the many others who followed them, books that gave Europeans conceptual possession of a world outside Europe they had hardly known but would soon possess in a more than merely conceptual way. Before being books, these voyages actually happened. Their having happened was essential to their mean- ing. They conferred authority on individual experience as Lambarde's "perambulation" of Kent or Carew's "survey" of Cornwall could never have done.

Still, in England the emergence of the two kinds, chorography and voyage, was nearly simultaneous and the generation most responsible for their production was the same. The first fifty years of the "age of discovery" passed with little English participation—John Cabot's trips across the north Atlantic being the major exception—and virtually no English publication.[1] In the early 1550s, the Willoughby-Chancellor search for a northeast passage, the founding of the Muscovy Com- pany, and the publication of Richard Eden's *Treatise of the New India* (1553) and *Decades of the New World* (1555) marked the beginning of a significant expansionist drive. But it was not until the 1570s and 1580s, when Francis Drake, John Hawkins, Martin Frobisher, Hum- phrey Gilbert, Walter Raleigh, and the younger Richard Hakluyt were all active, that England made a major contribution to either overseas travel or its literature. And these were, of course, the same decades that saw the publication of Lambarde's *Perambulation*, Saxton's atlas, and Camden's *Britannia*. This coincidence in time was coupled with a coincidence in theme. In their English versions, both chorography and voyage were parts of the larger generational project that is the subject of this book, the articulation of England itself. Chorographies described the body of England. Voyages showed England in action.

Insistence on the nation as ultimate actor is what distinguishes Richard Hakluyt's *Principal Navigations of the English Nation* from its chief continental counterparts. Neither Fracanzano da Montalboddo's *Paesi Novamente Ritrovati* (1507), the first important collection of voyages, nor Giovanni Battista Ramusio's *Navigazioni e Viaggi* (1550–59), which gave Hakluyt his model, nor even Theodore de Bry's two series of illustrated *Voyages* (1590–1634), which Hakluyt himself helped get started, confine their attention to the exploits of any one particular kingdom or nation, certainly not that of the compiler.[2] Though they regularly identify the nationality of the voyagers whose narrations they print, their interest is rather in the extra-European world and its description than in the political and cultural divisions of Europe itself. As Ramusio puts it, his aim is to replace Ptolemy, to provide a new geography for a new world.[3] Hakluyt shared this scientific interest. He was first lured into the work that resulted in his collections by the sight of maps and books of cosmography; he corresponded with many of the leading continental geographers; and he filled the geographical lacunae in the second edition of his *English Voyages* (his own short title for the book) with the travels of other nations. But his prime intent remained always to celebrate English navigation and to promote England's expansion abroad. In his patriotism, Hakluyt more nearly resembles Lambarde, Camden, and Drayton than he does Montalboddo, Ramusio, or de Bry. Like the English chorographers, Hakluyt claims to be sustained in his enormous task by "the ardent love of my country,"[4] and, like them, he expresses that love by holding up to his fellow countrymen an image of themselves.

Hakluyt's is not, however, the same England the chorographers show. The exigencies of the expansionist movement supported by printed voyages were different from those of the parliamentary and landowning interest chorography served, and the representational practices associated with the two kinds differed as well. The displacement of the monarch favored by chorography and by at least some elements of the chorographic community could not be a feature of a book like Hakluyt's. Indeed, Hakluyt's English successor, Samuel Purchas, made the favorable representation of monarchy central to his *Pilgrims* (1625).[5] Hakluyt is considerably less emphatic, so unemphatic that an absolutist could easily have been troubled by his book. But given the fact that kings licensed and often financed voyages of discovery, he could hardly exclude them. Nor could a promoter of expansion put quite the same value as did the chorographers on what purported to be the immemorial order of society. Though he might seek historical precedent for overseas travel, he could not disguise the essentially innovative quality of the enterprise he described. The discovery of a new world with new opportunities and new demands inevitably threatened the old hierarchy of power. Somehow that threat and its resolution would have to figure in his work, as it does in Hakluyt's. A collection of voyages had, furthermore, to concern itself, to a far greater degree than did a chorography, with other nations, whether European competitors or more distant commercial and/or military targets. Its England would of necessity be an England defined by its relations to those other more or less similar entities, an England reconstituted in response to a new global system of differences.

Hakluyt's task—the collective task of the various intersecting communities for which his name and his book stand as convenient markers—was thus not merely to record what the English had done and what the world was like, though these are the goals he explicitly set himself. He had also to reinvent both England and the world to make them fit for one another. This reinvention sometimes met harsh limits. No argument, however ingenious or convincing, for a navigable passage through North America to the East could overcome the intransigent realities of geography. And no promise of unlimited wealth could make successful colonists of gentlemen who refused to work.[6] But such limits could be known only by repeatedly bumping against them. That is what Hakluyt and the communities he represented did. They mapped the physical world and strove to impress on it the designs of collective desire. The fabled gold of Guiana proved to be only a fable. But the England that sought that treasure and the riches of all the world beside transformed itself, in part through the agency of representations like Hakluyt's, into a significantly different polity than it would otherwise have been.

What then are the lineaments of Hakluyt's England? And how do those features relate to the discursive practices and to the social, economic, and political interests that informed the *English Voyages*? I wish to approach these issues indirectly, by first asking similar questions of another text from another author and another country. Though Hakluyt's *Principal Navigations* is alone among the major European travel collections in making the nation the universal voyager, there are other accounts of overseas enterprise that concentrate on the accom-

plishments of just one country. Most of these are histories like Peter
Martyr's *De Orbe Novo* (1547–51) or Fernández de Oviedo's *General
History of the Indies* (1535). But the one I would like to consider is a
poem, *The Lusiads* (1572) of Luís de Camões, an epic account of
Vasco da Gama's first voyage to India. Camões was as much a propa-
gandist of empire as Hakluyt, and his book is as much a product of
what Camões himself identifies as "amor da pátria." The Lusitanians,
the sons of Lusus, the mythic founder of Portugal, are the Portuguese. The story of da Gama's voyage is their story. The Portuguese
nation is the subject of Camões's poem just as the English nation is
the subject of Hakluyt's collection. Similar questions can thus be
asked of each. One reason for doing so is that the answers are so
interestingly different. Comparing the two prevents us from thinking,
as we might otherwise do, that Hakluyt's formulations are either
natural or inevitable, helps us to discover the ideological construction
of his England.

But there is another reason as well. Setting Camões's *Lusiads*
against Hakluyt's *Voyages* reveals a system of differences in generic
form and sociopolitical formation that was active in the production of
both texts and that has remained active in their reception. Here I
cannot claim, as I could in comparing Spenser to Tasso or Coke to
Justinian, that the English author knew the foreign text when he
composed his own. There is no evidence that Hakluyt had read or
even heard of Camões. But Hakluyt did know the heroic genre in
which Camões wrote, and he was aware of its bearing on his project.
Indeed, he not only thought epic an appropriate response to the
"venture" of overseas expansion, he also included epic material in his
own more miscellaneous book. And if Hakluyt knew and included
epic, Camões knew and excluded the kind of voyage material that
dominates large parts of Hakluyt's text. Inclusion and exclusion—of
people as well as of generic forms—is what this system of differences
is all about.

Epic has, of course, already figured in an earlier chapter in a quite
different relation, in opposition to chivalric romance. We need not be
surprised to find its political valence suddenly changing. Something of
the same sort has already happened to *The Faerie Queene*. Opposed to
Gerusalemme Liberata in chapter one, it stood for a neofeudal dispersal of power from the crown to aristocratic champions like Leicester, Sidney, and Essex. But placed next to Drayton's *Poly-Olbion* in
chapter three, it looked rather like an advocate of royal absolutism.
Likewise epic, which in Tasso stood against romance and represented

the newly consolidated absolutist state, now joins with romance in a generic and sociopolitical formation whose signifying other is the unheroic pursuit of commercial gain. In the vast outpouring of writing concerning its overseas expansion, "Europe," in the words of Daniel Defert, "becomes conscious of itself, writes its own description and understands itself increasingly as the guiding principle of a planetary process, no longer simply a region of the world."[7] But this consciousness was from the first profoundly fissured. The Europe that wrote itself, the England and Portugal that wrote themselves, were divided both internally and externally along lines suggested by the opposition of voyage to epic. Choosing a genre (or being chosen by one) and understanding that genre within a particular system of differences also meant choosing (or being chosen by) a politics, choosing to endorse one distribution of power and wealth rather than another. What Europe was to be the guiding principle of this planetary process? And what Europeans? These are questions that representations like Camões's and Hakluyt's could not avoid addressing.

Class, Nation, and Camões

From the first words of his poem, Camões's choice of genres is clear: "As armas e os barões. . . . "[8] This is to be a Virgilian epic concerned with military accomplishment. But Camões has significantly altered Virgil's formula. "Arms and the men" takes the place of "arms and the man"—"Arma virumque." Despite the narrative centrality of Vasco da Gama, *The Lusiads* has no single hero. Instead it celebrates the deeds of a nation. There is, however, a peculiar and distinguishing exclusiveness to Camões's conception of the nation. For him, Portugal is identified with its "barões"—not its "men" or even its "heroes," though the word is often translated in both ways, but its "noblemen," its "barons." In choosing this term and making it plural, Camões enforces both the aristocratic and the nationalist ideology already strongly associated with the classical epic. But that very emphasis betrays a tension, an uncertainty imperfectly masked by assertiveness.

Camões had good reason for uncertainty. Despite his claims, da Gama's voyage does not quite satisfy the requirements of either class ideology or literary decorum. A classical epic, as the Renaissance understood it, was, above all, a poem of war. And the feudal nobility was just as firmly identified as a class devoted to war. But, as Voltaire was to object, da Gama never fights.[9] The arms are there. They are often mentioned, occasionally shown off, even fired once or twice. But except for a minor skirmish, they are never used in battle. "I came, I saw, I went home again" might have been da Gama's summary of his experience. So crucial was that coming and going to the Portuguese empire as it developed in the seven decades between da Gama's voyage and the publication of Camões's poem that Camões could hardly have put any other event at the center of his narrative. But still the very act of representing the Portuguese nation in an epic poem centered on an essentially peaceful, if hazardous, maritime voyage of discovery raised a potentially troubling question. Is this a properly heroic action, an action worthy of a class devoted to war? Is the nation that takes its identity from such an action a truly noble nation?

One way to deal with this problem, the way adopted nearly a century later by Milton in *Paradise Lost,* would have been to write a heroic poem against the ideology of the heroic poem, to turn the genre against itself, to sing a "better fortitude . . . unsung." This Camões does not do. Though he talks no less than Milton of his rivalry with the ancient poets and of the rivalry of his heroes with theirs, his "outro valor" (1.3) is not fundamentally "other." It is rather the same valor enacted on a larger stage. In keeping with this conservative intent, Camões attempts rather to conceal than to expose and exploit the difference between generic expectation and the story he has to tell. Da Gama's first voyage may have been marked by no significant battle, but it followed from many battles, the several centuries of heroic warfare by which Portugal was reclaimed as a Christian kingdom from the Moors and retained its autonomy from the encroachment of its Castilian neighbors, and it was itself followed by a no less glorious series of battles in the Indian Ocean and the Far East. The greater part of four of *The Lusiads*'s ten cantos is given over to the recital of these events, and da Gama's involvement as narrator, listener, and even participant helps divert attention from the incongruous peacefulness of his first voyage.

That incongruity does, however, hint at a still more fundamental suppression, a more significant refusal to acknowledge what the poem and the poet cannot help but know. What both know—what we all know—is that the Portuguese sailed around the Cape of Good Hope and across the Indian Ocean in search of a more direct access to the much desired wealth of the Orient. For that purpose, war was initially not needed and even subsequently it remained subordinate to a mercantile motive. It is this "base" motive, this quest for "vile reward" (1.10) that Camões will not acknowledge, whether in his heroes or in himself.

Rumors of wealth do nevertheless echo through the poem. Again and again we hear of the gold and spices, the medicinal drugs and precious jewels "que produze o aurífero Levante" (2.4). Indeed, in its descriptions of Calicut (7.35 and 41), Jiddah (9.3), and Malacca (10.123), *The Lusiads* goes so far as to present the outline of a theory which would equate long-distance trade with communal well-being, suggesting (perhaps subversively) in two of those instances that trade has "ennobled" the city that engages in it.[10] Clearly the hope of such wealth and such nobility is what makes the Portuguese so eager to reach the Indian coast. Others, even in the poem, have no difficulty discerning this motive. The natives of Mombasa suppose da Gama seeks "the rich merchandise of the golden East" (2.4), and the merchants of Jiddah recognize in him a rival for their Indian trade (9.4). But these perceptions are not shared by the Portuguese themselves. If commercial gain is their goal, neither they nor their poet ever says so. Instead, they repeatedly and insistently proffer a set of quite different motives, motives more compatible with the crusading ethos of a Christian *barão*. Da Gama and his companions voyage in search not of wealth but rather of honor, conquest, and the opportunity to spread the Christian faith.

The closest Camões comes to allowing the expression of a commercial interest occurs in a passage so hedged in with qualification and denial that it deserves some more particular attention. At his first meeting with the Zamorin, the ruler of Calicut, da Gama offers a "commercial" pact, a treaty of "peace and friendship" (7.62). Whatever the historical da Gama may have meant (the passage comes from Camões's chronicle sources), can the heroic, antimercantile da Gama of this poem really mean it? There is reason for thinking he doesn't. The offer contradicts not only the general spirit of the poem but also both the narrator's flat statement earlier in the same canto that the Portuguese have come "to plant the law of Christ and to give new customs and a new king" (7.15). But if he doesn't mean it, why does he say it? Is his offer merely a diplomatic lie, like the earlier lie he told the king of Malindi to avoid leaving his ship? I don't think so. It is rather a contradiction forced on Camões by the contradictions in his ideology and his material. Both the facts of history and the logic of his narrative require that da Gama meet the Zamorin. When they meet, da Gama must have something to say about why he is there. Unprepared to fight (and in history not having fought), he can hardly announce his "true" reasons: conquest and conversion. So Camões lets him say what the historical da Gama is supposed to have said and then does what he can to remove the force of that saying. He has da Gama conclude his description of the trade agreement which is to bind the Portuguese king and the Zamorin with the unlikely but ideologically saving claim that "yours will be the profit, his the glory will be found" (7.62).[11]

Profit—*proveito*—is as strongly negative a term in Camões's lexicon as *glory* and *fame* are positive. Desire for profit grows in the "base heart" (8.59) of the heathen ruler; the noble-hearted Portuguese seek only fame. Or at least in the ideal time of *The Lusiads,* a time less historical than mythic, they sought only fame. When, however, Camões considers his own age and his own experience, the sharp distinction between "them" and "us" breaks down. "No more, my Muse, no more," he concludes in Sir Richard Fanshawe's translation,

> my harp's ill strung,
> Heavy, and out of tune, and my voice hoarse:
> And not with singing but to see I've sung
> To a deaf people and without remorse.
> Favor (that wont t'inspire the poet's tongue)
> Our country yields it not, she minds the purse
> Too much, exhaling from her gilded mud
> Nothing but gross and melancholy blood.[12]

"She minds the purse / Too much." Portugal is overcome by a "gosto da cobiça" (10.145). "Favor," the gratuitous reward characteristic of a noble and courtly society, the reward figured in the Isle of Love to which Venus leads da Gama and his men, is denied. Instead, values that Camões never clearly defines but that seem strongly marked by a mercantile spirit have taken over.[13] Intent not merely on representing a Portugal that is, a Portugal that prefers *gloria* to *proveito,* Camões aims to bring such a nation into existence by showing it an ideal image of its heroic and nonmercantile self. From this perspective, his misrepresentation even of the past, his suppression of the commercial motive that directed the Portuguese to the Indies and the Far East, comes to seem a hortatory representation of what should have been and what should be—if, that is, Portugal is to deserve a poet like Camões.

Camões's own densely conflicted subjectivity is the measure of the distance between the actual Portugal and its heroic ideal. In the poem only the Zamorin, caught between fear of invasion and hunger for profit, possesses a similarly rich inner life. As for da Gama, the poet's surrogate both as narrator of Portuguese history and as recipient of prophetic inspiration, he is as transparent as a ghost. He has no existence apart from the mission of state that fills him.[14] He is brought into his own historical narrative, the account of himself and his nation he gives the king of Malindi, as a function of a royal proclamation, itself the product of a god-sent vision. A heroic national destiny thus chooses its protagonist all unawares. For Camões it is just the other way around. As numerous passages of complaint and admonition make clear, he must invent from often resisting and unsuitable material a nation that will justify his heroic literary undertaking—an undertaking defined by the ancient antipathy of the epic to commerce.[15]

This, however, is greatly to exaggerate the hold of the past, and particularly of the literary past, on the present. A modern cultural movement, born in the very Italian centers of commerce whose monopolistic control of the eastern trade Portugal was successfully supplanting, was responsible for the renewed prestige of Greek and Roman literary forms. In imitating the ancients, Camões imitated the Italians. "*Os Lusíadas* is," as C. M. Bowra has remarked, "in many ways the epic of humanism."[16] But in being the epic of humanism, it is also the epic of an intense conflict in cultural values made more intense by the Portuguese expansion. In the course of the sixteenth century, according to the report of the modern economic historian of the Portuguese empire, Vitorino Magalhães-Godinho, "opposition continued without respite between the anticommercial attitude and ideological system on the one hand and the pursuit of profit and the effort to create material goods on the other."[17] On one side Godinho lets us hear the aristocratic archbishop, Dom Frei Bartolomeu, charging that "where there is a crowd of merchants and merchandise, cupidity, the root of all evil, is never absent," and on the other, the apothecary-adventurer, Tomé Pires, answering that "trading in merchandise is so necessary that without it the world could not go on. It is this that ennobles kingdoms and makes their people great, that ennobles cities, that brings war and peace."[18] Both voices speak in *The Lusiads,* but not with equal strength or authority.

"Of this country," Camões wrote sometime during his lengthy stay in India, "I can tell you it is the mother of corrupt villains and the stepmother of honorable men. For those who throw themselves into the pursuit of money always bob to the surface like inflated bladders, while those who take as their motto 'To arms, Mouriscote' . . . wither before they ripen."[19] Castilian *hidalgism* finds its Portuguese counterpart in the *fidalgism* of a passage like this. The "To arms, Mouriscote"—"à las armas, Mouriscote"—is particularly revealing. Taken from a Spanish chivalric poem, the line points to the nonhumanist literary sources of Camões's aristocratic ideology. Like Cervantes' mad *hidalgo,* the *caveleiro fidalgo* Luís de Camões sees himself and his experience through eyes trained by much reading of chivalric romance, and he projects that vision onto his poem.[20] The romantic tale of the Twelve of England, the perilous encounter with the giant Adamastor, the enchanted visit to the Isle of Love—episodes like these belong rather to the world of Rodomonte, Ruggiero, and Orlando than to that of *pius* Aeneas. In *The Lusiads* these two worlds, the world of chivalric romance and the world of Roman epic, worlds that Tasso was just then setting in opposition to one another, coalesce to exclude still more powerfully base mercantile cupidity. Literary reminiscence does difficult political work.

When da Gama offers the Zamorin the profit of their trade and keeps only the glory for the king of Portugal, he imagines systems of value that never touch. Glory is as clean as a poem, as clean as da Gama's transparent self. But in sixteenth-century Portugal things were messier. Overseas trade was a crown monopoly in which both king and nobles participated actively. This monopolistic policy, like Camões's poem, had an exclusionary intent. It kept the middle class weak and allowed the nobility, as Oliveira Marques has written, "to invest their new capital in land, in building . . . and in luxuries. As a result, the feudal structure of the country . . . was not essentially shaken by expansion."[21] Still, the threat of mercantile contamination persisted. The king of Portugal had himself "become a merchant"—a merchant whose commercial identity figured in his very title.[22] After da Gama's voyage, kings of Portugal styled themselves lords "of the conquest, navigation, *and traffic* of Ethiopia, Arabia, Persia, and India" ("domin[i] . . . conquistae, navigationis, *et commercii* Aethiopiae, Arabiae, Persiae, atque Indiae"). And the taint of so prevalent an activity inevitably marked the Portuguese people as well. By the early seventeenth century, a French visitor to India could say of them that they were "good merchants and good sailors, and that's all."[23] What a blow such a remark would have been to Camões! But by the time it was made, he had died and Portugal had fallen under the sovereignty of the king of Spain.

The preservation of Portuguese national autonomy, the exclusive identification of the nation with its aristocratic governing class, and the equally exclusive identification of that class with a heroic crusading ethos—these were the prime elements in the ideological program of *The Lusiads.* Many things would have urged this program on Camões: his own class identity, his experience as a soldier and government agent in North Africa, India, and China, the epic and romantic models on which he drew, the centuries of anti-Moorish warfare that had characterized Portugal's history, and the very real menace to class and to nation posed by both Portugal's geographic location and the effects of its rapid and enormous mercantile expansion. Like the other coastal peoples of Iberia—the Galicians, Catalonians, Valencians, and Andalusians—the Portuguese were constantly threatened by Castilian aspirations to peninsular hegemony. But unlike the others, the Portuguese had succeeded in preserving their independence by adopting the warrior mentality of their inland rivals.[24] Or so Camões seems to have thought. That is why he puts such emphasis on the shared crusading zeal of the two Iberian nations *and* on the many wars waged between them.[25] Portugal maintained itself by being more Castilian than the Castilians. But could it continue to do so as the center of a vast commercial empire?

As an extension of intra-Iberian rivalry and of anti-Moorish warfare, Portugal's penetration into the Indian Ocean fits the heroic pattern of its feudal history and thus deserves the epic representation Camões gives it. But as a commercial venture, it undermines the very basis of aristocratic Portuguese self-understanding. And though Camões chooses not to dwell on the simultaneous overseas expansion of Spain, preferring to compare da Gama and his Portuguese successors with the heroes of Homer, Virgil, and Ariosto than with Columbus, Cortés, or Pizarro, the vast territorial conquests of the Spanish, their establishment in the New World of a quasi-feudal system of land tenure, and their haughty disdain for trade must have made Portugal's commercial empire seem still less ideologically defensible. The Portuguese had won half the world but lost their own aristocratic souls. Some such suspicion combined with his own unhappy experience in the East, experience that seems to have included open conflict with the Portuguese trading community in Macao, goes far toward explaining why Camões expresses such ambivalence about the seagoing venture that forms the main subject of his poem.

It is in these terms, rather than merely as a conventional moral attack on overweening ambition, that I would read the famous episode of the old man of Restelo who erupts suddenly into the poem at the end of canto 4, just as da Gama is departing for India.[26] Though this "reverend father" seems to object to *any* venture in search of fame and is as resolute in his neglect of the mercantile motives of da Gama's voyage as is Camões himself, he does make a distinction between the traditional struggle against the neighboring infidels, which he allows, and this new undertaking, which he rejects. And he prophetically mocks that royal title, borne by the kings of Camões's own time, in which, as we have noticed, conquest, navigation, and trade were so compromisingly mixed. "Do you seek," he asks, "an uncertain and unknown fate so that fame will exalt and flatter you, calling you, with extravagant plenty, lord[s] of India, Persia, Arabia, and Ethiopia?" (4.101). Is it really fame itself the old man objects to, or rather this new commercial renown, renown tinged with infamy? When the poet addresses his readers and particularly his king, the difference between the two sources of fame is made clear, as is his preference for one over the other. He passionately attacks the corrupting influence of money and calls, with equal ardor, for renewed war against the Islamic rulers of neighboring North Africa.

Never has a king followed the recommendation of a poet with greater fidelity than King Sebastião followed that of Camões. But then the recommendation may itself have been made with a knowledge of the king's projects. Among the many pressures shaping *The Lusiads* there was also this. *The Lusiads* was written as a courtly poem in search of royal patronage, a poem that fit itself to the tastes of its dedicatee— who, in this case, was already bent on doing precisely what his poet told him to do. In 1578, six years after the publication of Camões's epic, King Sebastião led a great army to destruction on the sands of Alcazarquivir, where Sebastião himself died. Just two years later, after the brief reign of the tubercular Cardinal-King Henrique, Philip II of Spain assumed the Portuguese crown. Not until 1640 did Portugal regain its autonomy, and by then its place as the dominant European power in the Orient had been taken by the Dutch, a nation that was winning its independence from Spain just as Portugal was losing its. In its commercial expansion, republican Holland was, moreover, as eager to suppress all signs of aristocratic identity as Camões had been to suppress the marks of trade. The Dutch avoided territorial acquisition, made little attempt to spread their Protestant faith, called even their *de facto* colonial administrators "merchants," and produced no epic poem celebrating their overseas accomplishments.[27] They thus exemplify the triumph of those values Camões opposed just as clearly as Don Sebastião does the defeat of those he supported.

This crushing verdict of history has not, however, been ratified by the Portuguese people, who have embraced *The Lusiads* as their national poem—the prime literary representation of who they have been, who they are, and who they should be. Not even Shakespeare's position in the English-speaking world can rival that of Camões in his homeland. Statues of him are everywhere. Streets, squares, and ships are named for him. A national holiday commemorates him. His epic is the one inevitable school text. Illustrations of it decorate hotels and offices. Newspapers and magazines devote extensive space to its discussion. There can be few examples in history of a poet or of a poem more intimately linked with the identity of a nation than Camões and *The Lusiads* have been with that of Portugal.[28] Through the dark decades of subjection to Spain and the long centuries of colonial rule in Africa, Asia, and South America, the Portuguese were sustained and inspired by Camões's vision of their heroic destiny—a vision that even in 1572, when the poem was first published, blatantly contradicted the reality of its author's experience.

Commodity and Vent

Camões died on June 10, 1580. Philip II became king of Portugal two months later. Anticipating both events, Camões wrote, "All will see that so dear was my country that I was content to die not only in, but with it."[29] But as one career ended, another began. In England the younger Richard Hakluyt responded to Portugal's loss of autonomy with his first surviving work, "A Discourse of the Commodity of the Taking of the Strait of Magellanus" (1580). What to Camões must have seemed a consequence of the ignominious defeat of Portuguese chivalry, chivalry he had urged onto the field where it perished, was to Hakluyt a threat of national isolation. "The peril that may ensue to all the princes of Europe if the king of Spain be suffered to enjoy Portugal with the East Indies is . . . a matter of great and grave consideration," he wrote. And the menace to England was particularly keen. "Whenever the rule and government of the East and West Indies and their several isles and territories shall be in one prince, they neither will receive English cloth nor yet care for any vent of their commodities to us, having then so many places of their own to make vent and interchange of their commodities."[30]

Unlike Camões, Hakluyt thinks in economic terms, in terms of "vent" and "commodity." His suggestion of the three principal ways that "without great charge and without open war" England can respond to this challenge tells still more of this mode of thought. He advises, "(1) that the Strait of Magellanus be taken and fortified, inhabited and kept; (2) that the Isle of St. Vincent in Brazil and the soil adjoining be taken and kept; [and] (3) that the northeast trade be discovered with all speed and drawn to trade" (*Corr.* 1.140). His object was to break Spain's power with two bold strokes, one to the south and the west, the other to the north and the east. "The Strait of Magellan is," he claims, "the gate of entry into the treasure of both the East and West Indies" (*Corr.* 1.140). From this vantage point, the English would soon make themselves the masters of "all the golden mines of Peru and all the coast and tract of that firm of America upon the Sea of Sur" (*Corr.* 1.142). In this enterprise St. Vincent would serve as a way station and source of supply. As for the other stroke, the discovery of a northeast passage to the East, it would not only provide a market for English cloth but also "cut Spain from the trade of the spicery, to the abating of her navy, her wealth, and high credit in the world" (*Corr.* 1.144).

To measure the full audacity of this plan, we need to remember that in 1580 England did not control a square inch of territory outside the British Isles. The preceding decades had seen a sharp increase in English maritime activity, culminating in Drake's circumnavigation, which was even then underway. But the one established and moderately successful long-distance trading connection, the relationship with Russia, was already in decline and was further menaced, as Hakluyt points out, by the unstable political situation in Moscow. The only other likely opening, a direct trade route to Turkey, had not yet been developed. Unlike the Portugal of Camões, which by papal donation possessed half the world and which, in actual fact, exercised effective control over coastal territory and major trade routes from Brazil to the Moluccas, Hakluyt's England had no overseas empire and comparatively little overseas experience. Even a half dozen years later Hakluyt could be embarrassed by questions from his continental acquaintances about English inactivity at sea. Thus where Camões reflects back on a period of almost incredible accomplishment, Hakluyt is driven by the fear of national exclusion and shame. Camões can afford to worry about a distortion of values that has resulted from rapid expansion; Hakluyt is preoccupied with the sheer need to expand.

From our perspective, Hakluyt's proposals in this first pamphlet appear both more likely and less likely than they could have to his contemporaries. We know that in the next century England would in fact surpass the commercial strength of both Spain and Portugal. But we know too that the establishment of an English garrison in the Strait of Magellan would have been far more difficult than Hakluyt supposed—the Spanish tried and failed just a short while later—and that with sails and wooden hulls the northeastern passage could not have been navigated. Still, neither the general plausibility nor the particular implausibility of Hakluyt's project is as significant as the glimpse it affords us at the very beginning of his career of the global reach of his thought, including as elements in his response to a European dynastic event all the world from China to Peru.

Like Hakluyt, Camões belonged to a generation whose imagination had been shaped by the voyages of discovery. He had himself traveled around Africa to India and the Far East, and he ends his poem with a vision of the terrestrial globe informed by those experiences. But however he actually got his geographical knowledge, he presents the world from a celestial vantage point, as a body fully known and neatly contained within the familiar Ptolemaic cosmos. The conservatism that would reinforce aristocratic preeminence is apparent here as well. To Hakluyt the world appears rather as a field of uncertain and potentially unsettling enterprise. Odd bits of land are to be taken, colonies planted, populations moved, passages explored, trades opened. His reports come not from the all-knowing gods but rather from the partial experience of individual mariners and traders. Drake's men have told him of the fresh water and victual in the Strait of Magellan, and he has developed his ideas about the northeast from the reports of the Muscovy Company. His later collections are compendia of information of this sort, information organized by geographical region for the easy use of travelers and strategic planners. In his *Voyages,* historical narrative is proleptic. It anticipates by enabling future accomplishment.

Who is to be the agent of this accomplishment? A certain ambiguity marks this early treatise. Hakluyt slips back and forth from monarchs to nations in a way that suggests they are interchangeable. "The Russian" means the czar; "the Spaniard" means any native of Spain. "All princes of Europe" are menaced by the king of Spain, but "the Portugal nation" needs particular assistance (*Corr.* 1.140, 142, 139, and 140). The same uncertainty applies to England. Passive constructions leave it unclear whether the king or the nation will take and fortify the Strait of Magellan, take and keep the Isle of St. Vincent, discover the northeast and draw it to trade. But even this ambiguity, particularly in a text addressed to the court, is significant. It suggests a conceptual fluidity that would be essential to Hakluyt's representation of England, a fluidity that would be difficult to match in France, Spain, or Portugal. Still more significant, however, is his understanding of England as an essentially economic entity, a producer and consumer of goods. Though variously modified, this conception persists through

his subsequent work, including the two editions of the *Principal Navigations*. Exploration, military action, colonization: all must be made
to serve the overriding objective of economic well-being.

In a brief and informal memorandum like the "Discourse on the
Strait of Magellan," this economic conception of the nation appears in
its least qualified form. It is equally clear in the writings of Hakluyt's
elder cousin and namesake, Richard Hakluyt of the Middle Temple,
under whose tutelage the editor of the *Principal Navigations* began
his geographical studies. "Since all men confess (that be not barba-
rously bred) that men are born as well to seek the common commodity of their country as their own private benefit . . . " begins one of the
elder Hakluyt's several important "notes of instruction." And before
many lines we discover that "of many things that tend to the common
benefit of the state . . . no one thing . . . is greater than clothing [i.e.,
trade in cloth]" (*Corr.* 1.184). There then follows a detailed discussion of English clothmaking and the ways it may be improved by a
close study of the Turkish trade. This particular document was addressed to "a principal English factor at Constantinople." The elder
Hakluyt's other papers, most of which his cousin published in one or
another of his collections, have a similarly practical intent. They concern North American colonization, Persian dyestuffs, the northeast
passage, the Levant trade, and the Virginia enterprise and are directed
to those immediately involved. But whatever the particular object, the
general understanding remains the same. Commerce is the life of both
England and the world.

In its representation of England and its representation of the world,
the younger Hakluyt's *Principal Navigations* conveys a similar message. Its size (834 folio pages in the 1589 edition, expanding to over
two thousand in 1598–1600), the number of voyages it records (93
in 1589, 216 in 1598–1600), the number of supporting documents it
prints (159 in 1589, 378 in 1598–1600), its historical scope (fifteen
hundred years in the first edition, sixteen hundred in the second), and
its geographical coverage (the greater part of the known world in both
editions) testify to England's "great trade and traffic in trade of merchandise" (*Corr.* 1.55) and work to augment that trade by inspiring
and informing future enterprisers and adventurers.

I do not by this mean to suggest that every one of those voyages
and every one of those supporting documents concern trade. Many
obviously do not. As Hakluyt himself points out in his preface to the
1589 edition, most of the medieval English voyages he prints were
directed to the Holy Land and were undertaken, whether by pilgrims

or crusaders, "principally for devotion's sake according to the time" (*PN* 1.xxv). Nor are such uncommercial motives confined to the middle ages. Even the elder Hakluyt in his pamphlet for the Virginia enterprise could list as the first three "inducements to the liking of the voyage":

1. The glory of God by planting of religion among those infidels.
2. The increase of the force of the Christians.
3. The possibility of the enlarging of the dominions of the queen's most excellent majesty and consequently of her honor, revenues, and of her power by this enterprise. (*Corr.* 2.327)

But if motives like these, motives that would have pleased even Camões, head his list, they are followed by twenty-eight others that concern commercial activity. And this latter group determines all the elder Hakluyt's practical advice. When, for example, he catalogs the various "sorts of men which are to be passed in this voyage," he specifies thirty-one different skills and trades, from fishermen and salt-makers to shipwrights and painters, but he includes no minister of the gospel (*Corr.* 2.336–38). Conversion, if it is to happen at all, will follow and serve commerce rather than the other way around.

A similar seeming complexity of motive in the work of the younger Hakluyt generally resolves itself in a similar way. He charges, for example, in the dedication to Philip Sidney of his first collection, the *Divers Voyages* of 1582, that "if hitherto in our own discoveries we had not been led with a preposterous desire of seeking rather gain than God's glory, I assure myself that our labors had taken far better effect."[31] But, as the context makes clear, *gain* here means short-term gain of the sort Frobisher's men sought in hunting for gold rather than finding out the northwest passage, and *God's glory* means the long-term gain that would come from well-established colonies and secure commerce with the East. It is in this, as well as in the more obvious spiritual sense, that, as Hakluyt goes on to say, "Godliness is great riches and that if we first seek the kingdom of God all other things will be given unto us." Those "other things," the "lasting riches [that] do wait upon them that are zealous for the advancement of the kingdom of Christ," evidently include not only the treasure of heaven but also "the most noble merchandise of all the world," the trade of Cathay.

To dismiss such religious claims as mere humbug would surely be wrong, though Hakluyt himself, when referring to the Spanish and Portuguese, had little compunction about doing so. The Iberians, "pretending," he says, "in glorious words that they made their discoveries chiefly to convert infidels to our most holy faith (as they say), in deed and truth sought not them but their goods and riches." Coming just a few lines after his own glorious words, this charge can as easily confirm as erase our doubt. But even if Hakluyt could himself see through motives like those he professes, that does not make the profession any less necessary or any less significant. Resistance to an open acknowledgment of commercial designs, like the resistance we encountered in Camões, exists too, though at a much lower level, in Hakluyt. And when the audience becomes socially more elevated, as it is in this letter to Sidney, the level of resistance also rises. Addressing a merchant of London in his notes on the Turkish trade, the elder Hakluyt easily and perhaps automatically drops all mention of propagating the faith. Finding a vent for English cloth is service enough to the commonwealth. But when he or his cousin writes for a larger, more general audience, especially one that includes members of the landowning aristocracy, they become aware that something else needs to be said. If their conception of the nation is fundamentally economic, it is not a conception they can always admit—not even, I would guess, to themselves.

Camões, as we noticed, was a member of the lesser nobility, a Portuguese *caveleiro fidalgo*. The Hakluyts were situated rather differently. Though they descended from Herefordshire gentry and retained connection with their country origins, their own lives were centered in London. The elder Richard Hakluyt was a lawyer, a member of the Middle Temple; his younger cousin was a clergyman, the son of a member of the Skinners' Company.[32] Close relations with the merchant community of London—and, for the younger Hakluyt, that of Bristol where he held a prebend—are evident in the work of both. The elder Hakluyt's memoranda were, for the most part, produced for the particular use of the great trading companies, and the younger Hakluyt drew heavily on the archives of these companies in assembling his *Voyages*. Merchants' interests and attitudes were shared by both. Without some such connection, their image of England would have been very different.

But if a concrete relation to the merchants who were carrying English commerce into parts of the world it had never before known is a necessary condition for the Hakluyts' representation of England, it is not a sufficient one. For merchants themselves in these years lacked a conceptual vocabulary that would have permitted them to assign special value to their own activities. So concludes an impressive recent study by Laura Stevenson of merchants and craftsmen in Elizabethan popular literature. While the older, negative stereotype of the merchant as a greedy usurer waned in the last decades of the sixteenth century, no more favorable image emerged—or rather none that would serve to distinguish merchants from the aristocratic leaders of society. Instead of praising merchants for their diligence, thrift, or financial talent, as their successors a hundred years later would do, Stevenson's popular authors "praised them for being 'magnanimous,' 'courtly,' 'chivalric' vassals of the king." As she demonstrates, "the labels Elizabethan authors attached to men of trade . . . reveal that they never sought to consolidate the social consciousness of these men by appealing to bourgeois values. Elizabethan praise of bourgeois men was expressed in the rhetoric—and by extension, in terms of social paradigms—of the aristocracy."[33]

Writing an epic poem addressed to a crusading king, Camões had good reason actively to suppress the commercial side of Portugal's overseas expansion. But even without such reason, in less obviously class-minded genres and addressing an audience that included many merchants, Elizabethan writers fell back on a strategy not altogether unlike his. Where he celebrates a mercantile voyage of discovery in terms borrowed from epic warfare, they dress merchants themselves in the rhetorical (and sometimes in the literal) garb of chivalric knights. For at least a few years, "gentle" merchants and clothiers in armor appeared as familiar figures in the popular literature of Elizabethan England. Clearly, the producers of these images—poets, players, printers, preachers, and pamphleteers—felt some need to show the leading members of the urban commercial class in a more positive way than had been customary. The extraordinary growth and diversification of the English economy, particularly as a result of increased overseas trade, required new forms of expression, as they required new forms of economic organization. On the organizational level, the rapidly proliferating array of joint-stock companies met this need. On the expressive level, the merchant heroes of Elizabethan popular literature performed an analogous function. The one provided capital; the other, ideological support. But economic reorganization seems to have been easier than social reevaluation. For all their debt to predecessors like the Merchant Adventurers, the joint-stock companies set an essentially new course from which there was no turning back.[34] The merchant hero was, in contrast, an unstable and short-lived paradox, an attempt to deny change even while expressing it, a reassertion of traditional social values and a familiar social hierarchy in the very midst of their subversion.

In its representation of commercial activity, Hakluyt's *Voyages* managed to slip past the conceptual barriers that otherwise confined not only the popular writers studied by Stevenson but also Hakluyt himself, barriers that could make him prefer "glory" to "gain" in a way strongly reminiscent of Camões. Far the greater part of its first two volumes—those concerned with voyages to the north and northeast and to the south and southeast[35]—are given over to the activities of merchants, their agents, and their "servants." And even in the thick third volume, which deals with the new world in the west, an area where gentlemen and mariners were the dominant figures, merchants play a conspicuous role. Furthermore, the voices we hear in all three volumes are often those of the merchants themselves, for their reports are among the most frequent documents in Hakluyt's collection. They are thus doubly brought into unaccustomed prominence, both as actors and as authors.[36] Sometimes they earn the right to this attention, as do the merchant heroes of Elizabethan popular literature, by behaving like aristocrats. Merchant ships engage in battle against "strong and warlike" opponents (*PN* 1.xliv), and the merchants themselves not only fight valorously but also perform with dignity and skill as ambassadors before monarchs all over the world. But they accomplish even these "gentle" actions in the course of avowedly commercial voyages, and they spend far more of their time acting specifically as merchants: finding out likely trade routes, analyzing markets, securing charters and commercial privileges, ordering and carrying goods, mastering foreign systems of coinage, weight, and measure, setting up "standing houses," hiring factors and other employees, engaging in actual trade. In no body of writings published in England in the sixteenth century—and, so far as I know, in none published elsewhere in Europe—were merchants and their doings presented more fully or more favorably or with less ideological constraint than in Hakluyt's three volumes of *Navigations, Voyages, Traffics, and Discoveries.*[37]

Something powerful and powerfully disruptive goes on in Hakluyt's text as a result of his larger project of demonstrating and encouraging English expansion, something that he could not himself have easily acknowledged. To what should we attribute this feat? In part at least to the fact that Hakluyt's real interest lay elsewhere. Unlike Stevenson's popular writers, Hakluyt had only incidentally undertaken the task of praising merchants. His intention was rather to describe the world and to show England active in it. And for that purpose mercantile voyages were among his richest sources. To omit them would be to leave large gaps in his description. But including them inevitably altered the picture. Not only did they make it more complete, they changed its essential character. Seen through the eyes of merchants, the world emerged as a vast network of markets offering unlimited commodities and vent, and England itself emerged as the aggressive commercial entity required from the first by Hakluyt's strategic thinking. As Hakluyt formulated his argument in the early "Discourse on the Strait of Magellan," what mattered most to England was finding buyers for its cloth and suppliers for its needs. In his various prefatory addresses to the *Voyages,* a strong but less sharply defined English presence in the world seems enough. But whichever way he puts it, mercantile activity assumes a prominence that can hardly help but upset the usual assessment of the relative importance of various social groups within the English polity. If England's "wealth and honor," as the tirelessly repeated formula has it, depend above all on overseas trade, then it follows that merchants are exceptionally important Englishmen, perhaps no less important than their traditional superiors, the landowning gentry and aristocracy.

Merchants, Gentlemen, and Their Genres

People of all sorts, from the queen and her councillors to common soldiers and seamen, contributed to the Elizabethan expansion. But the initiation, organization, and financing of most voyages remained in the hands of just two groups, merchants and gentlemen. Voyages to Russia, Turkey, and the East Indies were primarily the work of the merchants. Gentlemen, particularly west-country gentlemen connected to the Gilberts and Raleighs, dominated the attempts at western planting.[38] The two Hakluyts were similarly divided. The lawyer did most of his consulting for the eastward-bound merchants; the preacher did most of his, particularly in the 1580s, for gentlemen with colonial designs in the west. The *Principal Navigations,* shaped by its scientific goal of describing the whole world and by its nationalist ambition of showing England active everywhere, represented both groups and both regions.

The differences between merchants and gentlemen should not be exaggerated. As William Harrison remarked, merchants "often change estate with gentlemen, as gentlemen do with them, by a mutual conversion of the one into the other."[39] And members of both groups participated in many of the same projects. Nevertheless, a sense of class difference persisted. Harrison insists on it and so do those other Elizabethans who tried to describe the social structure of their country, Richard Mulcaster, Sir Thomas Smith, and William Camden. However they chose to divide the various categories of Englishmen— and they by no means agreed about every detail—each located gentlemen and merchants in quite distinct classes and each made it clear that the former was superior to the latter. Such differences in status were, moreover, seen to be seconded by differences in interest, even with regard to a common undertaking like overseas expansion—as this account of a text reprinted by Hakluyt suggests: "In 1583, writing in support of a project for the colonization of Newfoundland, Sir George Peckham considered it 'convenient that I do divide the adventurers into two sorts: the noblemen and gentlemen by themselves, and the merchants by themselves.' He said he had heard that in fact two companies were going to be established, one for each class. And he shaped the propaganda accordingly. For the gentry he stressed the fine climate, the conditions favorable to landowners, the crops that could be produced, and the excellent hunting. . . . For the merchants he provided a list of over seventy commodities which could bring them profit."[40]

Theodore K. Rabb, from whose book *Enterprise and Empire* I have taken this summary of Peckham's views, argues that, though Peckham may have been wrong about the gentry's hunger for land, he was right that fundamental differences separated them from merchants as investors. Where merchants were motivated by a relatively uncomplicated desire for profit, gentlemen needed the impulse of glory. Gentlemen chose to support riskier and more glamorous ventures, exploration and colonization rather than settled trade. And they were more strongly influenced by ideas of national enterprise. "One needs," Rabb writes, "only to turn from the minutes of the staid and solidly merchant East India Company to the records of the exuberantly hopeful and optimistic Virginia Company to appreciate the difference. The great trading corporation pursued its profits singlemindedly. Discussions of national prestige were entirely absent: in fact, it had to be reminded by the government of its national obligations; and even the tracts written in its behalf dealt more with economics than glory. The literature relating to the Virginia Company, on the other hand, was full of the most lofty and ambitious sentiments: Indians were going to be converted, Spain was going to be frustrated, and England's fame was going to be spread abroad."[41]

Such differences in content were associated with precisely the different generic forms we have been considering. Dedicating his edition of Peter Martyr's *Decades* (1587) to Sir Walter Raleigh, Hakluyt promises that Raleigh's endeavors in Virginia will win him, "if not a Homer, yet some Martyr—by whom I mean some happy genius—to rescue your heroic enterprises from the vasty maw of oblivion" (*Corr.* 2.369). Heroic enterprises demand a heroic treatment. Hakluyt himself worked to make sure the demand would be met. Several years earlier, he had recruited his Oxford "bedfellow," the young Hungarian humanist Stephan Parmenius, to memorialize in Latin verse the Newfoundland expedition of Raleigh's half-brother, Sir Humphrey Gilbert. Both Parmenius and Gilbert died on the voyage, but Parmenius's embarkation poem, *De Navigatione,* survived to appear in the *Principal Navigations,* where it was joined by yet another heroic poem, George Chapman's *De Guiana, Carmen Epicum,* an English blank-verse celebration of Raleigh's "discovery" of Guiana.

These poems bear a striking resemblance to Camões's *Lusiads*—a resemblance that testifies not only to the persistence of heroic convention but also to a shared aristocratic ideology. When Chapman addresses "you patrician spirits that refine / Your flesh to fire," he makes clear the class bias common to all three; and when he attacks "gold-made men as dregs of men," he expresses the antimercantile attitude that is the reflex of that bias (*PN* 10.448). Each poem is, furthermore, marked by the same stylistic as well as social elevation, the same proclamation of inspiration, the same prophetic vision of empire, the same rarified evocation of boundless wealth, the same neglect of commerce, the same nationalist emphasis, and the same identification of the nation with the monarch and the arms-bearing nobility. Whatever the differences between Portugal and England, between Camões and Hakluyt, they have at least this much in common. Nor is the epic strain in the *Principal Navigations* confined to these isolated bits of verse. Elements of it recur in many of the individual voyages and in Hakluyt's own prefatory statements, where he can, for example, link Raleigh's colonial enterprises with the medieval "heroical intents and attempts of our princes, our nobility, our clergy, and our chivalry" (*PN* 1.lxv) in much the way that Camões linked da Gama's voyage with the crusading warfare of Portugal's feudal nobility.

But in Hakluyt's case, the volume he introduces with these evocations of aristocratic glory is filled with records of mercantile profit and loss. Though recognized by no system of poetics, commerce, like conquest, has its genres, and they too are amply represented in

Hakluyt. At the opposite pole from the epic poem, with its elaborate narrative structure and its careful hierarchical ranking of gods and heroes, is the bare list of commodities to be bought or sold in some distant part of the world. Here, as in the still more frequent commercial letters and notes, the profit motive is taken for granted and all attention is focused on the practicalities of trade.

Consider, for example, this brief extract from a letter sent by John Newbery from Babylon to Master Leonard Poore in London: "Since our coming hither we have found very small sales, but divers say that in the winter our commodities will be very well sold. I pray God their words may prove true. I think cloth, kerseys, and tin have never been here at so low prices as they are now. Notwithstanding, if I had here so much ready money as the commodities are worth, I would not doubt to make a very good profit of this voyage hither, and to Balsara, and so by God's help there will be reasonable profit made of the voyage. But with half money and half commodity may be bought here the best sort of spices and other commodities that are brought from the Indies, and without money there is here at this instant small good to be done." The letter concludes with a list of "prices of wares as they are worth here at this instant":

> Cloves and maces, the batman, 5 ducats.
> Cinnamon, 6 ducats, and few to be gotten.
> Nutmegs, the batman, 45 medines, and 40 medines maketh a ducat.
> Ginger, 40 medines.
> Pepper, 75 medines.
> Turbetta, the batman, 50 medines.
> Neel, the churle, 70 ducats, and a churle is 27 rottils and a half of
>   Aleppo.
> Silk, much better than that which cometh from Persia, 11 ducats and a
>   half the batman, and every batman here maketh 7 pound and 5
>   ounces English weight. (PN 5.455–56)[42]

In itself there is perhaps nothing very remarkable about this letter. How else would one expect a merchant to write? But still, this representation of the world as a great field of commodities, each in flux, each identified for the "instant" by exotic measures of quantity and price, is as much the product of cultural work as an epic poem. One is as ideological as the other. In place of the epic's resistance to social change, its attempt to figure the present as a version of the mythic past, the commercial letter makes all value depend on a constantly changing market, a market whose very operative terms—*batman, medine, churle, rottil*—suggest acceptance of a kind of cultural dislocation that epic refuses. Or perhaps it would be better called cultural undifferentiation, for in a letter like this we see something of what Marx talked of as the abstracting and undifferentiating force of money. Here the world of distinct and differentiated objects and cultures, including the distinction of self and other, begins to melt before the common denominator of ducats and medines. This meltdown is not unresisted. Newbery can still distinguish between what English goods will bring on the Babylonian market and what they are really worth. But even this is a long way from the absolute differentiation of them and us that Camões or Chapman attempt to erect and maintain.

In directing critical attention to this letter, I am granting it a privilege not ordinarily accorded commercial documents. This is the kind of treatment that in our culture is reserved for poems. But in his own time Hakluyt already did something very like this. By printing both poems and letters in the same collection and the same format—a handsome black-letter folio (fig. 12), with decorated capitals, marginal notes, contrasting type for titles and proper names: in short, the format Elizabethan printers used for their most prestigious books—he implicitly assigned comparably lofty status to each. Gilbert's voyage to Newfoundland with its accompanying embarcation poem and the Newbery-Fitch voyage to the East Indies with its accompanying commercial letters appear as equivalent parts of a single expansionist project. Both are voyages of the English nation.

Class differences do nevertheless persist in the reception of Hakluyt's text, as they did in the communal enterprise he represented. In the 1840s, to take an example from a period two and a half centuries after the original publication of the *Voyages*, the Hakluyt Society was founded, according to D. B. Quinn, as "a typical expression of free trade optimism." But no sooner had the society's first publications appeared than they were roundly damned by J. A. Froude, the Victorian "prophet of imperial revival," who rather hailed the *Voyages* as "the prose epic of the modern English nation"—a kind of Camões for the nascent British empire. Hakluyt changed, as Quinn puts it, "in the period of the new imperialism of the late nineteenth century from the great free trader"—in effect, a merchants' Hakluyt—"to the protagonist of nationalistic empire"—a gentlemen's Hakluyt.[43] Nor, though Froude's characterization of the *Voyages* as the prose epic of the English nation has been so often repeated and elaborated that it has attained almost the status of unquestioned fact, did that transformation quite settle the issue. Reviewing the secondary literature on

Hakluyt, L. E. Pennington has noticed a continuation into our own century of the split between commercial and imperial readings. "Insofar as historians of all shades have generalized on Hakluyt's motives, they have," Pennington writes, "tended to divide into two camps: those who have seen his thinking as essentially concerned with the high strategy of international politics, usually with religious overtones"—the gentlemen's version—"and those who have viewed him as essentially a pragmatist interested in promoting the economic advancement of England"—the merchants' version.[44]

A shifting and unstable system of differences thus yields a certain measure of continuity. Different social classes, different motives for expansion, and different representational practices in the sixteenth century are at least partially replicated in nineteenth- and twentieth-century differences in reading. Free-traders and imperialists repeat, albeit with significant changes in emphasis and ideological commitment, the differences between merchants and gentlemen that divided both Elizabethan culture and Hakluyt's text. The *Principal Navigations,* like Camões's *Lusiads,* is a scene of ongoing struggle, a place of cultural production and reproduction. And like *The Lusiads,* it defines the field of contest in national terms. The nation thus emerges as a transcendent and itself uncontested point of reference. In this, the two achieve a similar end. But Hakluyt differs from Camões in making trade and traders so obvious and so valued a part of the nation. What Camões excludes, he includes. Without denying difference, his book bridges it. The *Principal Navigations* brings merchants into the nation and brings gentry into trade. Given the ideologically dominant position of the erstwhile warrior aristocracy, this is an accomplishment of considerable moment, one that significantly redrew the parameters of social consciousness, helping to bring about the nineteenth- and twentieth-century arguments over trade and conquest reported by Quinn and Pennington. And if Hakluyt did not himself quite make all this happen, his book does nevertheless provide the most notable testimony to an enabling change in which it undoubtedly participated.

Some more detailed consideration of the relations of merchants and gentlemen in Hakluyt's text and in the Elizabethan expansion should make clearer the modalities of that participation. As Stevenson

Facing Page
12. John Newbery's letter to Leonard Poore as it appears in the second edition of
Richard Hakluyt's *Principal Navigations of the English Nation*
(1599). Huntington Library.

Giles Porter and mafter Edmund Porter, went from Tripolis in a fmall barke to Iaffa, the fame day that we came from thence, which was the 14 day of this prefent, fo that no doubt but long fince they are in Ierufalem: God fend them and vs fafe returne. At this inftant J haue receiued the account of M. Barter, and the reft of the rings, with two and twentie duckats, two medines in readie money. So there is nothing remaining in his hands but a few bookes, and with Thomas Boftocke J left certaine fmall trifles, which J pray you demaund. And fo once againe with my hearty commendations J commit you to the tuition of the almightie, who alwayes preferue vs. From Aleppo the 29 of May 1583.

Yours affured, Iohn Newberie.

Another letter of Mafter *Newberie* to the aforefaide M. *Poore*, written from *Babylon.*

MY laft J fent you, was the 29 of May laft paft from Aleppo, by George Gill the purfer of the Tiger, which the laft day of the fame moneth came from thence, & arriued at Feluge the 19 day of June, which Feluge is one dayes iourney from hence. Notwithftanding fome of our company came not hither till the laft day of the laft moneth, which was for want of Camels to cary our goods: for at this time of the yeere, by reafon of the great heate that is here, Camels are very fcant to be gotten. And fince our comming hither we haue found very fmall fales, but diuers fay that in the winter our commodities will be very well fold, J pray God their words may proue true. J thinke cloth, kerfies & tinne, haue neuer bene here at fo low prices as they are now. Notwithftanding, if J had here fo much readie money as the commodities are woorth, J would not doubt to make a very good profite of this voiage hither, and to Balfara, and fo by Gods helpe there will be reafonable profite made of the voiage. But with halfe money & halfe commoditie, may be bought here the beft fort of fpices, and other commodities that are brought from the Indies, and without money there is here at this inftant fmall good to be done. With Gods helpe two dayes hence, J minde to goe from hence to Balfara, and from thence of force J muft goe to Ormus for want of a man that fpeaketh the Indian tongue. At my being in Aleppo J hired two Nazaranies, and one of them hath bene twife in the Indies, and hath the language very well, but he is a very lewde fellow, and therefore J will not take him with me.

The beft fort of fpices at Babylon, Balfara, Ormus.

Here follow the prices of wares as they are worth here at this inftant.

CLoues and Maces, the bateman, 5 duckats.
Cynamom 6 duckats, and few to be gotten.
Nutmegs, the bateman, 45 medins, and 40 medins maketh a duckat.
Ginger, 40 medins.
Pepper, 75 medins.
Turbetta, the bateman, 50 medins.
Neel the churle, 70 duckats, and a churle is 27 rottils and a halfe of Aleppo.
Silke, much better then that which commeth from Perfia, 11 duckats and a halfe the bateman, and euery bateman here maketh 7 pound and 5 ounces English waight. From Babylon the 20 day of July, 1583.

The prices of fpices at Babylon.

Yours, Iohn Newberie.

Mafter *Newberie* his letter from *Ormus*, to M. *Iohn Eldred* and *William Shals* at *Balfara.*

RIght welbeloued and my affured good friends, J heartily comend me vnto you, hoping of your good healths, &c. To certifie you of my voiage, after J departed frō you, time wil not permit: but the 4 of this prefent we arriued here, & the 10 day J with the reft were committed to prifon, and about the middle of the next moneth, the Captaine wil fend vs all in his fhip for Goa. The caufe why we are taken, as they fay, is, for that J brought letters from Don Antonio. But the trueth is, Michael Stropene was the onely caufe, vpon letters that his brother wrote him from Aleppo. God knoweth how we fhall be delt withall in Goa, and therfore if you can procure our mafters to fend the king of Spaine his letters for our releafement, you fhould doe vs great good : for they cannot with iuftice put vs to death, It may be that they will cut out our throtes, or keepe vs long

in

has shown, Elizabethans who praised merchants did so in terms borrowed from the aristocracy. Hakluyt repeats that process, dressing
craftsmen and merchants in figurative robes of honor, but he also
comes close to reversing it. In the 1598 dedication of the revised
Voyages, he commends Charles Howard, the lord high admiral of
England, first for his "ancestors' honors" and then for his "own heroical actions" (*PN* 1.xxxiii). The latter include the eminently warlike
defeat of the Spanish Armada in 1588. But, as his only example of the
former, Hakluyt mentions an investment made by Howard's father in
the Muscovy Company. Commercial and military ventures here blend
under a single set of values. Both contribute to the well-being of the
nation and both adorn even a member of the aristocracy. To the
"gentle merchants" of Thomas Deloney and of Stevenson's other
popular authors, Hakluyt thus adds, though without using the term,
the "mercantile gentleman." That such a term could not have been
used in a favorable way, that even now it retains a strong negative
valence, suggests how powerful the ideology Hakluyt evades really
was. The adjectives of status, "gentle" and "noble" on the one side
and "mercantile" and (worse) "mercenary" on the other, have still
never come close to reaching connotative parity.

Already in the sixteenth century, that asymmetry was, however,
balanced by another. In the overseas expansion, which for Hakluyt
represented the greatest modern achievement of the English nation,
merchants played a far larger (if less conspicuous) part than gentlemen. The entry of English landowners, like the elder Howard, into
the world of trade and commercial investment was undoubtedly, as
T. K. Rabb has argued, a matter of great consequence. It distinguished England from most other countries of early modern Europe,
distinguished Elizabethan and especially Jacobean England from the
England that preceded it. Yet even Rabb must concede that "merchants were clearly the vital driving force behind England's expansion."[45] And K. R. Andrews, in the most recent general survey of that
expansion, echoes Rabb's conclusion. "The main driving force of the
movement was," he writes, "commercial, even though the types of
people interested and their particular aims, methods, and attitudes
varied considerably."[46] A predominantly commercial movement that
nevertheless involved large numbers of gentlemen (some twelve hundred between 1575 and 1630 by Rabb's count)[47] and was made to
seem essential to England's "honor"—this is the image that emerges
from the work of these historians. But it was an image first presented
on a large scale by Hakluyt. His book superimposed the ideological

and economic asymmetries of his culture to represent and to enforce a coupling of classes in an enterprise he defined as national.

The best way to experience this remarkable superimposition is to read Hakluyt's collection, whether in the first or second edition, whole. The extraordinary variety of documents, ranging from those epic fragments of Parmenius and Chapman to commercial lists like Newbery's, suggests an equal variety in the nation that produced them. For the most part, the interaction of these various discourses and of the different sorts of people responsible for them is left to happen in the reader's mind by the force of juxtaposition. Hakluyt's *Voyages* has its effect by paratactic accumulation rather than by some more obviously willed hypotaxis. If Hakluyt does succeed (and in large measure did succeed historically) in bringing merchants into the nation and bringing gentry into trade, it is most often by appearing not to try, by gathering and printing material needed to accomplish a quite different end, that of presenting, as I have said, a description of the world and proof of England's active place in it. But occasionally his comprehensive gathering does lead him to include a voyage or an ancillary document that works its own hypotaxis, that makes explicit the social differences and relations that are elsewhere left unspecified. Sir George Peckham's "True Report of the Newfound Lands," which Rabb described, is one such document. Another is Clement Adams's account of "The New Navigation and Discovery of the Kingdom of Moscovia."

Written in Latin by a "schoolmaster to the queen's henchmen," first published as a separate book in 1554, mentioned a year later by Richard Eden in his *Decades,* then reprinted and translated into English by Hakluyt in 1589, Adams' narrative applies humanist eloquence to the task of describing a maritime and commercial voyage. Instead of the usual abrupt opening (e.g., "The ships departed from Plymouth the second day of October . . . "), Adams' lengthy first sentence provides a full analysis of the circumstances from which the Willoughby-Chancellor expedition emerged: "At what time our merchants perceived the commodities and wares of England to be in small request with the countries and people about us and near unto us and that those merchandises which strangers in the time and memory of our ancestors did earnestly seek and desire were now neglected and the price thereof abated, although by us carried to their own ports, and all foreign merchandises in great account and their prices wonderfully raised, certain grave citizens of London and men of great wisdom and careful for the good of their country began to think with themselves how this mischief might be remedied" (*PN* 2.239). As in Hakluyt's own later "Discourse on the Strait of Magellan," the good of the country is identified with a favorable balance of trade. But here the principal actors, those who perceive the problem and seek a solution, are specifically merchants, "grave citizens of London." They recall the prosperity that overseas expansion has brought Spain and Portugal, find out and consult Sebastian Cabot, settle on a voyage "for the search and discovery of the northern part of the world," organize themselves into a company, seek investors, provide for the building of ships, and engage the "captains and governors" to lead the expedition.

Only at this point do gentlemen appear in the narrative. "One Sir Hugh Willoughby, a most valiant gentleman, and well born," is chosen as captain general of the fleet and, at the recommendation of "Master Henry Sidney, a noble young gentleman and very much beloved of King Edward," Richard Chancellor is made pilot major. Gentlemen thus grace and support a project that is essentially mercantile in its origins and its aims. "I cannot but greatly commend," Sidney is made to say in a formal oration directed to the assembled merchants, "your present Godly and virtuous intention in the serious enterprising (for the singular love you bear to your country) a matter which, I hope, will prove profitable for this nation and honorable to this our land. Which intention of yours we also of the nobility are ready to our power to help and further" (*PN* 2.242). Such commendation not only asserts an ideologically difficult coupling of profit with honor (remember Camões's insistent dividing of those qualities: "De ti *proveito*, e dele *glória* ingente"), it enacts that union. But the particular terms of the enactment remain significant. Honor does not arise out of profit as a quality intrinsic to it. Rather it is added on. The representative of honor, the *adolescens nobilis,* comes from the court to the mercantile seekers of profit. The two groups and the two qualities remain distinct, needing as a third term to enable their union the "nation" or "country." National interest alone makes a commercial venture like that of the Merchant Adventurers a fit subject for humanist eloquence and courtly patronage. It alone makes profit honorable.

The relationship of classes so clearly articulated here by Adams is implicit through much of Hakluyt. Merchants typically initiate projects with which gentlemen or the attributes of gentlemen then become associated. In Hakluyt's collection of voyages, as in the more recent accounts by Rabb and Andrews, the main "driving force" of the expansionist movement is commercial. But this shifting and unstable cultural milieu sometimes prompted even the gentle initiators of overseas projects to accept an economic explanation of their behavior. Chapman may have sung the glory of Raleigh's Guiana expedition in a way that etherealized gold and left little place for trade, but Raleigh himself could on occasion confound the motives of conquest and commerce and blur the line between gentlemen and merchants. "Whosoever commands the sea, commands the trade," he wrote in his *Discourse of the Invention of Ships*, "whosoever commands the trade of the world, commands the riches of the world, and consequently the world itself."[48] And in discussing the possibility of a royal marriage with a family descended from merchants, he remarked, "It is true that long ago they were merchants; and so was King Solomon too. The kings in old times . . . traded with nature and with the earth, a trade by which all that breathe upon the earth live. All the nobility and gentry in Europe trade their grass and corn and cattle, their vines and their fruits. They trade them to their tenants at home, and other merchants adventure them abroad."[49] Where all wealth (and indeed all life) derives from trade and where all men are traders, an economic conception of the nation is "natural" and inevitable. That Raleigh and his various supporters, including Chapman and Hakluyt, were not always consistent in maintaining such a conception is again testimony to the strength of the aristocratic ideology against which it was struggling to assert itself.[50] But Hakluyt's *Voyages* does represent, despite its many countermoves, a fundamentally new alignment of power in England, one in which merchants and mercantile activity had an ever increasing share.

Spain's Tyrannical Ambition

In Raleigh's heady talk of commanding the world through trade, an aristocratic idea of universal conquest piggybacks on a mercantile notion of universal commerce. For sixteenth-century Englishmen, both were conditioned by the preeminent accomplishment of Spain. When the Merchant Adventurers gathered in the 1550s to consider the decline in their trade, the example of Spain suggested a remedy. When Hakluyt urged action in the Strait of Magellan and the northeast passage, Spanish hegemony prompted his bold response. When Raleigh undertook to settle Virginia and exploit Guiana, Spanish success and the Spanish threat shaped both his plan and his rhetoric. Like Portugal, which fell to the dynastic claims of Spain, and Holland, which came into existence in opposition to Spanish overlordship, England necessarily defined itself and the character of its overseas expansion in terms of its relation to Spain.

For England, as for Portugal and Holland, simple freedom from Spanish dominance was the first requirement of national self-realization. And that freedom was far from secure. Once in the course of England's sixteenth-century expansion it had virtually been lost, and in the year before the *Voyages* first appeared it was again severely menaced. In 1553 Sir Hugh Willoughby and Richard Chancellor sailed in search of the northeast passage from an England ruled by the staunchly Protestant boy-king Edward and the anti-Spanish regent Northumberland. Two years later, Chancellor returned to find the throne shared by the half-Spanish Mary and her Spanish husband, Philip. In that latter year, Richard Eden, who in 1553 had dedicated his first book on America to "the right high and mighty prince, the duke of Northumberland," brought out his *Decades of the New World* with a dedication to the "potentissimus ac serenissimus Philippus, ac serenissima potentissimaque Maria." "Stoop, England, stoop," Eden wrote in his address to the readers, "and learn to know thy lord and master, as horses and other brute beasts are taught to do."[51] Only Queen Mary's infertility and death saved England from the accomplishment of that beastlike humiliation. But in the 1580s, the execution of another Queen Mary, Mary Queen of Scots, raised once again the menace of Spanish rule—this time through armed invasion. Little more than a half century earlier the great empires of Mexico and Peru had fallen to Spain, and within the previous decade a similar fate had overtaken Portugal and its East Indian possessions. Why not England? With the defeat of the Armada, the most pressing threat passed, but through the remainder of Elizabeth's reign, war with Spain continued to be the prime conditioning element in England's expansion.

The ideological relation of England to Spain was further complicated, as was that of neither Portugal nor Holland, by an awkward mix of similarity and difference. Like Spain in both religion and aristocratic heritage, Portugal could figure itself, as Camões does in *The Lusiads*, as a rival in a common imperial project. Unlike Spain in both religion and class structure, Holland could develop as Spain's antithesis, as a bourgeois commercial nation with no explicit imperial ambition. Neither of these positions quite suited England. England was Protestant and had an active if not fully acknowledged merchant class. But it was also a nation with a strong aristocratic identity and tradition, a nation whose most glorious memories were of feudal conquest and crusading zeal. England could thus feel comfortable neither in a complete repudiation of the Spanish model nor in an unqualified imitation of it.

Two arguments for American colonization, Sir George Peckham's "True Report of the Newfound Lands" and Hakluyt's own "Discourse of Western Planting," reveal both the intensity of the preoccupation with Spain and the conceptual problems that arose from it. Emulation is the theme of Peckham's "Report." "Why," he asks, "should we be dismayed more than were the Spaniards, who have been able within these few years to conquer, possess, and enjoy so large a tract of the earth . . . ? Shall we . . . doubt [God] will be less ready to assist our nation . . . than he was to Columbus, Vasques, Nunes, Hernando Cortes, and Francis Pizarro?" (*PN* 8.123–24 and 131). But if Spain provides the model, it has also made that model suspect. As a member of a prominent Catholic family, Peckham says little of that darker side of Spain's accomplishment. For him, it is enough that Spain has spread the Christian faith abroad and increased its own wealth at home. England should, he suggests, do likewise. But even Peckham feels compelled to argue at length and with much biblical citation for the lawfulness of colonization. Hakluyt's account of Spanish behavior in the New World suggests why Peckham might have felt such justification was needed. Quoting freely from the recently translated *Relación de la Destruycíon de las Indias* of Bartolomé de las Casas, Hakluyt proclaims the "most outrageous and more than Turkish cruelties" of the Spanish "in all the West Indies" (*Corr.* 2.257). "The Spanish," he says, "have not done in those quarters these forty years be past, neither yet do at this present, ought else than tear [the Indians] in pieces, kill them, martyr them, afflict them, torment them, and destroy them by strange sorts of cruelties, never either seen or read or heard of the like . . . so far forth as of above three millions of souls that were in the Isle of Hispaniola . . . there are not now two hundred natives of the country" (*Corr.* 2.258).[52]

Spain's destruction of the New World natives was only the most dramatic example of a tyranny that seemed intent on spreading itself over the entire world. This ambition, Hakluyt shows, is no more than what the Spanish have themselves advertised. In the dedication of his *Decades*, Peter Martyr advised Emperor Charles that from the wealth of the Indies "shall instruments be prepared for you whereby all the world shall be under your obeisance," and Fernández de Oviedo, in his *History of the Indies*, told the emperor much the same: "God hath given you these Indies . . . to the intent that your majesty should be the universal and only monarch of the world" (*Corr.* 2.244–45 and 312). Coming into the gallery of the governor's house in San Domingo a half century later, Drake and his men found an emblem to the same effect, the arms of the king of Spain with "a globe containing in it the whole circuit of the sea and the earth whereupon is a horse standing on his hinder part within the globe and the forepart without the globe, lifted up as it were to leap, with a scroll painted in his mouth, wherein was written these words in Latin: *Non sufficit orbis,* which is as much to say as the world sufficeth not" (*PN* 10.114). Drake's bold depredations in the Caribbean and the Pacific mocked this overweening ambition, and the various English schemes for western planting, Hakluyt's among them, were meant to bridle it still more effectually. But both depended for their particular rhetorical force on being seen as parts of a movement that was essentially different, one that had no such universalist ambition.

For a country whose only overseas possession was the often rebellious neighboring island of Ireland, first conquered centuries earlier, such renunciation would, one supposes, have come easily. But that appears not to have been the case. No one was more eloquent or outspoken in his condemnation of Spanish ambition than Raleigh, but surely his notion of commanding the world by controlling the seas bespeaks an imagination infected with ideas of universal conquest. Knowledge of Spain's triumphant accomplishment could turn even a poetic meditation on England's past into a fantasy of what might have been. Had only the English managed to avert the civil wars of the fifteenth century, Samuel Daniel writes in the 1595 edition of the poem he devoted to those wars, they, not the Spanish, would have "joined the western empire" to their continental conquests and would now be in position "to march against the earth's terror Ottoman."

> The proud Iberus' lord not seeking how
> T'attain a false-conceived monarchy,
> Had kept his barren bounds and not have stood
> In vain attempts t'enrich the seas with blood.[53]

England's loss was the Spaniard's gain. But from this heroic and aristocratic perspective (Daniel imagines Essex and Mountjoy in the role of conquering protagonists of England's imperial glory), there is no essential difference between England and Spain.

In its very form, its systematic representation of the whole of a hitherto unknown world, a book like Hakluyt's expresses and inspires similar dreams of universal dominance. Something of this sort had from the first been the effect of the new maps and globes that began appearing in the wake of Columbus's discoveries. One maker of those early maps, Robert Thorne, an English merchant "who dwelt long in the city of Seville in Spain," wrote Henry VIII in 1527 to urge that he occupy some of the new "empty" space. "Out of Spain they have discovered all the Indies and seas occidental, and out of Portugal all the Indies and seas oriental. . . . So that now rest to be discovered the . . . north parts, the which, it seemeth to me, is only your charge and duty"—a duty imposed, Thorne argues, by the "natural" desire of "all princes . . . to extend and enlarge their dominions and kingdoms" (*PN* 2.161 and 159). From the new cosmography, conquest follows inevitably. If one European prince does not seize the great unclaimed regions of the newly mapped world, another will. Hakluyt's own global imaginings, beginning with his "Discourse of the Strait of Magellan" and continuing on through the two editions of his *Principal Navigations,* similarly derive from this new map-conditioned sense of the world, a sense that his work made more widely available in England.

But in Hakluyt that sense is qualified, as it isn't in Thorne or Daniel or Peckham, by a sense of England's difference from Spain. Hakluyt's England defines itself in opposition to Spanish tyranny, Spanish cruelty, and Spanish ambition. And for that purpose the inclusion of so many mercantile voyages is crucial. If Spain's behavior in the New World has given conquest a bad name, trade has not been similarly tainted. "For who doubteth," writes Peckham, "but that it is lawful for Christians to use trade and traffic with infidels and savages, carrying thither such commodities as they want and bringing from thence some part of their plenty" (*PN* 8.97)? In a letter to the emperor of China concerning the "honest and lawful custom of traffic in all countries" (*PN* 11.420), Elizabeth herself confirms such ideas. The pursuit of trade rather than conquest becomes a sign of England's virtuous difference.

No one in any document gathered by Hakluyt argues for free and unrestricted trade, though Hakluyt himself does use the term "free trade of merchandise" (*PN* 1.xlviii). But this trade, like all other between civil states, is licensed and privileged by royal charter. It is made free by proper authority. What was so offensive about the Spanish was their absolute denial of trade to such vast and lucrative markets. "For the conquering of forty or fifty miles here and there and erecting of certain fortresses, [they] think to be lords of half the world, envying that other should enjoy the commodities which they themselves cannot wholly possess" (*PN* 6.141). It was in testing the limits of this

Spanish prohibition that John Hawkins, carrying a cargo of slaves to the settlements of the Caribbean, had his celebrated conflicts with the Spanish, conflicts that did much to inflame anti-Spanish feeling. Against such tyrannical intransigence even piracy, like that of Hawkins and Drake, seemed well justified.

Drake's daring and successful raids on Spanish settlements and shipping contributed greatly to England's sense of maritime accomplishment—as did the defeat of the Armada and the burning of Cadiz. Heroic encounters of this sort fill Hakluyt's *Voyages,* particularly in its much enlarged second edition. If England in the sixteenth century never succeeded in establishing a permanent settlement of its own in the New World, it did nevertheless manage to humble the proud Iberian conquerors, thus proving Hakluyt's contention that Spain's "might and greatness is not such as *prima facie* it may seem to be," for "some of his countries are dispeopled, some barren, some . . . far asunder also held by tyranny" (*Corr.* 2.251). What Drake and the others exposed was not merely the material weakness of the Spanish empire—a "dissembling and feeble scarecrow" (*Corr.* 2.252) upheld only by American gold—but the weakness of tyranny itself.

In his "Description of Florida," translated by Hakluyt and four times published at Hakluyt's instigation,[54] René Laudonnière makes that anti-imperialist argument in historical and theoretical terms. Travel "into far and remote regions" for the purpose of trade or the exportation of excess population serves, according to Laudonnière, the genuine interests of the traveling country. Travel for the purpose of planting, as the Romans did, "not only their ensigns and victories, but also their laws, customs, and religion in those provinces which they had conquered by force of arms" is ultimately self-destructive. It leads to the "ruin and overthrow" of the country that undertakes it. "These," he claims with obvious reference to Spain, "are the effects and rewards of all such as being pricked forward with their Roman and tyrannical ambition will go about thus to subdue strange people: effects, I say, contrary to the profit which those shall receive which only are affectioned to the common benefit, that is to say, to the general policy of all men, and endeavor to unite them one with another as well by traffic and civil conversations, as also by military virtues and force of arms, whenas the savages will not yield unto the endeavors so much tending to their profit" (*PN* 8.446–47).

Laudonnière's may seem a distinction with little difference. In each case, one people subjects another to its will—if necessary, by force of arms. But to Laudonnière (and presumably to Hakluyt) the difference was large and essential. Where the Romans (and Spaniards) pursued "universal monarchy," Laudonnière would seek only mutual profit, "an end so much more commendable as it is far from all tyrannical and cruel government" (*PN* 8.447). Trade does not alone define this antityrannical overseas project. Finding a home for excess population, bringing the "strange . . . country to civility," reducing "the inhabitants to the true knowledge of our God," all figure in Laudonnière's program, as they do in Hakluyt's. But since these goals are also shared by the Romanlike imperialists, trade remains the chief distinguishing sign. Here, without quite rejecting values like those that shaped Camões's *Lusiads,* Laudonnière sets them on their head. To seek profit, he seems to suggest, is the best way to temper an excessive desire for glory, the "Roman and tyrannical ambition . . . to make [one's] name immortal" (*PN* 8.447).

In these texts one sees the emergence of an anti-imperialist and even anti-aristocratic logic of mercantile nationalism. But if Hakluyt would seem at times to be approaching an argument of this sort, an argument that would set trade and nation *against* conquest, settlement, and imperial dynasty in much the way that he sets England against Spain, he never reaches it. The strength of the dynastic conception was too great, the association of honor and conquest too firm, the practical dependence (in at least some parts of the world) of even trade on settlement and armed coercion too obvious for him to tie the nation exclusively to trade. Nevertheless, his book does make it possible to imagine an England not merely competing with Spain for the same prize of universal dominance, but opposing itself to empire and working instead to construct a world of distinguishable and sovereign economic entities—that is, a world of nation-states—capable of entering into relations of trade with commercial England. Pushed by the need to differentiate England from tyrannical and Catholic Spain, Hakluyt's text moves toward an anti-imperialist—indeed, anti-colonialist—logic of economic and cultural nationalism. This is the Hakluyt the Hakluyt Society was founded to perpetuate. And though it is not the only Hakluyt, it is one that arises almost inevitably from the textual practices by which his book did its promotional work.

Posthumous Writings and Rewritings

Any one of a large number of books from the next couple centuries—starting with Samuel Purchas's massive continuation of Hakluyt, *Hakluytus Posthumus, or Purchas His Pilgrims*—might be taken as evidence of the change of attitude brought about by Hakluyt's *Voyages* and by the commercial expansion to which it contributed.[55] But none that I know registers that change more unequivocally than Thomas Mun's *England's Treasure by Foreign Trade,* the treatise that gave mercantilist theory its classic formulation. Written in the mid-1620s, though not published until 1664, Mun's little book brings into sharp focus ideas of class and nation that we have seen emerging in Hakluyt.[56]

For Mun, as for Hakluyt, the traditional ruling class, the landed aristocracy, provided the inevitable standard of value. If merchants are to be honored, it is as members of a "noble profession."[57] But now, as was never possible in Hakluyt or in the work of those Elizabethan contemporaries of Hakluyt, the popular writers who praised merchants, men of trade are preferred to nobles, and they are preferred not for their magnanimity and valor, but for qualities intrinsic to their commercial activity, for diligence, thrift, and worldly knowledge. Indeed, Mun presents such qualities as autonomous and self-sufficient. No other set of duties than the specifically commercial ones he enumerates need be considered in defining either the ideal merchant or the true national interest. And from this it follows that merchants, not aristocrats, are the proper governors of a modern state. "It is therefore," he writes, "an act beyond rashness in some who do disenable their counsel and judgment (even in books printed) making them uncapable of those ways and means which do either enrich or impoverish a commonwealth, when in truth this is only effected by the mystery of their trade." The defensive edge in this sentence is sharpened by Mun's characterization of England as a country where the traditional nobility does not practice trade and where those who do are "not so well esteemed as their *noble vocation* requireth."[58] But clearly the very existence of his treatise, the very fact that in England in the 1620s such thoughts were thinkable, suggests that a significant change in the estimation of merchants had already taken place.

And that change depended in its turn on another, on one so successful that, unlike the somewhat tendentious claim for merchants, it required no argument. Throughout his book, Mun simply assumes that the nation or kingdom (terms he uses interchangeably), as a purely economic unit, should be the basis of all calculations of relative honor and worth. The balance of trade is always the balance of a nation's trade. The nation is always the entity enriched or impoverished by a surplus or deficiency of exports. There had been medieval anticipations of this idea. The anonymous fifteenth-century *Libelle of*

English Policy, first printed by Hakluyt, is one of the clearest. And it was of course to go on dominating economic thought for centuries. Adam Smith's *Wealth of Nations* (1776), to cite only the most conspicuous example, both accepts it and, in its chapter "Of Colonies," makes explicit the anti-imperialism latent in the notion of economic nationalism. National prosperity, Smith argues, derives rather from trade—now explicitly free trade—than from the maintenance of monopolistic political and economic control over conquered and colonized territories. The establishment of colonies—Hakluyt's plantations—is in this view only a way of extending the world system of trading nations, a way of expanding the field in which commercial activity can take place.[59]

Neither this economic understanding of a nation's interest nor the accompanying sense of the superiority of merchants appears in anything like an unqualified way in Hakluyt, whether in individual voyages and documents or in the collection as a whole. Nor does the clear expression of these ideas, when it does finally come, settle the issue. As the reports of Quinn and Pennington on the nineteenth- and twentieth-century reception of Hakluyt suggest, powerfully conflicting groups and interests continued to struggle for interpretive possession of his text, just as they struggled for the domination of overseas activity itself. But for such ideas to emerge at all, representations like Hakluyt's were needed. Their depiction of merchants as rightful and important emissaries of the nation enabled the kind of positive statements and grand schematic elaborations that we find in Mun, Smith, and the many other economic theorists of the last four centuries.

In one of those odd convergences by which history constantly rewrites itself, the representational and ideological systems that found expression in Hakluyt even managed to produce a wonderfully apt misreading of Camões. In 1776, the year of both *The Wealth of Nations* and the American Declaration of Independence, William Julius Mickle, Camões's only eighteenth-century English translator, advertised *The Lusiads* as "the poem of every trading nation, . . . the epic poem of the birth of commerce."[60] How, one wonders, could any reader of Camões, much less a translator, so miss the point? But in 1776, in an England that controlled the Indian commerce da Gama had opened, trade *was* the point. So massively overdetermined was Mickle's reading that it appears almost with an air of inevitability. Two centuries of overseas trade and, no less important, two centuries of discourse prompted by trade had made Camões's anticommercial meaning as invisible to Mickle as Mickle's meaning would have been to Camões or his original courtly Portuguese readers. Nor is *The Lusiads* a wholly innocent victim of this bizarre twist in the hermeneutic spiral. Commerce and its relation to national identity are, after all, central to *The Lusiads*. It is simply that Camões worked to suppress what Mickle strove to exalt. Much the same can be said of their mutually contradictory understandings of Portuguese history. In Mickle's view, Prince Henry the Navigator was "born to set mankind free from the feudal system and to give the whole world every advantage, every light that may possibly be diffused by the intercourse of unlimited commerce" (p. xii). Camões, on the contrary, saw the spread of that very feudal system and the religion that supported it as Portugal's mission. But, again, both accept that the point at issue was as much the structure of power at home as its extension abroad.

The differences between the aristocratic Portuguese poet and his middle-class English translator over issues whose stake they nevertheless identify alike include their sense of the heroic genre in which both wrote, the genre to which, as we have seen, Hakluyt's *Voyages* has in the last century and a half been regularly assimilated. To Camões, an "epic of commerce" would have seemed a ridiculous paradox. He seized on the ancient heroic genre precisely because it so obviously legitimated the military ethos of the feudal nobility to which he belonged. For Mickle, who bemoaned "the uncommercial and dreadful consequences of wars unjustly provoked" (p. cv), the revival of ancient learning, signaled by the return of the epic, served rather to bracket the dark age of feudalism between two periods of enlightenment and trade. But on the incompatibility of commerce with the feudal system and the resulting impossibility of basing a stable literary or national identity on some combination of the two, they would have agreed.

More eclectic than either and more deeply involved in the practicalities of overseas expansion, Hakluyt would not easily have accepted this agreement. Nevertheless his text is caught, as theirs are, in the historic conflict of classes, of interests, and of representational forms by which the world of Camões's nostalgic imagination gave way to the eighteenth-century world of Mickle and his contemporary Adam Smith. To call that text "the prose epic of the modern English nation," as J. A. Froude and a host of imitators have done, may be to misname it almost as badly as Mickle misnamed *The Lusiads*. Yet it is by such misnamings that the ideological construction of the nation—and the powerfully hidden reaffirmation that prior to and independent of all its constructions the nation does in fact exist—goes on.

And even the misnamings are the products of material and textual forces not unlike those that produced the works they misname.

To say this may, however, seem to suggest that against these misnamings we might set true names. I want in conclusion to dispel this positivist implication, for in this discursive field there are no true names. What is at stake is not truth but success. Do the names stick? Do men and women behave as though they lived in the kind of community Camões or Hakluyt or Mickle or Froude name? From Columbus on, written voyages tell not only what happened when some captain and crew sailed to some distant land. They also tell what world those happenings require and suppose: what structures of identity, what division of power, what representational practices—all matters that Europe's expansion could not help but unsettle. For Europe to transform itself from its medieval isolation and marginality to the position of world dominance that it is only now beginning to lose demanded much prospective and retrospective renaming. It is to this process that Camões, Hakluyt, and their interpreters have contributed. They enforced the emerging nationalist bias of Europe's expansion and struggled over the nation's identity. In our own age of decolonialization and international economy, even the positive side of this accomplishment begins to appear increasingly problematical. Though nationalism may still be the most powerful ideological force in the world (Europe's most widely accepted cultural export), nations no longer seem quite so natural as they once did. But that, I would suggest, is all the more reason for questioning the ideological strategies of the texts that first helped elevate the nation to the privileged position it has so long enjoyed.

5

STAGING EXCLUSION

Mr. WILLIAM
SHAKESPEARES
COMEDIES,
HISTORIES, &
TRAGEDIES.

Published according to the True Originall Copies.

LONDON
Printed by Isaac Iaggard, and Ed. Blount. 1623.

THE FIRST PART OF THE CONTENTION BETWIXT THE two famous Houses of York and Lancaster, the play we now know as *Henry VI, part 2,* opens, as do many of Shakespeare's plays, with a spectacle of royal and aristocratic power. "Flourish of trumpets: then hoboys. Enter King, Duke Humphrey, Salisbury, Warwick, and Beauford, on the one side; the Queen, Suffolk, York, Somerset, and Buckingham, on the other."[1] The king, the queen, a cardinal, four dukes, a marquis, and two earls. This élite parade might be taken as an emblem of Shakespeare's England, the England Shakespeare presents and represents. In Shakespeare's English history plays—and *The Contention* may well be the first of them—England seems often to be identified exclusively with its kings and nobles.[2] The story of their conflicts and conquests is its story. No one else matters. But before this scene is over, another vision asserts itself, one that will not again emerge so clearly in Shakespeare's work for nearly a quarter of a century, and then only briefly.[3] Duke Humphrey—the "good Duke Humphrey" of the play's original title page—is, according to the accusation of his rival, Cardinal Beauford, favored by "the common people." And not many lines later the earl of Salisbury, one of Duke Humphrey's chief supporters, talks of joining together "for the public good," for "the profit of the land." To bear oneself "like a noble gentleman" is, Salisbury implies, to serve the interests of "the commons." "The people" are thus made fundamental to the nation's identity and to the legitimacy of its governing order. So foreign is this view both to the discursive modes we have been regarding so far and to the greater part of Shakespeare's own dramatic production that it demands some special notice. Why should it emerge here at all? And why does it find no greater echo in Shakespeare's subsequent representations of England?

The obvious, if trivial, answer to the first question is that Duke Humphrey's special relation to the common people emerges in this play because it had already emerged in the play's sources. Grafton's *Chronicle* had spoken of "the good duke of Gloucester . . . loved by the commons," and Foxe in his *Acts and Monuments* had portrayed the "good duke" as "a supporter of the poor commons."[4] But neither

Grafton nor Foxe goes quite so far as Shakespeare. Neither presents solidarity with the commons in opposition to aristocratic ambition as a principle underlying political legitimacy. Surely this extrapolation from an individual attribute to a general principle is significant. And more significant still is the fact that these sentiments were expressed on a public stage. Whatever Duke Humphrey's identification with the common people may have meant in Grafton or Foxe, it meant something different in the theater.

We do not know with any certainty when *The Contention* was first produced, what company acted it, or in what playhouse it appeared. The most likely estimates date it 1590 or 1591, assign it to Lord Strange's Men, and place it in the Theater or the Rose. But we do know enough of the theatrical milieu of the early 1590s to say that there was a strong popular element in both the play's production and reception. Its author was a commoner, its actors were commoners, the greater part of its audience were commoners.[5] On all three sides they came from the ninety-five percent of the English population that found little representation in the works of Spenser, Coke, Camden, Drayton, or Hakluyt and that had little access to such works. *The Faerie Queene, The Institutes, Britannia, Poly-Olbion,* and *The Principal Navigations,* like the chronicle histories which preceded and informed them, were all printed books. Indeed, all but *The Faerie Queene* and *Britannia* made their first appearance as handsome and expensive folio volumes, and the two exceptions quickly grew up to that imposing stature. Each of these books made its primary appeal to a narrowly defined community, whether courtly, legal, landowning and antiquarian, or mercantile and adventuring. But they shared a more general limitation. Their audiences were highly literate and at least relatively well-to-do. No one but the literate and well-to-do could read or buy such books. And their representations of England were similarly exclusive. Neither in form nor in content did they wander far from the culture of learning and privilege.

In their long and vigorous afterlife, Shakespeare's plays have also assumed the marks of distinction and exclusivity, qualities which they in turn confer on their consumers. Their appearance in the first folio of 1623 signaled this arrival.[6] But that is not where they began. They began in the playhouses of Shoreditch and Southwark, performed by "rogues and vagabonds" to "an assembly of tailors, tinkers, cordwainers, sailors, old men, young men, women, boys, girls, and such like."[7] Or so contemporary enemies of the theater suggested. The reality was more complex, complex enough to have encouraged at least one recent scholar to reverse this degrading characterization and claim that the playgoers of late sixteenth- and early seventeenth-century London were predominantly privileged.[8] Not many experts have accepted this reversal, but clearly the original audiences for Shakespeare's plays were more varied and more socially distinguished than the hostile critics of his own time would allow.[9] At court performances, the queen herself was a regular auditor, and gentlemen frequented public playhouses no less assiduously than they did the bookstalls of Fleetstreet and St. Paul's. But in the playhouses they were joined by a less privileged multitude, a multitude from whose ranks the players, the playwrights, and the playhouse owners had themselves come and to whose ranks they, for the most part, still belonged. Shakespeare was the son of a small-town glover. The family backgrounds of the other leading dramatists at the time when *The Contention* appeared were similarly modest. The fathers of Chettle, Greene, Kyd, Marlowe, Munday, and Peele were a dyer, a saddler, a scrivener, a shoemaker, a draper, and a clerk. Robert Wilson's burial notice identifies him as "a yeoman (a player)."[10] The Burbages, who built the Theater and eventually supplied Shakespeare with his leading actor, had been joiners. Philip Henslowe, landlord and manager of the Rose, began his London career in the service of a dyer. As for the common run of players, "most," in the words of one contemporary, "have been either men of occupations, which they have forsaken to live by playing, or common minstrels, or trained up from their childhood to this abominable exercise and have now no other way to get their living" (*ES* 4.218).

The mixed social identity of Shakespeare's audience and the largely artisanal identity of his collaborators and competitors have prompted several of the most influential twentieth-century studies of the Elizabethan theater. In one of the best of them, *Shakespeare and the Rival Traditions,* Alfred Harbage set the socially inclusive public theater against its more exclusive private competitor. Where the former was, in Harbage's words, the "theater of a nation," a theater that both catered to and provided a sympathetic representation of the English nation in all its social variety, the latter was the theater of a restricted group, the privileged. "The difference between the popular and the select drama is," Harbage suggested, "the difference between social consciousness and class animosity."[11] Subsequent studies have cast considerable doubt on the sharp distinction Harbage makes between the public theaters and their repertories and the private theaters and theirs. The clearest differences now seem rather to be between one company and another, wherever they played, and one moment and another, whatever the company or theater. But Harbage's sense of a significant bond linking the social structure of the theatrical institution to the form and content of its plays has persisted, as have many of his leading terms. Robert Weimann in his important book on *Shakespeare and the Popular Tradition in the Theater* makes conspicuous use of the phrase "theater of a nation," and it recurs, with a slight alteration, as the title of Walter Cohen's *Drama of a Nation*.[12] Both Weimann and Cohen write from a Marxist perspective, and both find more tension even in the public theater repertory than Harbage was inclined to acknowledge. But both nevertheless continue to emphasize the socially "composite" nature of the Elizabethan theater and to give considerable importance to the popular (or artisanal) element of that composite, an element that has been privileged in other ways by such critics as C. L. Barber in *Shakespeare's Festive Comedy* and Michael Bristol in *Theater and Carnival*.[13]

Besides their shared concern for the relation between the sociology of the theater and its dramatic products, their shared insistence on the role of the popular, and their shared recognition of a "national" dimension to this complex cultural amalgam, these studies agree, whether explicitly or implicitly, that the particular social and dramatic configuration that they variously describe changed decisively sometime around 1600. For Harbage, the crucial event was the reopening of the private theaters in 1599 and 1600. Others point to the building of the Globe in 1599 and the Fortune in 1600, the emergence of a third adult company at the Boar's Head and Rose in about 1600, the replacement of Will Kemp by Robert Armin as Shakespeare's clown in 1599, and the increasing prominence around the turn of the century of a new generation of playwrights, including Jonson, Chapman, Dekker, Marston, and Middleton. As well as altering much else, the Essex revolt in 1601, followed two years later by the death of Elizabeth, further altered the conditions of playing. And the altered conditions coincided with a marked shift in generic preferences, as the national history play and romantic comedy gave way to satire, city comedy, tragedy, and eventually tragicomedy and romance. How the particular changes are linked to one another, which are cause and which are effect, which necessary and which accidental, are questions that lend themselves to no easy resolution, but it is clear that together these changes mark the end of the moment that gave rise to *The Contention* and that sustained the sequence of plays that followed from it.[14]

If *The Contention*'s opening vision of an aristocracy committed to the service of the commons had a particular dependence on and resonance within the theatrical setting in which it first occurred, that setting had been substantially altered by the first decade of the seventeenth century. But more than that (and here I am going well beyond the warrant of the major studies of Shakespeare and popular culture), the English history play, particularly as practiced by Shakespeare, was itself an instrument devised to achieve the very transformation in the theater's institutional role that would render the genre and much of what it stood for dispensable. I don't suppose that Shakespeare began writing English history plays to kill the history play. But he may well have begun writing them to secure for himself and his fellows a position that would no longer require such strategies, a position quite unlike the one they occupied in 1590.

The time at which *The Contention* was written was in its own way no less decisive for the history of the English stage than 1600. It was marked, at least in London, by a radical narrowing and focusing of professional theatrical energies. In 1590, the boys' companies were shut down and the adult companies began sifting down toward the two that a few years later survived to share a nearly decade-long monopoly as the Chamberlain's and Admiral's Men. But, more important, the players' theater was becoming what retrospectively looks like an authors' theater. For us, of course, the most significant of the new dramatic "authors" is Shakespeare himself. But initially his position was much more in the tradition that had up to then dominated the professional adult companies, the tradition represented in the 1580s by Richard Tarlton, Robert Wilson, and the Queen's Men. Like Tarlton and Wilson, Shakespeare was a player who collaborated in generating the plays his company put on. But others—the "university wits" most prominent among them—were being engaged and being recognized solely as writers. The difference between writer and player had always been characteristic of the boys' companies, and even the adult companies had occasionally acquired a play text from a writer who was not also a player. What happened in the late 1580s and early 1590s was a shift in the weight of production and recognition toward the new nonplayer writers. A sharply increasing proportion of public-theater plays (and after 1590 that was the only kind) was being produced by men who had no other theatrical function than to write, and a sharply increasing share of public attention (at least in that part of the public that has left written records) was being paid to the texts as texts and to the authors as authors.

This new age declared itself most unequivocally in Marlowe's rejection for *Tamburlaine* (1587) of the "jigging veins of riming mother-

wits / And such conceits as clownage keeps in pay." And the declaration was reaffirmed in 1590 by Marlowe's printer who commended
the "eloquence of the author that writ" *Tamburlaine* unto the "wis-
doms" of his "gentlemen readers" and scorned the "fond and frivo-
lous gestures" that deformed the play when it appeared on stage.[15]
Presumably Marlowe himself was kept in pay by clownage, by the
clownish players who produced *Tamburlaine* and the clownish spectators who came to see it. But he, like his shepherd protagonist,
aspired to a higher station. In 1589 Nashe expressed similar aspiration
and similar scorn of the players, and Greene repeated the sentiment a
year later.[16] For both, the gentility of poets and of poetry was endan-
gered by their subjection to the begging rabble of players. And when
in 1592 Greene warned "those gentlemen, his quondam acquaintance
that spend their wits in making plays"—Marlowe, Nashe, and Peele—
of "an upstart crow, beautified with our feathers, that with his tiger's
heart wrapped in a player's hide supposes he is as well able to bombast
out a blank verse as the best of you," he left no doubt concerning
which side of the opening divide between gentlemen poets and mechanical players he would put Shakespeare.[17] Though Greene and the
others were no better born than Shakespeare, they had won the right
to gentility along with a university degree—and that, they would have
us believe, made all the difference. The very uncertainty of gentle
status so precariously established may have lent a special urgency to
their claims. But whatever the reason, these men constructed a self-
presentational dialectic in which the author was defined by his social
superiority to the institution for which he wrote.

As Peter Stallybrass and Allon White have recently pointed out,
"the extremes of high and low have a special and powerful symbolic
charge."[18] In setting "high astounding terms" against "jigging veins,"
printed texts against staged plays, gentlemen poets against common
players, Marlowe, Nashe, Greene, and their fellow university wits tried
to ignite that symbolic charge in such a way as to project themselves
out of the base company of theatrical clowns and into the orbit of
gentility. Where the players' theater had featured a union of high and
low, the kind of union represented in *The Contention*'s opening assertion of a bond between the lord protector and the common people,
the newly emerging authors' theater asserted difference. It founded its
own legitimacy on the very gap the players' theater bridged—an operation made easier by a tradition of learned (and sometimes not so
learned) complaint focusing precisely on the popular theater's trans-
gressions of hierarchy.

The most familiar of these complaints is Sidney's attack (echoed by George Whetstone and Joseph Hall) on the mingling of kings and clowns.[19] The mere fact of representing a monarch and a lowly commoner together on stage violated a decorum that was both political and aesthetic. But the players' theater mixed high and low in other ways as well, all of them objectionable. As members of the public-theater audience, clowns sat in judgment on kings. In such a setting, kings were, as Shakespeare's Henry V later complained, made "subject to the breath / Of every fool."[20] But in the theater the very breath by which that complaint was voiced came from a "fool," the common player who acted the role of the king—a transgression that brought its own complaint. "For a mean person to take upon him the title of a prince with counterfeit port and train" falls, Stephen Gosson charged, "within the compass of a lie" (*ES* 4.217). And still another transgression occurred when a play came to court. "It is not convenient," argued the members of the London corporation in one of their many antitheatrical petitions to the privy council, "that [the players] present before her majesty such plays as have been before commonly played in open stages before all the basest assemblies in London and Middlesex" (*ES* 4.300). Exposure to a base assembly, or even to a play that a base assembly had witnessed, might breed semiotic contagion. To be an author was to remove oneself as far as possible from such contagion. It was to identify oneself with the high and to spurn the low.

The problem was that the terms would not stay fixed. In the decades prior to 1590, the adult companies had achieved unsettling prosperity. Indeed, after the charge that playhouse crowds spread plague and fostered insurrection, the most frequent complaint about the theater was that players were making money. As early as the 1570s, William Harrison proclaimed it "an evident token of a wicked time when players wax so rich"; Gosson complained a few years later of players who "jet under gentlemen's noses in suits of silk"; and in 1587 a now anonymous correspondent told Sir Francis Walsingham that "it is a woeful sight to see two hundred proud players jet in their silks where five hundred poor people starve in the streets" (*ES* 4.269, 204, 304). The players' wealth was particularly galling to the poor university men who wrote for them. "A player!" exclaims Greene's Roberto to the well-dressed stranger who has just offered him a job in the *Groatsworth of Wit* (1592). "I took you rather for a gentleman of great living, for if by outward habit men should be censured, I tell you, you would be taken for a substantial man" (12.131). And a decade later the unemployed graduates in *The Second Part of the Re-*

turn from Parnassus (1603) find themselves in a similar situation and express similar surprise:

> And must the basest trade yield us relief?
> Must we be practiced to those leaden spouts,
> That nought do vent but what they do receive?[21]

This was to reverse the hierarchy on which these gentleman-scholars based their identity. It made the low the patrons of the high. "Some fatal fire hath scorched our fortune's wing," lament the *Parnassus* gentlemen, "And still we fall, as we do upward spring." Vertical polarities govern their metaphor. But where they expected to rise, they find they have fallen. The poor players, the representatives of "the basest trade," are on top—an inversion fraught with the menace of universal catastrophe. As Gosson put it in *Plays Confuted* (1582), "in a commonweal, if private men be suffered to forsake their call-ing"—as the craftsmen-turned-players had done—"because they de-sire to walk gentleman-like in satin and velvet with a buckler at their heels, proportion is so broken, unity dissolved, harmony confounded, that the whole body must be dismembered and the prince or the head cannot choose but sicken" (*ES* 4.218–19).

This then was the institutional setting for Shakespeare's English history plays. Those plays were the products of an essentially artisanal theater—or rather of a theater whose leading members were of artisa-nal origin but had abandoned "work," as the familiar charge ran, for the more lucrative pleasures of "play."[22] It was a theater patronized and protected by the crown and the higher nobility but dependent for a great part of its income on a popular audience, a theater whose very success put extraordinary pressure on its class identity. Men as wealthy and famous as Edward Alleyn and Richard Burbage, men who trium-phantly impersonated kings and emperors before the queen herself, could hardly be treated as rogues, beggars, and vagabonds—yet that, according to some accounts, is precisely what they were.[23] And the pressure, as we have seen, did not come only from without, from city fathers and Puritan preachers. The theater was riven by internal ani-mosities that set the new breed of university-educated poets against the professional players for whom they wrote. The theater was thus both powerfully inclusive, mingling in every aspect of its operation high and low, and powerfully exclusive, basing the very self-definition of one important group within it on opposition to presumably less elevated collaborators and to a large part of the audience. Both these tendencies, the inclusive and the exclusive, existed at once. Both were built into the institutional structure of the theater itself. But they were not evenly distributed over time. From the Queen's Men of Tarlton and Wilson to the King's Men of Shakespeare and Burbage (to say nothing of Beaumont and Fletcher), there was a marked shift from inclusion to exclusion, from public to private, from "hodge-podge" to "art." In that transition, the 1590s was the crucial decade, the decade of maximum tension.

The persistent concern with status which marked virtually every response to the theater in the 1590s focused with particular intensity on Shakespeare. The "upstart crow" of the early 1590s, he was the darling of fools and gulls in the Parnassus plays of 1600 and 1601. As the player-poet who presented the most direct competition to the scholar-poets at their own specialty of producing artful and learned theatrical texts, the player-poet who could "bombast out a blank verse" with the best of them, Shakespeare became an indigestible lump in the craw of the new authors' theater. He had either to be swallowed or spat up, assimilated as an author or rejected as a player. The process of assimilation is suggested by the succession of printed texts of Shakespeare's plays, including the 1609 quarto of *Troilus and Cressida*—"a new play, never staled with the stage, never clapper-clawed with the palms of the vulgar"—and culminating in the 1623 folio and the many collected editions that have followed it. The rejection is found not only in Greene, the Parnassus plays, and perhaps the Posthaste of Marston's *Histriomastix* (1598), but also in various slurs from Ben Jonson, who was himself mocked on occasion for his brick-laying and acting. Particularly offensive must have been Jonson's parodic allusion in 1599 to Shakespeare's recently acquired badge of gentility. "Non sans droit," read the motto on the Shakespeare coat of arms. "Not without mustard," replied Jonson.[24] The commoner's condiment was the player's only right. That Shakespeare should have exposed himself to such a taunt, that he should have sought officially to better his station and to brave out the grab with such a motto, testifies to his social insecurity, an insecurity that permeates his sonnets. Whatever the institutional constraints and contradictions that marked the 1590s, they worked themselves out in the particular experience of this ambitious, sensitive, and supremely talented man.

Shakespeare did not invent the English history play. According to most estimates, *The Famous Victories of Henry V* (1586) appeared several years before *The Contention*.[25] But Shakespeare did make a larger contribution to that genre than anyone else, and he used it more fully to respond to the ongoing crisis of the theater and its sociopolitical identity. If powerful institutional forces made *The Contention*'s initial vision of popular inclusion almost inevitable, equally powerful forces were pushing the other way. The new and highly successful genre of the national history play was caught between the two. It thus served at a crucial moment in the history of the English stage as a site of individual and collective struggle and self-legitimation.[26] In this it resembles the generic forms that have concerned us in previous chapters: chivalric romance, legal reports and institutes, maps, chorographical descriptions, and overseas voyages. But here the subsequent fate of both the contested social formation and the particular texts lends a special urgency to our inquiry. In the last two centuries popular sovereignty has become the governing ideology of most of the world's nation-states, and Shakespeare's history plays have remained a paradigmatic expression of Anglo-British national self-understanding. That Shakespeare and the other dramatists of the 1590s do provide some access to the popular has surely contributed to their continuing appeal. But, as we have noticed, the Elizabethan theater's popular associations were in its own time among its most controversial features.

How then has this struggle worked itself out? I would suggest that it hasn't. The English history play is still a scene of contention.[27] If, however, no stable resolution has ever been achieved regarding the popular element either in the drama of the 1590s or in the nation Elizabethan drama represented and to some extent continues to represent, it is nevertheless the case that the drama, or at least the Shakespearean part of it, encodes a significant symbolic action. It moves in the direction of greater exclusion, which is also the direction of an authors' theater as Marlowe, Nashe, Greene, Marston, and the other university wits were defining it. The structural conditions for Shakespeare's posthumous elevation to the rank of major canonical poet were to this extent prepared by his own early work. That work—and particularly the national history play—redefined both the theater and the nation and, in so doing, made a place in the established hierarchy of value for the author Shakespeare became.

Popular Revolt

No one below the rank of earl appears on stage in the opening scene of *The Contention*. No one above the rank of joiner appeared on stage in the opening scene of *The Contention*. Both these statements are true. The first refers to the represented action. Its verb in the present tense suggests that this would be so whenever or by whomever the play were to be produced. The second, with its verb in a past tense, refers to the actors engaged in a particular performance that is supposed to have taken place in one of the London playhouses sometime around 1590 or 1591. The gap between them is the space any historically formalist reading must attempt to fill.

The play itself offers some pointers. Beginning with those references to the commons in the opening scene, it never goes long without recalling the vulgar multitude. This recollection includes a significant commoner participation in the play's action, a participation to which I will want to return. But it also has a powerful symbolic dimension. Not only are the contending groups of nobles distinguished from one another by the degree to which they support the "king and common weal"—an often repeated formula that at least implicitly includes the commons—but they define themselves both individually and collectively with reference to commoners. For them all, whatever their stance on other issues, nobility is primarily a term of difference. They insist less on what they are than on what they aren't. And what they aren't is common. "Let pale-faced fear keep with the mean-born man," declares the duke of York; Gloucester denies having "a base ignoble mind"; Queen Margaret fears having her image made "an alehouse sign." The strong negative valence of these differentiating allusions is replicated in many direct characterizations of commoners. Crowding four such terms into one line of verse, York calls Peter Thump "Base dunghill villain and mechanical." The people as a whole fare little better. In the mouths of various nobles, they are the "abject people," the "giddy multitude," the "envious people," the "rude multitude," "rude unpolished hinds," the "trait'rous rabble," "base peasants." And when nobles abuse one another, they use much the same language. In the opinion of Queen Margaret, the duchess of Gloucester is a "base-born callet"; the duke of Suffolk addresses the earl of Warwick as "Blunt-witted lord, ignoble in demeanor" and suggests that Warwick's mother must have taken "into her blameful bed / Some stern untutored churl"; Suffolk and his pirate captors exchange a whole string of status insults: "lousy swain," "jady groom," "forlorn swain," "base slave," "kennel, puddle, sink," "paltry, servile, abject drudges," "villain," "lowly vassal," "vulgar groom," "vile Besonians"; even the false noble Jack Cade, the leader of the people, can call Alexander Iden a "burly-boned clown"; and Richard Crookback says much the same by means of an action, as he leaves the slaughtered body of the duke of Somerset under "an alehouse' paltry sign."

Nothing in all this distinguishes *The Contention* from any other Shakespearean play. Those other plays, like most Elizabethan literature, are obsessively concerned with status. In a newly mobile and variously unsettled society, matters that could once have been taken almost for granted had constantly to be readjusted and reasserted—and much of the adjusting and asserting was inevitably nasty.[28] But it is nevertheless useful to be reminded how such nastiness functioned and how prevalent it was. If Shakespeare and his fellows, whether we think of those fellows as other players or other playwrights, needed a model for social self-promotion, this was it. The high declared itself high by spurning the low. No feeling of national solidarity across the classes could be expected to prevail against the demands of this fundamental strategy. But how then do we account for the fact that this play, so thickly crammed with class slurs, was written, played, and viewed by base, abject, ignoble villains, grooms, and clowns? Did none of them notice that they were themselves the objects of the abuse they were so generously handing out and so eagerly taking in? Or was the point precisely that they were not its objects, that their very participation in this rite of noble flouting vaccinated them? Much of the status abuse—terms like *villain, clown, churl, hind, peasant, swain*—refers specifically to countrymen. Perhaps the city dwellers who populated the theaters thought themselves exempt. But if so, it must have been an uncomfortable and unstable exemption, for this conceptual universe allotted no terms, whether favorable or unfavorable, specifically to them. Between the extremes of high and low, noble and base, there was only semiotic vacancy, a noplace without meaning. And at least some of the players and theatergoers who inhabited that noplace must have known that in attacks on the theater they were both regularly assimilated to the villains and clowns, almost never to the nobles.

The Contention does, however, contain a strong counterdiscourse, a discourse of popular protest and popular power. In some five or six separate episodes, commoners intrude on the noble contentions that are the play's main subject. These intrusions begin with deferential petitioning but end in rebellion. Between the two are scenes of witchcraft (Margery Jordan), piety or its abuse (Saunder Simpcox), rage (at Duke Humphrey's murder), and retribution (against Suffolk). Nobles manipulate and control these expressions of the popular. But there does nevertheless remain a significant residue of political otherness, enough to provide the basis for an alternate system of value, one in which the theater would have its part. Instead of acting as a shill for aristocratic exclusiveness, this theater would go on mingling kings and clowns in a way that made clear their interdependence and reciprocal interests. The commons themselves, as Shakespeare presents them in the first three acts of *The Contention,* are not single. But neither are they negligible. A semiotic necessity for the nobility, which exists as a class only by virtue of its difference from the commons, commoners also wield considerable power: the power of immemorial rights and customs, the power of opinion, the power of witchcraft and popular religion, the power of organized resistance and coercion.

It is this last—organized resistance and coercion—that marks *The Contention*'s best-known episode of commoner action, Jack Cade's rebellion, an episode that fills most of the last third of the play. Up to this point, the play's opening vision of a mutually beneficial union of top and bottom, of king (or lord protector) and commons, has been consistently reaffirmed as a political ideal, even as it has been undermined as an historical reality. Duke Humphrey has been deposed and murdered, but the political values he represented have gotten the play's endorsement. The lower-class petitioners discover genuine threats to both their rights and the king's position. The men of Bury, who call for Suffolk's downfall, are equally motivated by the true interests of the king and the commonwealth. And the pirates, who murder Suffolk, act in accordance with those interests. Even the conjuring and miracle scenes, by heightening our sense of Duke Humphrey's worth and the injustice of those who conspire against him, contribute to the pattern. If any Shakespearean play can be described as open and univocal in its political ideology, the first two-thirds of this one can. Against the negative and exclusionist strategy of noble self-aggrandizement stands the positive and inclusionist ideal of the king and commonwealth, the ideal associated *both* with Duke Humphrey *and* with a certain notion of the Elizabethan theater as a popular institution voicing a position consonant with its social identity. What Cade's rebellion does is to push that inclusionist ideal toward its own exclusionist extreme, at once enunciating its most radical implications and reducing it to absurdity.

The folio version of Cade's rebellion—and presumably the prompt book on which it was based—begins with a suggestive mixing of levels. Where the quarto stage direction reads, "Enter two of the rebels with long staves," the folio has "Enter Bevis and John Holland." And where the quarto speech tags read "George" and "Nick," the folio has "Bevis" and "Hol." From other records, we know that John Holland was an actor. Theater historians suppose that Bevis was too. If we think of the following lines, the opening lines of the first

scene of Cade's rebellion, as spoken simultaneously by two rebels and
by two actors, the theater's potential implication in the actions it
represented becomes difficult to ignore.

> *George/Bevis.* Come and get thee a sword, though made of a lath.
> They have been up these two days.
> *Nick/Holland.* They have the more need to sleep now, then.
> *George/Bevis.* I tell thee, Jack Cade the clothier means to dress the
> commonwealth, and turn it, and set a new nap upon it.
> *Nick/Holland.* So he had need, for 'tis threadbare. Well, I say, it was
> never merry world in England since gentlemen came up.
> *George/Bevis.* O miserable age! Virtue is not regarded in handicrafts-
> men.
> *Nick/Holland.* The nobility think scorn to go in leather aprons.
> *George/Bevis.* Nay more, the king's council are no good workmen.
> *Nick/Holland.* True. And yet it is said, labor in thy vocation; which is
> as much to say as, let the magistrates be laboring men; and therefore
> should we be magistrates.
> *George/Bevis.* Thou hast hit it; for there's no better sign of a brave
> mind than a hard hand. (4.2.1–20)

A few of these lines—the references to "their" having "been up these
two days" and to "Jack Cade the clothier"—belong only to the represented action. And in 1590 or 1591, "king's council" would have had
to be "queen's council." But otherwise the passage works for both
sets of speakers. A lath sword could as easily be a stage property as a
workman's weapon, the call to get a sword as easily a stage direction
as a summons to rebellion. What's more, the social status of Bevis and
Holland was much like that of George and Nick. And if their status
was the same, so may have been their opinions. Actors and characters
may have shared an animosity toward gentlemen, a sense of unre-
garded virtue, a feeling that laboring men should be magistrates. They
may even have shared a desire to rebel. Indeed, in speaking these lines
the actors may have thought of themselves as renewing a rebellion that
George, Nick, and their like had not managed to make successful a
century or two earlier.[29]

Something of this sort, without my emphasis on the specific social
identity of the Elizabethan theater, has recently been suggested by
Annabel Patterson. According to Patterson, Elizabethan plays, *The
Contention* among them, participate in a continuous tradition of radical protest, a tradition that stretches from the Peasants' Revolt in the
fourteenth century to the Sacheverell Riots in the eighteenth—and
beyond. Those plays preserve and repeat the basic tenets of what

Patterson, following Rosemond Faith, calls a "peasant ideology." As a concise example of this ideology and its theatrical embodiment, Patterson cites John Ball's sermon from the anonymous *Life and Death of Jack Straw* (1591):

> Neighbors, neighbors, the weakest now a days goes to the wall,
> But mark my words, and follow the counsel of John Ball.
> England is grown to such a pass of late,
> That rich men triumph to see the poor beg at their gate.
> But I am able by good scripture before you to prove,
> That God doth not this dealing allow nor love.
> But when Adam delved, and Eve span,
> Who was then a gentleman?

"Articulate here," she writes, "was an appeal to a principle of natural justice and equality, to a moral economy and a classless society, made memorable by an Edenic motto that, in the fifteenth century, had been passed by word of mouth around Europe."[30] Much the same could be said of the exchange I quoted from *The Contention*. If the Edenic allusion is not there, it will soon make its appearance in the mouth of Jack Cade, who responds to the accusation that his "father was a plasterer" by recalling that "Adam was a gardener" (4.2.132–34). And even in the opening exchange itself we find a reference to a happier time before the distinctions of class: "It was never merry world in England since gentlemen came up." The similarity between *Jack Straw* and *The Contention* is not fortuitous. Departing from the chronicle descriptions of Cade's Rebellion, which contain nothing of Patterson's "peasant ideology," Shakespeare based his version of these events on accounts of the much earlier Peasants' Revolt—perhaps on *Jack Straw* itself and certainly on the chronicle sources of *Jack Straw*. Shakespeare's Jack Cade thus more nearly resembles Wat Tyler and Parson Ball than he does his fifteenth-century namesake.

In making this substitution, Shakespeare contributed to the invention of the radical tradition Patterson evokes. As one encounters them in the chronicles, the Peasants' Revolt of 1381 and Cade's Rebellion of 1450 are ideologically discontinuous. They share no significant objectives or concerns. Shakespeare makes them mirror images of one another. He thus invites his audience, which was also the audience of *Jack Straw*, to see all popular revolts as essentially the same revolt, motivated by the same fundamental grievances, directed toward the same leveling end. A possible effect of this collation can be found a few years later in Thomas Heywood's *1 Edward IV* (1599), where the rebellious Falconbridge proclaims, "We do not rise like Tyler, Cade, and Straw, / Bluebeard, and other of that rascal rout."[31] Together Tyler, Cade, Straw, and Bluebeard constitute a single "rascal rout," a rout from which Falconbridge tries vainly to distinguish his own rebellion. Emphasis must be put on the *vainly,* for everything else in the scene points toward likeness rather than difference. Falconbridge's declaration is preceded by the familiar cry of "Liberty, liberty, liberty, general liberty," and it is followed by his own Cade-like promise of universal wealth.

> We'll shoe our neighing coursers with no worse
> Than the purest silver that is sold in Cheap.
> At Leadenhall, we'll sell pearls by the peck,
> As now the mealmen use to sell their meal. (p. 10)

Falconbridge, whose stage rebellion bears even less resemblance to its historical counterpart than Cade's does to its, is the captive of what by the mid-1590s was an established theatrical convention. His evocation of Jack Straw and Jack Cade serves rather to associate him and his fellow rebels with that convention than to distinguish them from it. Far from achieving a unique identity of its own, their rebellion collapses into yet another version of the perennial peasants' revolt, by which its stage representation was generated in the first place.

Finding a play based, as *Jack Straw* is, on the original Peasants' Revolt and finding scenes of the same sort in plays like *The Contention* and *1 Edward IV,* where the historical record would not have led one to expect them, lends support to the idea that there may have been a special relation between popular revolt and the theater. Clearly, a significant portion of the Elizabethan theater audience liked seeing such plays, and a significant portion of the players liked putting them on. To this degree, the theater was a willing bearer of a radically subversive peasant, or more generally commoner, ideology. Occasionally this willingness could get the theater into trouble. Sometime in the last decade of Elizabeth's reign, the master of the revels refused Henslowe's company the right to produce the collaborative *Sir Thomas More* (1595) with its depiction of the Ill May Day of 1517. "Leave out the insurrection wholly and the cause thereof," Edmund Tilney wrote in the margin of the manuscript. If the uprising were to figure in the play at all, it could only be "by a short report and not otherwise at your own perils."[32] Tilney clearly thought this dangerous matter. Some ten to twenty years earlier, a lord mayor of London considered the very "memory of Ill May Day" sufficient provocation for him to deny a license for a fencing exhibition to be held in the Theater on May Day eve (*ES* 4.293). What would he have thought had the proposed entertainment been a play *about* Ill May Day? Other mayors and aldermen were certainly not reluctant to see a connection between the content of plays and the disorder that periodically troubled their city. "Stage plays," one such group wrote to the lords of the privy council in 1595, "are so set forth as that they move wholly to imitation and not to the avoiding of those vices which they represent, which we verily think to be the chief cause . . . of the late stir and mutinous attempt of those few apprentices and other servants, who we doubt not drew their infection from these and like places" (*ES* 4.318). Given such provocation, the playhouses should, the city fathers argued, be torn down. Yet despite these objections and threats, scenes of rebellion like those in *Jack Straw, The Contention,* and *1 Edward IV* went on being written and played. Even Marston's *Histriomastix* has one. Was the public theater so committed to a program of radical change that it was willing to risk its very survival rather than renounce sedition?

The mention of *Histriomastix* should raise some doubt concerning this possibility—should, that is, were the other evidence adduced in the preceding paragraph not already so strikingly flimsy.[33] *Histriomastix* was not, after all, a public-theater play. None of the connections I have made between the socioeconomic identity of the theater and the radical popular ideology it sometimes expresses would apply here. The players of *Histriomastix* were either boys, who, whatever their politics, exercised no control over their scripts, or Inns-of-Court students, gentlemen by profession if not by birth. The author was himself a gentleman of the Middle Temple. And the greater part of the audience was at least as privileged. Few of these beneficiaries of gentility can have seriously wished to see the abolition of all social difference. Marston's theater founded itself on social difference, and his play directed much of its energy against the insufficiently exclusive popular theater. Yet his rebellious "russetings and mechanicals" express precisely the same peasant ideology that Patterson found in *Jack Straw*. They cry for liberty; they talk of equality; they threaten to "pluck down all the noble houses in the land"; they promise that "all shall be common"; they even remember that "we came all of our father Adam" (pp. 288–89). Must Marston then be enrolled in the tradition of John Ball and Wat Tyler? In some sense, he must. In repeating (with whatever mockery) the leveling program of those Ricardian rebels, he helped keep it alive. But clearly he thought of this not as a way of associating himself and his theater with the commons and their interests, but rather the reverse. It was a way of marking a difference. And if that was his intent, may it not also have been the intent of Heywood, Shakespeare, and the anonymous author of *Jack Straw*? Instead of being ideologically at one with George and Nick, perhaps Bevis, Holland, *and* Shakespeare were making fun of them.

No one who knows these plays and the criticism concerning them will be surprised by this suggestion. By most accounts, the plays are all rabidly opposed to the popular rebellion they depict. David Bevington's treatment of them is in this respect true to critical opinion generally. He puts *Jack Straw, The Contention, 1 Edward IV,* and *Sir Thomas More* together in a chapter called "Orthodox Reply"—the theater's orthodox reply to the "vox populi" that had marked some plays of the 1580s—and quotes Heywood's *Apology for Actors* (1612) in support of this conservative reading. Plays, wrote Heywood, should strive "to teach the subjects obedience to their king, to show the people the untimely ends of such as have moved tumults, commotions, and insurrections, to present them with the flourishing estate of such as live in obedience."[34] As early as 1592, Nashe insisted that this objective was already being met. "No play" to be seen in the London theaters of that time "encourageth any man to tumults or rebellion but lays before such the halter and the gallows" (1.214). If there was, as I have suggested, a special relation between popular revolt and the public theater, it was, these various accounts seem to reply, a relation of intense and unremitting hostility. But hostility is itself a form of relation, one no less significant than the solidarity it denies. Popular revolt, and perhaps popular culture generally, was the theater's dark other, the vestigial egalitarian self that had to be exorcised before a more gentrified, artful, and discriminating identity could emerge.

In *The Contention,* Shakespeare sets to the work of exorcism with savage zeal. His mockery of Jack Cade, in particular, is open and unmistakable.[35] Cade's appearance, his social pretension, his manner of speaking, his reforming ideas, his arbitrary brutality are all made to seem ridiculous. Even his followers mock him.

> *Cade.* My father was a Mortimer—
> *Dick.* He was an honest man, and a good bricklayer.
> *Cade.* My mother was a Plantagenet—
> *Dick.* I knew her well, she was a midwife. (4.2.39–42)

"O gross and miserable ignorance!" Sir Humphrey Stafford exclaims on hearing one of Cade's ludicrous outbursts, and we are presumably intended to agree. Mockery, rather than any desire to foment rebellion, explains why Shakespeare substituted the events of 1381 for those of 1450. Jack Straw's rebellion was easier to laugh at than Jack Cade's. As Heywood's Falconbridge realizes, the Peasants' Revolt, with its "rascal rout," was in itself discreditable. To be associated with it was to be branded as foolish and irresponsible—utterly incapable of governing.[36]

But Cade's Rebellion, as Shakespeare presents it, has a more pointed relation to the theatrical situation of the early 1590s. A minor touch of this sort comes with the passing suggestion that the rebels are puritanically inclined. In the course of a few speeches we hear them talk of "labor[ing] in thy vocation," of striking down "sin . . . like an ox" and cutting "impiety's throat . . . like a calf," of being "inspired with the spirit of putting down kings and princes" (4.2.16–36)—all cant phrases of radical religious dissent. Puritans were among the theater's most vociferous enemies. To associate them with rebels, an association made easy by the Anabaptist reputation as levelers and communists, was to label their antitheatricalism as seditious.[37] But not only are the theater's enemies rebellion's friends, but the reverse is true as well. Cade's special targets, "all scholars, lawyers, courtiers, gentlemen" (4.4.36), are precisely those whom Nashe was to identify a year later as the members of his ideal theater audience.[38] Here exclusivity meets exclusivity. Nashe, his fellow university wits, and the authors' theater they were working to establish would exclude all those below the rank of gentleman. Cade, despite his claim to a royal inheritance, would kill all those above the rank of a common working man. And if Cade's war on gentlemen would destroy the social and demographic foundation of the new authors' theater, his campaign against literacy would destroy its mode of production. When Cade has one man hung for knowing how to write and another beheaded for "erecting a grammar school," causing "printing to be used," and building "a paper mill," he implicitly sentences all authors, all readers, and the whole institutional structure that promotes and sustains their activities. There may be, as Patterson suggests, "a note of genuine ideological confusion" in Shakespeare's attack on Cade, an allowance of what his play would seem to disallow.[39] One cannot represent rebellion, however negatively, without permitting it to speak its discontent. Every one of the plays I have mentioned does as much. But *The Contention* constitutes an attack as well as representing one. It not only makes fun of Cade and his fellow rebels, it exposes popular rule as inimical to the very existence of the institution by which it and other plays like it were produced.

But more than choosing sides—and a member of Shakespeare's audience could certainly have resisted the play's promptings and chosen differently—*The Contention* eliminates the inclusionist position with which it seemed to begin. It divides peasants and craftsmen from their more privileged fellows and sets one group against the other. In this division any possibility of a national theater or a national culture based on the kind of union of top and bottom represented by Duke Humphrey in the play's first several acts is lost. The two groups are mutually exclusive. The nation, its interests, and its self-representational forms can be identified with one or the other, but not with both. Nor is the exclusionist move confined to this play. In keeping with it, Shakespeare eliminates the "good" Duke Humphrey, the people's Duke Humphrey, from his subsequent plays devoted to the reign of Henry VI.[40] In *The True Tragedy of Richard Duke of York,* the play the folio calls *The Third Part of Henry the Sixth,* the king himself blames dead Gloucester, *The Contention*'s archdefender of England's conquests, for the loss of France, and no one denies the charge. And in *Henry VI, part 1,* where we see the duke once again as lord protector, he shows none of that special regard for the people that characterized him in *The Contention.* As for the people themselves, they are rarely mentioned and hardly ever seen in either play—unless, of course, one counts as a representative of the people the shepherdess-warrior, Joan of Arc. But Joan is an enemy of England, a member of the French, not the English, nation. To judge from these plays, no commoner could represent England. It is as though Shakespeare set out to cancel the popular ideology with which his cycle of history plays began, as though he wanted to efface, alienate, even demonize all signs of commoner participation in the political nation. The less privileged classes may still have had a place in his audience, but they had lost their place in his representation of England. If Cade's rebellion forces a choice between mutually exclusive groups, it is clear which of the groups Shakespeare has chosen.

Such a choice is rarely final or definitive. This one had to be made over and over. What disappeared from history remained in comedy, where both native popular tradition and classical precedent justified it. And from comedy it made a return to history, only to be banished once more. One might, however, object that Shakespeare didn't banish anything or anyone, that he didn't efface or demonize or exorcise or perform any of the other acts I have been attributing to him. Instead, he wrote some plays in which various characters perform various acts. Duke Humphrey is strangled, Jack Cade stabbed and beheaded, Joan of Arc burnt at the stake not by Shakespeare but by the fifteenth-century Englishmen who are represented in his plays. Shakespeare simply retold their story. But, of course, he didn't "simply" retell anything. He chose what to tell and how to tell it. He even made up a fair amount. And, more than that, he performed acts of inclusion and exclusion that had an effect outside the fictional world of the plays, acts that became part of other stories, the histories of the English theater and the English nation. I don't by this mean to attribute excessive weight to Shakespeare's individual agency. He and his plays were constituted by the social and representational systems they participated in altering. And they have been the instrument of meanings they never intended. But neither do I want to deny Shakespeare all agency. As an actor-sharer-playwright in the most successful theatrical company England had ever known, he occupied a unique position, a position that his plays did much to create. He helped make the world that made him. And that making involved a redefinition both of the nation and of the place common people, the peasants and craftsmen who made up far the greater part of England's population, occupied in that nation. The "facts" of England's history would not have allowed Shakespeare to show a popular revolt toppling the monarchy and replacing it with a democratic republic—not, that is, so long as he remained within the genre of the English history play. But nothing intrinsic to the genre required the particular treatment he gave Cade's Rebellion. That treatment was one enabling act among many in the process by which Shakespeare became England's "national poet."

Carnival and Clowns

In *The Contention,* the first words we hear concerning Jack Cade associate him in a quite particular way with what we now call "popular culture." "I have seen / Him," says the duke of York, "caper upright like a wild Morisco, / Shaking . . . his bells" (3.1.364–66). A "Morisco" is a dancer, a performer of that most popular of popular dances, the morris, "the centerpiece," according to one critic, "of Elizabethan folk culture."[41] Morris dancing was a regular part of holiday merriment, of May Day, midsummer, and carnival. And in the 1590s morris dancing was the specialty of the theater's most celebrated clown, Will Kemp. From 1593 to 1599, Kemp and Shakespeare were both members of the lord chamberlain's company. Did their collaboration begin still earlier and include *The Contention?* No one can say with any certainty. Kemp did perform with Lord Strange's Men early in the 1590s, and so apparently did Shakespeare. Lord Strange's is the company usually credited with *The Contention*. So there is a possibility that Kemp "created" the role of Jack Cade or that the role was created for him and drew on his special talents as a morris dancer. But whether Kemp was Shakespeare's first Jack Cade or not, it does seem likely that the part was enacted by the company's clown and certain that Cade and his rebellion were seen in terms of carnival and carnivalesque misrule. The clown, a figure invented scarcely a decade earlier in the context of a newly emerging urban and professionalized entertainment business, and carnival, the ancient mainstay of a culture that had included all ranks of society, here converge and are linked with the history of popular rebellion. Whatever the nature of the theater's engagement with the "people," it involved both clowns and carnival.

In the fourteen or fifteen years between the building of the first permanent public theater in London and the first production of *The Contention*, the clown dominated the theatrical scene. In this players' theater, the clown was the chief player. And Richard Tarlton was the chief clown. By the force of his theatrical presence, Tarlton imposed himself on his contemporaries and became the center of a legend that was repeated and amplified for decades after his death. Shakespeare's clown, Will Kemp, and John Singer, the clown of the Admiral's Men, may have achieved comparable renown in the 1590s, but they did so by following Tarlton's lead. Tarlton invented the role of clown and brought it to such prominence that it became an inevitable part of virtually every public-theater performance. What then was Tarlton's clown? He was, of course, first a funny man, a man who could make an audience laugh. This the clown shared with such predecessors as the court fool and the morality-play Vice. But the clown was distinguished from both by his strongly marked class identity. As his name suggests, the clown was a countryman, a rustic. His familiar suit of russet, his buttoned cap, his tabor and pipe all proclaimed his status (fig. 13). And so too did his usual stance as the fall guy, the ignorant victim, who gets the best of his antagonists only through an accidental turn of wit. In the new public theater, with its largely urban clientele, Tarlton presented a figure his audience could both laugh at and laugh with. They could laugh *at* the oafish countryman, *with* the witty Tarlton.

An epitaph, published some thirty years after Tarlton's death, suggests both the lineage and the power of this representation:

Here within this sullen earth
Lies Dick Tarlton, lord of mirth,
Who in his grave, still laughing, gapes,
Sith all clowns since have been his apes.
Erst he of clowns to learn still sought,
But now they learn of him they taught.
By art far past the principal,
The counterfeit is now worth all.[42]

13. Richard Tarlton from an undated seventeenth-century copy of the woodcut
printed in *Tarlton's Jests* (1611). Tarlton appears in his familiar peasant's costume:
russet suit, buttoned cap, cloth shoes, tabor, and pipes. Huntington Library.

On a first reading—and perhaps on a second—the meaning of *clown* changes from the fourth to the fifth line. The clowns who have been Tarlton's apes are, we suppose, the likes of Kemp and Singer, the professional entertainers who learned their trade from Tarlton. But the clowns he learned from were not actors but rather common rustics, who are themselves now learning clownishness from his example. I don't suppose that anyone, including the author of this epitaph, really thought peasants learned to be peasants by imitating Tarlton. But something like that might almost have appeared to be the case. Tarlton's counterfeit proved so compelling that it may well have substituted itself for the reality it purported to imitate. Rustics came to be seen as Tarlton portrayed them. We have no way of knowing how any actual Elizabethan countryman reacted to this comic impersonation, but Robert Greene guessed the reaction would not have been favorable. Talking of the players, Greene's Cloth Breeches remarks that "such a plain country fellow as myself they bring in as clowns and fools to laugh at in their play, whereas they get by us, and of our alms the proudest of them all doth live" (*ES* 4.240).

In the last few words of Cloth Breeches's remark, we get another sample of the way the university wits habitually put down players. However proud they may have become, players remain beggars, dependent on the alms of mere rustics. But the statement as a whole points to another paradox. The players' theater of the 1580s both privileged and degraded the common people. Through the figure of the clown, commoners were made central to the stage and its representations. Sometimes this centrality could result in a genuinely radical expression of lower-class grievance. A remarkable instance occurs in *The Cobbler's Prophecy* (1590), a play written by Robert Wilson, the leading maker of playscripts in the 1580s and one of Tarlton's fellow players in the Queen's Men. Addressing a courtier, a gentleman, a scholar, and a soldier, Wilson's cobbler foresees a paradise of social inversion:

> Then these poor that cry,
> Being lifted up on high,
> When you are all forlorn,
> Shall laugh you loud to scorn. (ll. 332–35)

Considering that courtiers, gentlemen, scholars, and soldiers were well represented in the public playhouse audience, the gibe had a target close at hand. In plays given at court, Tarlton himself could be still more particular. Pointing at Sir Walter Raleigh during one such performance, Tarlton is reputed to have said, "See, the knave commands the queen" (*ES* 2.342). But in every instance the social and political criticism is combined with a demeaning role. The cobbler is a henpecked ignoramus, "contemptible and vile" (l. 1389), and Tarlton is always the clown—as another of his performances before the queen suggests.

> The queen being discontented, which Tarlton perceiving, took upon him to delight her with some quaint jest. Whereupon he counterfeited a drunkard and called for beer, which was brought immediately. Her majesty, noting his humor, commanded that he should have no more, for, quoth she, he will play the beast, and so shame himself. "Fear not you," quoth Tarlton, "for your beer is small enough." Whereat her majesty laughed heartily and commanded that he should have enough.[43]

Both the cobbler, a part no doubt taken by the clown, and Tarlton enjoy a privileged access to the monarch, and both use that access to express popular discontent. Even the comment about the queen's small beer has an edge to it. But the price of their freedom is self-abnegation. Were this just the familiar enabling pose of the court jester or licensed fool, it wouldn't much matter. The fool represents no one but himself. But the clown stands for all craftsmen and all peasants. When he is made ridiculous, so are they. And once having been made ridiculous, they are prime candidates for exclusion from a theater—and from a nation—that comes to pride itself on its elevation and seriousness.

Playing the drunkard, Tarlton reminds us that among the figures behind the clown is carnival. Indeed, his exchange with the queen reenacts the most familiar of carnivalesque scenarios, the battle of Carnival and Lent. The queen is cast as the lenten killjoy, serving small beer and curbing desire. Tarlton assumes the carnival role of bestial and unrestrained appetite. The result of their encounter is the transformation of discontent into hearty laughter, producing a reign of abundance. She "commanded that he should have enough." This festive transformation does not, however, upset the hierarchy of power. Hierarchy is, on the contrary, renewed and reinforced. The queen ends in happy control. But the ancient holiday script does nevertheless involve a moment of danger. In calling imperiously for beer, Tarlton usurps the queen's place, acts as though he were king. And in pointing out the weakness of her brew, he implicitly accuses her of niggardliness. Had she responded differently or had his complaint been less easily satisfied, the encounter might have ended in repression or rebellion.

In the beneficent form one finds in this anecdote, a form that achieves renewal without repression or rebellion, carnival has been seen to underlie much Elizabethan drama, including most prominently the comedies of Shakespeare's first decade, which was, of course, also the decade of his English history plays. Nor are comedy and history wholly distinguishable in this regard. The two parts of *Henry IV* figure along with *Love's Labor's Lost, Midsummer Night's Dream, The Merchant of Venice, As You Like It,* and *Twelfth Night* in C. L. Barber's classic study of carnival form in Shakespearean drama, *Shakespeare's Festive Comedy.* But, as Barber acknowledges, something goes wrong at the end of *Part Two.* Instead of the generous and joyous inclusion that should be the result of festive celebration, the play leads to harsh exclusion, to Hal's rejection of Falstaff.[44] I will want to return to this episode and examine its implications for our understanding of the symbolic action Shakespeare performed in his history plays. Here, however, it is enough to remember that Falstaff was not the only Shakespearean lord of misrule to be sacrificed to the forces of history. Jack Cade got there first. Cade's motto, "then are we in order when we are most out of order" (4.2.189–90), could be taken as the rallying cry for all carnival, where systematic inversion is the unruly rule. In *The Contention,* clowns take the place of kings, ignorance substitutes for learning, "hard hands" are confounded with "brave minds," and unbridled festivity proclaims a reign of plenty: "There shall be in England seven halfpenny loaves sold for a penny; the three-hooped pot shall have ten hoops, and I will make it a felony to drink small beer" (4.2.65–68). And, of course, carnival is severely punished. Cade is proclaimed an outlaw and hunted to his death. One wonders not only why in this play, as in *2 Henry IV,* Shakespeare would have treated festivity so harshly, but also why he would have established the connection between carnival and rebellion in the first place. Nothing in his chronicle sources—certainly nothing in the chronicle accounts of Cade's Rebellion—required the connection. Nothing suggested that Cade was a clown or that his rebellion took the form of festive misrule. Why did Shakespeare want it that way?

Before trying to answer this question, we should, however, depersonalize its subject, for in this regard Shakespeare's practice was the practice of the Elizabethan theater generally. In the theater, carnival and clowns were regularly a part of popular revolt. Tom Miller, one of

Jack Straw's chief lieutenants, is specifically identified as the clown in *The Life and Death of Jack Straw,* and their rebellion is full of the usual carnivalesque revelry. In *Edward IV* Spicing strikes the holiday note: "Rantum, scantum, rogues, follow your leader, Cavaliero Spicing, the maddest slave that ever pund spice in a mortar" (p. 19). In both plays, food, drink, and sex are constant preoccupations. And in both the grotesque body is much in evidence. "A small matter," says Tom Miller, "to recover a man that is slain, / Blow wind in his tail, and fetch him again."[45] Especially interesting in this regard is the riot in *Sir Thomas More,* for it began by resisting these conventions. As originally written, the episode did contain at least one notable symbolic inversion. The most forceful rebel leader is a woman, Doll Williamson, who enters wearing a shirt of mail, a headpiece, and a sword and buckler. But neither Doll nor any of the other rebels is at all clownish. Their grievances are well founded, the expression of them is cogent and even literate, and their strategy is carefully formulated. They use May Day festivity as a means of achieving their end. They are not themselves holiday revelers. The difference is that these rebels are Londoners. Whether because of the sensibilities of the London audience or because of the force of historical memory, their uprising cannot be so easily assimilated to the conventional pattern of peasant revolt. They are not clowns. But that resistance in itself tells us something important about the Elizabethan perception of festivity. Festivity is seen as status specific. In associating rebellion with carnival, the authors of *The Contention, Jack Straw,* and *Edward IV* label this kind of festive rebellion as *not* urban and *not* upper class.[46] They stigmatize and compartmentalize in such a way as to constitute an alien social formation that will centuries later be recovered as "the folk."

The resistance to convention in *Sir Thomas More* is thus highly significant. But no less significant is the fact that the resistance crumbles. In revisions of the original text, the rebellion is systematically carnivalized. Marginal additions in the hand of Thomas Heywood introduce a clown into the execution scene and a rewriting of the riot itself makes the clown one of the principal speakers. Opinions differ sharply over the intent of these changes. Most critics would probably agree with Carol Chillington's sense that the clown makes the rebels less threatening, less serious, less vulnerable to the censor's objection.[47] But not all would agree. Chillington ignores, according to David Wiles, "the plain fact that the clown is more seditious than anyone when he is made to sing: 'Shall we be held under? No! We are freeborn and do take scorn to be used so.'"[48] The clown *is* the most

seditious character in the play, the least cautious and the least re-
strained. But would Heywood and his fellows have revised scenes the
master of the revels had already marked for excision to make them
more offensive? It seems unlikely. However seditious their intent, this
group of experienced playwrights seems rather to have thought that
clownishness would make what had been unacceptable acceptable.[49]
Associating rebellion with clowns and with carnival made rebellion
both more radically subversive and less dangerous. But in addition to
that, it created an associative cluster that could then be manipulated
as a unit. Festivity discredited rebellion; rebellion discredited festivity;
and both discredited the clown and the common people he represented. In its inclusion of such materials, the Elizabethan history play
unquestionably participates in popular culture. But in its handling of
them, it prepares the way for a withdrawal from that culture. The
history play rehearses popular festive customs, as Prince Hal studies
his lowlife companions, so as to reject them.[50]

Which brings us back to Falstaff. Fat Jack—"that trunk of humors,
that bolting-hutch of beastliness, that swollen parcel of dropsies, that
huge bombard of sack, that stuffed cloak-bag of guts, that roasted
Manningtree ox with the pudding in his belly, that reverent Vice, that
grey Iniquity, that father ruffian, that vanity in years" (*1HIV*,
2.4.449–54)—has long been recognized as an embodiment of carnival.[51] And though it enters less often into interpretations of the part
or the play, Falstaff's identity as clown is only slightly less well established. Will Kemp played the part, and, as J. A. Bryant pointed out
many years ago, memories of Dick Tarlton helped shape it. Falstaff is,
in Bryant's phrase, "an immortalized Tarlton."[52] Thus when Hal
banishes Falstaff, both carnival and the clown feel the blow.

Hal's banishment of Falstaff is among the most frequently discussed episodes in all Shakespeare. And, as with all such episodes,
there is no agreement about how it should be taken. Is this the
proper and necessary return of order that must accompany Hal's
assumption of power? Or is it rather an intolerable narrowing of
sympathies?[53] And whether necessary or intolerable or both, is the
act Hal's alone or were Shakespeare, his theater, and his culture
implicated in it as well? "Hal's project," as Michael Bristol has defined it, "is eventually to break the rhythmic alternation between the
abundance of the material principle embodied in carnival and the
abstemious social discipline embodied in Lent by establishing a permanent sovereignty of lenten civil policy" (p. 206). Was that project
more widely shared? A suggestive homology from theatrical history

permits one to think that it may have been. The epilogue to *2 Henry IV* (1597) promises a continuation of the story "with Sir John in it," but when in *Henry V* (1599) the story does continue, Sir John is kept out. The usual explanation for this change in plan is that the clown who played Falstaff had left the company. In February of 1599, Will Kemp joined other members of the Chamberlain's Men in signing the Globe lease. By autumn of the same year, he was no longer included on the company's cast lists. There is no reason to think that the banishment of Falstaff caused this separation. But the fictional event does have a proleptic relation to the factual one. The banishment of carnival from the proximity of politic rule foreshadows the departure of Will Kemp from the Shakespearean theater. And when neither returns, the likeness is confirmed. Falstaff fails to appear in *Henry V,* though his death of a broken heart is reported. As for Kemp, he danced himself, in his words, "out of the world," away from the newly constructed Globe, where he was replaced by Robert Armin, a comedian who exchanged Tarlton and Kemp's role of plebeian clown for the socially unmarked part of court fool.[54]

Between the clown, the central figure of the old players' theater, and the playwright, the *sine qua non* of the emerging authors' theater, tension was inevitable.[55] A few months after Kemp's departure from the Chamberlain's Men, Hamlet pointed to its primary cause. "Let those that play your clowns speak no more than is set down for them, for there be of them that will themselves laugh to set on some quantity of barren spectators to laugh too, though in the mean time some necessary question of the play be then to be considered. That's villainous, and shows a most pitiful ambition in the fool that uses it" (3.2.38–45). "Villainous" is as much as to say "clownlike." The clown is by definition a villain. He is a churl, a hind, a swain, a peasant. Any competition with a gentle or (in this case) princely text from one of such lowly status is bound to show "a most pitiful ambition." The clown's role is to stay in his place, to confirm the superiority of his betters by his own submissive inferiority, to speak only when written for. Acting on his own, the clown appropriates the stage in a way inimical to the play and its necessary questions. Robert Weimann has called the clown's stage the *platea* and the author's the *locus.*[56] The *platea* Weimann identifies as the downstage area where the clown talks to and with the audience. The *platea* is a place of open exchange and improvisation, a place where the actor speaks more than is set down for him. In the upstage *locus,* the actors keep to the script. They imitate a written and iterable action. They do not take part in a unique and unpredictable event. On the *platea* ultimate authority belongs to the actor. In the *locus* it belongs to the author. From the author's perspective, the perspective Hamlet adopts in his instructions to the players, the *platea* is an illicit space, a space given over to unauthorized speech and action. In this respect the author's perspective was shared by the state. Without a fixed text, official censorship could have no effect.[57] The unitary voice of the author and the unitary voice of the state would gladly combine to exclude the clown's disruptive and discordant improvisation.

Improvisation did nevertheless flourish. It was the distinguishing mark of Tarlton, Wilson, and the players' theater to which they belonged. Though Tarlton and Wilson both produced scripts, both were especially admired for their "extemporal wit" (*ES* 2.342–45 and 349–50). And even in the 1590s some accommodation was made for impromptu clowning. Shakespeare wrote parts for Kemp—including the part of Falstaff—that conveyed an "improvisation effect" even as they eliminated the real thing. But, more important, in Shakespeare's theater, as in the competing theater of the Admiral's Men, a segment of each afternoon's entertainment was reserved specifically for that real thing, for the clown and his disruptive kind of playmaking. Following the dictates of the script, Cade may have been killed and Falstaff banished, but the clown returned triumphantly to the stage—a stage made all *platea*—to perform in a genre of his own, the stage jig. The alternation of carnival and Lent was thus maintained in defiance of the play's exclusionary, killjoy plot. And the people kept a place in the show, for the jig was a resolutely plebeian form, unfit, according to *An Invective against Tarlton's News out of Purgatory* (1590), "for gentlemen's humors."[58]

Tarlton himself seems to have established the theatrical jig. An anecdote from his *Jests* gives an idea of at least one of its elements. "I remember," writes the anonymous narrator, "I was once at a play in the country, where, as Tarlton's use was, the play being done, everyone so pleased to throw up his theme" (p. 28). These "themes" were pointed bits of verse, aimed often at Tarlton himself, to which he responded extemporaneously in a similarly aggressive vein. Drumming and satiric song were also part of his usual performance. Kemp inclined rather to dance and brief skits, a few of which found their way into print. In his great study of the Elizabethan jig, C. R. Baskervill lists the following titles, all of which were entered in the Stationers' Register between 1591 and 1595:

A New Northern Jig
The Second Part of the Jig between Rowland and the Sexton
The Third and Last Part of Kemp's Jig
A Merry New Jig between Jenkin the Collier and Nancy
A Ballad of Cutting George and his Hostess, being a Jig
A Pleasant Jig between a Tinker and a Clown
Kemp's Pleasant New Jig of the Broomman
Master Kemp's New Jig of the Kitchen-Stuff Woman
Phillips his Jig of the Slippers
*A Pretty New Jig between Francis the Gentlemen, Richard the Farmer,
  and their Wives*
Kemp's New Jig betwixt a Soldier and a Miser and Sim the Clown.[59]

From these titles alone, the strongly plebeian cast of the jig, Kemp's conspicuous association with it, and its probable lack of any direct connection with the plays that it followed should be evident. What the national history play with its increasingly élitist conception of the nation defeated, banished, or merely marginalized found its place in the jig: the broomman, the kitchen-stuff woman, the tinker, the collier, the farmer, the sexton, and the clown. Whether it favored singing or dancing, extemporaneous jesting or scripted comic wooing, the jig maintained the people's representation in the theater, giving them an independent last word in every performance.

Abundant evidence testifies to the enormous popularity of the jig, but there is also considerable evidence that the jig was anathema to the new authors' theater. Marlowe seems to have been thinking specifically of Tarlton when he inveighed against "the *jigging* veins of riming mother wits," and his successors, whether Marston ironically proclaiming that "the orbs celestial / Will dance Kemp's jig" or Guilpin stating more flatly that "whores, beadles, bawds, and sergeants filthily / Chant Kemp's jig," make their disapproval of Kemp still more explicit. Within a year of Kemp's departure from the chamberlain's company, Brutus invokes the jig to mark the distinction between soldiers and poets, "What should the wars do with these jigging fools" (4.3.137), and Hamlet uses it to characterize Polonius's poor taste, "He's for a jig or a tale of bawdry, or he sleeps" (2.2.500–501). Among partisans of the authors' theater, the jig continued to serve as a sign of difference for decades. In the dedication of *Catiline* (1611), Jonson praises the earl of Pembroke for countenancing "a legitimate poem" in "these jig-given times," and Massinger lets it be known that his *Roman Actor* (1626) is not for those who prize jigs:

"If the gravity and height of the subject distaste such as are only affected with jigs and ribaldry, as I presume it will, their condemnation of me and my poem can in no way offend me: my reason teaching me, such malicious and ignorant detractors deserve rather contempt than satisfaction."[60]

No less significant historically than these verbal gestures was the physical separation of the authors' theater from the jig. The jig had never had a place in the private playhouses, and after Kemp's departure it disappeared from the repertory of the Chamberlain's Men—which, given that his departure coincided with the move to the Globe, means that the Globe was in all likelihood a theater unsullied by the jig.[61] Was that why Kemp left? Was the author's theater and the hegemony of the script clamping down on him? Was that what the shift from the north of London to the Bankside meant to the clown? Three years earlier, the Chamberlain's Men had tried to establish themselves at the Blackfriars, but the attempt had been defeated by protests from the genteel inhabitants of that neighborhood. Had the company been successful, there would presumably have been no jig at their indoor theater, as there was none when they finally got to the Blackfriars in 1608. Clearly, they were hoping to move in a direction that would leave Kemp and his specialty behind. Did that move begin when they went to the Globe? If so, it is not surprising that Kemp should have chosen to remain in the north London theaters where the jig and its lower-class audience were still welcome.[62]

The fate of the jig is just one more indication of the alienation of the clown from the playwright, of the players' theater from the authors' theater, of the people from the nation and its canonical self-representations. In a recent paper, David Scott Kastan has nicely suggested the relation between the order of the play and the order of the state.

> The professional clown competes with the authorial voice for attention and control, producing a dialogic text in place of the monological scripted play. The formal unity that could be achieved only by subordinating subplot to main plot, commoners to aristocrats, comedy to history, by imposing, that is, the same hierarchies of privilege and power that exist in the state upon the play, is ruptured by the clown's refusal to be subordinated to the serious plot. His presence serves to counter the totalizing fantasies of power, to destabilize the hierarchies upon which they depend.[63]

Like many critics, Kastan wants to keep Shakespeare and the two parts of *Henry IV* on the dialogic side of this opposition. Hal banishes

Falstaff, Kastan would argue, the play doesn't. On one level, this is unquestionably true. Just as Annabel Patterson's "peasant ideology" is repeated every time *The Contention* is staged, so Falstaff reappears in every production of either part of *Henry IV.* He remains an integral and inalienable part of the play. And the popular, festive values he represents continue, through him, to exercise their power. The widespread, though far from universal, preference for Falstaff over Hal— the feeling that in banishing Falstaff Hal has indeed banished "all the world" (2.4.480)—is clear evidence of that power. If this be the condition for the establishment of orderly rule, say many spectators and readers, orderly rule isn't worth having. But it is also true that from his first appearance in *Part One* Falstaff is under suspended sentence. He is there to be banished. And that is Shakespeare's doing as much as it is Hal's. Shakespeare's play participates with Hal in a rite of exclusion that breaks the rhythmic alternation of carnival and Lent; it shares Hal's totalizing fantasy of power; it subordinates subplot to main plot, commoners to aristocrats, comedy to history. The proof of that participation is not, however, to be found in the text itself, which oscillates constantly in our apprehension of it according to the inclination of our tastes and interests. It is to be found rather in the events that surround and include the text: in the attempt Shakespeare and his company made to secure a private playhouse closer to the center of fashion and government, in their actual move from Shoreditch to the Globe, in the disappearance of Will Kemp from the company and the jig from its repertory, in the transformation of Shakespeare himself from player to author. Like the banishment of Falstaff, all those events both depend on and reaffirm the hierarchies of power and privilege that carnival and the plebeian clown sometimes reinforced but could also destabilize. By including Falstaff, the play maintained its stake in a popular theater that mingled kings and clowns, a theater that could imagine a political nation comprising both high and low. But in banishing him, it awoke and despised that dream.

Henry IV is not an allegory, certainly not an autobiographical allegory. Hal is not Shakespeare; Falstaff is not Kemp. But if one thinks of Falstaff as figuring many of the elements of the players' theater, particularly as it existed in the late 1580s when Shakespeare began his dramatic career, and of Hal as incorporating some of the attitudes and experiences of the newer authors' theater, a significant and signifying congruence between the play world and the theater world does emerge. Even this congruence is no allegory. Or, if it is, it is my allegory rather than Shakespeare's. The two parts of *Henry IV* are not *about* the theatrical situation in the late 1590s. They were *produced by* that situation. Their terms are its terms. In these plays Shakespeare and his company enacted a set of cultural oppositions that concerned them as men of the theater as much as they concerned the politic Hal. Like Hal, they had long been remembering "the poor creature, small beer" (*2HIV*, 2.2.10–11), and, again like him, they had reason to be ashamed of that remembrance. For both, the sense of a potentially redeeming national destiny conflicted—or seemed to conflict—with their continuing attachment to popular manners and popular politics, with their continuing attachment to the people. Hal's exclusionary act wasn't yet Shakespeare's or that of his company. But given what was to happen in the next few years, it seems likely that they were seriously trying it out.[64]

Losing the Common Touch

Shortly after his final appearance as Falstaff, Will Kemp danced "out of the world" and into a printed text. He left the Globe and became the author of a book celebrating his own heroic deeds. *Kemp's Nine-Days' Wonder* (1600) tells of the morris-dancing progress the ex-chamberlain's man made from London to Norwich, a feat of strength and endurance without precedent. Here Kemp goes solo. He frees himself from the theater and the script to do his own thing in his own way. But if we open the *Nine-Days' Wonder* expecting to find a Jack Cade or Jack Falstaff or even a latter-day Dick Tarlton finally liberated from the tyranny of the text, we will be disappointed. Outside the theater the clown is still less a figure of popular insurrection, still more firmly directed by the exigencies of professional performance, than he was in his scripted roles. There are, of course, memories of carnival in Kemp's book, as there were in the event it commemorates. The morris itself has such associations. And when Kemp introduces himself as "Cavaliero Kemp, headmaster of morris dancers, high headborough of heighs, and only tricker of your trill-lills, and best bell-shangles between Sion and Mount Surrey," we may for a moment think of the self-dubbed "Cavaliero" Spicing, Falconbridge's rebellious compan-ion in Heywood's *Edward IV*, and of other usurping, carnivalesque lords of misrule. But this thought does not last long. Unlike Spicing and the others, Cavaliero Kemp is no rebel. He is not even particularly unruly, as the remainder of his self-introductory sentence makes clear. "I . . . began," he says, "frolicly to foot it from the right honorable the lord mayor's of London towards the right worshipful and truly bountiful master mayor's of Norwich."[65] Kemp's dance is bounded by established and respected authority, authority that legitimates and rewards his performance.

Kemp takes over the popular to make it the ground for a new kind of popularity, that of the popular celebrity, the famous entertainer. His morris does not depend on any communal festivity, whether carnival, May Day, or midsummer. Nor is it linked to any social disturbance or protest. He begins his dance on what, in traditional terms, might seem a most unlikely day, the first Monday of Lent, and continues it on-and-off over the next several weeks with no particular regard for the holiday calendar. Instead of expressing holiday merriment or rebellious discontent, Kemp's morris is a measured and certified (he brings along an "overseer" for the purpose) athletic accomplishment, widely advertised in advance and designed to draw large and generous crowds. As a popular song said of his later dance across the Alps,

> He took pains
> To skip it.
> In hope of gains
> He will trip it.[66]

In other ways too, Kemp's performance distinguishes itself from the familiar inversionary pattern of popular festivity. Where the usual lord of misrule has a Falstaffian appetite for food and drink, Kemp prides himself on his sobriety and moderation. "My only desire was to refrain drink and be temperate in my diet" (p. 11). And where the usual lord of misrule scoffs at the law, Kemp is its arch-defender. When a group of thieves are taken in the crowd that greets Kemp in the town of Burntwood, he helps finger them and tells how he and his fellow players would punish such malefactors. "I justly denied their acquaintance," he says, "saving that I remembered one of them to be a noted cutpurse, such a one as we tie to a post on our stage for all people to wonder at when at a play they are taken pilfering" (p. 9). Kemp's only rivalry with a figure of the law again marks his difference from the unruly characters he played (or may have played) on stage. Dancing into Bury on a Saturday afternoon "at what time the right honorable the lord chief justice entered at another gate of the town, the wondering and regardless multitude, making his honor clear way, left the streets where he past to gape at me" (p. 17). One recalls Falstaff's competition with another chief justice in *2 Henry IV* and Jack Cade's enmity toward the whole legal profession in *The Contention*. But where Falstaff and Cade would make their own anarchic will the law

of England, Kemp merely counts the crowd. Though Kemp's commercialism, like the commercialism of the public theater, may in the
long run have been more radically disruptive than any popular revolt,
its aim was to profit by the system rather than to change it. If Kemp
and the players' theater he represented were rivals of Shakespeare and
the emerging authors' theater, they were rivals in a shared transformation of the popular into the commercial.

Still, there is a significant difference between the move Shakespeare
and his company made, first to the Globe and then to the Blackfriars,
and the move Kemp made. For all Kemp's hobnobbing with gentlemen, the crowd that followed him on his dance from London to
Norwich remained largely popular. And it was still a popular audience
that filled the playhouses where he performed when he returned to
London. That difference in audience was, moreover, matched by a
difference in the plays the audience saw. According to David Wiles,
the repertory of the company Kemp joined after leaving the
Chamberlain's Men was "markedly un-Shakespearean." "While
Shakespeare tends to legitimate heredity and the preservation of an
aristocratic order," plays put on by the newly organized Worcester's
Men, plays like *Sir Thomas Wyatt* (1602), *The Royal King and the
Loyal Subject* (1602), and *Sir John Oldcastle* (1599), "offer as hero a
man of the people at odds with the monarchy" (p. 40). Of particular
interest on Wiles's list of examples is *Sir John Oldcastle*. Here, after all,
is an English history play written specifically to correct a play by
Shakespeare in which Kemp himself had taken the offending part. *Sir
John Oldcastle* aims to restore the reputation of the proto-Protestant
martyr whose name had been used by Shakespeare for the character
who became Falstaff. "It is no pampered glutton we present," declares
the prologue,

> Nor aged counselor to youthful sin,
> But one whose virtue shone above the rest,
> A valiant martyr and a virtuous peer,
> In whose true faith and loyalty expressed
> Unto his sovereign and his country's weal,
> We strive to pay that tribute of our love
> Your favors merit.[67]

"True faith and loyalty" hardly sounds like Wiles's "man of the people
at odds with the monarchy." But if neither the titular hero of *Sir John
Oldcastle* nor the play itself opposes monarchy—and neither does—
both do nevertheless represent a very different understanding of En-

glish history and the English polity than do Shakespeare's history plays, an understanding that finds an echo both in many other plays produced at the theaters Henslowe controlled and in the popular narrative traditions that inform those plays.

One version of that difference has been described by Anne Barton in "The King Disguised: Shakespeare's *Henry V* and the Comical History."[68] Barton compares Henry's incognito visit to his troops on the eve of Agincourt with scenes from other history plays in which a disguised or unrecognized king meets his common subjects. *Sir John Oldcastle* furnishes one such example, Henry V's encounter with the clownish highwayman-priest, Sir John of Wrotham, the part Kemp would presumably have taken if he acted, as Wiles suggests he did, in this play. Other examples come from the anonymous *George a Greene, the Pinner of Wakefield* (1590), from Peele's *Edward I* (1591), and from Heywood's *Edward IV.*[69] What distinguishes Shakespeare's rendition of the scene from these others is the complete lack of rapport between his king and the commons. The Chorus in *Henry V* may effuse about the cheering effect of "a little touch of Harry in the night," but what we actually see is a bristling exchange between a defensive king and his acutely critical soldiers. Where the soldiers firmly define the king's responsibility for the men he has led into war, the king chops logic to evade responsibility. The scene thus represents antagonism, a clear difference of interests, rather than commonality between top and bottom, and it leads, as Barton remarks, to "Henry's only soliloquy in the play: a bitter examination of kingship itself and of the irremovable barriers isolating the monarch from a world of private men" (p. 92). Questioning such barriers—indeed, overcoming them—is precisely the function of the disguised king scenes in the other plays. Sir John of Wrotham, George a Greene, and Hobs, the tanner of Tamworth, meet their monarchs on terms of easy familiarity and likeness. And even in Peele's *Edward I,* Prince Lluellen of Wales, himself disguised as Robin Hood, establishes for a moment a kind of camaraderie with his enemy of England who comes in disguise to visit his greenwood haunt.

The mention of Robin Hood suggests the obvious source of these scenes. They come from the tradition of popular balladry. Robin Hood had been the favorite subject of English ballads as least as far back as the fourteenth century; George a Greene and the tanner of Tamworth had made ballad appearances as well; and Sir John of Wrotham, in his outlawry, his identity as a jolly wenching priest, and his chance encounter with the king, conforms to a familiar ballad type.[70] In English ballads, meetings of unrecognized kings and their subjects are particularly frequent. Edward I's encounter with Prince Lluellen in Peele's play merely recreates a visit another English king had paid to Robin Hood in the seventh and eighth fits of the "Gest of Robin Hood." Other ballads tell of similar meetings between King Alfred and a shepherd, Henry II and a miller, Edward I and a reeve, Henry VIII and a cobbler, James I and a tinker, William III and a forester.[71] "Conversations of this sort represent," Barton claims, "a fantasy . . . of a victimized agrarian class" (p. 97). They owe their popularity to a persistent illusion that the king, as the beneficent fount of justice, would right the people's wrongs if only he knew of them. But in the ballads and the plays that derive from them, the righting of wrongs is rarely at issue. More than a dream of justice, these stories represent a dream of commonality, of common interests and common humanity, between the ruler and the ruled. They denaturalize class difference and claim the king as one of their own.

But whatever the dream, Shakespeare's play unequivocally denies it. His king, despite a long apprenticeship in the taverns of London where he learned to "drink with any tinker in his own language during [his] life," is aware only of difference, and difference is what the audience sees enacted on stage. King Hal does not remember Falstaff, whose heart he has "killed" with neglect, does not remember Bardolph, whom he orders executed for petty thievery, and scarcely remembers his own humanity, which is squeezed to almost nothing by the burden, as he likes to think of it, of his office. He is a man who can threaten a defenseless town with rape and slaughter, can promise "shrill-shrieking daughters," "fathers taken by the silver beards, / And their most reverend heads dashed to the walls," "naked infants spitted upon pikes" (3.3.118–21), can actually order his soldiers to slit the throats of their prisoners—can do all this and still blame the victims. He is the centerpiece of what Barton chooses to call "tragical history." If one thinks of the radical divorce this play enacts between the king and his people, between the king and that part of himself that might share in the most fundamental concerns of the people, the play is indeed tragic. But in another, more familiar sense, "tragedy" is a very odd term to apply to *Henry V.* This is, after all, a great success story, the story of a triumphant "star of England." And the story ends in traditional comic fashion with a marriage.

No less odd is Barton's term for the other plays she discusses. She calls them "comical histories." *Comical* fits the meetings of the disguised kings and their subjects well enough. Those encounters are high-spirited and even funny. But in a broader sense only one of the plays, *George a Greene,* seems much like a comedy. The others are more nearly tragic in their narrative design. In Peele's *Edward I,* the Robin-Hoodlike Lluellen is killed in a battle with the English king, and the play results in the deaths of several of its other most attractive characters. The central figures of Heywood's *Edward IV,* Jane and Matthew Shore, die an excruciatingly painful death after long and unjustly inflicted suffering. And the protagonist of *Sir John Oldcastle* is headed for a still more explicit martyrdom, a martyrdom we are spared only by the disappearance of the second part of the play. And even in the part that has survived, Oldcastle's sufferings occupy the greater share of the action. Why would one call such plays comical?

For Barton *tragical* and *comical* are terms of value. Tragical is better than comical, just as Shakespeare is better than Peele, Heywood, Munday, Dekker, and Chettle. Tragical history is more "serious," "more consequential," "far more ironic and complicated" (pp. 116, 117, 99). Where comical history naively blinds itself with "wistful" illusion, the illusion that the king can or should share in the humanity of his common subjects, its tragical counterpart sees things as they are, sees the falseness of that illusion. Comical history is "attractive but untrue: a nostalgic but false romanticism" (p. 99). Unblinkered tragical history is mature and realistic. To argue this way is to accept as necessary and inevitable the very exclusion Shakespeare and his company put on stage, the exclusion of the common people both from the English nation and from what would come to be recognized as the canonical literature of that nation. Comical history, as Barton characterizes it, belongs to a distant and largely forgotten popular culture. It is recalled only to reaffirm by its difference the superiority of Shakespeare. Tragical history belongs to universal literature. It represents and participates in the sad, hard truths of power—and, in so doing, it triumphs. Barton records the triumph, celebrates it, perpetuates it. She names Shakespeare's English history plays "tragical" so as to reassert their canonicity. As for the comical histories, once they have served their purpose in this never-ending renewal of hierarchy, a hierarchy that is both literary and political, they can be sent back to the oblivion their "anachronistic ethos" so properly merits (p. 117).

Let's for a moment resist this easy condemnation. Barton is right. There *is* a broad and consistent difference between Shakespeare's representation of English history and the way that history gets represented by the dramatists who wrote for Henslowe. But the difference is not between tragedy and comedy. Shakespeare's English history plays are no more or less tragical or comical than the history plays produced by the Admiral's Men or Lord Worcester's Men. What then is the difference? What interests are we preferring when we prefer Shakespeare? Shakespeare's history plays are concerned above all with the consolidation and maintenance of royal power. The history plays Henslowe paid for give their attention to the victims of such power. Kings and their aristocratic rivals are what the audiences at Shakespeare's history plays see most. In the work of Munday, Chettle, Heywood, Dekker, and their collaborators, common people and their upperclass champions occupy the central place.

Disguised king scenes are one mark of the ballad-inspired histories, but they are only one such mark, and not the most frequent or most telling. These plays—and once we drop the disguised king scene as their single identifying trait the list can be greatly expanded—repeatedly focus on a character who is intensely loyal to the reigning monarch, who has a special relation to the common people, and who suffers as a victim of power. Sir John Oldcastle is such a figure, and so are Jane and Matthew Shore in Heywood's *Edward IV*. In *Sir Thomas Wyatt*, Lady Jane Grey, Guilford Dudley, and Wyatt himself, whose English patriotism finally proves more hardy than even his loyalty to Queen Mary, all show marks of the type, as does the Marshal in Heywood's pseudo-history *The Royal King and the Loyal Subject*. One might also list Robert, earl of Huntington, and his beloved Matilda in Munday and Chettle's two *Robin Hood* plays (1598), More in *The Book of Sir Thomas More*, Cranmer in Rowley's *When You See Me, You Know Me* (1604), and Princess Elizabeth in the first part of Heywood's *If You Know Not Me, You Know Nobody* (1604). Before the advent of the Admiral's Men, Thomas of Woodstock anticipated the type in the anonymous play that usually goes under his name (1592), and bits of it can be found in various characters in *Edward I* and *George a Greene*. This figure even had an early adumbration in Shakespeare, who may, in any case, have spent some time early in the 1590s working in the Henslowe environment.[72] The good Duke Humphrey, around whom cluster, as we have seen, a set of popular political values that have little place in Shakespeare's subsequent history plays, combines the loyalty, the suffering, and the common touch. But for Shakespeare this was a false start, a "comical" beginning, in Barton's term, to a series of plays that quickly turned "tragical." For the Henslowe playwrights, this was where they remained. More than civil war or foreign conquest (the favorite topics of Shakes-

peare), the innocent suffering of common people and their defenders
continued to preoccupy these dramatists. This was the experience that
governed their representation of England and its history.

Only a careful reading of a great many of these plays, both the
Shakespearean and the non-Shakespearean ones, can give a full appre-
ciation of how deep and pervasive their differences are. But comparing
Richard of Gloucester as he appears in Shakespeare's *Richard III* and
Heywood's *2 Edward IV* will furnish a quick sense of the most obvious differences. Both Richards are villains, but only Shakespeare's
delights and captivates us with his villainy. Shakespeare's play shares
Richard's fascination with power, his Machiavellian desire to domi-
nate. It makes us complicit in actions we know we should abhor.
Though Heywood occasionally imitates the crackling Ricardian rhet-
oric Shakespeare made so appealing, the magnetic thrill is gone.
Heywood's Richard, like his King Edward, is a pale and marginal
figure, certainly not the focal point of the play's emotional energy.
That place is reserved for the victims of royal power, for Jane and
Matthew Shore and the common people who befriend them. In *Richard III*, Shore's wife is the subject of a salacious running joke. In
Edward IV, she is the moral and affective center of the play, a character
who, in her appeal to the audience, overshadows the kings who seduce
and torment her. Similar differences show up when other same-reign
plays are set next to each other. Whether in defeat or in victory,
Shakespeare's Richard II and Henry V dominate the plays we know by
their names. The deposition of the first and the conquests of the
second provide the pathos and exhilaration that give the plays their
emotional force. But in *Woodstock*, Richard II is no more compelling
a figure than Edward IV or Richard III are in Heywood's *Edward IV*.
And in *Sir John Oldcastle*, Henry V gets still less attention. Instead of
reproducing Shakespeare's infatuation with kingly power, an infatuation that is often shadowed but never overcome by moral disapproval,
these plays eschew ambition and concern themselves with lower-
ranked characters who try to maintain their integrity, characters who
work to mitigate the effects of power on the common people. Like
Jane Shore, Woodstock and Oldcastle are mediators between the king
and the commons, and, again like her, they suffer for their virtuous
interference. Sympathy with that suffering, an emotion that has gotten these plays the reputation of being sentimental, rather than the
heady excitement of mystified kingship, is what they offer.

Even when the individual person of the king is less prominent, as in
the two parts of *Henry IV*, Shakespeare still keeps attention focused

on the monarchic office. Hal, Hotspur, and Falstaff, who claim our interest and sympathy in something of the way that Richard III, Richard II, and Henry V do, each represent the king. Taking turns playing the king in a mock meeting of father and son, Hal and Falstaff literally assume the king's part, but, as numerous critics have pointed out, all three also perform that role figuratively. Indeed, the two plays can easily be seen as a tightly woven tissue of analogical relations linking the four main characters—the king, the prince, the chief rebel, and the festive lord of misrule—to one another and to the king's deposed predecessor, Richard II. "For all the world," says King Henry to his son when they do actually meet,

> As thou art to this hour was Richard then
> When I from France set foot at Ravenspurgh,
> And even as I was then is Percy now. (*1HIV* 3.2.93–96)

But if Hal is like Richard in appearance, he more closely resembles his father in substance, a point the play has already established by having the two unconsciously echo one another's lines.[73] As for Falstaff, he is both a Richardlike prodigal and a Henrylike surrogate father to Hal: in both guises the designated, if unwilling, scapegoat in a sophisticated mimetic ritual. The narrative logic and figurative analogic of *1* and *2 Henry IV,* the syntagmatic and the paradigmatic planes of the two plays, concern the king, particularly in his impersonal corporate "body," almost exclusively. In this sense, whatever Falstaff's part may owe to traditions of popular festivity and improvisational clowning, Fat Jack stands less for any genuinely "common" other than for a negative permutation of power itself.

The same could not be said of the two Sir Johns, Sir John Oldcastle and Sir John of Wrotham, in the Henslowe company's answer to Shakespeare's Henriad. Rather than standing for the king, these characters, like the protagonists and clowns in Henslowe's other English history plays, stand apart from him. They meet the king on terms of significant and sympathetic difference, express loyalty to him from a position that is not simply an analogue of his own, suffer the effects of his sometimes misguided power as distinct subjects in their own abused right. What assimilation does take place in the Henslowe plays tends to move in the opposite direction from that in their Shakespearean counterparts—not the assimilation of the subject into the mystic body of the king but rather the assimilation of the king into the body of the people, as when Sir John of Wrotham companionably reminds the disguised King Henry of the king's thieving youth. Similar moments occur in other non-Shakespearean plays, in, for example, the meetings of three different King Edwards in three different plays with George a Greene, Lluellen/Robin Hood, and Hobs, the tanner of Tamworth. Such discovery of the commoner within the king is the function of the disguised king scenes. It is a discovery fundamentally at odds with Shakespeare's history plays, which remove the king from the people, mingling kings and clowns only when the latter can function as a type of the former, a lord of misrule whose banishment will effect the cleansing of the monarchic body and realm.

The disguised king scenes depend, as Barton argues, on ballads and other "folk" literature. But so do the scenes of suffering. Jane and Matthew Shore were as much ballad figures as was Hobs.[74] Their lamentations circulated in the same popular broadside format as did the story of his meeting with the disguised King Edward. Other broadside ballads recounted the sorrows of fair Rosamond, the Jane Shore of an earlier reign, told the grisly tale of Queen Elinor, a central figure in Peele's *Edward I*, repeated the plaints of Princess Elizabeth, Jane Grey, Guilford Dudley, Thomas Wyatt, and many other victims of Catholic persecution, and assimilated to their familiar patterns even figures of contemporary controversy. Immediately after his execution, the earl of Essex could be heard in numerous ballads, of which at least four have survived, lamenting his fate and protesting his love of both queen and commons.[75] To judge from these poems, Essex was another Gloucester, Woodstock, More, Oldcastle, or Huntington, a virtuous mediator between crown and people struck down by the inscrutable violence of power. In the ballad tradition, preoccupation with oppression and innocent suffering dates back at least to the fourteenth-century songs of Robin Hood and his outlaw band. These poems, like their sixteenth-century descendants, consistently position themselves on the side of the people. They thus provide a "people's history of England" in two senses: they were the history commoners heard and knew, and they were history from a commoner's point of view.[76] It is this people's history that the Henslowe companies staged. Their England and the England of the ballads were essentially the same.

Elizabethan ballads and plays do, however, differ from their medieval predecessors in eliminating any effective recourse to armed protest. There are no Robin Hoods, no outlaw righters of wrongs, in the later period. Not even Robin Hood himself, when he reappears in the noble guise of the earl of Huntington in the plays of Munday and Chettle, acts the violent part he played in the fourteenth- and fifteenth-century ballads. On stage, Wyatt's revolt is quickly put down. In the other plays, the central figures are not rebels but rather enemies of rebellion. George a Greene defends King Edward against the rebellious earl of Kendal; Woodstock, though sympathetic with the people's grievances, opposes the men of Kent and Essex when they rise up against Richard II; Matthew Shore fights valiantly against Falconbridge and his peasant band; Thomas More halts the Ill May Day uprising of the citizens of London; Sir John Oldcastle reveals the treachery of Cambridge, Scroop, and Grey and undermines the popular rebellion led in his name by Marley, the comic brewer; and even Sir Thomas Wyatt, before his own rebellion, is instrumental in defeating Northumberland and Suffolk in their attempt to supplant Queen Mary with Lady Jane Grey. Nor is the pattern that associates the commoners and their champions with the defense against rebellion limited to these plays. Though *Jack Straw* is not otherwise much like the Henslowe histories, it anticipates them in making a commoner, the lord mayor of London, the central figure in the defeat of rebellion. And in *The Contention* Shakespeare does something of the same sort when he has Alexander Iden, a yeoman of Kent, kill Jack Cade.[77] "Commons' love," as one of the characters in Peele's *Edward I* says, "is the strength / And sureness of the richest commonwealth."[78] Love and loyalty, rather than any effective resistance to royal power, is what these plays display. But in them the commons' love must often be maintained in the face of much abuse.

The central problematic of Shakespeare's history plays concerns the consolidation of monarchic rule. Legitimacy and efficacy are the main points at issue. Neither is of particular interest to the Henslowe dramatists. Their plays lack the elaborate genealogies that are such a prominent feature in all of Shakespeare's English histories. And they pay almost no attention to the strategies by which power is achieved and maintained. Even in Heywood's *Edward IV,* where a popular revolt is raised in the name of the deposed King Henry VI, the dominant attitude of the play accords with that of the Hobs, the tanner of Tamworth. "I am just akin to Sutton Windmill," Hobs tells the disguised King Edward. "I can grind which way soe'er the wind blow. If it be Harry, I can say, 'Well fare Lancaster.' If it be Edward, I can sing, 'York, York, for my money.'"[79] Hobs shares the instinctive and indiscriminate loyalty of the balladeers for whom every king, regardless of lineage or personal qualities, is "our king." Were such indifference universal, Shakespeare's history plays would lose their interest and their point. That they have not done so is testimony not only to

Shakespeare's remarkable artistry but also to our continuing fascination, despite large changes in the constitutional order, with the dynamics of power.[80]

But while achieving his obsessive and compelling focus on the
ruler, Shakespeare excluded another object of concern, the ruled.
Identifying himself, his plays, his company, and his audience with the
problematics of early modern kingship, he left out of consideration
the no less pressing problematics of subjecthood. To what extent can
the subject maintain a degree of autonomy and individual or communal integrity in the face of the growing power of the monarchic state?
This is an issue the Henslowe dramatists return to in play after play.
Caught between their loyalty to the crown and their adherence to a set
of values that the crown regularly violated, the protagonists of the
Henslowe history plays repeatedly find themselves forced into making
choices where either alternative is equally ruinous. Jane and Matthew
Shore, Robert, earl of Huntington, Sir John Oldcastle, Sir Thomas
More, the Marshal in Heywood's *Royal King and Loyal Subject,* and
Sir Thomas Wyatt are all obliged to choose in this way, and all but the
Marshal eventually die as a result of their choice. These plays are not
unconcerned with monarchic power. But, unlike Shakespeare's history plays, they represent such power from the point of view of those
who suffer its harshest consequences. Speaking over the dead body of
his wife an instant before his own death, Matthew Shore expresses
both the pain and the powerlessness of this familiar situation. "Oh,
unconstant world," he laments,

> Here lies the true anatomy of thee.
> A king had all my joy, that her enjoyed,
> And by a king again she was destroyed.
> All ages of my kingly woes shall tell.
> Once more, unconstant world, farewell, farewell. (1.189)

The kings are to blame, but kings are no more liable to retaliation than
the inconstant world. Effective resistance is impossible—indeed, unthinkable. Even at this point, Shore remains as loyal as he was ten acts
earlier when, in defense of King Edward's right, he fought
Falconbridge and the other rebels. But he is loyal to a power that
shares none of his bourgeois values, a power that has invaded and
destroyed his urban, domestic, and artisanal world, a power that has
more in common with the rebels than it has with him and his fellow
Londoners.

Like Sir Thomas More, Matthew Shore is a citizen of London. Sir

Thomas Wyatt and Sir John Oldcastle are Protestant or proto-Protestant martyrs. The situation of the citizen and the Protestant—both figures who identify strongly with the nation and its ruler but both of whom are intent on keeping some part of themselves and their community free from the encroachment of national power—is central to the Henslowe version of English history. Neither of these figures is of much interest to Shakespeare, at least not in the strongly favorable way characteristic of the Henslowe plays. This difference of interest reinforces those other differences by which Shakespeare and his plays attained their canonical exclusivity. The chief dramatist of the company that became the King's Men achieved his position as England's national poet by what he left out as well as by what he put in. And what he left out was precisely what most interested the dramatists who worked for Henslowe. Was this exclusion the result of a deliberate strategy of self aggrandizement? It is impossible to say. But the omission from Shakespeare's representations of England of a historical perspective associated with popular balladry was itself clearly intended. The opening scenes of *The Contention* show Shakespeare aware of such a perspective, and the disguised king scene in *Henry V* shows him subverting it. The difference that marks his plays, whether that difference was contrived to serve a particular literary and social ambition or not, was conscious and willed. And if that is so, it seems at least reasonable to assume that one departure was meant to facilitate another, that in departing from a popular representation of English history Shakespeare was also departing from a popular theatrical institution.[81] What Barton calls "tragical history" was, we may suppose, designed to serve the purpose it continues to serve in her essay. It was designed to elevate Shakespeare and his art out of the company of the base mechanicals with whom playwriting had inevitably associated him, designed to cleanse the dyer's hand.

Purged from Barbarism

A few years before the closing of the theaters, Richard Brome included the following exchange between a lord and a clown in one of his plays:

> *Lord.*   You, sir, are incorrigible, and
> Take license to yourself to add unto
> Your parts your own free fancy, and sometimes
> To alter or diminish what the writer
> With care and skill composed; and when you are

> To speak to your coactors in the scene,
> You hold interlocutions with the audients.
Clown. That is the way, my lord, has been allowed
> On elder stages to move mirth and laughter.
Lord. Yes, in the days of Tarlton and Kemp,
> Before the stage was purged from barbarism,
> And brought to the perfection it now shines with.
> Then fools and jesters spent their wits, because
> The poets were wise enough to save their own
> For profitabler uses.[82]

From the vantage point of 1630s, "the days of Tarlton and Kemp" could be seen as days of barbarism. Eliminating clownish improvisation had been one way of purging such barbarism, one way of making the stage fit for poets and lords. But it had been only one. Excluding the jig and the ballad had achieved a similar end. And so had the theatrical identification of carnival and traditional festivity with the "people" and the specter of popular revolt. Shakespeare and his English history plays participated in all these symbolic actions of containment and exclusion. They yearned for a "muse of fire," desired "A kingdom for a stage, princes to act, / And monarchs to behold the swelling scene," and set themselves in a very practical way to the work of gentrifying author, actors, audience, and nation. The playwright and his company exchanged their plebeian clown for a courtly fool, moved up the social scale from the Theater to the Globe to the Blackfriars, eliminated the jig from their repertory, gained a privileged place at court, and won the direct patronage of the king. As for the history plays they put on, they subjected commoners to a steady stream of abuse, turned radical protest to ridicule, undermined the sympathetic union of high and low, associated carnival with rebellion and clowns with criminal misrule, mocked or ignored the values of ballad history, and all the while celebrated (even as they questioned) the power and mystery of the crown.

The purging of the English stage from barbarism was, however, part of a much more general purgation. In the three centuries from 1500 to 1800, the aristocracy, the gentry, and the wealthier merchants, clergymen, and professional men of most parts of Europe purged themselves of the popular culture their ancestors had once shared with the lower orders. Peter Burke has called this process "the withdrawal of the upper classes" and has claimed for it an important social function. "As their military role declined," Burke writes, "the nobility had to find other ways of justifying their privileges: they had to show they were different from other people. The polished manners of the nobility were imitated by officials, lawyers, and merchants who wanted to pass for noblemen."[83] The theater was deeply involved in this process. Indeed, theatricality was essential to it. In a society where even aristocrats had to confirm their social identity by playing at being aristocratic, the theater became a school for social advancement and the actor became the very type of self-fashioning mankind. But for the theater and the actor to sustain these informative and paradigmatic roles they had themselves to join in the general upper-class withdrawal. Playhouses became less accessible to the lower classes, audiences became more exclusive, plays became more refined, actors and playwrights became more genteel. Or rather—since not all English playhouses, audiences, plays, actors, or playwrights experienced these elevating changes—some participated in the withdrawal, while others came to stand for that coarse, common, and vulgar culture from which the upper classes were withdrawing. When Shakespeare came to London in the late 1580s, there was, so far as we can tell, no marked social difference between, say, the Theater and the Rose. Both were socially suspect, but both attracted a mixed audience of gentlemen and commoners. By the end of his career, there was just such a difference between the Globe and the Blackfriars on the one hand and the Fortune or the Red Bull on the other, between Shakespeare's company and its rivals. That difference, a difference the new authors' theater had been working to establish at least since the advent of Marlowe and the university wits, provided the material basis for the reclassification of lowly plays as canonical poems. Sorting people into the opposed categories of gentle and common and sorting texts into the opposed categories of literature and trash thus proceeded together and depended on one another.

Enabling—and enabled by—these interlocking processes of social and literary discrimination was the theatrical representation of England. From the 1570s on, the younger Elizabethans had been driven in their writing of England by a sense of national inferiority, of national barbarity. In wondering "why . . . may not we, as else the Greeks, have the kingdom of our own language," Spenser gave expression to this sense. The English language was barbarous. And so was the form of verse most common in England. Ascham had said so with all the authority of his humanistic learning, and many others, both English and foreign, repeated the charge. Similar doubts attached themselves, as we have seen, to English common law. Again the models of civility were to be found elsewhere, in other times and other places. Barbarity reigned at home. And though barbarity was not so specifically the issue, the church too was haunted by the fear that truth and legitimacy might be found in Rome or Geneva more easily than in Canterbury, and proponents of overseas expansion feared the priority and superior strength of Spain. Even the chorographic project began with Camden's attempt to discover beneath the roads and villages of modern England traces of a more civilized Roman Britannia. For all these Elizabethans, the way to an acceptable national self led through self-alienation. They had to know themselves as the barbarous or inferior other, know themselves from the viewpoint of the more refined or more successful cultures of Greece, Rome, and contemporary Europe, before they could undertake the project of national self-making. In this sense, to be English was to be other—both before their work began and after it had been accomplished. Before, it was the otherness of the barbarian, the inferior. After, it was the otherness of the model of civility into which they had projected themselves.

In the theater this process of self-fashioning through self-alienation took a different form. Playwrights and actors expressed less anxiety concerning England and its barbarity, and more concerning the barbarity of the theater itself. If not by birth, then by virtue of the activities in which they were engaged, courtly poets, lawyers, clergymen, antiquaries, landowners, and overseas entrepreneurs were safely beyond the taint of popular association. The Elizabethan theater was popular by its very nature. Its inclusiveness made it suspect. Others could recuperate and value the barbarousness of their pursuits, as Daniel did in his *Defense of Rime* or Coke in his defense of English common law. After all, the Goths, though less cultivated than the Greeks and Romans, were nevertheless noble warriors. No specifically or strongly class-coded objection could be made to their cultural contributions. But a similarly recuperative or revaluative strategy was less easily available to those engaged in elevating the theater to the status of gentility and high art. The popular character of the theater was too obvious, its barbarity too close to home. A more radical corrective was thus required. One can still feel the resulting violence in Marlowe, Jonson, Marston, Chapman, Webster, and the many others who wrote against the theater even while they were writing for it. "O age," they charged, "when every scrivener's boy," "every artist-prentice," "every ballad-monger" might claim the stage as readily as they.[84] It was an age for purgation and withdrawal, not for recuperation and celebration.

Shakespeare's was a more subtle response. He was more deeply engaged with the theater than these other men, more dependent on it, less willing to set himself openly against it. But he did nevertheless participate in both the purgation and the withdrawal. Both are figured in his English history plays. Indeed, the cultural work these plays perform has everything to do with purgation and withdrawal. Yet, oddly, of all the discourses of Elizabethan nationhood we have considered so far, the theatrical is the one that gives greatest access to popular culture and popular political claims. It is in the theater, including the plays of Shakespeare, that we find the still vigorous expression of a radically leveling peasant ideology, in the theater that we find the surviving traces of carnival and clowns. A similar doubleness haunts the Shakespearean representation of monarchy. Shakespeare's history plays present, as do none of the other texts we have encountered, a preeminently royal image of England. The displacements variously effected by Daniel, Spenser, Coke, Camden, Drayton, and Hakluyt may have a counterpart in the history plays produced by the Admiral's Men and Lord Worcester's Men, but not in Shakespeare. For Shakespeare, England is a "sceptered isle," a "royal throne of kings." And yet, as his own contemporaries—indeed, his own plays—objected, the staging of England's royal history "made greatness familiar," subjected kings "to the breath / Of every fool." The exposure of kingship in a narrative and dramatic medium that not only displayed power but revealed the sometimes brutal and duplicitous strategies by which power maintained itself might be thought to subvert the structure of authority it ostensibly celebrated. But though the plays do bear a subversive potential, neither it nor their festive power of inversion have in fact often made themselves felt in any historically disruptive way. Instead, Shakespeare has stood, as he still stands today, for Royal Britain, for a particularly anachronistic state formation based at least symbolically on the monarch and an aristocratic governing class.[85]

Both the doubleness of Shakespeare's English history plays and the preponderantly royalist effect that they have had on England's self-understanding are related to the material conditions out of which they arose. Those plays were written for a theater that was patronized in one way or another by everyone from apprentices and countrymen to the king. Social success meant moving as strongly as possible from one end of this hierarchy of patrons to the other. We sometimes think of Shakespeare's as a moment of unique and irrecoverable equilibrium, a moment in which "Elizabethan players and playmakers succeeded . . . in forging a popular and professional drama that appealed to city, court, and country alike." And we often—and rightly—celebrate the "enormous range of human actions and cultural forms" that Shakespeare and his contemporaries managed to assimilate in their drama: "popular traditions of complaint, satire, and festive misrule; actions and opinions of socially marginal characters and groups—clowns, fools, madmen, transvestites, beggars, children, women; double plots and other aspects of dramatic construction which create social juxtapositions, parallels, and parodies; subversions of linguistic, logical, and social categories by such folk forms as jokes, parables, riddles, and prophecies."[86] But this is to neglect the part Shakespeare and his company took in upsetting that equilibrium, the efforts they made to exclude and to alienate the popular, the socially marginal, the subversive, and the folk. *Popular, marginal, subversive,* and *folk* were the very labels (or modern equivalents of the labels) from which they were striving to free themselves—signs of the barbarism they were purging from the theatrical institution they served, from the nation whose history they so memorably represented, from their own social identity.

No other discursive community I consider in this study was as far removed from the councils of power as the theatrical. Leading aristocrats and their humanist retainers, lawyers and churchmen, landowners and merchant adventurers all had a direct and significant influence on the great affairs of state. Playwrights and actors had little such influence, if any. Yet, because of that distance, their representations of England are at once the most popular and, in the case of those produced by Shakespeare and the Lord Chamberlain's Men, the most exclusively monarchic that his generation has passed on to us. In response to a complex set of conditions that included the artisanal identity of the theater itself, Shakespeare helped establish the new genre of the national history play and then gave that genre a singularity of focus that contributed at once to the consolidation of central power, to the cultural division of class from class, and to the emergence of the playwright—Shakespeare himself—as both gentleman and poet.

APOCALYPTICS AND APOLOGETICS

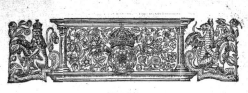

OF
THE LAVVES
of Ecclesiasticall
Politie.

Eyght Bookes.

By Richard Hooker.

Printed at London by *Iohn Windet*, dwelling at the signe of the
Crosse keyes neere Powles Wharffe, and are there
to be soulde

IN EDITION AFTER EDITION, JOHN FOXE'S MASSIVE
and enormously influential *Acts and Monuments* told Elizabethans of
the "trouble and persecution" of "the most valiant and worthy martyr
of Christ, Sir John Oldcastle, knight, Lord Cobham."[1] From Foxe,
Elizabethans learned of Oldcastle's attack in parliament on the papal
hierarchy and its temporal abuses, of his consequent pursuit by the
archbishop of Canterbury and the bishop of Rochester, of his fruitless
appeal to his former patron, King Henry V, of his trial for heresy and
his heroically forthright defense of his faith, of his condemnation,
imprisonment, and escape, of his betrayal and rearrest, of his death on
"the new gallows in St. Giles without Temple Bar . . . hanged and
burned hanging," a scene rendered unforgettable by one of the many
powerfully moving woodcuts that illustrated Foxe's book (fig. 14). Is
this the story Shakespeare imagined for his Sir John Oldcastle as he
began writing what is now *1 Henry IV*? When we look at Foxe's
picture of Oldcastle hanging over the fire, are we seeing the destined
end of Sir John Falstaff, "that roasted Manningtree ox with the pudding in his belly"? Obviously not. As the epilogue to *2 Henry IV* puts
it, "Oldcastle died a martyr, and this is not the man." And yet when
Shakespeare first chose the name and gave the character who bore it
language replete with the telltale phrases of Puritan spirituality, he
must have thought of the martyr. If he was not retelling Oldcastle's
story, if he was not renewing for the stage Foxe's celebration of this
fifteenth-century hero of the faith—and clearly he was not—he was
then mocking both the story and the use to which it had been put.
Mockery was precisely what the Henslowe dramatists (or whoever
commissioned their work) detected in Shakespeare's "Oldcastle"
plays. *The True and Honorable History of the Life of Sir John Oldcastle,*
a play based closely on Foxe, was their answer.

Shakespeare's inclusion/exclusion of the popular and the populace
has another side than the one I examined in the last chapter. The
popular, as Shakespeare represents it, is not only implicated in the
theater's attempt to elevate and purge itself, it is also deeply entangled
in the Elizabethan movement for religious reform. If both Jack Cade's
hard-handed rebels and Sir John Falstaff talk of "laboring in their

14. The martyrdom of Sir John Oldcastle from John Foxe's *Acts and Monuments*
(1563). Huntington Library.

vocation," it is because they share a common puritanical coloration.[2]
Many years ago, Brents Stirling argued that Shakespeare's hostility
toward popular political action was prompted by a fear of religiously
inspired radicalism, a radicalism that was thought to be particularly
prevalent among the lower orders. "Shakespeare's attack upon the
common mass for excesses of leveling, bungling, and instability was,"
Stirling concludes, "typical of a conservative position which sought to
discredit both moderate and extreme dissent."[3] In support of this
argument, he presents a large body of evidence demonstrating the link
defenders of the established church saw (or at least wanted their readers to see) between such lower-class rebels as Jack Cade, Jack Straw,
and Wat Tyler and Puritans, Presbyterians, and Anabaptists. In this
mix the secular and the religious were inevitably confounded. As the
anonymous *Rimes against Martin Marprelate* (1589) has it,
"Martin's mate Jack Straw would always ring / The clergy's faults,
but sought to kill the king." Any attack on the church could thus be
interpreted, and usually was interpreted, as an attack on the state.
Behind the anti-episcopal mask of a critic like Martin Marprelate was,

in the words of Bishop Thomas Cooper's *Admonition to the People of England* (1589), the rebellious face of "Martin Marprince, Marstate, Marlaw, Marmagistrate." In similar fashion, when opponents of Foxe wished to discredit his book, they argued that Oldcastle died a traitor as much as he did a heretic.[4] But if the unveiling could go one way, it could also go the other. Behind the mask of Marstate Cade or Marprince Falstaff, could be seen the face of the Marprelate Martinists and all their schismatic brood. Turning an aristocratic Lollard martyr into a fat, festive, clownish, Bible-quoting thief and lord of misrule was part of a strategy of rhetorical debunking that Shakespeare shared with bishops, archbishops, and a host of clerical and lay supporters of episcopacy.

Shakespeare's English history plays were not simply an intervention in an ecclesiastical dispute. Far more was—and is—going on in them than that. But, as their depiction of Cade and their choice of Oldcastle suggest, religion was not irrelevant to them. In sixteenth-century England, there was very little to which religion was irrelevant. *The Faerie Queene* may be a chivalric romance with all that implies concerning the appropriate distribution of power between monarch and nobles, but for long stretches it is also an apocalyptic allegory heavily dependent on Foxe.[5] Edward Coke may have been one of the staunchest defenders of the legal profession and one of the most assiduous readers of legal literature who has ever lived, but his own personal library contained half again as many books of divinity as it did books of law.[6] And though the Reverend Richard Hakluyt gave more time to his *Voyages* than to his ministry, he saw those *Voyages* as a way of propagating Christianity as well as expanding trade and empire. If one event more than any other determined the extraordinary sixteenth-century outpouring of writing about England—poetic, theatrical, legal, chorographical, historical, antiquarian, mercantile, or whatever—it was the separation of the English church from the church of Rome. And if one issue kept England unsettled both in the sixteenth century and the century to follow, it was the question of church government. In a recent paper, Conrad Russell has looked closely at those men who were active members of parliament in both the 1620s and 1640s to see if positions they took in the earlier decade would allow one to predict the side they would choose later. He examined attitudes regarding court and country, law and liberty, parliamentary privilege, prosecution of recusants, Buckingham, and the petition of right. On none was there a significant correlation between speeches delivered in the 1620s and party allegiance in the 1640s. Only religion provided an element of consistency. In the 1620s, future royalists thought religious reform had gone far enough; future parliamentarians thought it hadn't.[7] And since this was also the single most divisive issue of Elizabeth's reign, one can surmise (though Russell chose not to) that religious differences dating back eighty years and more gave ideological form to a conflict that eventually erupted into war. At the very least, Russell's findings confirm once again the sense that in early modern England the language of politics was most often the language of religion.

If Shakespeare's Henriad, a set of plays ostensibly concerned with the secular order of the English state, had a politico-religious function as well, so, in a far more obvious way, did the play written to answer it, the Henslowe *Sir John Oldcastle*. The exemplary tale of scripturally inspired resistance and martyrdom that Foxe had told and that Shakespeare mocked and strove to suppress is restored by the Henslowe playwrights. But this was not their only staging of Foxe. Rowley's *When You See Me, You Know Me* (1604), Dekker and Webster's *Famous History of Sir Thomas Wyatt* (1604), Heywood's *If You Know Not Me, You Know Nobody* (1605), and Dekker's *Whore of Babylon* (1607) all have a similar provenance.[8] The overlap between these plays and the "popular," "comical," or "ballad" histories I examined in the last chapter is extensive. All but the allegorical *Whore of Babylon* figured in that discussion. Of course, not every popular history took its plot from Foxe, but every Foxian play does share the interests and the values of the popular histories. Suffering at the hands of established power was, after all, both the sign of that dramatic subgenre and Foxe's subject. But the resemblance goes deeper. Like the popular histories, Foxe's book pays unusual attention to commoners. Many of his martyrs, from ancient apostles to modern Protestants, are common laborers and craftsmen. And the persecuting authorities, as Foxe represents them, often worry about the spread of heretical— that is, godly—ideas among the vulgar masses. Such worries are repeatedly expressed in Foxe's account of Oldcastle, where, in addition to being attacked for preaching, teaching, and publishing treatises, Oldcastle's Wycliffite collaborators are blamed for making ballads. Whatever may have been the case in Oldcastle's time, in the last half of the sixteenth century, ballads provided not only a people's history of England but also a people's martyrology, complementing and echoing Foxe's expensive and learned book. So when Henslowe's dramatists began drawing on Foxe, they were not abandoning the kind of history that had informed such earlier, non-Foxian plays as *George a Greene, Edward I, Edward IV, Robert, Earl of Huntington,* or *Sir Thomas More*. They were simply moving to a more religiously marked precinct of the same territory.

Following their lead, I wish to consider those books which represented England's religious and ecclesiastical identity most directly. These fall into two closely related but fundamentally diverse categories: apocalyptic and apologetic.[9] Foxe's *Acts and Monuments* is itself easily the most prominent and influential apocalyptic work. Anglican apologetic began with John Jewel's *Apologia Ecclesiae Anglicanae* (1562) and includes Jewel's *Defense of the Apology* (1570), John Whitgift's *Defense of the Answer to the Admonition* (1574), and John Bridge's *Defense of the Government Established* (1587). But here, too, one work, Richard Hooker's *Of the Laws of Ecclesiastical Polity* (1594–97), towers over the rest. No books, with the obvious exception of the English Bible and the *Book of Common Prayer*, have had a greater part in shaping England's religious self-understanding than Foxe's *Acts* and Hooker's *Laws*. Written at opposite ends of Elizabeth's long reign—Foxe's book in its first decade, Hooker's in its last—both were meant to reinforce the Elizabethan settlement in church and state. Both favor the Protestant separation from Rome; both support the monarch's supreme rule over the church of England; both are attached to an episcopal form of government. Yet in generic form and historical effect they differ markedly, no less markedly than do Shakespeare's history plays from the history plays produced in the Henslowe theaters. *Acts and Monuments* is fundamentally narrative in its structure. Hundreds of individual stories of persecution are subsumed within a larger story of church history based on the Book of Revelation. The *Laws of Ecclesiastical Polity* has a fundamentally argumentative structure. Following an introductory discussion of "laws and their several kinds in general," each of its remaining seven books responds to a specific charge that had been directed against the church of England by advocates of further reform.

Apparently accidental, these differences are in fact systematic. They are determined by profound differences in the historical conditions of production by which these two books came into being, and they have led to equally profound differences in reception. If we take the image of Sir John Oldcastle in torment as standing synecdochically for the true church as Foxe represents it, Hooker can be seen as no less intent than Shakespeare on obscuring that image and replacing it with another more amenable to the claims of stable hierarchy. But where Shakespeare's method shares the narrative design of Foxe and thus risks the kind of reversal that makes Falstaff's banishment a martyrdom, Hooker departs from both. Instead of contributing to the nation's story, he contributes to its thought. Unlike Foxe, Shakespeare, or any other writer I have considered in this book, Hooker has come to be known primarily as a thinker.[10] This difference carries a powerful ideological import. As a discursive genre, thought is no less fraught with meaning than story. I do not mean by this that any particular set of political beliefs is intrinsic to the form of either polemical ratiocination or storytelling—such capacious formal kinds can obviously become the bearers of widely differing meanings—but rather that in the particular historical situation in which Foxe and Hooker wrote, the very forms they adopted assumed a meaning that enforced, altered, or even contradicted their apparent aims. Those forms set the books against one another, making them advocates not for the single Elizabethan settlement both authors favored but for radically differing constructions—one apocalyptic, the other apologetic—of England's religious identity.

Antichrist and the Suffering Elect

Every now and then in the lengthy course of *Acts and Monuments,* Foxe draws attention to an episode he thinks more than usually significant. One of these is the "notable story of a faithful woman burned in Chipping-Sudbury" toward the end of Henry VII's reign by the action of the local diocesan chancellor, one Dr. Whittington. Foxe was unable to discover the woman's name. Nor did he have any information regarding her arrest, the specific beliefs for which she was condemned, or her behavior during her examination and execution. The interest of this story lies elsewhere, in the events that followed her burning. Here is how Foxe tells it:

> The sacrifice being ended, the people began to return homeward, coming from the burning of this blessed martyr. It happened in the meantime that, as the Catholic executioners were busy in slaying this silly lamb at the town's side, a certain butcher within the town was as busy in slaying of a bull, which bull he had fast bound in ropes, ready to knock him on the head. But the butcher (belike not so skillful in his art of killing beasts as the papists be in murdering Christians), as he was lifting his axe to strike the bull, failed in his stroke and smit a little too low, or else how he smit I know not. This was certain, that the bull, although somewhat grieved at the stroke, but yet not stroken down, put his strength to the ropes and brake loose from the butcher into the street, the very same time as the people were coming in great press from

the burning. Who, seeing the bull coming towards them and supposing him to be wild (as was no other like), gave way for the beast, every man shifting for himself as well as he might. Thus the people giving back and making a lane for the bull, he passed through the throng of them, touching neither man nor child, till he came whereas the chancellor was: against whom the bull, as pricked with a sudden vehemency, ran full butt with his horns and taking him upon the paunch gored him through and through and so killed him immediately, carrying his guts and trailing them with his horns all the street over, to the great admiration and wonder of all them that saw it. (4.128)

In the margin, Foxe adds two notes, one at the beginning of the passage, one at the end: "A comparison between butchers and the pope's murdering ministers" and "A rare and special example of the just punishment of God upon a persecutor . . . slain of a bull."

This story presents in stark and violent opposition the Roman church, enforcing its idolatrous beliefs and practices with all the punitive force of the state, and God's divine providence. "What man can be so dull or ignorant," Foxe exclaims, "which seeth not herein a plain miracle of God's mighty power and judgment, both in the punishing of this wretched chancellor, and also in admonishing all other like persecutors by his example to fear the Lord and to abstain from the like cruelty?" Power and judgment on one side answer power and judgment on the other. Misled by its reputation, by its vivid and well-known illustrations, by its popular title, and by dozens of latter-day abridgments, we expect the violence in Foxe's *Book of Martyrs* to go all one way. And certainly there is much to support that expectation. The persecution and martyrdom of those whom Foxe considers members of the true church of Christ are the book's most persistent subject. But God's punishment of persecutors makes a strong countertheme. Not every persecutor suffers, at least not in this world, but a great many do. Dr. Foxford, "a common butcher of the good saints of God," "died suddenly sitting in his chair, his belly being burst and his guts falling out before him" (5.64); David Beaton, "the cruel cardinal archbishop of St. Andrews," was murdered "and lay seven months and more unburied and at last like a carrion [was] buried in a dunghill" (5.636); Bishop Stephen Gardiner, "the bloody tyrant" of Queen Mary's reign, was struck down at table by God's "terrible hand . . . whereby his body being miserably inflamed within (who had inflamed so many good martyrs before) was brought to a wretched end" (7.593); others fall mad, hang themselves, are poisoned, drowned, burnt, hit by lightning, eaten by lice, or horribly stricken in various parts of the body. Nor are antichristian princes spared retribution. While godly rulers prosper, rulers who encourage persecution decline: "either their lives do not long continue or else they find not that quiet in the commonwealth which they look for" (4.130). Mary Tudor, whose reign was short and whose hopes were all disappointed, is the most recent and most telling example of such divine disapproval, but there are many others from pharaoh and the Roman emperors to Richard II and the Lollard-persecuting Lancastrian Henries.

Fundamental to apocalyptic as a narrative form is the continuing struggle between mighty opposites: Christ and Antichrist, God and Satan, the true church and the church of this world. But apocalyptic also has a predetermined plot, a plot cryptically imaged in the revelations of Daniel and St. John and historically embodied in the Egyptian and Babylonian captivities, the crucifixion and resurrection of Christ, and the sufferings and spread of the apostolic church. For the godly, triumph follows persecution. After "the manifold assaults, wars, and tumults of the princes of this world against the people of God" (1.87) comes the ultimate victory of Christ and his church. *Christus Triumphans,* the "apocalyptic comedy" Foxe wrote in the 1550s, retells the familiar story. Ecclesia and her children first suffer persecution from emperors and popes but are then joyously reunited with Christ. For the adherents of Antichrist, the plot goes the other way: from worldly exaltation to punishment. The frontispiece of *Acts and Monuments* shows both stories (fig. 15). On the right hand of Christ, the godly, who have undergone fiery martyrdom for their word-centered faith, are rewarded with the crown of salvation, while on Christ's left hand, papists suffer the damnation to which their idolatry inevitably leads. Foxe never promises that either a lasting reign of the godly or a permanent defeat of the ungodly will be achieved in this world. That long-expected consummation will come only with the end of time. But history does nevertheless offer many local intimations of the final victory, many signs of God's judgment and power—among them the grisly deaths of Dr. Whittington, Dr. Foxford, Cardinal Beaton, and Bishop Gardiner. These stories and the many others like them spread through the massive extent of Foxe's book help confirm a powerfully contested construction of reality. They reassure the suffering elect that the deaths of their fellow Protestants have not been in vain, maintain the apocalyptic hope on which such self-sacrifice depends, keep believers believing.

A marked dissimilarity separates the two kinds of violence Foxe depicts. The violence of Antichrist against the true church of Christ

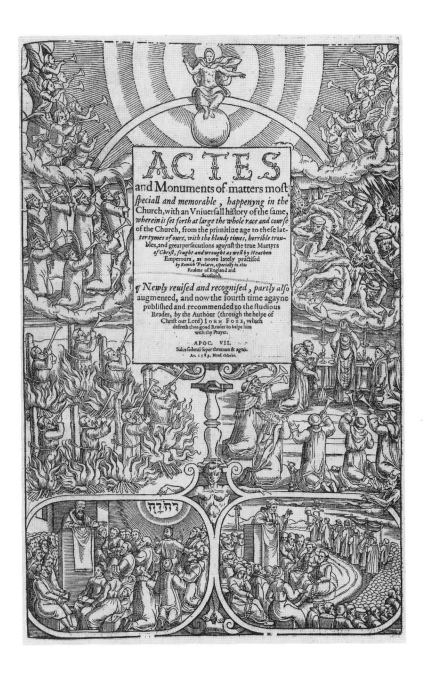

15. Title page from Foxe's *Acts and Monuments* (1583). Huntington Library.

and its members is carried out by willing human agents occupying offices of great worldly power. The violence of God is either direct or else mediated by unwitting actors, "pricked," like the bull of Chipping-Sudbury, "with a sudden vehemency." God's violence requires no institutional order. Underlying this dissimilarity is a double and potentially divided sense of communal identity. Foxe and his fellow believers owe their highest earthly allegiance to the prince whose subjects they are. Unlike papists and Anabaptists, who "agree in this point, not to submit themselves to any other prince or magistrate than those that must first be sworn to maintain them and their doings" (8.475), the godly put no condition on their allegiance. The king, they argue, is rightfully the head of both state and church. Officers of both are the king's and must be obeyed.[11] But the godly are also members of the true church of Christ, a church that in times of persecution and antichristian rule may have no officers and no institutional structure. Ideally these two communities merge. The visible church of which the king is the head should also be the local embodiment of Christ's invisible and universal church. This is what happened when Constantine made Christianity the religion of the Roman empire. And it happened again in England in Foxe's own lifetime during the few reforming years of Henry VIII and during the reigns of Edward VI and Elizabeth. At such a time the godly experience no conflict in their loyalty. They can obey both the laws of their prince and the word of God without scruple. And at such a time there is no need for religiously motivated violence from either God or the state. Persecution and divine retribution are equally unknown. But in the long history of the church such happy union has been the exception rather than the rule. More often than not, particularly in England in the two centuries since Wycliffe first spoke out against the pope and his false religion, princes have been "slaves and butchers" under the control of the papal Antichrist, and the godly have had no way to maintain their divided loyalty but through exile or martyrdom.

Foxe himself took the path of exile. The book that eventually became *Acts and Monuments* was begun in England in the aftermath of one persecution, continued on the continent during another, and completed back in England during a second reprieve. The works that most influenced Foxe had a similar provenance. John Bale, whose *Image of Both Churches* (1548) supplied the reading of the Book of Revelation on which Foxe depended, fled England first under Henry VIII and then again under Mary. As Bale recalled, St. John's Apocalypse had itself been written in exile. Inspired by this example, Bale saw exile as a divinely appointed vocation: "The forsaken wretched sort hath the lord provided always to rebuke the world of sin for want of true faith, of hypocrisy for want of perfect righteousness, and of blindness for lack of godly judgment. For naught is it not therefore that he hath exiled a certain number of believing brethren the realm of England, of the which afflicted family my faith is that I am one."[12] Most of the English apocalyptic writers of the first half of the sixteenth century, from John Frith to the annotators of the Geneva Bible, were of the same afflicted family.[13] The book that instructed believers "to flee from Babylon" had a particular relevance to the experience of these men.[14] Having fled, they found in Revelation a way of talking about their own community and about the community they had left behind.

Not that the kingdom of England belonged irredeemably to Babylon. Like Foxe, most of these men had known the rule both of Christ and of Antichrist in England. But, like his, their apocalyptic writings are far more strongly marked by the latter. Issues of church governance in a time of godly rule, what Hooker would call "the laws of ecclesiastical polity," command little of their attention. They concentrate instead on the identity and history of the two churches, the true and the false. In such accounts, exile and martyrdom become signs of truth. The church of Christ makes itself known, as it has done since Cain slew Abel, through its suffering.[15] And persecution becomes a sign of falsity. "For as he that in suffering patiently for the gospel of God is thereby known to be of Christ, even so in likewise is the persecutor of him known to be a member of Antichrist" (7.365). The result is to stigmatize as antichristian any regime that exercises in matters of religion the monopoly on institutional violence that defines it. Even when his own co-religionists were in power, Foxe argued against such state violence.[16] Citing such passages, historians have often described Foxe as an early advocate of religious toleration.[17] But there is another, more immediate explanation. As Foxe recognized, the very apocalyptic rhetoric that he and his fellow Protestant exiles had used with such effect against papists could be turned back on them once they returned home and adopted the persecutor's role. Indeed, if such signs betokened an existential reality, a switch in roles might require an altered understanding of truth itself. As a cynic might put it, lack of might makes right. To ward off the undermining effect of such a reversal, Foxe had to keep Elizabeth and her bishops from imitating Mary and hers, had to keep royal and ecclesiastical power from acting like themselves.

In the apocalyptic equation of persecutors with Antichrist and the

persecuted with Christ, the institutional power of the state, its kings
and queens and their governments, could rarely be placed on Christ's
side, almost never with the unanswerable conviction that attaches to
the martyr. Elizabeth nevertheless began her reign as an exception.
Her imprisonment under Mary, to which Foxe devotes many pages
toward the end of *Acts and Monuments,* identified her with those who
had suffered for their faith. She too was among the persecuted. And
so long as she refrained from burning those whom her church declared heretics, she remained an exception, one Foxe could boast of.[18]
But Foxe had a more positive reason for valuing Elizabeth, a reason
that also derives some of its force from apocalyptic tradition, though
not from the Book of Revelation itself. Like Constantine before her,
Elizabeth could be seen as a type of the Emperor of the Last Days, the
godly ruler who ends the persecution of the elect and institutes a
period of Christian peace. The strongest expression of this imperial
association appeared in the 1563 edition of *Acts and Monuments,*
where an initial letter C beginning the word *Constantine* contains a
portrait of Elizabeth triumphing over the papal Antichrist (fig. 16).[19]
In the dedication to the queen introduced by this decorated capital,
Foxe includes himself in the historical pattern. As Elizabeth is to
Constantine, so he is to the ecclesiastical historian and eulogist of
Constantine, Eusebius. And though this dedication was replaced by
another in subsequent editions, the idea persisted that Elizabeth had
been providentially appointed to the role of imperial restorer of the
faith in England, "through whose true, natural, and imperial crown,
the brightness of God's word was set up again to confound the dark
and false-visored kingdom of Antichrist" (7.466).

England's royal identity is built into the very structure of *Acts and
Monuments.* Though the book presents itself as a universal ecclesiastical history, its chronological frame is provided by the succession of
England's monarchs. After a first book devoted to the ten persecutions of the primitive church, each of the remaining eleven books
takes its title, its internal divisions, and/or its running titles from the
kings and queens of England. And when foreign events are included,
as they often are, they are made to fit under a rubric designating the
contemporary English ruler. In this, *Acts and Monuments* obeys one
of the controlling conventions, and with it the ideology, of secular
chronicle history. As we noticed in earlier chapters, chronicle history
is royal history. It identifies the land, the people, and the institutional
order, including here the institutional order of the church, with the
king. This is certainly not the way the history of the church would

have been presented by a Catholic. For such a writer, the government of the church itself, the series of papal reigns from St. Peter to the mid-sixteenth-century Paul, Piuses, and Gregory, would have supplied a universal frame, good for all nations. Foxe too thought the true church transcended national boundaries, but he could evoke no such all-encompassing institutional structure. Instead his Erastian insistence on the primacy of emperors and kings over all ecclesiastical

16. Queen Elizabeth enthroned in the capital letter C, dominating the defeated bishop of Rome, from the dedication to Elizabeth in Foxe's *Acts and Monuments* (1563). In the 1563 edition, this letter begins the word *Constantine*. In 1576 and all subsequent editions in Foxe's lifetime, the dedication was rewritten so that the word introduced by the decorated C was *Christ*. Huntington Library.

officers, including the bishop of Rome, reduced universal history to national dimensions. From an English perspective, England's royal history became the only established, institutional measure of time.

Emphasis must here be put on the limiting adjective *institutional,* for Foxe did make use of another organizational scheme, another measure of time, one that derived rather from the revelation of God than from the institutions of men. And this second organizational scheme both enforced and undermined the first. He divides all of church history into five periods of roughly three hundred years each:

> First, . . . of the suffering time of the church, which containeth about the time of three hundred years after Christ.
>
> Secondly, the flourishing and growing time of the same, containing other three hundred years.
>
> Thirdly, the declining time of the church and of true religion, other three hundred years.
>
> Fourthly, of the time of Antichrist, reigning and raging in the church, since the loosing of Satan.
>
> Lastly, of the reforming time of Christ's church, in these latter three hundred years. (1.87)

As Foxe's allusion to "the time of Antichrist . . . since the loosing of Satan" suggests, these categories are not merely descriptive. They are rather providential and were foretold, in at least their broadest outline, by St. John in the Book of Revelation. The crucial verses come from Revelation 20 where John tells how "the dragon, that old serpent, which is the devil and Satan" is to be bound for a thousand years and how "after that he must be loosed for a little season." In the 1563 edition of *Acts and Monuments,* Foxe, in agreement with the Geneva annotators and many other apocalyptic writers, dates the binding of Satan to the resurrection of Christ, which makes the time of his loosing include both the vast expansion of papal power under Hildebrand and Innocent III and the founding of the mendicant orders. But in later editions he altered his interpretation. Satan, he decided, had not been bound until the end of the ten persecutions of the primitive church and was not released until persecution began to rage again in the fourteenth century.[20] This change did not excuse Hildebrand and the rest. Foxe still insists that during the fourth age "the proud and misordered reign of Antichrist [began] to stir in the church of Christ" (2.105). But he can now neatly equate the two periods of Satan's freedom with the two periods of most intense persecution and can, as a result, more firmly identify the modern reformed church with its apostolic forebear.

But no less important, the change in Foxe's dating of the thousand-year binding of Satan increases the contribution of England to the history of the true church. The earthly instrument of Satan's binding is now Constantine, a Briton by birth and education, and the first victims of Satan's loosing are the English followers of Wycliffe. Nearly thirty years ago, in what is surely the best known modern interpretation of Foxe, William Haller argued that *Acts and Monuments* was responsible for establishing the idea that England was an "elect nation," a nation set apart by God to lead mankind back to true religion.[21] Since then, many scholars have contested Haller's reading. The idea of England as an elect nation did not, they claim, really take hold before the 1640s and cannot be found at all before Thomas Brightman's *Apocalypsis Apocalypseos* of 1609. To see it in Foxe is mere anachronism. Far from being an "apocalyptic nationalist," Foxe was "adamant in [his] support of a universal meaning" in church history.[22] On the issue of Foxe's apocalyptic nationalism, Haller's critics are certainly right. Foxe does say that the church is "universal and sparsedly through all countries dilated" (1.5), and he reads the Book of Revelation with reference to that universal church rather than to the particular nation of England. But he also grants England a quite extraordinary place in the universal scheme, a place that is significantly augmented by his idiosyncratic understanding of Revelation. Though he may never claim, as Milton will some eighty years later, that when God decrees "some new and great period in his church," he first reveals "himself to his Englishmen," he does nevertheless supply the evidence on which such a notion depends.[23] In his account, Constantine and Wycliffe, Englishmen both, mark two of the greatest periods in God's church, the binding and loosing of Satan. Clearly, their Englishness had something to do with their election.

As one reads through *Acts and Monuments* in the 1570 edition or any of those subsequent to it, one experiences two marked shifts of emphasis, shifts that coincide with the activity of Constantine and Wycliffe. During the first age, the church exists apart from the state and in tacit, though never active, opposition to it. The persecuted and their imperial persecutors are the chief actors. With the coming of Constantine, church and state enter into a strong symbiotic relationship with one another. For the next thousand years, attention belongs almost exclusively to emperors, kings, and popes. Except for the Albi-

gensians and Waldensians, there is no autonomous community of
faith, none at all in England. During this period, English identity
depends wholly on the succession of England's kings. But with the
loosing of Satan and the rise of Wycliffe, a new configuration emerges,
a new community of faith, once again apart from the state. Kings'
reigns are still important markers in the progress of England's history,
and kings themselves, whether as persecutors or champions of the true
church, remain highly significant figures. But they are now eclipsed in
importance by the believers, and particularly by the suffering believers. Accounts of individual interrogations and martyrdoms, each set
off by its own heading, now dominate the book. Where kings were,
martyrs now are. And because this last age, after the loosing of Satan,
occupies 1,822 of the book's 2,314 pages and includes virtually all the
stories for which the book is remembered, its representations have
been easily the most powerful and lasting. The community it defined
is the community to which Foxe's sympathetic readers are instructed
to pay their primary allegiance.

Authority in this community derives neither from the king nor
from an ecclesiastical establishment but rather from the word of
God—which, by the middle of the sixteenth century, meant the Bible
printed in English.[24] Translation and the new technology of print had
made God's word accessible, without clerical intervention, to all who
could read or who could find someone to read to them. The result was
to threaten the hierarchical order of both church and state. Suddenly,
those who had been disempowered felt themselves empowered; those
who had been dependent experienced a new spiritual independence.
Acts and Monuments testifies repeatedly to this newly acquired power
and independence. The bodies of the godly may still be subject to the
old governing order, but their minds quite clearly are not.

In the years immediately following its first publication, the vernacular Bible served as a great and irresistible leveler. The community it
created, the community whose stories Foxe told, included, alongside
a few gentlemen and a larger number of scholars, many of whom had
themselves arisen from humble social origin, a multitude of common, unlearned men and women. In *Acts and Monuments*, wives,
widows, and maidens, merchants and craftsmen, husbandmen, laborers, and servants are subjected to the same interrogations, answer
with the same articulate and informed conviction, die with the same
fortitude as their social betters. And many of them proudly call attention to their humble station. "I was an honest poor man's daughter,"
Alice Driver tells the chancellor of Norwich, "never brought up in

the university, as you have been, but I have driven the plow before my father many a time" (8.495). Tyndale had said that, by the strength of his biblical translations, "he would cause a boy that driveth the plow to know more of the scripture" than learned doctors of the church did (5.117).[25] In Alice Driver or Rawlins White, an illiterate Welsh fisherman who had the Bible read to him by his son, or John Bernard, a Bible-reading agricultural laborer, or the dozens of others like them, Tyndale's ambition has been realized. If these people can defeat university-educated men at the very sort of dialectical confrontation for which those men have been specially trained, it is because they speak out of God's word, not out of the imaginings of men.[26] Poverty and simplicity thus join martyrdom as signs of Christ's true church. As scripture asserts and as Foxe often recalls, "God hath chosen the foolish and weak things of this world to confound the wise and mighty ones, and things that are not to bring to naught things that are" (8.310).

This reversal of hierarchy did not go unnoticed by Foxe's detractors. In the words of the Jesuit Robert Parsons, the martyrs of *Acts and Monuments* are a "contemptible and pitiful . . . rabblement," "rags and rotten clouts cast out to the dunghill, as they well deserve."[27] Such language may recall familiar Shakespearean characterizations of common people: the "trait'rous rabble," "paltry, servile, abject drudges," "base dunghill villain[s] and mechanical[s]." And that recollection may further suggest how unlike Shakespeare's Foxe's lower-class men and women are, as unlike as Falstaff is to Sir John Oldcastle. Here are no clowns, no bawds, no giddy, carnivalesque rebels. Like Foxe himself, his martyrs know precisely what obedience they owe the established order and what obedience they owe God. And they speak their knowledge with force and clarity. In response to the charge that he was a traitor for denying "the higher powers," John Fortune, a blacksmith from Hintlesham in Suffolk, replied, "I am no traitor, for St. Paul saith, 'All souls must obey the higher powers,' and I resist not the higher powers concerning my body. But I must resist your evil doctrine wherewith you would infect my soul" (8.162). Fortune is one of twelve commoners Parsons ironically identifies as Foxe's "greatest disputers." The others are a cook, a cowherd, a young artificer, a tailor, an ironmaker, and six women, including Alice Driver. That such people are represented as defending themselves with such skill is, Parson contends, self-evident proof of Foxe's mendacity.[28] The comic malapropism, the confusion and illogicality, of Shakespeare's lower-class characters corresponds to a reality that Foxe

violates at the cost of his credibility.[29] But what then do we make of
the extraordinary wealth of documentary evidence Foxe presents, the
hundreds of detailed eyewitness accounts? And what do we make of
the still more compelling evidence of the martyrdoms themselves?
Not even Parsons can deny that these men and women died, nor that
they died for a faith whose basic tenets and whose source of authority
they understood and could express. The printed Bible in English
served to constitute a new social reality in which unlearned commoners were able to argue on an equal footing with doctors of the church,
a new social reality that Foxe represents and that Parsons and Shakespeare resist.

Benedict Anderson has described nations as "imagined communities," communities whose members do not know and have for the
most part never seen one another but who nevertheless have a strong
sense of belonging together, and he has credited print and the spread
of literacy in the vernacular with a significant part in their development.[30] The "invisible church" of Foxe and the other apocalyptic
writers is just such an imagined community. Its members are readers
who imagine themselves in invisible fellowship with thousands of
other readers, particularly with those who encounter the word in the
same vernacular translation. Like the nation, this imagined community does not necessarily coincide with the state. Indeed, the state may
frustrate its ambition to achieve a visible institutional embodiment of
its own, may hunt down and persecute its members. But where the
imagined community does not coincide with the state, it saps the
state's legitimacy and the legitimacy of the social hierarchy that constitutes the power structure of the state. In terms of the imagined
community, "gospelers" like Alice Driver and John Fortune have
more real authority, a stronger claim on truth, than do the bishops
and diocesan chancellors who judge them or the secular officers who
execute them. When Alice Driver says of the sacrament that, "seeing
it is a sign, it cannot be the thing signified also" (8.494), she attacks
the mystery of a "real presence" that invested church and state as well
as bread and wine.[31] And she does so in the name of a printed book
among whose readers she numbers herself: "For in all my life I never
heard nor read of any such sacrament in all the scripture." As a reader,
she belongs to an invisible and imaginary community whose reality is
constituted by the deferral of sign to signified.

Such deferral takes the narrative form of a projection from persecution to an unseen triumph, a triumph that was figured but not ex-

hausted by Elizabeth's assumption of the English throne. In the vernacular Bible, English readers not only encountered God's word, they also learned of the working of the word in time, of the narrative structure of revelation. For Bale, Foxe, and many of the other Henrician and Marian exiles, the Apocalypse was itself the prime source of narrative self-understanding. But other biblical narrations, from Abel, Jacob, and the chosen people to Christ and the apostles, enriched and reinforced the apocalyptic pattern. In suffering persecution and exile, these English Protestants could feel themselves part of an invisible church that stretched back to the beginning of human history and that would triumph with the end of time. Nor was their narrative participation in the invisible church wholly passive. The interest they felt in finding a scriptural model for their experience was matched by their eagerness to tell their own stories. *Acts and Monuments* is the product of a powerful and widely shared narrative impulse, the product of an enormous communal effort to record the sayings and doings of the martyrs and their persecutors. To this effort the martyrs themselves were among the chief contributors. Ralph Allerton, who for want of ink wrote an account of his interrogation with his own blood, is only the most dramatic example. Dozens of others wrote and then managed to smuggle out of prison the extraordinarily full records Foxe eventually printed. Given the number of these accounts and their length, one cannot help imagining the ecclesiastical prisons of England during the persecuting years of Henry and Mary as a vast penal scriptorium in which the incarcerated were condemned to write until they burned. But for these Protestant martyrs writing was no punishment. It was rather an expression of defiance and hope, an act of participation in an imagined community formed by the printed word and monumentalized in it. When in the 1570s the convocation of Canterbury ordered that copies of *Acts and Monuments* be placed in each cathedral church along with the English Bible, the circuit was complete.[32] From printed book back to printed book, from narrative back to narrative, the word had done its work.

That work included breaking the Roman church's ideological hold on England. Foxe and the martyrs he celebrates obeyed "the higher powers" in everything but this: despite official prohibitions, they continued to propagate the word and continued to tell their own story. If the foolish and weak things of this world were to confound the wise and mighty ones, if things that are not were to bring to naught things that are, it was by the force of this production and reproduction of

narrative. And for this purpose print was essential. Foxe in particular
was keenly aware of the militant function of print. In a section on "the
invention and benefit of printing," he argues "that either the pope
must abolish printing or he must seek a new world to reign over, for
else, as this world standeth, printing doubtless will abolish him"
(3.720). He does not suggest that print will also overthrow secular
rulers who resist God's word, but the implication can easily be drawn.
To this extent he was not merely a bystander in the struggle between
Christ and Antichrist. He and the many others, including the martyrs
themselves, who served his narrative project were active participants in
that struggle—more like the bull of Chipping-Sudbury than the pas-
sively wonderstruck crowd.

Acts and Monuments suggests a much stronger identification between Foxe, the once exiled spokesman for the persecuted and suffering elect, and the wounded bull of Chipping-Sudbury than Foxe himself could have easily admitted.[33] In making a dumb beast (or a
sudden illness, or a bizarre accident) the instrument of God's violent
judgment, Foxe keeps intact that godly submission to higher powers
that is an essential part of his Erastian Protestantism. The bull kills Dr.
Whittington. The godly remain passive. After yielding themselves to
Dr. Whittington's power and to the power of the state, the onlookers
yield themselves (no doubt with greater pleasure) to the spectacle of
Whittington's destruction. But Foxe's storytelling and the storytelling of the community to which he belongs, including their telling and
retelling of biblical story, do constitute an active intervention in the
apocalyptical struggle they claim only to observe. The violence of the
wounded bull and the violence of Foxe's antipapal narratives are
closely allied. Both are prompted by a botched job of butchery, and
both aim at the swollen paunch of ecclesiastical authority. Despite its
passivism and its professions of obedience, *Acts and Monuments* thus
becomes part of the double apocalyptic story it tells. It is both a
product of persecution and an instrument of divine retribution.
Through its emphasis on the church in England, it contributes to the
making of a specifically English community of faith. And through its
celebration of Constantine and Elizabeth, it enforces England's imperial identity. But it devotes far the greater part of its narrative energy,
far the greater part of its enormous length, to the conflict between the
godly and the established authority of church and state. It thus gives
its "invisible" English church a strongly oppositional identity, an identity founded on suffering and resistance and profoundly antithetical to
the hierarchical order of the English state.

Defending the Ecclesiastical Polity

The narrative and dramatic impulse of *Acts and Monuments* finds vivid expression in the book's best known lines. As the fire touches the faggots piled around them, Hugh Latimer addresses Nicholas Ridley: "Be of good comfort, master Ridley, and play the man. We shall this day light such a candle, by God's grace, in England as I trust shall never be put out" (7.550). One recent critic has called *Acts and Monuments* an *ars moriendi,* a book of holy dying.[34] A passage like this—and there are many of a similar sort—shows the martyrs themselves aware of the exemplary role they play. They perform as on a stage, providing both a testimony of their faith and a model for those who may be called to suffer in their turn. But *Acts and Monuments* is also something else, something more polemical. These deaths deliberately inscribe themselves in the ongoing struggle between Christ and Antichrist, a struggle that here takes on a specifically local thrust.[35] The candle Latimer and Ridley light by their fiery deaths will shine "in England" and in support of an English Protestant church. It is a struggle these martyrs obviously expect to win. With the help of divine grace, they will turn apparent defeat into victory. As they experience it, apocalyptic is not only a discourse of suffering. It is also—and most importantly—a discourse of hope and even triumph.

Like *Acts and Monuments,* Hooker's *Laws of Ecclesiastical Polity* is a polemical book. But it does not share Foxe's hopeful and triumphant commitment to narrative. On the contrary, its best known passage does all it can to avert change, to keep things just as they are.

> Now if nature should intermit her course and leave altogether, though it were but for a while, the observation of her own laws; if those principal and mother elements of the world, whereof all things in this lower world are made, should lose the qualities which now they have; if the frame of that heavenly arch erected over our heads should loosen and dissolve itself; if celestial spheres should forget their wonted motions and by irregular volubility turn themselves any way as it might happen; if the prince of the lights of heaven, which now as a giant doth run his unwearied course, should as it were through a languishing faintness begin to stand and to rest himself; if the moon should wander from her beaten way, the times and seasons of the year blend themselves by disordered and confused mixture, the winds breathe out their last gasp, the clouds yield no rain, the earth be defeated of heavenly influence, the fruits of the earth pine away as children at the withered breasts of their mother no longer able to yield them relief, what would become

of man himself, whom these things now do all serve? See we not plainly
that obedience of creatures unto the law of nature is the stay of the
whole world?[36]

Anxiety, not hope, animates this passage. No longer a heroic role in an
apocalyptic drama ("play the man"), "man" is here a poor middling
creature threatened by change and by disobedience, caught between
unruly masters and unruly servants—masters and servants who dis-
concertingly turn out to be one and the same. Strict hierarchy is
supposed to be the rule. All things have a predetermined place and
must stay in it. But Hooker's rhetorical "ifs" make it clear that obedience cannot be taken for granted. The celestial spheres will perhaps
not forget their wonted motion, but humans are not so reliably law-
abiding.

Neither Hooker's attachment to order nor his fear of disorder are
unusual in this period. E. M. W. Tillyard's *Elizabethan World Picture,*
which first drew special attention to this passage, and the *Norton Anthology of English Literature,* which gave it great currency, both present
Hooker's views as representative of what virtually all Elizabethans
thought and feared, and both print as confirming evidence closely similar passages from Shakespeare and from the official *Book of Homilies.*[37]
But it is important to note that each of these celebrations of order is
specifically defensive. Each responds to a quite immediate threat of
insubordination: Ulysses' speech on degree to factional disarray in the
Greek army, the "Homily on Disobedience" to the Northern Rebellion of 1570, Hooker's *Laws* to Puritan attacks on the established
church. Such language belongs to an instrumental rhetoric. It works
to disable certain ideas and actions and to enable others. This does not,
of course, mean that no one really believed it. Had these notions enjoyed no currency or credibility they could have had no persuasive
effect, and their authors would not have bothered to use them. But
such ideas were nevertheless evoked more readily by those who opposed change than by those who favored it. One hears little of cosmic
order and its relation to human obedience in the apocalyptic discourse
of Foxe's reformers and martyrs. Unlike Hooker, they were more likely
to identify the hierarchy of church and state with the body of Antichrist
than with natural law and the great chain of being. And their view was
no less central to the Elizabethan world picture than his.

Both Foxe and Hooker wrote in support of the Elizabethan settlement. But by 1593, when the first four books of the *Laws* were
published, that settlement was faced with quite different opponents

and was sustained by a quite different sense of itself than had been the case thirty years earlier when the first English edition of *Acts and Monuments* came out. So recent was its escape and so precarious its position that the Elizabethan church of 1563 could still think of itself as a persecuted church. Its chief enemy was still the international church of Rome; its chief danger, the possibility of another change in rule and another papal restoration. By 1593, all that had changed. Rome, backed by the power of Spain, was still a menace. But the main impetus for change now came from within the English Protestant community, from Presbyterians and separatists. After the vestments controversy of the 1560s, the admonition controversy of the 1570s, and the Marprelate controversy of the 1580s, the established church no longer spoke with the voice of reform. Though both sides could on occasion use the apocalyptic rhetoric of Revelation, opponents of the official state church clearly found the substance and the mode of Foxe's martyrology more congenial than did its defenders. In his controversy with Archbishop Whitgift, Thomas Cartwright, the leader of the Presbyterian party, pays special homage to Foxe, brags of having read over the *Book of Martyrs* with far greater diligence than has the archbishop, and tries to claim Foxe for his side.[38] And in his unpublished writings, Henry Barrow, the separatist leader, adopts the formal devices of Foxe's martyrs to report his own interrogation by the lord chancellor, the lord treasurer, and the archbishop of Canterbury. Nor is it only Foxe's method that Barrow takes over. When he identifies the archbishop to his face as "a monster, a miserable compound . . . neither ecclesiastical nor civil, even that second beast spoken of in the Revelation," Barrow behaves just as Foxian heroes from Oldcastle to Ridley had done.[39] That Foxe himself would in all likelihood have disowned both Cartwright and Barrow is less important than their obvious attraction to his apocalyptic construction of religious experience. By the 1590s, apocalyptic belonged more to dissenters than it did to conformists. And conformists were compelled to adopt the language of apology.

Over the course of its more than thirty years in power, the once persecuted church had become a persecuting church. Along with eight other dissenting ministers, Cartwright was arrested in 1590. In 1595, he left England for the greater security of the island of Guernsey. Barrow and his separatist colleague John Greenwood were executed for sedition in 1593. The near coincidence of these dates with the 1593 publication of Hooker's *Laws* is no accident. In that year, parliament passed the first regulations since the time of Queen Mary directed specifically against Protestant nonconformity. The author of this legislation was Edwin Sandys, son of the archbishop of York and chief sponsor of Hooker's work. It is unclear whether either Sandys or the episcopal hierarchy had any direct part in the original formulation of Hooker's project. C. J. Sisson argued that they did. Hardin Craig and W. Speed Hill have shown that they may not have.[40] But Sandys certainly did pay for the printing of the first four books of the *Laws,* and he made sure the work came out in time to help with his campaign for antireform legislation. Hooker's defense of the established church was part of a large and deliberate movement of reaction and repression led by Archbishop Whitgift and supported by the queen. Hooker may sometimes have been uncomfortable with the hard polemical edge Sandys encouraged him to give his work, with the specificity of topical rejoinder that was an expected element in Elizabethan controversial writing.[41] But if he preferred the general to the particular, there can nevertheless be little doubt that the generalities he marshaled with such skill arose from a situation in which rational argument made common cause with coercive state power.

But state power did not necessarily mean public acceptance. That is why Hooker needed Sandys's financial support. Without it, no printer could be found willing to publish his book. "Books of that argument and on that part were," the printers alleged, "not saleable."[42] *Laws of Ecclesiastical Polity* favored the established church government; the reading interests of the book-buying public did not. This could not have surprised Hooker. After years of rivalry in the pulpit of the Temple with the Puritan lecturer Walter Travers, Hooker knew which way popular sentiment was likely to go. As he remarked in the opening sentence of book 1, "He that goeth about to persuade a multitude that they are not so well governed as they ought to be shall never want attentive and favorable hearers. . . . Whereas on the other side, if we maintain things that are established, we have . . . to strive with a number of heavy prejudices deeply rooted in the hearts of men, who think that herein we serve the time and speak in favor of the present state because thereby we either hold or seek preferment" (1.56). Time-serving was never a charge Foxe had to contend with. Nor did Foxe have any trouble finding a printer. Despite its size, *Acts and Monuments* was one of the great publishing successes of the sixteenth century. From 1563 to 1583, it went through four ever-expanding English editions, and, not counting abridgments, it was printed five more times in the next hundred years. With Sandys's help, the first four books of Hooker's *Laws* were published in 1593. A fifth book, again subsidized, appeared in 1597. Additional copies of the first four books were printed in 1604 to be sold with remaining copies of book 5, but in 1611 many of these were still in Sandys's possession. Publishing interest in the *Laws* did then pick up. Five editions of the first five books appeared between 1611 and 1639, but books 6 and 8 were not printed until 1648 and book 7 came out only in 1662. Some seventy years thus passed from the time Hooker first approached printers with the manuscript of his *Laws* until a version of the whole work was made available.

Differences in publishing history between Foxe's *Acts* and Hooker's *Laws* would not mean much were they not linked to a set of more systematic differences, including the difference between apocalyptic and apologetic. During his continental exile, Foxe worked in a printshop. In *Acts and Monuments* he celebrated the invention of print and mocked Catholic attempts to ban books. And he represented a community largely created and sustained by the circulation of printed books. Both the scripturalism and the social leveling that find such effective expression in *Acts and Monuments* depend on the new technology of print. Though Hooker also wrote with the intention of being printed, he had a very different relation to Protestant print culture. The scripturalist contention that the Bible contains an absolute and unchangeable prescription for godly church government is the chief target of his attack. And the notion that individual lay readers, whatever their educational background or social class, should be able to pronounce on matters of religion with an authority equal or even superior to that of bishops and archbishops seems to him little short of absurd. Of "the common sort," "the vulgar sort," "the multitude," "the simple and ignorant" (1.14–16), Hooker is as contemptuous as either Shakespeare or Parsons. Mere acquaintance with scripture certainly does not qualify such unlearned people to participate in the governance of an ecclesiastical polity. On the contrary, since their Bible reading is determined by preconceptions supplied by their Calvinist leaders, it is in fact no reading at all and can claim no independent authority.

With mordant wit, Hooker describes and discards the whole set of interpretive devices by which apocalyptic discourse, including the discourse of Foxe's *Acts and Monuments,* constructed and justified its antagonistic relation to the established church. The opposition of Sion and Babylon, of Christ and Antichrist, of the godly and the worldly, of the persecuted and the persecutor are all turned to ridicule. Armed with such notions, enemies of ecclesiastical hierarchy are able to resist any argument, however reasonable.

Show these eagerly affected men their inability to judge of such matters, their answer is "God hath chosen the simple." Convince them of folly, and that so plainly that very children upbraid them with it, they have their bucklers of like defense: "Christ's own apostle was accounted mad. The best men evermore by the sentence of the world have been judged to be out of their right minds." When instruction doth them no good, let them feel but the least degree of most mercifully tempered severity, they fasten on the head of the Lord's vicegerents here on earth whatsoever they anywhere find uttered against the cruelty of blood-thirsty men, and to themselves they draw all the sentences which scripture hath in the favor of innocency persecuted for truth. (1.19–20)

Hooker here undermines one of the central elements of apocalyptic hermeneutics: the inclination to read present conflicts as a reenactment of conflicts in the biblical past, the inclination to understand both as episodes in the continuing struggle of Christ against Antichrist. He thus denies what Foxe would have seen as the unchanging narrative design of history. Sometimes truth does favor the simple; sometimes the godly are accounted mad; sometimes persecution wrongly afflicts righteousness. But not always. "If that must needs be the true church which doth endure persecution and not that which persecuteth," Hooker quotes Augustine as arguing, "let them ask of the apostle what church Sara did represent when she held her maid in affliction" (1.20). A persecuting church can also be a true church. Scriptural narrative supplies no sure way of distinguishing one from the other.

Against Foxe, the apocalyptic historian, one can set Hooker, the apologetic historicist. Debora Shuger has recently made a similar distinction with reference to Hooker's Puritan opponents: "In place of the Puritans' analogical ground, Hooker's arguments stress historical context; in place of the normative example, they emphasize circumstantial particularity. It is absolutely characteristic of Hooker's mode of analysis to trace a historical narrative to demystify the text or practice in question by exposing its circumscribed and contingent origins." But, as Shuger remarks, "the purpose of such demystification . . . is *not*"—or at least is not always—"to discredit the rule or practice but to legitimate it."[43] Hooker defends the ecclesiastical order of the church of England by historicizing both it and the alternatives to it. He begins this procedure in an aggressively demystifying vein with the model his Presbyterian opponents hope to impose on England, that of Calvin's Geneva. Far from being the single, necessary form of church government ordained by God himself and described in holy writ, the

Calvinist discipline was merely a contingent response, perhaps the best response possible, to the uniquely anarchic situation in Geneva. In England, where political conditions are altogether different, there is no need to follow that example. But if Genevan practice has no ultimate and unchanging sanction, neither has English practice. Its basis in long-established tradition is one argument in its favor, an extraordinarily strong argument for so conservative a writer as Hooker, but not an unanswerable one. Traditions themselves took their beginning from the specificities of some particular historical moment. Should those specificities change, should the tradition no longer serve the great ends of order and salvation, it would have to be abandoned.

In Hooker's account, such historical contingency touches all but those few, largely noncontroversial articles of faith that truly are necessary for salvation. Everything else, including the episcopal governance of the church under the supreme regency of the king, could be altered were it convenient to do so. But rarely in Hooker, never with regard to the current practices of the church of England, does such alteration in fact appear convenient. His most sustained defense of things as they are comes in the long book 5 where he takes up in detail Puritan objections to English church buildings, to the order of the English church service, and to the English ministry. Unlike Foxe, who avoided extensive discussion of the *Book of Common Prayer* (already a source of contention among the Marian exiles) and devoted long, debunking discussions to the Roman service ("declaring . . . how and by whom this popish or rather apish mass became so clampered and patched together with so many divers and sundry additions"—6.368), Hooker takes the very form of the English prayerbook as the structural matrix for his argument and welcomes the papal origin of many of its elements. To disqualify one or another feature of the mass, Foxe thought it enough to name the pope who introduced it. Hooker disagrees. "To say that in nothing they may be followed which are of the church of Rome were," he argues, "violent and extreme. . . . As far as they follow reason and truth, we fear not to tread the self same steps wherein they have gone and to be their followers" (2.121). Once he has entered a world of historical contingency and left behind the apocalyptic confrontation of Christ and Antichrist, Hooker is free to ask which practices "can be sufficiently proved effectual and generally fit to set forward godliness" (2.34) and maintain those regardless of their origin.

Hooker's church, the community he and his book represent, has a quite different relation to history than does Foxe's apocalyptic church. Where Foxe's community of the godly relives or, perhaps better, participates in a history whose fundamental narrative design is always the same, Hooker's community is the product of a historical process in which no moment is quite like any other. Foxe supports a religion of the word, for it is in the word that the essential apocalyptic narrative is told and retold. Hooker favors rather a sacrament-centered religion, a religion best expressed and best experienced in "solemn and serviceable worship" (2.31).[44] I suggested earlier that of all English books only the Bible and the *Book of Common Prayer* have had a greater effect on English religious self-understanding than Foxe's *Acts* and Hooker's *Laws*. What we begin to see here is that the *Book of Common Prayer* bears much the same relation to Hooker's *Laws* as the English Bible does to Foxe's *Acts*. As the Bible is the essential book of sacred narrative, so the *Book of Common Prayer* is the essential book of worship. The biblical Acts of the Apostles finds its continuation in *Acts and Monuments,* and the prophecies of Revelation are realized there. In the *Laws of Ecclesiastical Polity,* the order of worship established in the *Book of Common Prayer* is repeated; the centrality of worship, maintained and defended. Foxe represents an invisible, or at least underground, community of Bible readers, a community brought into occasional visibility by persecution or, more rarely, by the support of a godly ruler. Hooker represents a thoroughly visible community of worshippers, a community identified by large and handsome church buildings, by an established ministry with a formal hierarchy of ecclesiastical officers, and by a set and publicly observed order of service. Where members of Foxe's church experience God's presence most intensely while reading his word alone or in small groups, members of Hooker's experience that presence through the sacrament of Christ's body and blood, celebrated by an ordained minister in a consecrated building as part of a congregation brought together, if not by devotion, then by the coercive power of the state. Where Foxe's church opposes the world, Hooker's replicates the world and its governing structure.

As Hooker understands them, the laws of ecclesiastical polity belong neither to the invisible church, which is known only to God, nor to the whole of the visible church on earth, which has no single corporate structure, but only to those particular visible churches constituted by some individual "politic society"—by, for example, the kingdom of England. Though not the same, the invisible church and the visible church are each one. Ecclesiastical polities are many. As they differ in circumstances, so they differ in law. It is thus possible for the episcopal government of the church of England and the presbyterian government of the church of Geneva to be equally legitimate. What appeals to Hooker about both is their institutional capacity to enforce internal uniformity. For if individual ecclesiastical polities may legitimately differ from one another, no similar allowance is made for difference within such polities. The idea that the same state might contain several churches is abhorrent to Hooker. "We hold," he wrote, "that . . . there is not any man of the church of England but the same man is also a member of the commonwealth; nor any man a member of the commonwealth which is not also of the church of England" (3.319). Foxe too had thought of church and state as ideally congruent. "Because God hath so placed us Englishmen here in one commonwealth, also in one church, as in one ship together," he wrote in an address "to the true and faithful congregation of Christ's universal church with all and singular members thereof wheresoever congregated or dispersed through this realm of England," "let us not mangle or divide the ship, which being divided perisheth" (1.xxiv). But Foxe's very definition of his intended audience, "the true and faithful congregation," suggests that some Englishmen might not belong. Hooker puts no such conditions on membership. "Impious idolaters, wicked heretics, persons excommunicable, yea, and cast out for notorious improbity" (1.198)—all belong and all are subject to whatever laws the commonwealth enacts to maintain its internal self-likeness. Such positive laws are "the deed of the whole body politic" (1.27–28) and are binding on all its members.

Hooker is not in any direct way responding to Foxe, whom he never mentions. His opponents are the Presbyterians, Travers and Cartwright, to whom he adds, whenever he plausibly can, the hated separatists: Brownists, Barrowists, Familists, and Anabaptists. Foxe in 1563 and Hooker in 1593 wrote, as I have said, on behalf of the same Elizabethan settlement. But an apocalyptic discourse and an apologetic discourse nevertheless clash at many points—and at none so resoundingly as when each represents the national religious community. For the apocalyptic writer, that community threatens constantly to divide into two: an invisible church of Christ and a visible church of Antichrist, a persecuted church and a persecuting church. With regard to the things of this world, the former owes the latter obedience. But with regard to the things of the spirit, it must resist. By making the invisible church wholly unknowable, the apologist denies the legitimacy of such resistance. Because men and women cannot know the invisible church of Christ and thus cannot know whether they themselves are members of it or not, they cannot act on its behalf. The only church to which they obviously belong is the visible church established in their own politic society, and for Englishmen that means the church of England. To its laws they must submit both body and spirit. Authority in Foxe's apocalyptic church resides ultimately with the individual believer, with the individual reader of God's word. Authority in the apologetic church of Hooker belongs to the state, which, though itself a wholly contingent product of history, provides the institutional setting in which orderly public worship and thus the saving transmission of grace can take place.

To a large extent these same differences, or others very like them, divide any apocalyptic and apologetic writers, not just Foxe and Hooker. Apocalyptic is always a discourse of struggle; apologetic, at least when used in defense of an established state church, always a discourse of order. But Foxe and Hooker each gave a unique generic twist to the discursive mode he practiced and, in so doing, greatly increased its impact. Foxe, as we have already noticed, joined apoca-lyptic, which for Bale and the Genevan translators had remained in the form of biblical commentary, to history and narrative. Hooker's de-parture was no less decisive. He elevated apologetic to the rank of thought. Where his chief predecessors, Bishop Jewel and Archbishop Whitgift, had shaped their work as a detailed, point-by-point rebuttal of their Catholic and Puritan opponents, Hooker argues from first principles and remains, particularly through the first four books, on a level of high abstraction. As Brian Vickers has remarked, the *Laws of Ecclesiastical Polity* is "the first coherent large-scale prose treatise in English,"[45] the first English book to demand serious consideration as philosophy, consideration it has received in large measure. *The Political Ideas of Richard Hooker, Richard Hooker and Contemporary Political Ideas, The Place of Hooker in the History of Thought, The Medieval Con-tribution to Political Thought: Thomas Aquinas, Marsilius of Padua, Rich-ard Hooker,* and *Reason and Revelation in Richard Hooker* are the titles of some of the twentieth-century studies that have been devoted to Hooker. Even the Germans have been willing to consider Hooker *als denker.*[46] Though it is not unusual for church historians to claim that Hooker got most of his ideas from such earlier apologists as Jewel and Whitgift, no one writes books with titles like these about them.[47] Nor is the twentieth century alone in recognizing Hooker's special claim. Izaak Walton reports that for his "clear demonstration of reason" Hooker was already regarded early in the seventeenth century as the first English writer who "deserved the name of author."[48] Clearly this reputation, whether in his time or in ours, owes as much to the form of Hooker's work as it does to any particular idea or ideas it contains. But how has the "form of thought," if that is what it is, Walton's "clear demonstration of reason," affected Hooker's apologetic project? And how has it altered his representation of England?

The most obvious effect of Hooker's philosophic manner has been to lift the author, his book, and the cause he defended above the timebound scuffle of Elizabethan ecclesiastical controversy and into the unchanging realm of ideas.[49] This, according to Walton, was the fate predicted for him by both a pope and a king. After hearing the first book of Hooker's *Laws* translated into Latin, Pope Clement VIII exclaimed, "There is no learning that this man hath not searched into, nothing too hard for his understanding . . . His books will get reverence by age, for there is in them such seeds of eternity that, if the rest be like this, they shall last till the last fire shall consume all learning." King James said much the same: "I observe there is in Mr. Hooker no affected language, but a grave, comprehensive, clear manifestation of reason. . . . Doubtless there is in every page of Mr. Hooker's book the picture of a divine soul, such pictures of truth and reason, and drawn in so sacred colors, that they shall never fade but give an immortal memory to the author."[50] Now, popes and kings are not usually thought to be especially acute judges of philosophical reasoning. If their opinions are worth citing—and Walton clearly feels that they are—it is because Hooker's elevation is as much social as it is intellectual. Hooker defended the royal and episcopal church of England against Puritan opponents whose strongest appeal, both he and Walton insist, was to the unreasoning and vulgar multitude. A mark of his success is that his own audience is of a very different sort. And the success was more widely shared. Just as England could take pride in having a poet like Spenser, a dramatist like Shakespeare, a legal oracle like Coke, or a scholar like Camden, so it could take pride in Hooker's philosophic accomplishment. But what is true of all these writers, that their success contributed not only to a generalized national pride but more specifically to the ideological strength of some particular group within the national community, is still more obviously true of Hooker. He is the philosopher of the church of England, his work the proof that this apparently time-serving and worldly amalgam of religion and politics is capable not merely of coercing obedience (something Hooker is at pains to justify) but of being defended rationally.

Hooker's move from Jewel's and Whitgift's kind of direct controversy to a more detached and elevated form of argument had a powerful rhetorical effect. By means of this tactical recourse, Hooker decisively altered the feel of the argument. No longer did the combatants appear to be on quite the same plane. Instead of setting one faith against another—faith in the church against faith in the word—one of the contestants now assumed a vantage point at least nominally independent of faith, a vantage point from which the claims of both could be assessed. That this assessment, as Hooker manages it, is far from even-handed, that its conclusion is in fact decided before he ever begins, does nothing to destroy the rhetorical appeal of the move. Nor does it keep it from substantively altering Hooker's representation of England.

Foxe's apocalyptic discourse opened a gap between the temporal state and the ultimate sanction God's word confers on the godly. Hooker's apologetic discourse opens the gap still wider. Indeed, Hooker makes the gap, as Foxe never did, unbridgeable. In denying the scripturalist claims of his Puritan opponents, Hooker also denies any comparable claim that might be made on behalf of the settlement he defends. It is not that absolute values are lacking. Eternal law, the law by which God orders his own actions; natural law, "which ordereth natural agents"; law celestial, "which angels do clearly behold"; divine law, the revealed law of God—all these come directly from God (1.63). But human law, the law that governs commonwealths and their churches, has no such origin, can pretend to no such certainty. Though striving to align itself with these others, human law must remain content with mere probability and expediency. Reason will deliver no more. "The laws of well-doing are," Hooker claims, "the dictates of right reason." But in actual practice, "amongst so many things as are to be done, there are . . . few the goodness whereof reason in such sort doth or easily can discover" (1.79–80). Hooker felt the loss. He longed for the kind of certainty Foxe's martyrs seemed so easily to feel, certainty concerning God's ultimate justice and one's own salvation.[51] But even in these areas certainty was hard to come by. And in matters of governance, whether in church or state, it was wholly unavailable. The Puritans' sense that God's word read by the light of the spirit had given them an absolute pattern for church government was founded, Hooker thought, on an insane, perhaps diabolical, delusion. But their "fervent earnestness," their "overplus of strength in persuasion," could be matched by no similar conviction on the side of reason (1.17–18). Instead of conviction, Hooker had to make do with convenience. Instead of godliness, with disabused worldliness. Between God's law and England's, his apologetic discourse finds a space that reason can only hope to fill.

Hooker's first readers could not have been as sharply aware of this space as we are, for it opens most obviously between the first books and the last two—between, that is, the books published in the 1590s and those that became available only in the middle decades of the seventeenth century. After a prefatory swipe at the Calvinists, the *Laws of Ecclesiastical Polity* begins with a comforting assertion of the God-given order of things. The order is menaced, but it is solid and comprehensive. Not until the last books does one become fully aware that this God-given order has only a probable relation to either episcopacy or royal supremacy, that bishops and kings owe their position not to heavenly appointment but to human law, to an act, that is, of the body politic. But if Hooker's first readers could not easily see the space opened by his rational apologetic, the gap between the state and its divine legitimation, it became shockingly clear when the last books were finally published. In response, the newly restored, high-church bishops of the 1660s, unable to dismiss so authoritative a champion of the royal and episcopal cause, tried to define the apparent ideological gap between the first books and the last as marking the difference between a true Hooker and a false. Clearly, someone had tampered with his manuscripts. A man so loyal "to his prince whilst he lived," one whose work had been praised by King James and recommended at his death by King Charles, could not have spoken "that language for which the faction then fought, which was to subject the sovereign power to the people."[52] Walton's *Life*, written at the bishops' behest, supports this claim. It canonizes the true Hooker and gracefully banishes the false.

Without doubting the authenticity of the last books, some twentieth-century scholars have also thought them inconsistent with the first.[53] When faced with the realities of Tudor government, Hooker was, they argue, unable to sustain the philosophic principles with which he began. He was forced to abandon the high scholasticism of Thomas Aquinas for the politic secularism of Marsilius of Padua. More recently, even this inconsistency has been denied. "In fact," writes W. D. J. Cargill Thompson, "one of the most notable features of book 8"—the book on royal supremacy—"is the extent to which its arguments continually relate back to ideas that Hooker had developed in earlier parts of the *Laws:* his concept of the church as a 'politic society' had first been adumbrated in book 1 and forms one of the two

main pillars of his general defense of the church of England; his theory
of the identity of church and commonwealth follows logically from his
definition of the visible church in book 3; his insistence that the royal
supremacy is based on human rather than divine law reflects his belief
that political authority is derived from the people and that no single,
uniform system of government is prescribed for all 'politic societies.'"54 Despite various hesitations and countercurrents in Hooker's
development of it, this seems an accurate account of his argument. Yet
the sense of disjunction remains. As one reads the *Laws of Ecclesiastical
Polity* from the first book to the last, the seemingly solid high ground
of reason opens leaving little but discredited tradition and coercive
authority to maintain things as they are. Hooker's argument may be
logically consistent with itself, but it is not consistent with the rhetorical elevation to which it had seemed to aspire. Rational apologetic
transcends controversy only to reveal that controversy cannot be transcended.

Like Foxe's *Acts and Monuments*, Hooker's *Laws* makes it possible
to imagine two quite different Englands, two quite different English
churches. On the one hand, there is an England of kings and bishops
and solemn worship, an England aligned with the universal and im-
mutable law of God. On the other, there is an England of probability
and uncertainty, an England of fallible human reason and political
controversy. The first is the England those Restoration bishops were
trying to restore, the England they supposed they saw in Hooker's
first five books. The second is the parliamentary England from which
they had so recently escaped, the England that seemed still to speak in
books 7 and 8. But, different as they appear, these two Englands are,
as Hooker conceives of them, not in fact separable. The first derives
from the second. Hooker was, in this regard, as much a parliamentar-
ian as Coke. "The parliament of England," he wrote, "together with
the convocation annexed thereunto, is that whereupon the very essence of all government within this kingdom doth depend. It is even
the body of the whole realm" (3.401). As the head of that body, the
king can refuse laws passed by parliament, but he cannot make law on
his own, for "the lawful power of making laws to command whole
politic societies of men belongeth so properly unto the same entire
societies that for any prince or potentate of what kind soever upon
earth to exercise the same of himself . . . is no better than mere tyranny" (1.102).55 As Bracton put it in a maxim Coke quoted to an
enraged King James and that Hooker repeats, "Rex non debet esse
sub homine, sed sub deo et lege" (3.332). What matters most here are

not, however, the particular constitutional arrangements Hooker thought appropriate for England but rather his sense of the church as a politic society dependent for its very institutional existence on the consent of its members. In that consent Hooker hoped always to hear an echo of God. "The general and perpetual voice of men is as the sentence of God himself" (1.83–84). But, as he knew, most human laws are neither general nor perpetual. They apply to single societies and change with time. Furthermore, the consent by which they are enacted is not easily had, almost never without controversy. Apology itself is a genre born of controversy. And in the case of Hooker's apology, it was immediately put to work in a controversial cause, securing the consent needed to pass the quite particular and time-bound human laws Sandys had written controlling Protestant recusancy. The curious mix of detachment and involvement, of philosophy and polemic, one finds here is characteristic of Hooker. Hooker tries paradoxically to put an end to controversy by allowing controversy, joins arms against difference and change by showing how essential difference and change are to all human institutions. No wonder the ecclesiastical polity he defined seems sometimes at odds with itself.

In the Body of the Beast

Apologetic and apocalyptic are both internally cleft. Apologetic is split between rational transcendence and polemical engagement, between an ideal of stasis and the reality of change. Martyrdom and imperium, suffering and power, divide apocalyptic. Out of these internal divisions significant differences in communal ideology and experience can arise—and have in fact arisen historically. One need think only of Cart-wright and Whitgift in the 1580s, both claiming an interest in Foxe, or of Lockean Whigs and high-church Tories a century or more later, both pretending derivation from Hooker. But despite the significance of these internal differences and despite the way in which they could occasionally expand to fill (or at least seem to fill) the whole discursive space, they are far less important than the differences that continued to pit apocalyptic against apologetic. As we have noticed, the Restoration bishops had some difficulty with the last books of Hooker's *Laws*, but they had no question that his apologetic discourse in defense of episcopacy and royal supremacy favored their side. Determining Foxe's allegiance was more difficult. Bishop John Hall and his anti-episcopal adversary John Milton lodged competing claims to Foxe in the 1640s, just as Whitgift and Cartwright had in the 1580s. But, to the right of

Bishop Hall, Laudians were as certain that Foxe was not on their side as their Restoration successors were that Hooker was on theirs. Archbishop Laud himself blocked the reprinting of *Acts and Monuments,* and John Pocklington, the king's chaplain, referred to the martyrs in Foxe's Protestant calendar as "traitors, murderers, rebels, and heretics."[56] Over the next several centuries, in scores of editions that have added Quakers, Baptists, Methodists, even American Congregationalists to what their author/editors continue to call *Foxe's Book of Martyrs,* that book has become ever more closely associated with evangelical enthusiasm, staunch anti-Catholicism, and persistent dissenting reform. In the meantime, Hooker has been unofficially canonized, in the words of Peter Lake, "as the patron saint of 'Anglicanism'" —a position he "undoubtedly deserves," Lake writes, "not because he personified or expressed existing 'Anglican' attitudes and values but because he, more than anyone else, invented them."[57]

Within the communities that embraced them, Foxe and Hooker represented largely distinct, though sometimes overlapping, English churches, churches their books helped bring into existence. One of these churches, dispersed through a wide variety of evangelical sects, was identified with a scripturally inspired and sometimes disruptive movement of God's word through time. The other, established in a single, official church of England, took its identity from a particular institutional order and a particular order of service. Where one had a fundamentally diachronic and narrative sense of itself, the other imagined itself synchronically and liturgically. Where one was drawn toward an ever-receding apocalyptic horizon, the other remained apologetically attached to a tradition that abandoned as little of the sacred residue of the past as it could. And where one leveled distinctions of rank and gender, the other was intent on preserving a seemly hierarchy in both church and state. The Foxian church relied for its maintenance on printing, preaching, and tales of persecution. Its Hookerian rival depended on ritual performance and official coercion. These differences resulted in sharply differing discourses of nationhood. In Foxe's apocalyptic mode, the true nation, though it often aspires to statehood, hardly ever coincides with the state. Instead, its most prized Englishness, the Englishness of Wycliffe and Oldcastle, of Tyndale and Latimer, of Alice Driver and John Fortune, realizes itself in resistance to the state and in suffering at the state's hands. In Hooker's apologetic vein, national identity is inseparable from state power. Together nation, state, and church are defined by a single set of laws, the laws of an indivisible politic society.

Such abstract terms of difference could be multiplied at great length. And each of the terms could and should be qualified. Foxe, for example, when pleading for a peaceful unity of church and state, could ignore the social leveling implicit in his apocalyptic discourse and urge that "every man serve with diligence and discretion in his order, wherein he is called" (1.520). And Hooker, equally oblivious to the demands of his hierarchical principles, could argue that the laws, including those by which the king claims his supremacy over church and state, are based on a consent that, at least in theory, includes the whole population, even its less privileged members. But here I want neither to multiply the terms nor to qualify them. Instead I want to give some sense, however briefly, of what subsequent works formed within the framework of each of these discursive communities might be like, for what matters most is not the abstract pattern itself but rather the historical intersection of that pattern with individual and communal experience. How were apologetic and apocalyptic lived and perpetuated? My examples come from two men who were both active in the second half of the seventeenth century: Izaak Walton, the biographer of Hooker, and John Bunyan, tinker, Baptist lay-preacher, and author of some of the most widely read works of evangelical spirituality ever written. Walton called his *Complete Angler* "a picture of my own disposition," and Bunyan presented *Grace Abounding* as a spiritual autobiography.[58] The discursive formation of such deliberately self-reflective works as these, their relation to the larger generic patterns that inform them, should give us a particularly good idea of what it meant to inhabit and be inhabited by an apologetic or an apocalyptic construction of world and self.

Walton's *Complete Angler, or the Contemplative Man's Recreation* was first published in 1653, four years after the execution of Charles I, at a time when royalists and Anglicans could speak their views only with indirection. Like Hooker's *Laws*, *The Complete Angler* is an apologetic work. It can, however, not quite say what it is apologizing for. Ostensibly the subject is "fish and fishing." *The Complete Angler* defends the contemplative man's favorite recreation against the aspersions of hunters and hawkers, who consider fishing "heavy," "contemptible," and "dull" (p. 11). But a reader does not need much penetration to discover that anglers are Anglicans and that fishing bears a close relation to Anglican piety, also stigmatized as heavy, contemptible, and dull. I do not mean to suggest that Walton and his friends, most of them sequestered Anglican clergymen, did not in fact enjoy fishing. So far as one can tell, they did. But in their correspondence fishing came to be associated with a whole complex of values that the civil wars had challenged and eventually overthrown.[59] Fishermen, Walton tells us, are the direct descendents of the first apostles, Peter, Andrew, James, and John. "And it is to be believed that all the other apostles, after they betook themselves to follow Christ, betook themselves to be fishermen too" (p. 37). From this one might easily conclude that bishops and other ministers of an apostolic church, like the recently disestablished church of England, are by rights "brothers of the angle," as the apostles were. When Walton defends fishermen, he thus inevitably defends high churchmen as well.

In *The Complete Angler,* Walton's allusions to ecclesiastical politics are, for the most part, veiled. But occasionally he allows himself a more open reference, as, for example, when in the 1655 edition he introduces a poem in praise of the *Book of Common Prayer,* "our good old service-book."[60] By the 1650s, parliament had outlawed the *Book of Common Prayer.* But the prayerbook remained as central to Walton's religious experience as it had been to Hooker's. Walton's *Life of Herbert,* first published in 1670, ten years after the return of the king and the bishops to power, contains a strong defense of the English prayerbook, one that refers directly to Hooker, and an attachment to the official order of service unites all five of the *Lives,* those of Donne, Wotton, and Sanderson as well as Hooker and Herbert. Donne is made to praise "the power of church music" and the "public duty of prayer"; Wotton is presented as the opposite of those whose consciences "boggle at ceremonies"; and Sanderson laments "that the parliament had taken upon them to abolish our liturgy, to the scandal of so many devout and learned men, and the disgrace of those many martyrs who had sealed the truth of it with their blood" (pp. 53, 129, 338). This last sentence would seem to draw on the authority of Foxe, but Foxe's martyrs died opposing an order of service, the Catholic mass, not defending one. The world of Walton's Anglican saints is rather the world defined in Hooker's fifth book, a world of "solemn and serviceable worship." But these men resemble Hooker in more than their attachment to the *Book of Common Prayer* and to the royal and episcopal order that maintained it. They also share, at least in Walton's account, Hooker's systematic dislike of controversy. "Disputandi pruritus ecclesiarum scabies"—"the itch of disputation will prove the scab of the churches" (p. 128–29)—is the epitaph Sir Henry Wotton orders for his tombstone. *The Complete Angler* gives literary form to such attitudes. The transcendence Hooker achieves through his appeal to reason finds a strong rhetorical equivalent in Walton's pastoral removal of himself and his friends from the turmoil and strife of civil and religious conflict. Piscator's last words are a blessing "upon all that are lovers of virtue, and dare trust in his providence, and be quiet, and go a angling" (p. 215). For Walton and his brothers of the angle, apologetic was as much a way of life as a discursive form.

In 1666, Walton's *Life of Hooker* appeared as the introduction to a new printing of the *Laws of Ecclesiastical Polity*. It remained in that privileged position in edition after edition through the nineteenth century. In the self-reinforcing interplay by which communities of discourse alter and perpetuate themselves, Hooker made Walton who remade Hooker. Still more complete, however, is Bunyan's absorption into the text of Foxe. In many of those abridged and augmented nineteenth- and twentieth-century reprintings of *Act and Monuments*, "An Account of the Life and Persecutions of John Bunyan" appears in its proper chronological place following accounts of the Henrician and Marian martyrs. And to tighten the circle still further, these Foxian renditions of Bunyan's story tell how, when he was imprisoned for preaching God's word without a license, "he was solaced by the two books he had brought with him, the Bible and Foxe's 'Book of Martyrs.'"[61] Bunyan enters the *Book of Martyrs* bringing the *Book of Martyrs* with him. But of course it was in some sense the *Book of Martyrs* that got him there in the first place. Bunyan's behavior, the behavior that led to his arrest and imprisonment, was shaped by the very discourse of apocalyptic Christianity to which Foxe had so largely contributed. And that shaping effected more than behavior, for it was from within that tight net of apocalyptic discursivity that Bunyan produced such works as *Grace Abounding* (1666), *The Pilgrim's Progress* (1678), *The Life and Death of Mr. Badman* (1680), and *The Holy War* (1682). Nor does the process stop there. Those books have subsequently joined the two that Bunyan carried with him into prison in working to perpetuate the discursive community to which he belonged. As J. H. Plumb has remarked, the Bible, *Acts and Monuments,* and *The Pilgrim's Progress,* "often the only books which the illiterate, the semiliterate, and the literate poor ever knew in any detail," have burned a "sense of progress and destiny into the unconscious mind of the British people."[62]

The work of Bunyan's that is closest to the kinds of documents Foxe prints is not, however, *The Pilgrim's Progress* or any of the other books I have mentioned. It is rather the brief *Relation of the Imprisonment of Mr. John Bunyan* (1661) that, since the eighteenth century, has often been printed with *Grace Abounding*. Here, as Henry Barrow had done in the 1590s and as a host of Marian martyrs did before him in the 1550s, Bunyan wrote a detailed account of his arrest, examination, and imprisonment. Some things have clearly changed since the sixteenth century. Bunyan's examiners are secular justices not bishops, doctors, and diocesan chancellors. He is threatened with execution, but there is no mention of burning. And he is blamed not for denying the real presence of Christ in the sacrament of the altar but for refusing to attend services conducted according to the prescripts of the English *Book of Common Prayer.* But much remains the same. Like so many of his Foxian predecessors in a similar situation, Bunyan consciously models his behavior on that of Jesus and Paul; he calls his inquisitors vassals of Satan; he remembers that "God had rejected the wise and mighty and noble and chosen the foolish and base"; he thinks it better to be one of "the persecuted than the persecutors"; he sets the "church of God" against the established church of England; he willingly submits to the king's justice, denying that he has any intention of disturbing "the peace of the nation"; and he cites scripture constantly, taking its authority as absolute in all matters of worship and church government.[63] Asked why he does not follow the common prayerbook, he responds, "Because it was not commanded in the word of God" (p. 116). Neither Foxe nor Hooker is ever mentioned in Bunyan's *Relation,* but both are implicated. Only once does Bunyan cite an authority other than the Bible. When told he must give up preaching, he responds, "Sir, . . . Wycliffe saith that he which leaveth off preaching and hearing of the word of God for fear of excommunication of men, he is already excommunicated of God and shall in the day of judgment be counted a traitor to Christ" (p. 122). As the modern editor of the *Relation* informs us, Bunyan learned what Wycliffe had said from Foxe, whom he quotes verbatim. The connection with Hooker is less direct but no less significant. The law under which Bunyan was arrested and prosecuted, a law to which he refers only by its date of enactment, "the 35th of Elizabeth" (p. 121), is the very law Sandys got through parliament with the help of Hooker's apology. If Foxe's book shaped Bunyan's life in a positive way, reinforcing the narrative patterns that were fundamental to his apocalyptic Christianity, Hooker's shaped it in a negative way. The *Laws of Ecclesiastical Polity* justified the parliamentary action which led to Bunyan's imprisonment and thus to the writing of most of the books for which he is now remembered.

Setting books like Bunyan's *Relation, Grace Abounding,* and *Pilgrim's Progress* against Walton's *Lives* and *Complete Angler* suggests communities that, despite their shared (or divided) Englishness, have only a negative relation to one another. They are socially, economically, and culturally separate. And with the departure of many dissenters for a new England beyond the sea, they were often physically separate as well.[64] But, as we have noticed in other chapters, even a negative relation can have great and lasting significance. Indeed, such negativity, such deliberate and decisive alterity, is the very basis of signification. These communities take their meaning from their differences. So far as I know, Bunyan and Walton neither met nor read one another's work. The groups to which they belonged were too sharply removed from one another to make such contact likely. But in his arrest and imprisonment Bunyan did encounter the values Walton defended, and during a brief period of liberty he made clear his unyielding opposition to them: "I followed my wonted course of preaching, taking all occasions that was put into my hand to visit the people of God, exhorting them to be steadfast in the faith of Jesus Christ and to take heed that they touched not the common prayer" (p. 129). For Bunyan, steadfastness in "the faith of Jesus Christ" and avoidance of "the common prayer" are the positive and negative poles of a single religious identity. Walton was no less clear about the otherness he deplored. In *The Complete Angler* he can only allude to his enemies,[65] but in the *Lives* he is more direct, condemning at length those turbulent and nonconforming ministers by whose means "the common people became so fanatic as to believe the bishops to be Antichrist and the only obstructors of God's discipline" (p. 166). Anglican and dissenter, as they developed in apologetic and apocalyptic discourse, are terms of difference—difference from one another. And if for Foxe the newly established church of England belonged on the side of apocalyptic narrative, it was easy enough for subsequent readers to translate that Protestant state-church into the antichristian position hitherto occupied by the church of Rome.

Differences between the state-church and the various dissenting churches continued to function as a decisive element in the experience of England and the peoples of the English diaspora for the next several centuries. And the generic representation of those differences in apocalyptic and apologetic continued to shape that experience. The religious discourse of English nationhood, like the poetic, legal, chorographic, mercantile, and theatrical discourses, was thus productively fissured. But differences in religion had the most immediate and violent effect. If Conrad Russell is right in arguing that attitudes toward religious reform were the single consistent element dividing men who became royalists in the 1640s from those who became parliamentarians, then civil war was the work of these differences. Feeling that reform has gone far enough, the defining position of Russell's royalists, is precisely the apologetic stand; expecting it to go further, as the parliamentarians did, is characteristic of apocalyptic. But to suggest that these opposed discursive modes remained impervious to one another, that they met only at a hostile border, would be seriously misleading. Bunyan and Walton, as nearly pure types of the two as one could find, were perhaps closed to any mutually contaminating influence. There did, however, exist others who, at least intellectually, inhabited both communities at once, others in whom the conflicting languages of apocalypse and apology combined to produce a discourse that could not easily be identified with either. The most remarkable of these hybrid figures is Thomas Hobbes. In *Leviathan* (1651), a book published just two years before *The Complete Angler,* Hobbes responded to the divisions of civil war with an apocalyptic apology for a state he defiantly likened to that great fish of whom God asked Job, "Canst thou pierce his jaws with an angle?"[66] Hobbes offers no peaceful resolution to the opposition between apologetic and apocalyptic, no neat Hegelian synthesis. Instead, his *Leviathan* defines "the matter, form, and power of a commonwealth ecclesiastical and civil" in terms that preempt and subvert both Anglican apologetic and Puritan apocalyptic.

Historians of English religious and political thought have sometimes claimed that Hobbes took an occasional idea from Hooker.[67] It is no less likely that he studied Foxe. The effects that interest me here do not, however, depend on any such direct connection. Wherever he met them—and for a man situated as Hobbes was, not meeting them would have been impossible—apologetic and apocalyptic, as broad discursive fields of force, shaped and divided his work, including most obviously *Leviathan*. According to J. G. A. Pocock, *Leviathan* is governed by two quite different "structures of authority," one philosophic and synchronic, the other religious and diachronic.[68] The first determines the form of Hobbes's argument in books 1 and 2, the only books normally regarded by students of political thought. The second takes over in books 3 and 4. As Pocock points out, this second is fundamentally apocalyptic. It depends on a reinterpretation of biblical prophecy and posits a "God of revelation and faith" who "acts upon men only through history and is present to them only in history." The first, with its ahistorical "God of nature and reason," is no less closely tied to the rhetorical practices of institutional apologetic, practices made familiar to us by Hooker's *Laws*. *Leviathan* is thus cut up the middle, just as the English religious and political community was. Books 1 and 2 are concerned with nature, reason, order, and the coercive establishment and maintenance of stable, defensible institutions of government. Books 3 and 4 talk instead of the kingdom of God and the kingdom of darkness, of the ministry of Moses and the second coming of Christ. But different as the two halves of his book appear, Hobbes was not merely a passive sounding board for the conflicting religio-political discourses that severed England. He actively rewrote both apologetic and apocalyptic to produce an argument that accords with neither.

Years later, in *Behemoth* (1680), Hobbes gave his own explanation for the divisions that had rent the English church. "After the Bible was translated into English," he wrote, "every man, nay, every boy and wench, that could read English thought they spoke with God almighty and understood what he said, when by a certain number of chapters a day they had read the scriptures once or twice over. The reverence and obedience due to the reformed church here, and to the bishops and pastors therein, was cast off, and every man became a judge of religion and an interpreter of the scriptures to himself."[69] Evidence to support this historical explanation could easily be found in Foxe, but the attitude agrees with Hooker and Walton. Hobbes had as little respect for unlearned gospelers as did either. But he does nevertheless take those gospelers seriously enough to think that they must be answered in their own terms. As he says in the dedication to *Leviathan,* readings "of holy scripture . . . are the outworks of the enemy, from whence they impugn the civil power."[70] Those outworks must be destroyed, not as Hooker or Walton would destroy them, by dismissing prophetic revelation as an unreliable authority in matters of worship and government, but by reinterpreting revelation itself. Hobbes opposes apocalyptic with *both* apologetic *and* apocalyptic. He first constructs a model commonwealth according to the dictates of nature and reason, and then, by means of his own reading of God's prophetic word, opens a space in which that commonwealth can function. Readers uninterested in revelation have long thought that the second operation can simply be ignored, that for all philosophic purposes we can stop reading *Leviathan* at the end of book 2. Perhaps they are right. Apocalyptic is not particularly philosophic. But to ignore Hobbes's immersion in apocalyptic is to ignore the ways in which apocalyptic attitudes shape even his philosophic representation of the state. Fundamental to the impression the book has made, to the shock and disapproval it willfully provokes, is an apocalyptic attitude toward the product of its own philosophic and apologetic analysis.

When Hobbes called his ideal state "Leviathan," he invested it with the terrifying and inhuman strength that in apocalyptic discourse belongs to Antichrist. Leviathan is not the Beast of the Apocalypse. Its source is the Book of Job. But it is a beast nevertheless. For centuries, Lollards and Protestant sectarians had identified the persecuting officers of church and state with "the body of the beast." *Acts and Monuments* is full of such charges. Now Hobbes accepts the charge. State and church *are* the body of the beast, a body that includes us all. Forming such a body and giving it absolute power is, Hobbes argues, the only way of escaping the otherwise inevitably destructive consequences of our natural inclination to prey on one another. "This," he writes, "is the generation of that great Leviathan, or rather (to speak more reverently) of that mortal god, to which we owe, under the immortal God, our peace and defense" (p. 119). But Hobbes cannot speak reverently of this politic idol. It inevitably provokes revulsion as well as assent. It may be needed, but it cannot be loved. "By this authority," he continues, "given him by every particular man in the commonwealth, he hath the use of so much power and strength conferred on him that, by terror thereof, he is enabled to form the wills of them all to peace at home and mutual aid against their enemies abroad." Peace and security are much to be desired; terror and coercion are not. How can the state achieve one without the other? In Hobbes's view, it can't. Terror and coercion are the necessary conditions for peace and security. There is no place in *Leviathan* for the religious dissent that arises from Foxe's invisible church. But neither is there much allowance for the saving patina of apostolic tradition that Hooker and Walton gave ecclesiastical power. Yet Hobbes's book drew on the discursive practices of both apocalyptic and apologetic. And like both, it was engaged in the broader discourse of early modern nationhood. When in 1534 parliament declared that England was and always had been an empire and that its king was supreme head of both church and state, it invented Leviathan. Hobbes merely recognized and named the novel beast. This monstrous creature, this mortal god, this demonically powerful other, is, he insists, the representation of a truly sovereign state. "No power on earth can be compared to him."

This last sentence comes from Job 41.24 and is quoted in Latin across the top of the frontispiece Hobbes designed for *Leviathan* (fig. 17). In this image we see the visible form of apology, the bal-

17. Title page from Thomas Hobbes's *Leviathan* (1651). Huntington Library.

anced and ordered symbols of state and church—sword and crozier, castle and church, coronet and miter, canon and thunderbolts, trophies of war and tools of argument, battle and disputation—arrayed under the imperial crown. But here too we see the looming, apocalyptic figure of Leviathan himself, monstrously towering above the land, his body composed of a multitude of obedient subjects turned to face their sovereign head. Apology, this frontispiece might seem to suggest, has always been a defense of some such figure as this "mortal god," a defense of what dissenters could only call Antichrist. Chorography, we remember, took the monarch off the map. Coke's institutes of common law, Spenser's chivalric romance, Hakluyt's voyages, and the history plays of the Henslowe companies all do something similar. They make place for the land and its owners, for lawyers, nobles, and merchants, for common suffering subjects. Foxe's apocalyptic narrative works a similar displacement. It puts martyrs in the place of kings. Like Shakespeare and Hooker, Hobbes restores the deposed sovereign. The England he imagines is necessarily identified with an absolute governing order. The alternative is unceasing war of all against all, the very negation of commonwealth.

But in one regard there is no difference between these various discourses of nationhood. Every discourse of nationhood is also a discourse of self. In representing England, these writers represent themselves. Their individual authority depends on the authority they attribute to the social and political entity of which they are part. Every man, says Hobbes, belongs in the body of Leviathan. But every man is also an author of Leviathan.[71] All the apparent displacements of rule, all the apparent defenses of it, are so many forms of self-writing. The face that peers out from our various constructions of the nation is inevitably our own. For those who were prepared to recognize it—or rather to recognize him—Hobbes made this point in a particularly telling way. He had his own features engraved on the face of Leviathan.[72] In giving up his right to govern himself, as he says we must all do when we author Leviathan, Hobbes gives up nothing at all. He is the sovereign for whom he apologizes; he, the apocalyptic other with whose ungodly body he merges. In Hobbes's writing of the nation, perhaps in all national self-writing, self-alienation and self-aggrandizement are one.

Afterword

ENGENDERING THE NATION-STATE

I am tempted to leave Hobbes with the last word. The union of self and state he represents in the figure of Leviathan and the absolute power he claims for that "mortal god" realize and expose premises that have been at work throughout the early-modern writing of England. Inasmuch as the discourse of nationhood is a discourse of unity and uniformity, Hobbes has pushed it to a logical conclusion. But once he has reached that conclusion, we may be inclined to back away in dissatisfaction. Not only is the need for terror and coercion too nakedly asserted, but at the extreme point to which Hobbes has taken us we may doubt that we are still in a discourse of nationhood at all. Nothing about the figure he imagines is specifically English. Rather than representing England, his mortal god represents a political order that could and, according to Hobbes, should be instituted anywhere and everywhere. Less concerned with community and national particularity than with rule and an abstract system of order, *Leviathan* belongs not to a discourse of the nation but to a discourse of the state. The distinction would perhaps have been lost on Hobbes himself and would certainly have been lost on his Elizabethan predecessors. Their writing of what has since become known as the "nation-state" made available representations from which such a divided conceptualization could arise. But as we look back on those representations from a perspective afforded by subsequent reflection, we can see differences of nation and state shadowing many of the formal and textual oppositions that have been at the center of our attention.

When Spenser aspires to have the kingdom of his own language, he hopes to imitate the imperious power of the state; when Harvey defies such usurpation and tyranny in the name of the English people, their privileges, liberties, and immemorial customs, he evokes the language of nationhood. In claiming that English common law, as opposed to Roman civil law, is "connatural to the nation," Sir John Davies takes a similarly "nationalist" stand, and so do the chorographers in their displacement of chronicle. As first chronicle and then "politic history"

295

focused more and more sharply on the state and the story of its growing power—its "improvement," as Daniel put it, "of the sovereignty"—chorography responded on behalf of the "country" from which nationhood arises.[1] To judge by their titles, *The Faerie Queene* and *The Principal Navigations of the English Nation* might seem to be on opposite sides of the state/nation divide, but in their departure from epic both assume a more national than statist posture. In neither is there anything quite like the single, divinely inspired and royally decreed project that leads to the Christian delivery of Jerusalem in Tasso or the Portuguese discovery of a sea-route to India in Camões. Both the chivalric adventures of Spenser's knights and the overseas ventures of Hakluyt's merchants and gentlemen are related to state interests but not fully directed by them. A similar split marks the theatrical representation of England's history. Where Shakespeare's English history plays focus on the establishment and maintenance of monarchic state power, the Henslowe plays attend rather to a nation that is found at the margins of such power. And in the church, Hooker answers the apocalyptic nationalism toward which Foxe's *Acts and Monuments* was at least implicitly, if not willingly or consciously, tending with an analysis of state power that goes a long way toward Hobbes's kind of abstract political theory.

In compiling this list I have done little more than add "state" to formulations that I made earlier in terms of the monarchy. But to the extent that the state was almost indistinguishably identified in this period with the crown (an identification that, as both Hooker and Hobbes acknowledge, is rather contingent than necessary), the addition seems appropriate. State/nation, court/country, king/people, sovereign/subjects—if these pairs cannot be neatly mapped onto one another, neither can they be sharply distinguished. In each, the left-hand term represents the governing order; the right-hand term, that which is governed. And in each, the right-hand term contains a multiplicity of interests and energies that escapes the simple subordination suggested by such binary couplings. Historically, it may be, as recent students of nationalism have argued, that "nations more often follow states than precede them,"[2] but, once given shape by the state, the nation makes claims of its own, serves as a semi-autonomous source of identity and authority. Whatever historical research may have taught us to the contrary, we still think "instinctively" of the state as deriving from and depending on the nation. And if that reversal was not fully accomplished in the early modern period, early modern representations did nevertheless prepare the way for it.

But they did more than that. They also associated nation and state with some of the most fundamental ordering principles of their culture and ours. Compare, for example, Hobbes's frontispiece with Drayton's (see figs. 17 and 8). The all-powerful state, as represented by Hobbes, is a man, erect, in armor, wearing an imperial crown, bearing a sword and crozier in his outstretched hands. He rises above the land and dominates it. The fruitful nation, as depicted by Drayton, is a woman, seated, dressed in a loosely draped gown, one breast exposed, holding a cornucopia and a scepter. She is enclosed in a triumphal arch occupied by the men who have fought for possession of her. Rather than dominating the land, she wears it. In other representations, the gendering of state and nation is complemented or replaced by identifications based on class, on high and low. Many of Foxe's English martyrs, including some of the most memorable and articulate of them, are women and men of lower status. Indeed, Foxe presents the prominent inclusion of such people among the persecuted as proof that his is a "true" church. Authority in Hooker's ecclesiastical polity is, on the contrary, wholly in the hands of men of recognized position—with the single inescapable exception of the queen. The epic depiction of overseas expansion, like the Shakespearean depiction of English history, is similarly focused on upper-class men, on what Chapman calls "patrician spirits."[3] But Hakluyt's representation of the "English nation" allows much space to ordinary merchants (Chapman's "dregs of men"), while the Henslowe history plays identify England with people like Jane and Matthew Shore, Doll Williamson, and Jane Grey. The inclination toward class inclusiveness can also be found in Harvey's defense of the "quiet company of words that so far beyond the memory of man have so peaceably enjoyed their several privileges and liberties without any disturbance or the least controlment," and both class and gender are evoked in William Fulbecke's comparison of English common law to Roman civil law as "rather popular than peremptory . . . rather embraced than persuaded."[4] In short, those discursive forms that emphasize state over nation, power over custom and individual conscience, are also more upper-class and male. Those that emphasize nation over state include—and even identify with—women and commoners. From this perspective, the two issues I identified at the beginning of this book—the issue of power and the issue of inclusion—coalesce. Inclusion emerges as an inverse function of power. The more intensely a discursive form concentrates on the centralized power of the state the more exclusionist it is likely to be with regard to class and gender. And, conversely, the more inclusive it is, the greater the place it gives women and commoners, the less concerned it will be to assert the prerogatives of monarchic rule.

There is, however, one large and obvious exception to this pattern: Spenser's *Faerie Queene*. After all, the Faery Queen is herself a woman and so are those other representatives of powerfully centralized monarchic rule, Lucifera, Philotime, Acrasia, Radigund, and Mercilla, while such upper-class men as Arthur, Redcross, Guyon, Artegall, and Calidore represent the centrifugal forces of the chivalric nation.[5] But if Hobbes and Drayton, as opposite extremes, reveal one pattern running through the Elizabethan writing of England, Spenser, by confounding that pattern, reveals another. Again and again these writers imagine Elizabeth on both sides of the boundary dividing nation from state. For Spenser she is Belphoebe, the martial huntress, as well as Gloriana, the Faery Queen; for Foxe and the Henslowe dramatists she is both a persecuted member of the true church and the church's Constantine-like imperial protectress; and for Hakluyt she is both a private investor in and the royal licenser of the voyages he records. Others—Coke, Camden, Drayton—looked back to her reign for an image of the union of nation and state that King James's absolutist pretensions threatened to disrupt. The anomalous fact, as these men were growing up and beginning (and in many instances also finishing) their work, that the English monarch was a woman both shaped and enabled much of what they wrote. Elizabeth's presence on the throne kept categories from closing, allowed for an open exchange between a still dynastic state and a discursively subdivided nation. When in 1603, in his first speech to parliament, King James proclaimed, "I am the husband, and all the whole isle is my lawful wife; I am the head, and it is my body,"[6] he removed all such ambiguity. He erected an impermeable barrier and put himself firmly on one side, his subjects on the other. Elizabeth's declaration years earlier that she too was married to her people required rather than forbad passage across the barrier. She was both husband and wife, and so was the nation. The androgyny—a "weak woman's body" and "the heart of a king"—that held such a large place in the queen's royal self-presentation made room for a similarly liberating and empowering doubleness on the part of her culturally mobile male subjects.[7] They could both serve the state and write the nation—serve the state by writing the nation. Spenser's effusive praise and subtle displacement of the queen is only one example, the one that focuses most sharply on Elizabeth herself, of a strategy that was often replicated in his generation. It was a strategy far more readily available to the subjects of a queen, particularly a queen who used gender as a shifting marker of her own royal claims, than it would have been to the subjects of a king, than it in fact was to the subjects of either Henry VIII or James I.

The sex of their monarch was one determining element in the generational location of the younger Elizabethans. Others include the Henrician separation from Rome, the midcentury reversals in church and state, the increasing rivalry with Spain, the Protestant isolation of England, the spread of humanist learning, the growing market for printed books and theatrical entertainment, the conspicuous development of strong national literatures in Italy, France, and Spain, the mounting anxiety about England's own backwardness and barbarity, the explicit calls in preceding generations and in their own for the kind of writing they undertook, and the unexpected clogging of other, more commonly traveled paths to preferment and promotion. Whichever of these we choose to emphasize—and the list could easily be extended—the resulting accomplishment stands as a pointer to a unique set of conditions that gave men of middling status and humanist education, men born at or shortly following the midcentury, the task of laying the discursive foundations both for the nation-state and for a whole array of more specialized communities that based their identity on their relation to the nation and the state. When Spenser and the others were born, England could claim no poet since Chaucer of major standing; by the time they died, English poetry could rival that of any language, ancient or modern.[8] At their births, English common law was unwritten and in vulnerable disarray; by the time the last of them died, England's law had been embodied in texts worthy to stand by Justinian's authoritative *Corpus Juris Civilis*. In the same eighty years and largely through their efforts, England was mapped, described, and chorographically related to its Roman and medieval past; the voyages of the English nation were gathered and printed, and an ideological base was laid for England's colonial and mercantile expansion; English history was staged before thousands by newly founded professional acting companies performing in newly constructed playhouses, and a national dramatic literature was provided with its most enduring works; and, finally, a church of England was established, challenged, and defended with unprecedented authority and sophistication. The men who accomplished these tasks engendered (even as they gendered) a national cultural formation that has not only survived for the last four centuries on the British Isles but has served as a sequentially engendering paradigm for nations throughout the world.

Unity is one mark of that formation. However much they may have resisted the centralizing forces of the monarchic state, these men helped solidify and thicken the lines that separate one nation from another. As a result of their efforts, poetry, law, chorographic and antiquarian study, trade, colonial expansion, and economic activity generally, drama, and even religion were all given a single, apparently coterminous national base that replaced the various overlapping local and international jurisdictions that had previously predominated in one cultural field or another. But if unity is one mark of the early modern nation-state, diversity is another. The different discursive forms and communities in and by which the nation-state was written provided competing and even contradictory ways of being English, a repertory of parts rather than a single role. John Bunyan's Englishness may have been largely defined by a Foxian apocalyptic discourse; Izaak Walton's, by a Hookerian apologetic ordering of experience. But most literate and mobile Englishmen belonged to several discursive communities, were traversed by a plurality of nationalist discourses. Their identity was constructed *within* particular forms and communities, but also *across* them. John Selden was at once a member of Camden's Society of Antiquaries, the annotator of Drayton's *Poly-Olbion,* and Coke's parliamentary collaborator in his struggles with King Charles on behalf of the common law. Fulke Greville contributed to the quantitative movement, patronized Daniel, Camden, and Speed, and wrote his own politic history of Elizabeth's reign, his *Life of Sir Philip Sidney.* And Edwin Sandys not only paid for the printing of Hooker's *Laws* but was also among the most active promoters of overseas expansion.

Again we need to put Hobbes and Drayton together. Hobbes represents a hegemonically unified state. To claim autonomous authority for the church or the law or any other communal formation apart from the state itself was to him unacceptable. All must submit to the undivided and unquestionable will of the sovereign ruler. Drayton, as the title of his poem suggests, represents multiplicity. Though only the monarchic order of the state can explain the limits of his chorographic description, he keeps that order carefully out of sight and concentrates instead on local particularity and local difference. He sings the "varying earth" and the equally varying peoples who have occupied it. The nation-state is an unstable and precariously balanced union of the two, of Hobbes's unified state and Drayton's multiple nation. Individual and communal identity are constructed at their intersection.

In chapter three, I characterized *Poly-Olbion* as a *discordia concors*. If we give full weight to both the discord and the concord, the same formula can serve for the nation-state. In the history of England and of all other nation-states, discord has been both real and inescapable. The civil wars of the mid-seventeenth century—wars which prompted Hobbes's call for absolute government—provide only the most obvious example of a continuing struggle between conflicting interests and conflicting discursive shapings of the nation. Those who thought religious reform had gone far enough and those who thought it hadn't, those who set the king above the law and those who reversed that ordering, those who favored the court and those who favored the country all acted out differences that had been given generic form in the course of the Elizabethan writing of England. But if the formal differences on which the nation-state was founded could provoke civil war and continue even now to fuel political conflict, the assemblage of those differences around the unifying concept of the nation-state has done much to keep conflict in check. Concord has, after all, been as characteristic of the nation-state as discord. The nation-state has thrived in those polities where it first emerged and has spread widely beyond its European home because it alone has provided the psychic and material support required by a restless commercial and industrial society.

The culturally uprooted young men who began writing England in the last decades of the sixteenth century opened a discursive space for dozens of uprooted generations to come. They thus set in motion a nationalist *discordia concors* that remains an object of desire to peoples throughout the world: a seemingly unique basis of freedom, of social and economic progress, of reintegrated identity. To study the early modern construction of the nation-state is to understand more fully the strength and the appeal of this complex cultural formation, but it is also to unmask the nation's claim to a "natural" or "immemorial" origin, its claim to having always been there waiting to join the state in a marriage of love rather than convenience. Neither the nation nor the state has always been there. Both were constituted and have been continually reconstituted in an ongoing exchange between individual needs, communal interests, and discursive forms, an exchange that continues to be driven, as it was in sixteenth-century England, by alienation and emulation—forces antithetical to the nation's fundamental sense of its distinguishing and enabling self-likeness.

Notes

Introduction

1. The two dozen men mentioned in this opening paragraph were born in the following years: William Camden in 1551; Edward Coke, Walter Raleigh, John Speed, and Edmund Spenser in 1552; Richard Hakluyt in 1553; John Cowell, Fulke Greville, Richard Hooker, John Lyly, and Philip Sidney in 1554; Lancelot Andrewes in 1555; George Peele in 1556; Henry Finch and William Warner in 1558; George Chapman in 1559; Francis Bacon and Edwin Sandys in 1561; Samuel Daniel and Michael Drayton in 1563; John Hayward, Christopher Marlowe, and William Shakespeare in 1564. John Norden, the author of *Speculum Britanniae*, was born in 1548, three years before Camden, but in his writing of England he followed Camden's lead. My emphasis in this opening paragraph and throughout the book is on the generational specificity suggested by these dates, but I can't say "all were written by men" without being conscious as well of gender specificity. For historical reasons too obvious to enumerate, the Elizabethan writing of England was "men's work," though, as I will suggest at various points, such men's work was in this generation both shaped and enabled by the presence of a female monarch.

2. *The Works of Edmund Spenser: A Variorum Edition*, edited by Edwin Greenlaw et al., 11 vols. (Baltimore: Johns Hopkins Press, 1932–57), 10.16.

3. This work can be found in *The Elizabethan Prodigals* (Berkeley: Univ. of California Press, 1976) and *Self-Crowned Laureates: Spenser, Jonson, Milton and the Literary System* (Berkeley: Univ. of California Press, 1983).

4. Compare King James's formula, "king, people, law" (law here representing the cultural system, as language does in Spenser), in the preface to his *Basilicon Doron*, in *The Political Works of James I*, edited by C. H. McIlwain (Cambridge: Harvard Univ. Press, 1918), p. 7.

5. I owe this suggestion to Patricia Fumerton.

6. On the perceived insufficiency of the English language in the sixteenth century, see Richard Foster Jones, *The Triumph of the English Language: A Survey of Opinions Concerning the Vernacular from the Introduction of Printing to the Restoration* (London: Oxford Univ. Press, 1953).

7. G. R. Elton, *The Tudor Revolution in Government: Administrative Changes in the Reign of Henry VIII* (Cambridge: Cambridge Univ. Press, 1953), p. 3.

8. I have taken the phrase "generational location" and much of my understanding of the cultural functioning of generations from Karl Mannheim's "The Problem of Generations" in his *Essays on the Sociology of Knowledge*,

edited by Paul Kecshemeti (London: Routledge, 1952), pp. 276–322. I briefly discuss the relation between the kind of semiotically oriented analysis I practice and generational history in the introduction to *Self-Crowned Laureates*, pp. 14–20. Both *Self-Crowned Laureates* and its predecessor, *The Elizabethan Prodigals*, have a strong generational emphasis.

9. Jonathan Goldberg's *James I and the Politics of Literature: Jonson, Shakespeare, Donne, and Their Contemporaries* (Baltimore: Johns Hopkins Press, 1983) provides the most extreme statement of this position, but a similar insistence on royal power and its virtually hegemonic influence on the discursive practices of Elizabethan and Jacobean culture is characteristic of much of the best and best-known new-historicist work. Even a short list would have to include Stephen Orgel's *Illusion of Power: Political Theater in the English Renaissance* (Berkeley: Univ. of California Press, 1975), Stephen Greenblatt's *Renaissance Self-Fashioning: From More to Shakespeare* (Chicago: Univ. of Chicago Press, 1980) and *Shakespearean Negotiations: The Circulation of Social Energy in Renaissance England* (Berkeley: Univ. of California Press, 1988), Leah Marcus's *The Politics of Mirth: Jonson, Herrick, Milton, Marvell, and the Defense of Old Holiday Pastimes* (Chicago: Univ. of Chicago Press, 1986) and *Puzzling Shakespeare: Local Reading and Its Discontents* (Berkeley: Univ. of California Press, 1988), Leonard Tennenhouse's *Power on Display: The Politics of Shakespeare's Genres* (New York: Methuen, 1986), and Louis Montrose's *The Subject of Elizabeth: Relations of Power and Cultural Practices in Elizabethan England* (Chicago: Univ. of Chicago Press, forthcoming).

10. For a brief but suggestive discussion of medieval state formation in England, see Philip Corrigan and Derek Sayer, *The Great Arch: English State Formation as Cultural Revolution* (Oxford: Basil Blackwell, 1985), pp. 15–42. The more general issue of royal absolutism is the subject of Perry Anderson's *Lineages of the Absolutist State* (London: New Left Books, 1974).

11. Ernest Gellner, *Nations and Nationalism* (Ithaca: Cornell Univ. Press, 1983).

12. Peter Burke, *Popular Culture in Early Modern Europe* (New York: Harper Torchbooks, 1978).

13. Anthony Giddens usefully distinguishes between traditional, "class-divided" societies, in which, despite "massive divisions of wealth and privilege between the dominant class and the majority of the population, class conflict is not a major axis of group formation and not a source of the major transformative influences shaping social change," and "capitalist" society, in which class differences are less marked but class conflict is endemic. See *The Nation-State and Violence: Volume Two of a Contemporary Critique of Historical Materialism* (Berkeley: Univ. of California Press, 1987), p. 64. This corresponds roughly to Gellner's distinction between agrarian and industrial societies. For both, the nation-state is uniquely associated with the more recent socioeconomic order, whether "capitalist" or "industrial." For a discussion of the invention of culture and its association with modern nation building, see *The*

Invention of Tradition, edited by Eric Hobsbawm and Terence Ranger (Cambridge: Cambridge Univ. Press, 1983).

14. F. J. Levy, *Tudor Historical Thought* (San Marino: Huntington Library, 1967), p. ix.

15. "More coherent" for us. Our sense of coherence is a product of the "rational" order of the modern nation-state. The sharp focus of Bacon's *Henry VII* or Daniel's *History of England* would probably have seemed incoherent, or at least arbitrarily and indefensibly limited, to the author of *Polychronicon.*

16. Samuel Daniel, *The Collection of the History of England* in *The Complete Works in Verse and Prose,* edited by Alexander B. Grosart, 5 vols. (London: Spenser Society, 1885–96), 4.77. The passage from which the phrase is taken nicely illustrates Daniel's sense of the historical difference of his own age from the not very distant past and his analytic focus on those conditions which contributed to the growing strength of the state. The Tudor century was, he wrote, "a time not of that virility as the former, but more subtle and let out into wider notions and bolder discoveries of what lay hidden before. A time wherein began a greater improvement of the sovereignty, and more came to be effected by wit than the sword. Equal and just encounters of state and state in forces and of prince and prince in sufficiency. The opening of a new world, which strangely altered the manner of this, enhancing both the rate of all things by the induction of infinite treasure and opened a wider way to corruption, whereby princes got much without their swords. Protections and confederations to counterpoise and prevent ever-growing powers came to be maintained with larger pensions. Ledger ambassadors first employed abroad for intelligences. Common banks erected to return and furnish moneys for these businesses. Besides strange alterations in the state ecclesiastical: religion brought forth to be an actor in the greatest designs of ambition and faction."

17. For a useful summary of some of these theories, see Anthony D. Smith, *Theories of Nationalism* (London: Duckworth, 1971). In using the verb *imagine* here and in preceding paragraphs, I am thinking of Benedict Anderson's *Imagined Communities: Reflections on the Origin and Spread of Nationalism* (London: Verso, 1983). And in speaking of "transitional men," I am once again aware that this is a gender-exclusive term. The liberating mobility conferred on some men by their humanistic education was not generally available to women, particularly not to women of lower status.

18. John Speed, *The Theatre of the Empire of Great Britain,* 2 vols. (1611), sig. O2.

19. Stephen Greenblatt provides a similar description (p. 7) of the "profound mobility" of the six figures he discusses in *Renaissance Self-Fashioning,* two of whom, Spenser and Shakespeare, also appear on my list. In the later part of the sixteenth century, individual self-fashioning and national self-fashioning were strongly dependent on one another and both in turn depended on the mobility that was already the experience, as Greenblatt shows in the

first chapters of his book, of some men in the early part of the century, well before the nation became the favored terminus for such restless energies.

20. *The Works of Michael Drayton,* edited by J. William Hebel, 5 vols. (Oxford: Shakespeare Head Press, 1931–41), 2.310.

21. Roy Strong quoted by Corrigan and Sayer, *The Great Arch,* p. 55.

22. The date of foundation of these groups are: the Camden Society, 1838; the Parker Society, 1840; the Shakespeare Society, 1841; the Hakluyt Society, 1846; the Spenser Society, 1867; and the Selden Society, 1887.

23. There may be some doubt concerning the "Elizabethan" genuineness of Coke's *First Institute,* a book published two kings and twenty-five years after Elizabeth's death. I here count as Elizabethan any works written by men born in the 1550s and 1560s, men who came of age midway through Elizabeth's reign and whose sense of the world was set long before she died—which does not of course mean that Coke's *First Institute* is not also Jacobean and Caroline.

24. I list here only the countries that successfully put together something like a nation-state in the early modern period. In many ways, the Italian city-states prepared the discursive structures that enabled this accomplishment, but Italy itself did not achieve national unity until much later.

25. Debora Kuller Shuger, *Habits of Thought in the English Renaissance: Religion, Politics, and the Dominant Culture* (Berkeley: Univ. of California Press, 1990), p. 11.

Chapter One

1. Acton's manuscript notes from which this quotation is taken are printed in Herbert Butterfield, *Man on His Past: The Study of the History of Historical Scholarship* (Cambridge: Cambridge Univ. Press, 1955), p. 212.

2. On the nineteenth-century Greek revival, see Frank M. Turner, *The Greek Heritage in Victorian Britain* (New Haven: Yale University Press, 1981). For a study of Victorian medievalism, see Mark Girouard, *The Return to Camelot: Chivalry and the English Gentleman* (New Haven: Yale Univ. Press, 1981). Turner opens his book with the quotation from Acton that also opens this chapter.

3. Emile Benveniste, quoted by John A. Armstrong, *Nations before Nationalism* (Chapel Hill: Univ. of North Carolina Press, 1982), p. 5.

4. *The Works of Edmund Spenser: A Variorum Edition,* edited by Edwin Greenlaw, C. G. Osgood, et al., 11 vols. (Baltimore: Johns Hopkins Press, 1932–57), 10.16.

5. Though we often call Petrarch "the first Renaissance man," he was considered medieval by sixteenth-century English writers. Roger Ascham counts Chaucer and Petrarch among the "Gothians" (*The Schoolmaster,* edited by Lawrence V. Ryan [Ithaca: Cornell Univ. Press, 1967], pp. 146–47), and Samuel Daniel, pushing Petrarch back "three hundred years before"

Reuchlin, Erasmus, and More—that is, more than a hundred years further back than he in fact belongs—presents him as proof of medieval learning (*Poems and A Defence of Ryme,* edited by Arthur Colby Sprague [1930: rpt. Chicago: Univ. of Chicago Press, 1965], pp. 140–41).

6. Later in the same letter, Harvey repeats this opposition in still more explicitly political terms: "Now for your *heaven, seaven, eleaven,* or the like, I am likewise of the same opinion, as generally in all words else. We are not to go a little farther, either for the prosody or the orthography (and therefore your imaginary diastole nothing worth) than we are licensed and authorized by the ordinary use and custom and propriety and idiom and, as it were, majesty of our speech, which I account the only infallible and sovereign rule of all rules. And therefore having respect thereunto, and reputing it petty treason to revolt therefro, dare hardly either in the prosody or in the orthography either allow them two syllables instead of one, but would in writing, as in speaking, have them used as monosyllaba" (10.475). As they assume the majesty of infallible rule, use and custom are here made sovereign, leaving little place for a more active royal lawgiver.

7. Ascham, *The Schoolmaster,* p. 151.

8. I depend here on Derek Attridge's discussion of pronunciation in his *Well-Weighed Syllables: Elizabethan Verse in Classical Metres* (Cambridge: Cambridge Univ. Press, 1974), pp. 21–40. Attridge's book provides the best introduction available to the quantitative movement in Renaissance England.

9. The peremptory quality of this reforming action puts it firmly on the civil-law side of the English-Roman opposition as it was understood in the legal community. In his comparison of the two legal systems, William Fulbecke characterized the common law as "rather popular than peremptory, rather accepted than exacted, and rather embraced than persuaded" (*A Parallele or Conference of the Civill Law, the Canon Law, and the Common Law of this Realme of England* [1601], sig. 🖋 i^v). As the product of an imperial decree, the civil law stood on the other side of this set of opposing terms. In the next chapter, I discuss the relation of the two legal systems and their part in the construction of English national self-understanding.

10. In *Elizabethan Critical Essays,* edited by G. Gregory Smith, 2 vols. (Oxford: Clarendon Press, 1904), 1.137 (Stanyhurst), 1.240 and 266–90 (Webbe), and 2.117–41 (Puttenham).

11. "Master Stanyhurst (though otherwise learned) trod a foul, lumbering, boisterous, wallowing measure in his translation of Virgil. He had never been praised by Gabriel [Harvey] for his labor if therein he had not been so famously absurd." Nashe in Smith, *Elizabethan Critical Essays,* 2.240.

12. *Ben Jonson,* edited by C. H. Herford, Percy Simpson, and Evelyn Simpson, 11 vols. (Oxford: Clarendon Press, 1925–52), 6:493. I have adopted a few minor variants from the earliest edition cited by Herford and Simpson in their textual notes.

13. See, for example, *The Works of Thomas Nashe,* edited by Ronald B. McKerrow and F. P. Wilson, 5 vols. (Oxford: Clarendon Press, 1958), 2:250.

14. The issues raised in this paragraph are central to my *Elizabethan Prodigals* (Berkeley: Univ. of California Press, 1976).

15. G. K. Hunter, *John Lyly: The Humanist as Courtier* (London: Routledge, 1962), pp. 1–35. For a discussion of the more positive effect of the court on poetry, see Daniel Javitch, *Poetry and Courtliness in Renaissance England* (Princeton: Princeton Univ. Press, 1978).

16. I discuss the relation of the two parts of *Euphues* in greater detail in *The Elizabethan Prodigals,* pp. 58–78.

17. Smith, *Elizabethan Critical Essays,* 2.116.

18. Sidney, *An Apology for Poetry,* edited by Geoffrey Shepherd (Edinburgh: Nelson, 1965) pp. 140 and 139.

19. *The Complete Works in Verse and Prose of Samuel Daniel,* edited by Alexander B. Grosart, 4 vols. (London: Spenser Society, 1885–96), 1.280.

20. Daniel, *Poems and A Defence of Ryme,* edited by Sprague, p. 81. (Quotations from Daniel identified by page number in the text are from this edition.) Daniel's reference to England as "thrust from the world" echoes a much-cited phrase from Virgil's first eclogue, "toto divisos orbe Britannos." In a chapter that includes an interesting discussion of Daniel, Gerald M. Maclean surveys English allusions to this phrase from the late-sixteenth to the mid-seventeenth century (*Time's Witness: Historical Representation in English Poetry, 1603–1660* [Madison: Univ. of Wisconsin Press, 1990], pp. 64–126). Clearly, the Roman sense of Britain—*ultima Britannia,* they called it—as far removed from the center of civilization contributed significantly to English self-alienation in the sixteenth century.

21. *The Works of Thomas Campion,* edited by Walter R. Davis (Garden City, NY: Doubleday, 1967), p. 291.

22. Daniel, *Complete Works,* edited by Grosart, 1.153. In his fourth volume of *Reports* (1604), the first to be published after James became king of England, Sir Edward Coke made a very similar attack on legal innovation, one that, like Daniel's, is quite clearly directed at the new king. Together Coke's preface and Daniel's small volume testify to the fear—a fear which persisted through much of James's reign—that the king would try to alter the fundamental laws of England, replacing English common law with the Roman civil law practiced in Scotland. In the face of that menace, English national self-consciousness became increasingly intense.

23. See *The Invention of Tradition,* edited by Eric Hobsbawm and Terence Ranger (Cambridge: Cambridge Univ. Press, 1983).

24. Attridge, *Well-Weighed Syllables,* pp. 127–28.

25. Jonathan Goldberg discusses the king's taste for the Roman in *James I and the Politics of Literature* (Baltimore: Johns Hopkins Univ. Press, 1983). See especially chap. 4, "The Roman Actor."

26. On the architecture of Penshurst and its relation to Jonson's poem, see Don E. Wayne, *Penshurst: The Semiotics of Place and the Poetics of History* (Madison: Univ. of Wisconsin Press, 1984).

27. The opposition between Roman civil law and English common law is

central to F. W. Maitland's *English Law and the Renaissance* (Cambridge: Cambridge Univ. Press, 1901). I discuss Maitland's thesis in the following chapter.

28. Quoted in *Spenser: The Critical Heritage,* edited by R. M. Cummings (New York: Barnes and Noble, 1971), pp. 260–61.

29. Richard Hurd, *Letters on Chivalry and Romance (1762),* edited by Hoyt Trowbridge, The Augustan Reprint Society, nos. 101–2 (Los Angeles: Clark Library, 1963), p. 56.

30. These quotations come from Thomas Rymer, Joseph Addison, Samuel Cobb, and John Dennis. See Cummings, *Spenser,* pp. 206, 224, 232, and 229.

31. Sidney, *Apology,* p. 133.

32. Daniel quoted by Cummings, *Spenser,* p. 77.

33. For some of those other enemies of romance, see Robert P. Adams, "Bold Bawdry and Open Manslaughter: The English New Humanist Attack on Medieval Romance," *Huntington Library Quarterly* 23 (1959/60): 33–48.

34. Ben Jonson, *The Complete Masques,* edited by Stephen Orgel (New Haven: Yale Univ. Press, 1969), pp. 148–49. Norman Council discusses this passage in the context of the humanist opposition to chivalry in "Ben Jonson, Inigo Jones, and the Transformation of Tudor Chivalry," *ELH* 17 (1980): 259–75. See also Roy Strong's more recent treatment of the passage in *Henry, Prince of Wales, and England's Lost Renaissance* (London: Thames and Hudson, 1986), pp. 141–43. As Strong points out, Jonson's text is pulled two ways at once, a division that may well reflect differences between Prince Henry and his father.

35. For a general discussion of this development, see Arthur B. Ferguson, *The Articulate Citizen and the English Renaissance* (Durham, NC: Duke Univ. Press, 1965).

36. J. H. Hexter discusses the antiaristocratic bent of More, Erasmus, and other early sixteenth-century Christian humanists in his introduction to *Utopia* in the *Yale Edition of the Complete Works of St. Thomas More* (New Haven: Yale Univ. Press, 1965), pp. xxiii–cxxiv. On the relation of Erasmus and his *miles christianus* to the "burgher" culture of the Low Countries, see Simon Schama, *The Embarrassment of Riches: An Interpretation of Dutch Culture in the Golden Age* (Berkeley: Univ. of California Press, 1988), pp. 326–28.

37. Spenser's extensive borrowings from *Gerusalemme Liberata* in the 1590 *Faerie Queene* provide powerful evidence of his close study of Tasso's poem. For a list of these borrowings, see Veselin Kostić, *Spenser's Sources in Italian Poetry: A Study in Comparative Literature* (Belgrade: Filoloski Facultet Beogradskog Univerziteta Monografije, 1969).

38. *Godfrey of Bulloigne: A Critical Edition of Edward Fairfax's Translation of Tasso's* Gerusalemme Liberata, edited by Kathleen M. Lea and T. M. Gang (Oxford: Clarendon Press, 1981). Unless otherwise indicated, subsequent quotations from *Gerusalemme Liberata* are from this translation.

39. Sergio Zatti, "Cultural Conflict as Military Encounter in the *Jerusa-*

lem Delivered," paper read to the Southern California Renaissance Conference (1983). I have also drawn in my discussion of Tasso on Zatti's book, *L'Uniforme Cristiano e il Multiforme Pagano: Saggio sulla "Gerusalemme Liberata"* (Milan: Il Saggiatore, 1983). The phrase "secret solidarity" in the next sentence is borrowed from Zatti.

40. Hurd, *Letters on Chivalry*, p. 79.

41. Mervyn James, *Society, Politics and Culture: Studies in Early Modern England* (Cambridge: Cambridge Univ. Press, 1986), p. 460.

42. Of the twelve pre-1590 editions of the *Gerusalemme Liberata* listed in the British Library catalog, seven, including the 1581 Ferrara edition and every edition published after 1581, contain the author's allegory. Another, Parma 1581 (British Library 1073.g.31.(1.)), clearly had access to it and used it as the basis for its allegorizations of individual cantos. The allegory is lacking only in the unauthorized and incomplete edition of 1580 and the Parma (British Library 1489.p.12), Casalmaggiore, and Lione editions of 1581. It is thus probable that in reading Tasso's poem, Spenser would also have read the allegory.

43. *Godfrey of Bulloigne*, p. 90. The following two quotations in this paragraph come from pp. 88 and 93.

44. James Nohrnberg, *The Analogy of* The Faerie Queene (Princeton: Princeton Univ. Press, 1976), pp. 61–63.

45. Arthur B. Ferguson surveys some of this opposition to the chivalric revival in *The Chivalric Tradition in Renaissance England* (Washington: Folger Shakespeare Library, 1986), pp. 83–106.

46. I assume here some acquaintance with the large body of scholarship that has recently been devoted to the Elizabethan chivalric revival. In addition to the work of Ferguson, McCoy, Esler, and James, cited in the notes immediately surrounding this one, see Frances A. Yates, *Astraea: The Imperial Theme in the Sixteenth Century* (London: Routledge, 1975); Roy Strong, *The Cult of Elizabeth: Elizabethan Portraiture and Pageantry* (London: Thames and Hudson, 1977); and Alan Young, *Tudor and Jacobean Tournaments* (London: George Philip, 1987).

47. Richard C. McCoy, "'Yet Little Lost or Won': Chivalry in *The Faerie Queene*," paper delivered at Modern Language Association Convention in Houston (1980). Since the completion of this chapter, McCoy's important work on Elizabethan chivalry has appeared in book form. See *The Rites of Knighthood: The Literature and Politics of Elizabethan Chivalry* (Berkeley: Univ. of California Press, 1989).

48. Richard C. McCoy, "'A dangerous image': The Earl of Essex and Elizabethan Chivalry," *Journal of Medieval and Renaissance Studies* 13 (1983): 313–29. All the quotations and most of the information in this paragraph are taken from McCoy's article. For the quotations, see pp. 315, 316, 319, 322, and 313. Similar arguments concerning Essex are made by Arthur Ferguson, *Chivalric Tradition*, pp. 73–74, by Anthony Esler, *The Aspiring Mind of the*

Elizabethan Younger Generation (Durham, NC: Duke Univ. Press, 1966), pp. 87–99, and by Mervyn James, *Society, Politics and Culture,* pp. 416–65.

49. In his "Prothalamion," ll.146 and 150–51 (8.261).

50. Zatti remarks that "the *Jerusalem Delivered* closes historically the season of the chivalric poem" ("Cultural Conflict"). The characterization of the Essex revolt as the last English "honor revolt" comes from James, *Society, Politics and Culture,* p. 416.

51. James, *Society, Politics and Culture,* p. 458.

52. In his article on Burghley in *The Spenser Encyclopedia,* edited by A. C. Hamilton (Toronto: Univ. of Toronto Press, 1990), pp. 121–22, Mark Eccles describes Spenser's antagonistic relationship with the lord treasurer. Especially interesting for the purposes of this chapter are Spenser's attacks on Burghley in *Mother Hubberds Tale* for underrating "Nobilitie" and for failing to reward men of learning (by which Spenser meant poets) and soldiers. Eccles neglects, however, to mention that Spenser's association with the Sidney-Leicester-Essex faction helped determine his opposition to Burghley.

53. Quoted by Conyers Read, *Lord Burghley and Queen Elizabeth* (London: Jonathan Cape, 1960), p. 538.

54. R. C. Strong and J. A. van Dorsten, *Leicester's Triumph* (Leiden: Leiden Univ. Press, 1964), p. 3.

55. An exception is Michael Leslie's *Spenser's 'Fierce Warres and Faithfull Loves': Martial and Chivalric Symbolism in* The Faerie Queene (Cambridge: D. S. Brewer, 1983). But even Leslie ignores the broader and more pervasive effects of chivalric romance to concentrate on the moral, religious, and historical significance of chivalric symbolism and knightly combat in specific passages. He is, as every academic literary critic must be, an obsessive close reader. Needless to say, for most of us this obsession is more institutional than individual.

56. Thomas Warton, *Observations on the Fairy Queen of Spenser,* 2 vols. (1754; 2nd ed. corr. and enl. London: Dodsley, 1762), 1.3.

57. This view has been elaborated in two book-length studies: Thomas H. Cain, *Praise in* The Faerie Queene (Lincoln: Univ. of Nebraska Press, 1978) and Robin Headlam Wells, *Spenser's* Faerie Queene *and the Cult of Elizabeth* (London: Croom Helm, 1983).

58. Michael O'Connell discusses these two figures and their likeness to Queen Elizabeth in *Mirror and Veil: The Historical Dimension of Spenser's* Faerie Queene (Chapel Hill: Univ. of North Carolina Press, 1977), pp. 52–54 and 105–7.

59. "The political culture of the [medieval] world of honor was," as Mervyn James has written in *Society, Politics and Culture,* "essentially pluralist. There was little room for the concepts of sovereignty, or of unconditional obedience, and such other *étatiste* notions. . . . Honor societies revered kingship, but the place which will and autonomy occupied in the honor code implied the possibility of changing one's master, if he could no longer be freely and honorably

served. Seen in terms of honor . . . kingship constituted one authority (admittedly the dominant one, whose claim to 'faithfulness' was the widest and most inclusive) among a number. . . . It was only gradually, and during the Tudor period, that the realm and the community of honor came to be identical, presided over by a crown whose sovereign authority constituted the only kind of 'lordship' which effectively survived" (pp. 327–28).

60. This substitution has often been noticed. I discuss it briefly in *Self-Crowned Laureates* (Berkeley: Univ. of California Press, 1983), pp. 92–96. It should be noted that in this passage from Book 6 Spenser's resistance to the monarch comes not from the aristocratic position that underlies chivalric romance, but rather from still another position—neither monarchic nor aristocratic—that is Spenser's as poet. Calidore, the chivalric knight, is as unwelcome and disruptive a figure on Mt. Acidale as the queen. This passage, where for the only time in *The Faerie Queene* Spenser appears in the pastoral guise of Colin Clout, has strong affinities with Colin's other poems, with *The Shepheardes Calender* and *Colin Clouts Come Home Againe,* and more generally with the large and miscellaneous collection of poems that Spenser published in the 1590s between the first and second installment of *The Faerie Queene.* I think particularly of *The Teares of the Muses, Mother Hubberds Tale, Muiopotmos,* the *Amoretti,* and *Prothalamion.* Though these works share with *The Faerie Queene* an engagement in the systems of patronage and power that centered on the queen and the greater nobility, they also express a considerable measure of alienation from both—alienation that grounds itself on the autonomous authority of poetry. Paradoxically, it is in the poem that most fully realizes Spenser's laureate ambition that he is most caught up in the sometimes conflicting, sometimes mutually supporting claims of the crown and the aristocracy and least able to represent the claims of poetry itself.

61. In addition to Lucifera, Philotime, and Mercilla, one might consider the emasculating Amazon Radigund and even the captivating witch Acrasia as types of Elizabeth in her effect on the knights who were drawn to her court. Spenser could easily have disavowed such identifications. Perhaps he never thought of them. But they are readily activated by the cultural field in which *The Faerie Queene* was produced and first received, a cultural field characterized by England's subjection to a powerful female monarch. For discussions of that cultural field, see Louis Adrian Montrose, "'Shaping Fantasies': Figurations of Gender and Power in Elizabethan Culture," *Representations* 2 (1983): 61–94, and Leah S. Marcus, *Puzzling Shakespeare: Local Reading and Its Discontents* (Berkeley: Univ. of California Press, 1988), pp. 51–105.

62. The moralization of politics and the displacement of lineage as the prime source of honor are central themes of Mervyn James's *Society, Politics and Culture.*

63. This impossibility is illustrated by the efforts of the baseborn Braggadocchio to learn horsemanship, "a science / Proper to gentle blood" (2.4.1). Compare young Tristram, whose knightly behavior shows him to be "borne of noble blood" (6.2.24) despite his rude upbringing.

64. *The Correspondence of Sir Philip Sidney and Hubert Languet,* edited by Steuart A. Pears (London: William Pickering, 1845), p. 154.

65. On the value of lineage and heroic endeavor, the poet is less certain than his poem. In *The Teares of the Muses,* he mocks in the name of learning those "mightie Peeres" who "onely boast of Armes and Auncestrie." Such mockery has no place in *The Faerie Queene.* As I suggest in note 60 above, Spenser's major poem was not the site of his strongest or most explicit claims for the autonomy of poetry.

66. Sir John Fortescue, *De Laudibus Legum Anglie,* edited by S. B. Chrimes (Cambridge: Cambridge Univ. Press, 1942), p. xvii.

67. *The Poetical Works of John Milton,* edited by Helen Darbishire, 2 vols. (Oxford: Clarendon Press, 1952), 1.3–4.

68. *Complete Prose Works of John Milton,* edited by Don M. Wolfe et al., 8 vols. (New Haven: Yale Univ. Press, 1953–82), 3.542.

69. I discuss this move at greater length in the Milton chapter of *Self-Crowned Laureates* (esp. pp. 231–52) and in "Milton Reads the King's Book: Print, Performance, and the Making of a Bourgeois Idol," *Criticism* 29 (1987): 1–25.

Chapter Two

1. Thomas Starkey, *A Dialogue between Reginald Pole and Thomas Lupset,* edited by Kathleen M. Burton (London: Chatto and Windus, 1948), pp. 174–75.

2. See G. R. Elton, "Reform by Statute: Thomas Starkey's *Dialogue* and Thomas Cromwell's Policy," *Proceedings of the British Academy* 54 (1968): 165–88. While arguing against Henry's having received the *Dialogue,* which he considers incomplete, Elton does present evidence that even in this form it circulated among Cromwell's supporters and may have had an effect on some Cromwellian legislation. In dismissing the usual understanding that Starkey "advocated the simple replacement of the common law by the civil law of Rome" as a misreading, Elton is, however, himself guilty of misreading. The *Dialogue* does advocate that replacement, though it also advocates codification of existing English law as a less satisfactory but still desirable solution to the uncertainty characteristic of legal practice in England. That the suggestion of codification should arise from a Romanist critique of English law is itself highly significant. It is from the "Roman" point of view that the unwritten character of English law seems most objectionable.

3. Frederic William Maitland, *English Law and the Renaissance* (Cambridge: Cambridge Univ. Press, 1901), p. 22.

4. Among the most prominent critics of Maitland's thesis are W. S. Holdsworth, *A History of English Law,* 16 vols. (London: Methuen, 1903–66), 4.252–85; G. R. Elton, "The Political Creed of Thomas Cromwell," *Transactions of the Royal Historical Society,* 5th series, 6 (1956): 78, and "Reform by Statute," pp. 176–77; H. E. Bell, *Maitland: A Critical Examination and*

Assessment (Cambridge, Mass.: Harvard Univ. Press, 1965), pp. 130–37; and S. E. Thorne, "English Law and the Renaissance," in *La Storia del Diritto nel Quadro delle Scienze Storiche* (Florence: L. S. Olschki, 1966), pp. 437–45. Reinterpretations and positive reevaluations of Maitland's argument have been proposed by W. H. Dunham in a review of Bell's *Maitland, Yale Law Journal* 75 (1966): 1059–64, and Dafydd Jenkins, "English Law and the Renaissance—Eighty Years On: In Defence of Maitland," *Journal of Legal History* 2 (1981): 107–42.

5. J. H. Baker, "English Law and the Renaissance," *Cambridge Law Journal* 44 (1985): 46–61. This essay has been reprinted in Baker, *The Legal Profession and the Common Law: Historical Essays* (London: Hambledon Press, 1986), pp. 461–76.

6. John Selden, *The Historie of Tithes* (1618), pp. 478 and 480. The following quotation concerning the equal antiquity of all systems of law comes from Selden's 1616 edition of Fortescue's *De Laudibus Legum Angliae,* sig. C1. For a careful discussion of these texts and Selden's other early writings, see Paul Christianson, "Young John Selden and the Ancient Constitution, ca. 1610–18," *Proceedings of the American Philosophical Society* 128 (1984): 271–315.

7. J. H. Baker, *The Reports of John Spelman,* 2 vols. (London: Selden Society, 1978), 2.50.

8. Further evidence of the growing cosmopolitanism that marks the difference between Baker's two assessments of Maitland is furnished by Gino Gorla and Luigi Moccia, "A 'Revisiting' of the Comparison between 'Continental Law' and 'English Law' (16th to 19th Century)" and Luigi Moccia, "English Attitudes to the 'Civil Law'," *Journal of Legal History* 2 (1981): 143–56 and 157–68. Daniel R. Coquillette's articles, cited in note 22 below, are also symptomatic of this shift.

9. Despite my introductory declaration of having been surprised by evidence that, in at least one instance, forced me to tell a story I did not want to tell, this inclination has no doubt shaped the present book in ways that are quite beyond my knowing but that will be retrospectively visible should any sufficiently distant future reader care to look. The authorial "I" is multiply constituted and wants contradictory things.

10. Maitland, *English Law,* pp. 10 and 52–53. See also H. D. Hazeltine's preface to Sir John Fortescue, *De Laudibus Legum Anglie,* edited by S. B. Chrimes (Cambridge: Cambridge Univ. Press, 1942), p. xvii.

11. Quoted by S. E. Thorne, "English Law," p. 440. See also Elton's discussion of Morison in "Reform by Statute," pp. 177–80.

12. J. G. A. Pocock, *The Ancient Constitution and the Feudal Law* (1957; enlarged ed. Cambridge: Cambridge Univ. Press, 1987), p. 56. On the more general issue of the insularity of English legal scholarship in this period, see Donald R. Kelley, "History, English Law and the Renaissance," *Past and Present* 65 (1974): 24–51. A criticism of Kelley's argument by Christopher Brooks and Kevin Sharpe can be found, together with Kelley's response, in *Past and Present* 72 (1976): 133–46.

13. The enormous increase in litigation during Elizabeth's reign no doubt gave greater urgency in the later period to the sense that England's law needed reform. See C. W. Brooks, "Litigants and Attorneys in the King's Bench and Common Pleas, 1560–1640," in *Legal Records and the Historian,* edited by J. H. Baker (London: Royal Historical Society, 1978), pp. 41–59.

14. *The Works of Francis Bacon,* edited by James Spedding, 14 vols. (London: Longmans, 1857–74), 10.3. Volumes 8–14 of this edition are often cited as volumes 1–7 of *The Letters and Life of Francis Bacon.* I have not followed this practice.

15. The following passages, which I have arranged in approximate chronological order, provide a good idea of both the persistence and the character of Bacon's ideas concerning the writing of English law: "Opening of Speech on Motion for Supply" (8.213–14); *Gesta Grayorum* (8.339–40); *Maxims of the Law* (7.313–87), *The Advancement of Learning* (3.475–76); "A Preparation toward the Union of Laws" (7.731–43); "A Speech . . . [on] a Motion Concerning the Union of Laws" (10.336); "Commentarius" (11.74 and 94); "Letter to King James" (13.59–60); "A Memorial touching the Review of Penal Laws and the Amendment of the Common Law" (12.84–86); "Proposition . . . touching the Compiling and Amendment of the Laws of England" (13.61–71); *Advertisement touching an Holy War* (7.14); and *De Augmentis Scientiarum* (5.88–110). Despite extraordinary personal and historical changes from the 1590s to the 1620s, Bacon's views on this topic remained remarkably consistent, so consistent that I have felt free to draw on various passages in summarizing his views without regard for chronology.

16. Bacon's interest in the institute as the crucial genre for the writing of national law was widely shared in early modern Europe. There have been a number of valuable surveys of this literature: Klaus Luig, "The Institutes of National Law in the Seventeenth and Eighteenth Centuries," *Juridical Review* n.s. 17 (1972): 193–226; Alan Watson, *The Making of the Civil Law* (Cambridge, Mass.: Harvard Univ. Press, 1981), pp. 62–82, and "Justinian's Institutes and Some English Counterparts," *Studies in Justinian's Institutes,* edited by P. G. Stein and A. D. E. Lewis (London: Sweet and Maxwell, 1983), pp. 181–86; F. H. Lawson, "Institutes," *Festschrift für Imre Zajtay,* edited by R. H. Graveson et al. (Tübingen: Mohr, 1982), pp. 333–55; John W. Cairns, "Blackstone, An English Institutist: Legal Literature and the Rise of the Nation State," *Oxford Journal of Legal Studies* 4 (1984): 318–60; and the introduction to *Justinian's Institutes,* edited by Peter Birks and Grant McLeod (Ithaca, New York: Cornell Univ. Press, 1987), pp. 7–26. See also A. W. B. Simpson's discussion of institutional writing in relation to other forms of legal literature in "The Rise and Fall of the Legal Treatise: Legal Principles and the Forms of Legal Literature," *University of Chicago Law Review* 48 (1981): 632–79.

17. In his first parliamentary speech in 1593, Bacon claimed that "nothing should tend more to the eternal praise of her majesty" (8.214) than a general abridgment of the law, and he was still saying much the same thing

under a new monarch more than twenty years later. "After I had thought of many things," he wrote to King James in 1616, "I could find, in my judgment, none more proper for your majesty as a master, nor for me as a workman, than the reducing and recompiling of the laws of England" (13.62). Such "lawgivers" as Justinian, to whom he regularly points as the most obvious example, stand only behind "founders of estates" in the "degrees of sovereign honor." They are *principes perpetui,* for they continue to rule "after their decease in their laws" (13.64). It is to this eminence that he urged first Elizabeth and then James to aspire. With few exceptions, all the texts in which Bacon argued for the rewriting of the law—his *Maxims,* his *Advancement of Learning,* his "Preparation toward the Union of Laws," his "Memorial touching the Review of Penal Laws," his "Proposition touching the Amendment of the Laws," and his *De Augmentis Scientiarum*—were addressed to the monarch. Even in his private notes, he thought of the king as his eventual audience: "Persuad. the k. in glory, *Aurea condet saecula.* New laws to be compounded and collected; lawgiver *perpetuis princeps*" (11.73–74). And when he slipped his familiar plea for a rewriting of the law into the script of the revels he prepared for the "readers and ancients" of Gray's Inn, he directed it to a fictional Prince of Purpoole (8.339–40). With the support of the monarch, who is the "soul of the law" (8.313), his project would prosper. Without that authorizing support, it had neither hope nor meaning.

18. W. S. Holdsworth, *A History of English Law,* 16 vols. (London: Methuen, 1903–66), 5.399.

19. Wilfred Prest, "The Dialectical Origins of Finch's *Law,*" *Cambridge Law Journal* 36 (1977): 343. On the relation between Finch and Justinian, see Alan Watson, "Justinian's Institutes and Some English Counterparts," *Studies in Justinian's Institutes,* edited by P. G. Stein and A. D. E. Lewis (London: Sweet and Maxwell, 1983), pp. 181–86.

20. On the *Interpreter* affair, see J. P. Sommerville, *Politics and Ideology in England, 1603–1640* (London: Longman, 1986), pp. 121–27. The more general opposition between absolutist and common-law notions of rule that figures largely in this chapter is a principal subject of Sommerville's valuable book.

21. Abraham Fraunce, *The Lawiers Logike* (1588), sig. ¶¶1–1ᵛ.

22. Quoted by Brian P. Levack, *The Civil Lawyers in England, 1603–1641: A Political Study* (Oxford: Clarendon Press, 1973), p. 123. For an excellent discussion of civilian attitudes toward the common law, see Levack's chapter on "The Laws of England," pp. 122–57. The contribution of civilians to English legal thought has been surveyed in a series of articles by Daniel R. Coquillette. Particularly relevant to the concerns of this chapter are the first two articles in the series: "Legal Ideology and Incorporation I: The English Civilian Writers, 1523–1607" and "Legal Ideology and Incorporation II: Sir Thomas Ridley, Charles Molloy, and the Literary Battle for the Law Merchant, 1607–1616," *Boston University Law Review* 61 (1981): 1–89 and 315–71.

23. *The Political Works of James I,* edited by Charles Howard McIlwain (Cambridge, Mass.: Harvard Univ. Press, 1918), p. 62.

24. Henry Finch, *Nomotexnia* (1613), sig. ¶iii^v. I am grateful to G. W. Pigman for directing my attention to the echo from Virgil.

25. John Cowell, *The Interpreter* (1607), sig. *3.

26. W. O. Hassall, *A Catalogue of the Library of Sir Edward Coke* (New Haven, Conn.: Yale Univ. Press, 1950), nos. 422, 435–39, 445, 459, 461, 464, 466, 469, 486–91, and 745. For Finch's *Nomotechnia,* see p. xxiin56.

27. Hassall, *Catalogue,* p. 38.

28. Catherine Drinker Bowen describes this volume in *The Lion and the Throne: The Life and Times of Sir Edward Coke* (Boston: Little, Brown, 1956), pp. 424 and 549–50. I adopt Bowen's translation of Coke's Latin. For the original, see Hassall, *Catalogue,* no. 745.

29. Peter Stein discusses Bacon's *Maxims* in relation to the Roman tradition in *Regulae Juris: From Juristic Rules to Legal Maxims* (Edinburgh: Edinburgh Univ. Press, 1966), pp. 170–76.

30. The printed reports are surveyed by Theodore F. T. Plucknett, "The Genesis of Coke's Reports," *Cornell Law Quarterly* 27 (1942): 190–213. For a discussion of both manuscript and printed reports, see L. W. Abbott, *Law Reporting in England, 1485–1585* (London: Athlone Press, 1973).

31. J. H. Baker describes the three extant manuscripts and speculates concerning the contents of the other four in "Coke's Note-Books and the Sources of his Reports," *The Legal Profession and the Common Law,* pp. 177–204.

32. I quote Coke's *Reports* by volume and signature from the following first editions: 1 (1600); 2 (1602); 3 (1602); 4 (1604); 5 (1605); 6 (1607); 7 (1608); 8 (1611); 9 (1613); 10 (1614); and 11 (1615). The present quotation is from 1.¶ iii–iii^v.

33. Sir John Hayward, *A Treatise of Union of the Two Realmes of England and Scotland* (1604), sig. C2.

34. James cited the maxim *rex est lex loquens* in his parliamentary speech of 1607 (*Political Works,* pp. 291 and 299). The maxim was also used by Lord Chancellor Ellesmere, who attributes it specifically to "some grave and notable writers of the civil law" (*A Complete Collection of State Trials,* edited by T. B. Howell, 21 vols. [London: Longman, 1816], 2.693). For Coke's *judex est lex loquens,* see 7.biv.

35. In Louis A. Knafla, *Law and Politics in Jacobean England: The Tracts of Lord Chancellor Ellesmere* (Cambridge: Cambridge Univ. Press, 1977), p. 190.

36. As examples of Coke's hyperbolical praise of all legal things English, consider the following: he calls the Inns of Court "the most famous university for profession of law only . . . that is in the world" (3.Div^v), Littleton's *Tenures* "a work of as absolute perfection . . . as any book that I have known written in any human learning" (10.div^v–v), English lawyers nonpareils of "honesty, gravity, and integrity" (2.¶v), and English law "the most ancient and best inheritance that the subjects of this realm have" (5.Avi).

37. The essays of Plucknett and Baker cited in notes 30 and 31 above

illustrate the lawyers' emphasis; the intellectual historians' emphasis can be found in Pocock's *Ancient Constitution,* pp. 30–69, and Sommerville's *Politics and Ideology,* pp. 86–111.

38. Sir John Davies, *Le Primer Report des Cases . . . en Ireland* (1615), sig. *1^V.

39.Bowen, *The Lion and the Throne,* p. 378. The first and last quotations in the next paragraph also come from Bowen, pp. 379 and 388.

40. Knafla, *Law and Politics in Jacobean England,* p. 297. The conflict in 1616 between Egerton's Court of Chancery and Coke's common law jurisdiction has been expertly surveyed by J. H. Baker in "The Common Lawyers and the Chancery: 1616," *The Legal Profession and the Common Law,* pp. 205–29.

41. Six months after Coke's fall, Bacon was still expressing concern over the *Reports.* "I did call upon the judges' committee also," he wrote Buckingham in May of 1617, "for the proceeding in the purging of Sir Edward Coke's *Reports,* which I see they go on with seriously" (13.199).

42. Two additional volumes appeared posthumously in 1658 and 1659, but these were not prepared for publication by Coke, contain only cases heard prior to the loss of his judicial position, and include no authorial preface.

43. Bowen, *The Lion and the Throne,* p. 484. Bowen seems to have assembled this "speech," which accurately represents things Coke said even though he may never have produced this particular string of words as a single utterance, out of a variety of sources. See, for example, the different reports of Coke's interventions in the House of Commons on March 29, 1628, in *Commons Debates 1628,* edited by Robert C. Johnson and Maija Jansson Cole, 3 vols. (New Haven: Yale Univ. Press, 1977), 2.187–209.

44. *Justinian's Institutes,* translated by Birks and McLeod, pp. 33 and 36.

45. *Calendar of State Papers, Domestic, 1629–1631* (London: Longman, 1860), p. 490.

46. Baker, "Coke's Note-Books," pp. 196–98.

47. *Reports* 10.dv, and *Institutes* 1.¶3^V. Except where otherwise indicated, I quote Coke's *Institutes* from the following editions: Part 1 (1628); part 2 (1642); part 3 (1644); and part 4 (1644). For all of part 1, except the preface, I quote leaf rather than signature numbers, with "a" for recto and "b" for verso. These leaf numbers from the first edition supply the standard reference system for subsequent editions.

48. *Institutes* 1.394b.

49. In his article on Littleton in *The Interpreter,* John Cowell quoted the French civilian François Hotman's opinion of the *Tenures* as "confused, clumsy, and ridiculous." According to Cowell, English law generally was equally subject to scorn. It "has hardly escaped," he wrote, "among foreigners the blame of barbarism" *(Institutiones Juris Anglicani* [1605], sig. A4).

50. The two versions of this remark that I have here combined read: "I shall have estate in my land, and be tenant at will for my liberty. Littleton never discovered that," and "Shall I be tenant for life of my land and at will for my liberty?" *Commons Debates 1628,* pp. 195 and 209.

51. Davies, *Le Primer Report,* sig. *4^{v}–5.

52. Hassall, *Catalogue,* no. 469. I have not seen this volume, which was published in Lyon in 1559, but I have seen the presumably similar 1555 Geneva edition with Accursius' glosses.

53. Baker, "English Law and the Renaissance," p. 59.

54. The many branching diagrams that later readers (Coke among them) have produced to describe the contents of Littleton's *Tenures* are testimony to its systematic, synchronic quality. Ideally, it can all be seen at once. No comparable representation of Coke's commentary would be possible. Instead of systematizing, it disrupts system, introducing dimensions that a diagram cannot show. For a collection of branching diagrams based on Littleton, see *The First Part of the Institutes of the Laws of England,* 2 vols. (Philadelphia: Robert H. Small, 1853), 1.xli and xliii–lx.

55. Roger North, *The Lives of the Norths,* 3 vols. (London: Henry Colburn, 1826), 1.21n. William Blackstone, *Commentaries on the Laws of England,* 4 vols. (1765–69; facs. rpt. Chicago: Univ. of Chicago Press, 1979), 1.73. And Holdsworth, *A History of English Law,* 5.482n1.

56. Coke's reluctance in this regard was quickly violated. "The undeniable importunity of some especial friends" pushed the printer into supplying a "table" to the *First Institute* as early as its second edition in 1629, just a year after the first. See the note to that effect on the title page to the second edition, a reproduction of which heads this chapter.

57. Thomas Hobbes, *A Dialogue between a Philosopher and a Student of the Common Laws of England,* in *The English Works,* edited by Sir William Moleworth, 11 vols. (London: Bohn and Longman, 1939–45), 6.14–15. In response to the lawyer, who quotes this passage from Coke, the philosopher (obviously Hobbes himself) says: "Do you think this to be good doctrine? Though it be true that no man is born with the use of reason, yet all men may grow up to it as well as lawyers; and when they have applied their reason to the laws (which were laws before they studied them, or else it was not law they studied) may be as fit for and capable of judicature as Sir Edward Coke himself, who, whether he had more or less use of reason, was not thereby a judge, but because the king made him so. And whereas he says, that a man who should have as much reason as is dispersed in so many several heads could not make such a law as this law of England is, if one should ask him who made the law of England, would he say a succession of English lawyers or judges made it, or rather a succession of kings? And that upon their own reason, either solely, or with the advice of the lords and commons in parliament, without the judges or other professors of the law? You see therefore that the king's reason, be it more or less, is that *anima legis,* that *summa lex,* whereof Sir Edward Coke speaketh, and not the reason, learning, and wisdom of the judges. But you may see that quite through his *Institutes of Law* he often takes occasion to magnify the learning of the lawyers, whom he perpetually termeth the sages of the parliament or of the king's council. Therefore, unless you say otherwise, I say that the king's reason, when it is publicly upon advice and

deliberation declared, is that *anima legis;* and that *summa ratio* and that equity, which all agree to be the law of reason, is all that is or ever was law in England since it became Christian, besides the Bible."

58. From the posthumous *Twelfth Reports,* quoted by Roland G. Usher in "James I and Sir Edward Coke," *English Historical Review* 18 (1903): 664. Usher casts considerable doubt on the accuracy of Coke's account but none at all on the fact that Coke would have wanted to be known as having said something like this to the king.

59. Compare *Reports* 3.Cii, where Coke talks of the "coherence and concordance" that emerges from the yearbooks and concludes from this that "without question *lex orta est cum mente divina,* and this admirable unity and consent in such diversity of things proceed from God, the fountain and founder of all good laws and constitutions." In knowing the laws of England, the lawyer knows the mind of God. Thus to say that the king is under God and the law is a redundancy. God and the law are, for all practical purposes, one. For a discussion of Coke's notion of artificial reason, see Charles Gray, "Reason, Authority, and Imagination: The Jurisprudence of Sir Edward Coke," in *Culture and Politics: From Puritanism to the Enlightenment,* edited by Perez Zagorin (Berkeley: Univ. of California Press, 1980), pp. 25–66.

60. That "breaking through" was in fact the experience of reading Coke is suggested by the advice Jeremiah Gridley gave the young John Adams. "You must conquer the *Institutes.* The road to science is much easier now than it was when I set out; I began with *Coke Littleton* and broke through" (Bowen, *The Lion and the Throne,* p. 514).

61. See, for example, James's 1616 speech in Star Chamber where he insisted that "the absolute prerogative of the crown . . . is no subject for the tongue of a lawyer." Elsewhere in the same speech, James denied the countervailing secrecy of the law. "Though the laws be in many places obscure and not so well known to the multitude as to you," he said to his judges, "and that there are many parts that come not into ordinary practice, which are known to you because you can find out the reason thereof by books and precedents, yet know this, that your interpretations must always be subject to common sense and reason"—by which he clearly meant subject to him. "For," as he continued, "I will never trust any interpretation that agreeth not with my common sense and reason, and true logic; for *Ratio est anima legis* in all human laws without exception" *(Political Works,* pp. 333 and 332).

62. In this section I have respected King Charles's censorship and the legal profession's choice and have concentrated only on Coke's *First Institute.* Looking across the sections that head Coke's four volumes, we can, however, see form expressing itself in another way, one that both reinforces and complicates what we have already noticed. Part 1 begins with fee simple, the strongest claim on real property recognized by English common law; part 2, with *Magna Carta,* the earliest of the statutes Coke discusses and the most important; part 3, with "the highest and most heinous crime of high treason" (3.B2); and part 4, with "the high and most honorable court of parliament"

(4.B2). The strongest, the earliest, the most heinous, and the most honorable: these are each the supreme exemplars of the categories to which they belong. And each, in one way or another, implicates the king. All land derives ultimately from the king. There is in England no allodial land, no land held outright by anyone but the king. He alone could be said not to be a tenant. In similar manner, "all liberties," including those set forth in *Magna Carta,* "at the first were derived from the crown" (2.B3). As for high treason, it concerns the king directly—his life, his lineage, his seals and coin, his chief officers, and his peace. And the king sits in parliament, summons it into session, and prorogues it at will. In each case, the supreme legal exemplar depends on the supremacy of the crown. But in each the crown is also limited. The king cannot reclaim the lands or liberties that derive from him. The law of treason protects both the king and the subject. No offense but those named in the statute of 25 Edward III can be punished as treason. And parliament must pass any new law for it to take effect. The king cannot legislate on his own. If the order of Coke's *Institutes,* both the order of its four volumes with respect to one another and the order of the materials in each, represents the order of the state, it is an order under law.

63. Thomas Jefferson quoted by Julian S. Waterman in "Thomas Jefferson and Blackstone's Commentaries," *Illinois Law Review* 27 (1933): 635.

64. George Sharswood quoted on an advertising sheet in *The First Part of the Institutes of the Laws of England,* 2 vols. (Philadelphia: Robert H. Small, 1853).

65. J. H. Thomas, *A Systematic Arrangement of Lord Coke's First Institute* (Philadelphia: Robert H. Small, 1827). On Blackstone's similarity to Justinian, see Cairns, "Blackstone, An English Institutist." The political ideology of Blackstone's *Commentaries* and its relation to the book's formal arrangement has been discussed by Duncan Kennedy, "The Structure of Blackstone's Commentaries," *Buffalo Law Review* 28 (1979): 205–382. Kennedy's important article neglects the intertextual associations of Blackstone's organizational scheme with Justinian and his successors.

Chapter Three

1. Among those earlier maps was one (which has not survived) by Saxton's own mentor, the Yorkshire clergyman John Rudd. Others were drawn by George Lily, Laurence Nowell, and Humphrey Lhuyd. See Sarah Tyacke and John Huddy, *Christopher Saxton and Tudor Map-Making,* British Library Series no. 2 (London: British Library, 1980), pp. 7–11.

2. British Library, G. 3604.

3. R. A. Skelton, *Saxton's Survey of England and Wales with a Facsimile of Saxton's Wall-Map of 1583* (Amsterdam: N. Israel, 1974), p. 22.

4. Coming from a different direction, Victor Morgan has reached a similar conclusion in two overlapping articles, "The Cartographic Image of 'The Country' in Early Modern England," *Transactions of the Royal Historical So-*

ciety, 5th series, 29 (1979): 129–54, and "Lasting Image of the Elizabethan Era," *The Geographic Magazine* 52 (March 1980): 401–8. The former supplies more evidence; the latter states its conclusion more boldly.

5. J. R. Hale quoted in J. B. Harley, "Meaning and Ambiguity in Tudor Cartography," in *English Map-Making, 1500–1650*, edited by Sarah Tyacke (London: British Library, 1983), p. 26. I have profited from Harley's suggestive and informative discussion of "cartographic semantics." Of further interest to those who wish to associate the reading of maps with contemporary interpretive theory are Harley's "Silences and Secrecy: The Hidden Agenda of Cartography in Early Modern Europe," a paper read at the 12th International Conference on the History of Cartography (Paris, 1987); "Maps, Knowledge, and Power," in *The Iconography of Landscape*, edited by Denis Cosgrove and Stephen Daniels (Cambridge: Cambridge Univ. Press, 1988), pp. 277–312; and "Deconstructing the Map," *Cartographica* 26 (1989): 1–20. I responded to the last of these papers in "Dismantling to Build," *Cartographica* 26 (1989): 98–101.

6. Skelton, *Saxton's Survey*, p. 16. Harrison stops at "so perfectly."

7. Skelton, *Saxton's Survey*, p. 16.

8. Skelton, *Saxton's Survey*, p. 17. Skelton's translation. Skelton mistakenly gives 1584 as the date of this edition.

9. These documents are all reprinted by Skelton, *Saxton's Survey*, pp. 15–16.

10. See Ifor M. Evans and Heather Lawrence, *Christopher Saxton, Elizabethan Map-Maker* (Wakefield: Wakefield Historical Publications, 1979), pp. 15–17.

11. In the case of Saxton's maps, the person most responsible for their existence was in all likelihood none of the three we have so far mentioned— not the queen, Seckford, or Saxton—but rather William Cecil, Lord Burghley, who for many years before Saxton's commission had been known for taking "especial pleasure in geographical maps" and for knowing "how to make good use of them in [his] office" (Skelton, *Saxton's Survey*, p. 15); who was the chief signatory of the various governmental decrees favoring Saxton's labors; who was master of the Court of Wards to which Seckford was promoted; whose particular needs determined the order, timing, and specific content of Saxton's survey; and who received, annotated, and even corrected the proofs as they emerged from the press. See Skelton's discussion of Burghley's part in the Saxton survey (p. 8) and the detailed description of Burghley's map-book in Evans and Lawrence, *Saxton*, pp. 143–47.

12. The phrases regarding the use of maps are from Thomas Blunderville and John Dee, both quoted in Morgan, "Lasting Image," pp. 405–6.

13. The full-page coat of arms seems to have been Norden's way of appealing for patronage. The description of Middlesex was dedicated to Elizabeth and a copy of Hertford (British Library, G. 3685) was presented to her. The manuscript description of Essex (1594), presented to the earl of Essex, gives a page to that nobleman's coat of arms (British Library, Additional

Manuscript 33769) and the manuscript description of Windsor (1607) does the same for James, its dedicatee (British Library, Harleian Manuscript 3749). Interestingly, while the map in the Essex volume does bear the royal arms, none of those in the Windsor volume do.

14. *The Works of Michael Drayton,* edited by J. William Hebel, 5 vols. (Oxford: Shakespeare Head Press, 1931–41), 4.vi*. Subsequent references to this edition will be included in the text.

15. On Coke, see J. G. A. Pocock, *The Ancient Constitution and the Feudal Law: A Study of English Historical Thought in the Seventeenth Century* (Cambridge: Cambridge Univ. Press, 1957), chaps. 2 and 3. As it happens, Drayton himself shared Coke's devotion to the continuity of British institutions, as he makes clear in *Poly-Olbion.* But, unlike Coke's, his representation of Britain finally relegates dynastic and institutional continuity to a secondary role.

16. *The Complete Works in Verse and Prose of Samuel Daniel,* edited by Alexander B. Grosart, 4 vols. (London: Spenser Society, 1885–96), 4.102 and 133.

17. I would suggest, though with some hesitation, that even the ugly distortion in the drawing of Britain, the squat lower limbs and the elongated torso, may have been intended. This distortion allows Britain's gown to assume a shape roughly approximating the outline of England and Wales, as one sees it on Saxton's map.

18. The most recent discussion of the Renaissance discovery of the self, Stephen Greenblatt's *Renaissance Self-Fashioning: From More to Shakespeare* (Chicago: Univ. of Chicago Press, 1980), subjects the whole notion to a passionately ironic reexamination. There is, however, no irony in the patriotic fervor of the best known account of the Elizabethan discovery of England, A. L. Rowse's *The England of Elizabeth* (New York: Macmillan, 1951), pp. 31–65.

19. For an interpretation of Jacobean literature that does all it can to support this absolutist view, see Jonathan Goldberg, *James I and the Politics of Literature* (Baltimore: Johns Hopkins Univ. Press, 1983).

20. Transcribed from British Library, G. 3685.

21. From a letter dated July 10, 1618, printed in Richard Parr, *The Life of James Ussher* (1686), p. 65 (letters are paginated separately).

22. Kevin Sharpe, *Sir Robert Cotton, 1586–1631: History and Politics in Early Modern England* (Oxford: Oxford Univ. Press, 1979), p. 32.

23. The most thorough study is Linda Van Norden's "The Elizabethan Society of Antiquaries," (Ph.D. diss., Univ. of California, Los Angeles, 1946). See also Van Norden, "Sir Henry Spelman on the Chronology of the Elizabethan College of Antiquaries," *Huntington Library Quarterly* 13 (1949/50): 131–60, and the discussions by May McKisack, *Medieval History in the Tudor Age* (Oxford: Clarendon Press, 1971), pp. 155–69; F. J. Levy, *Tudor Historical Thought* (San Marino: Huntington Library, 1967), pp. 163–66; and Sharpe, *Cotton,* pp. 17–32.

24. This petition is printed in *A Collection of Curious Discourses,* edited by Thomas Hearne, 2 vols. (London, 1771), 2.324–26.

25. Sir Henry Spelman, quoted by Van Norden in "The Elizabethan Society of Antiquaries," p. 74.

26. On the delight Englishmen took in maps, see Morgan, "Lasting Image," pp. 405–6.

27. Bernard H. Newdigate discusses Drayton's attitude toward James in *Michael Drayton and His Circle* (Oxford: Shakespeare Head Press, 1941), pp. 124–35.

28. A decade later, the names of Camden and Greville were once again significantly linked when they founded the first two chairs of history at Oxford and Cambridge, respectively. See Kevin Sharpe, "The Foundation of the Chairs of History at Oxford and Cambridge: An Episode in Jacobean Politics," *History of Universities* 2 (1982): 127–52.

29. See Joan Grundy, *The Spenserian Poets* (London: Edward Arnold, 1969), where all three are discussed. David Norbrook describes the political attitudes of the seventeenth-century Spenserians in *Poetry and Politics in the English Renaissance* (London: Routledge, 1985), pp. 195–214.

30. On this nostalgia for the age of Elizabeth, see Richard F. Hardin, *Michael Drayton and the Passing of Elizabethan England* (Lawrence: Univ. Press of Kansas, 1973) and Anne Barton, "Harking Back to Elizabeth: Ben Jonson and Caroline Nostalgia," *ELH* 48 (1981): 706–31. In "Two Elizabeths? James I and the Late Queen's Famous Memory," *Canadian Journal of History* 20 (1985): 167–91, D. R. Woolf shows that memories of Elizabeth could also be used by James and those who supported his policies.

31. For an illuminating general discussion of the strategy of self-protective indirection that I am here describing, see Annabel Patterson, *Censorship and Interpretation: The Conditions of Writing and Reading in Early Modern England* (Madison: Univ. of Wisconsin Press, 1985).

32. See K. Tillotson, "Drayton, Browne, and Wither," *TLS* (November 27, 1937): 911.

33. Camden called Saxton, who was by profession a surveyor and was usually designated as such, an "excellent chorographer" (*optimus chorographicus*), and Saxton himself, as we have noticed, specified his relation to his maps with the tag "Christophorus Saxton descripsit." As for Drayton, the subtitle of his *Poly-Olbion*, like the subtitle of Camden's *Britannia*, calls the work a "chorographical description," and the initial lines of its opening argument tell us that "the sprightly Muse her wing displays / And the French Islands first surveys" (4.1).

34. Georges Edelen discusses this medieval tradition in his introduction to Harrison's *Description of England* (Ithaca, New York: Cornell Univ. Press, 1968), pp. xvi–xviii.

35. John Speed, *The Theatre of the Empire of Great Britain,* 2 vols. (1611), sig. A1.

36. Skelton, *Saxton's Survey,* pp. 11–12.

37. Thomas Habington, *A Survey of Worcester,* edited by John Amphlett, 2 vols. (Oxford: Parker, 1895), 1.34, and Thomas Westcote, *A View of Devonshire in MDCXXX,* edited by George Oliver (Exeter: William Roberts, 1845), p. 448.

38. John Coker of Mapowder, *A Survey of Dorsetshire* (1732), p. 79.

39. Coker, *Dorsetshire,* p. 23; William Camden, *Britain,* translated by Philemon Holland (1610), sig. R2; Richard Carew, *The Survey of Cornwall,* edited by F. E. Halliday (London: A. Melrose, 1953), pp. 116–19; George Owen of Henllys, *The Description of Pembrokeshire,* edited by Henry Owen (London: Clark, 1892), p. 41; and Westcote, *Devonshire,* p. 382.

40. Carew, *Cornwall,* p. 138.

41. For an account of Carew's parliamentary service and a description of the constituencies he represented, see P. W. Hasler, *The House of Commons, 1558–1603,* 3 vols. (London: History of Parliament Trust, 1981).

42. Owen, *Pembrokeshire,* p. 9.

43. Carew, *Cornwall,* p. 151.

44. William Lambarde, *A Perambulation of Kent* (Chatham: W. Burrill, 1826), p. 7.

45. Lambarde, *Perambulation* (1596), sig. Ll4^v. In 1576 he had written "antiquities" rather than "topography," an indication that his own sense of what he had done became clearer over the years, particularly as a result of Camden's *Britannia,* which he goes on in 1596 to laud. See also Sir William Dugdale, *The Antiquities of Warwickshire* (1656), sig. a3.

46. See Barbara C. Ewell, "Drayton's *Poly-Olbion:* England's Body Immortalized," *Studies in Philology* 75 (1978): 297–315. In this article, Ewell develops a hint supplied by Angus Fletcher, who claimed that "it could be shown that *Poly-Olbion* is, with *The Faerie Queene* and *Paradise Lost,* one of the most comprehensive and powerful of English sublime poems, though failure to understand its allegorical use of the body image has kept it from any general public favor." See Fletcher, *Allegory: The Theory of a Symbolic Mode* (Ithaca, New York: Cornell Univ. Press, 1964), p. 236n.

47. In chapter one, I discuss the way in which Spenser qualifies this praise by attributing a similar monopoly of honor to a negative figure of monarchic rule, Mammon's daughter Philotime. But despite such qualifications, it is nevertheless true that the monarch is a far more significant figure in *The Faerie Queene* than in *Poly-Olbion.*

48. The royal equivalent of such poetic prerogative is the king's summoning of parliament, some of whose members have such names as "Essex," "Leicester," "Surrey," and so on. Like the poet, the king assembles the land in a single meeting place in defiance of the normal limitations of geography.

49. See the Charwell's praise of rivers at the end of the Tame-Isis wedding (4.309–10). The passage recalls Spenser only to suggest its difference.

50. Camden, *Britain,* sig. P5^v, and Carew, *Cornwall,* p. 164. It is interesting to note in this regard that William Burton, who himself used alphabetical listing in his *Leicestershire,* was the first to call Leland's notes "itineraries."

He read the signs of the genre as he knew it back into its predecessor. See *The Itinerary of John Leland,* edited by Lucy Toulmin Smith, 5 vols. (London: G. Bell, 1907–10), 1.1n.

51. Dugdale, *Warwickshire,* p. 421; Westcote, *Devonshire,* p. 275; and Coker, *Dorsetshire,* p. 40.

52. Simon Erdeswicke, *A Survey of Staffordshire* (1723), p. 122.

53. Grundy, *Spenserian Poets,* p. 134.

54. Compare, for example, the use of *progress* at 4.30 and 4.397.

55. Quoted in J. E. Neale, *Elizabeth I and Her Parliaments, 1584–1601,* 2 vols. (London: Cape, 1953–57), 2.119. Compare *The Political Works of James I,* edited by Charles Howard McIlwain (1918; rpt. New York: Russell, 1965), pp. 5 and 310. Christopher Pye discusses the relation of visibility to power in "The Sovereign, the Theater, and the Kingdome of Darknesse: Hobbes and the Spectacle of Power," *Representations* 8 (1984): 85–106.

56. See G. R. Crone, *Maps and Their Makers: An Introduction to the History of Cartography* (1953; rpt. Hamden, Conn.: Archon, 1978), pp. 85–91. In twentieth-century France, still the most powerfully centralized country in the Western world, maps and chorographic descriptions do function not only as instruments of bureaucratic control but also as representations of a centrifugal ideology. This becomes explicit in at least one modern chorography, Georges and Régine Pernoud's *Tour de France Médiéval* (Paris: Stock, 1982), whose announced purpose is to present the "other" France, the non-Parisian, nonclassical, nonbureaucratic France of provinces and villages. It is also, I think, often the effect of the omnipresent Michelin maps and guides.

57. In the sixteenth and seventeenth centuries, Netherlanders led Europe in the production and use of maps. They furthermore provided the specific models for Saxton and Speed and, through the efforts of Ortelius, the incitement for Lhuyd, Lambarde, and Camden. Svetlana Alpers discusses the ideology of Dutch mapping in *The Art of Describing: Dutch Art in the Seventeenth Century* (Chicago: Univ. of Chicago Press, 1983), pp. 119–68.

58. James R. Akerman and David Buisseret, *Monarchs, Ministers, and Maps: A Cartographic Exhibit at the Newberry Library* (Chicago: Newberry Library, 1985), p. 13. Pedro de Esquival's survey was, interestingly enough, undertaken in the same decade as Saxton's. The differing fortunes of the two suggest something of the differing politics of the two countries.

59. For an account of the relation of maps to the modern bureaucratic state, see Chandra Mukerji, *From Graven Images: Patterns of Modern Materialism* (New York: Columbia Univ. Press, 1983), pp. 79–130.

60. Camden, *Britain,* sig. æ4; Speed, *Theatre,* 1.sig. ¶4; and Stow, *A Survey of London,* edited by Charles Lothbridge Kingsford, 2 vols. (Oxford: Clarendon Press, 1908), 1.xcviii.

61. The widespread use in Caroline England of the term *country* to designate those who opposed the court has been thoroughly documented by Perez Zagorin in *The Court and the Country: The Beginning of the English Revolution* (New York: Atheneum, 1970). Though my argument does not

depend on anything like a full acceptance of Zagorin's notion of a well-developed country party in the 1620s and 1630s, it does suppose (in opposition to the views of many "revisionist" historians) that the civil wars of the mid-seventeenth century did have causes that antedate 1640. In this I agree with the general position developed by Lawrence Stone in *The Causes of the English Revolution, 1529–1642* (London: Routledge, 1972), with many of the specific arguments presented by Christopher Hill in his *Intellectual Origins of the English Revolution* (Oxford: Clarendon Press, 1965), and with the more recent, postrevisionist, arguments of J. P. Sommerville in *Politics and Ideology in England, 1603–1640* (London: Longman, 1986).

Chapter Four

1. For a survey of Elizabethan and Jacobean publications concerned with overseas travel, see John Parker, *Books to Build an Empire: A Bibliographical History of English Overseas Interests to 1620* (Amsterdam: N. Israel, 1965) and two books by E. G. R. Taylor, *Tudor Geography, 1485–1583* (London: Methuen, 1930) and *Late Tudor and Early Stuart Geography, 1583–1650* (London: Methuen, 1934).

2. Montalboddo's *Paesi Novamente Ritrovati* was first published in 1507. The three volumes of Ramusio's *Navigazioni* came out between 1550 and 1559. For a description of their contents, see George B. Parks, *The Contents and Sources of Ramusio's "Navigationi"* (New York: New York Public Library, 1955). De Bry's *Voyages* were issued between 1590 and 1634 in two series, the *Large Voyages* concerning America and the *Small Voyages* concerning the East Indies. The first two *Large Voyages,* Thomas Hariot's *Virginia* (1590) and René Laudonnière's *Florida* (1591) were both produced in response to Hakluyt's prompting. For a full list of the de Bry volumes, see the "Catalogue of the de Bry Collection of Voyages in the New York Public Library," *Bulletin of the New York Public Library* 8 (1904): 230–43.

3. See Ramusio's dedicatory epistle to Hieronimo Fracastoro.

4. Richard Hakluyt, *The Principal Navigations Voyages Traffiques and Discoveries of the English Nation,* 12 vols. (Glasgow: MacLehose, 1903–5), 1.xxxi. Subsequently cited as *PN* in the text.

5. James Boon discusses Purchas's royalism in *Other Tribes, Other Scribes: Symbolic Anthropology in the Comparative Study of Cultures, Histories, Religions, and Texts* (Cambridge: Cambridge Univ. Press, 1982), pp. 156–61.

6. Edmund S. Morgan, "The Labor Problem in Jamestown, 1607–1618," *American Historical Review* 76 (1971): 595–611.

7. Daniel Defert, "The Collection of the World: Accounts of Voyages from the Sixteenth to the Eighteenth Centuries," *Dialectical Anthropology* 7 (1982): 16. See also Defert's "Collections et Nations au XVIe Siècle," in *L'Amérique de Théodore de Bry,* edited by Michèle Duchet (Paris: Editions du CNRS, 1987), pp. 47–67. My thanks to Frank Lestringant for generously supplying me with a copy of the Duchet volume.

8. *Os Lusíadas* is quoted from Luís de Camões, *Obras Completas,* edited by Hernani Cidade, 5 vols. (Lisbon: Livraria sá da Costa, 1946–47). Quotations are identified in the text by canto and stanza. Except where otherwise indicated, translations are based on those of Leonard Bacon, *The Lusiads* (New York: Hispanic Society of America, 1950).

9. Voltaire is quoted by William Julius Mickle in the introduction to his translation, *The Lusiad; or, The Discovery of India. An Epic Poem* (Oxford: Jackman and Lister, 1776), p. cxxii. It should be noted that on the subject of Camões, Voltaire is not a very reliable witness. His objection in this instance has, however, been repeated with greater respect for Camões's text by Georges Le Gentil, *Camoëns: L'Oeuvre épique et lyrique* (Paris: Hatier-Boivin, 1954), pp. 51–52.

10. "Calecu . . . / Cidade já por trato nobre e rica" (7.35) and "Malaca por empório ennobrecido" (10.123).

11. David Quint discusses this line in a brilliantly suggestive article on the ideological differences between epic and romance, "The Boat of Romance and Renaissance Epic," in *Romance: Generic Transformation from Chrétien de Troyes to Cervantes,* edited by Kevin Brownlee and Marina Scordilis Brownlee (Hanover, N.H.: Univ. Press of New England, 1985), pp. 186–87. Despite my admiration for this fine article to which I am significantly indebted, I must take issue with its central argument. I am not convinced that the main opposition between epic and romance corresponded to the social and political cleavage between the nobility (and/or landed gentry) and merchants. As I suggest in chapter one, the epic/romance split seems rather to be a scene of contention between the newly consolidated monarchic state and a latter-day feudal dispersion of power. In *The Lusiads,* as I will argue, epic and romance join to oppose mercantile activity, activity that found its generic representation in voyages of the kind Hakluyt published.

12. Sir Richard Fanshawe's translation of *The Lusiads,* edited by Geoffrey Bullough (Carbondale, Ill.: Southern Illinois Univ. Press, 1963), p. 334.

13. See, for example, his execration on gold (8.96–99) or his account of Cupid's campaign against those who give their affection to things designed "for use and not for love" (9.25).

14. That this thinning out of "heroic subjectivity" was the product of the exigencies of the early modern state is argued by Neil Larsen and Robert Krueger in "Homer, Vergil, Camões: State and Epic," *I & L: Ideologies and Literature* 2.10 (1979): 69–94.

15. On this antipathy, see Quint, "The Boat of Romance," pp. 187–88.

16. C. M. Bowra, *From Virgil to Milton* (London: Macmillan, 1945), p. 138. See also the essays collected in *Camões à la Renaissance* (Brussels: Editions de l'Univ. de Bruxelles, 1984).

17. Vitorino de Magalhães-Godinho, *L'Economie de l'empire Portugais aux XVe et XVIe siècles* (Paris: S.E.V.P.E.N., 1969), pp. 834–35.

18. For Pires, I follow the translation of Armando Cortesão, *The Suma Oriental of Tomé Pires,* 2 vols. (London: Hakluyt Society, 1944), 1.4.

19. "Da terra vos sei dizer que é mãe de vilões ruins e madrasta de homens honrados. Porque os que se cá lançam a buscar dinheiro, sempre se sustentam sobre água com[o] bexigas; mas os que sua opinião deita *á las armas, Mouriscote* . . . antes que amadureçam, se secam" (*Obras Completas,* 3.245–46).

20. In the opening chapter of *O Strange New World* (New York: Viking Press, 1964), Howard Mumford Jones describes how Europeans' reading of romance conditioned their response to the New World. See also Irving A. Leonard, *Books of the Brave* (New York: Gordian Press, 1964).

21. A. H. de Oliveira Marques quoted by Larsen and Krueger, "Homer, Vergil, Camões," p. 83.

22. Robert Thorne in *PN* 2.165. An instance of the Portuguese king's title can be found in *PN* 5.63.

23. François Pyrard de Laval quoted by Godinho, *L'Economie,* p. 834.

24. Pierre Vilar discusses the relation between the "dry and warlike" Spain of the interior plateau and the "rich and fleshy" surrounding provinces in the first chapter of his *Histoire de l'Espagne* (Paris: Presses Universitaires de France, 1958).

25. Bowra remarks (*Virgil to Milton,* p. 91) that "in the south-western corner of Europe the Portuguese nation . . . had to secure its independence against two main enemies, the Moors and the Spaniards. That is why the three battles which Camões presents at some length are Ourique, where in 1139 the nation was born in battle against the Moors, Salado, where in 1340 Affonso IV helped the king of Castile to rout the Moors, and Aljubarrota, where in 1385 João I defeated a Spanish attempt to conquer Portugal."

26. For a recent discussion of this episode and the varying interpretations of it, see Gerald M. Moser, "What Did the Old Man of Restelo Mean?" *Luso-Brazilian Review* 17 (1980): 139–51.

27. See J. H. Parry's chapter on "The Sea Empires of Portugal and Holland," in *The Age of Reconnaissance: Discovery, Exploration, and Settlement* (1963; rpt. Berkeley: Univ. of California Press, 1981), pp. 242–57.

28. Two volumes prepared to commemorate the 400th anniversary of Camões's death testify to his extraordinary place in Portuguese culture: *Estudos sobre Camões: Páginas do* Diário de Noticias *Dedicadas ao Poeta no 4º Centenário da sua Morte* (Lisbon: Imprensa Nacional, 1981) and *Camões e a Identidade Nacional* (Lisbon: Imprensa Nacional, 1983). The first is a collection of articles that appeared in a leading Portuguese newspaper; the second, a collection of addresses by some of Portugal's most prominent writers and intellectuals.

29. Quoted by Aubrey F. G. Bell, *Luis de Camões* (Oxford: Oxford Univ. Press, 1923), p. 65.

30. *The Original Writings and Correspondence of the Two Richard Hakluyts,* 2 vols. (London: Hakluyt Society, 1935), 1.139 and 143. Subsequently cited in the text as *Corr.*

31. *Divers Voyages Touching the Discovery of America* (1582), sig. ¶2ᵛ.

Divers Voyages has been edited in a facsimile edition, with an introductory volume entitled *Richard Hakluyt, Editor,* by David B. Quinn (Amsterdam: Theatrum Orbis Terrarum, 1967).

32. On the family background of the two Hakluyts, see George Bruner Parks, *Richard Hakluyt and the English Voyages* (New York: American Geographical Society, 1928), pp. 25–30, 233–38, and 242–45.

33. Laura Caroline Stevenson, *Praise and Paradox: Merchants and Craftsmen in Elizabethan Popular Literature* (Cambridge: Cambridge Univ. Press, 1984), p. 6.

34. For a history of the joint-stock companies, see William Robert Scott, *The Constitution and Finance of English, Scottish, and Irish Joint-Stock Companies to 1720,* 3 vols. (Cambridge: Cambridge Univ. Press, 1910–12).

35. The order of these volumes changed from the first to the second edition. In the first, the southern voyages come first; in the second, the northern voyages take their place.

36. Hakluyt's successor, Samuel Purchas, remarked on the role merchants play in books like the ones he and Hakluyt assembled. "Soldiers and merchants [are] the world's two eyes to see itself," he proclaimed on the title page of his *Pilgrims* (1625), and in the body of the work he said that "the actors" of the voyages he was collecting are "the authors, and the authors themselves the actors of their own parts, arts, acts, designs" *(Hakluytus Posthumus or Purchas His Pilgrimes,* 20 vols. [Glasgow: MacLehose, 1905–7], 2.286).

37. As if in response to the large amount of commercial material that his project compelled him to print, Hakluyt inserted the word *traffics* into the title of the second edition. The title of the first edition had referred only to navigations, voyages, and discoveries.

38. Kenneth R. Andrews discusses these differences in *Trade, Plunder, and Settlement: Maritime Enterprise and the Genesis of the British Empire, 1480–1630* (New York: Cambridge Univ. Press, 1984), pp. 9–10 and 17–22.

39. Quoted by Stevenson, *Praise and Paradox,* p. 80. See also Stevenson's useful discussion of the various Elizabethan descriptions of the class divisions of England, pp. 79–91.

40. Theodore K. Rabb, *Enterprise and Empire: Merchant and Gentry Investment in the Expansion of England, 1575–1630* (Cambridge, Mass.: Harvard Univ. Press, 1967), p. 35.

41. Rabb, *Enterprise and Empire,* pp. 39–40.

42. Of the unfamiliar terms in this passage, *batman, medine, turbetta, neel, churle,* and *rottil,* the *OED* defines only three, *batman* ("an oriental weight"), *medine* ("a silver half-dirhem"), and *neel* ("obs. form of *anil*"), and quotes this passage as the earliest instance of each. Among themselves, Elizabethan merchants had learned to speak a language that was not altogether English.

43. D. B. Quinn, "Hakluyt's Reputation," in *The Hakluyt Handbook,* edited by D. B. Quinn, 2 vols. (London: Hakluyt Society, 1974), 1.147–48.

44. L. E. Pennington, "Secondary Works on Hakluyt and His Circle," *The Hakluyt Handbook,* 2.588–89.

45. Rabb, *Enterprise and Empire,* p. 68.

46. Andrews, *Trade, Plunder, and Settlement,* p. 6. Similarly George Bruner Parks argues "that the merchants were all-important and that the 'seadogs' and colonizers alike were their agents" *(Richard Haklulyt,* p. 88, n. 1).

47. Rabb, *Enterprise and Empire,* p. 27.

48. *Works of Sir Walter Raleigh,* edited by T. Birch, 2 vols. (London: R. Dodsley, 1751), 2.80. I owe this and the following quotation from Raleigh to Christopher Hill, *Intellectual Origins of the English Revolution* (Oxford: Clarendon Press, 1965), pp. 165–70, where Hill discusses Raleigh's ideas concerning commerce and labor.

49. *Works,* 1.276–7.

50. A surprising example of the strength of aristocratic ideology comes from John Milton's *Brief History of Moscovia.* Introducing an abridgment of Clement Adams's account of the Willoughby-Chancellor voyage, Milton remarks, "The discovery of Russia by the northern ocean, made first of any nation that we know by Englishmen, might have seemed an enterprise almost heroic, if any higher end than the excessive love of gain and traffic had animated the design." Apparently for Milton, trade (which in the next sentence he calls an "evil occasion") and heroic endeavor are utterly irreconcilable *(The Complete Prose Works of John Milton,* edited by Don M. Wolfe et al., 8 vols. [New Haven: Yale Univ. Press, 1953–82], 8.524).

51. Richard Eden, *The Decades of the New World,* rpt. in *The First Three English Books on America,* edited by Edward Arber (Birmingham, 1885), p. 52. (In quoting Eden's Latin, I turn his datives into nominatives.) Despite the apparently pro-Spanish content of Eden's dedication and preface, it seems likely that his purpose was to goad Englishmen into competing with the Spanish in the New World.

52. Hakluyt's part in the spread of anti-Spanish propaganda has been discussed by William S. Maltby in *The Black Legend in England: The Development of Anti-Spanish Sentiment, 1558–1660* (Durham, N.C.: Duke Univ. Press, 1971), pp. 61–75.

53. Samuel Daniel, *The Civil Wars,* edited by Lawrence Michel (New Haven: Yale Univ. Press, 1958), p. 311.

54. In French in Paris (1586); in his own English translation in London (1587) in Theodore de Bry's illustrated Latin version in Frankfort (1591); and again in English in the second edition of the *Principal Navigations* (1600).

55. For a discussion of the more distant discursive consequences of European expansion, see Louis Dumont, *From Mandeville to Marx: The Genesis and Triumph of Economic Ideology* (Chicago: Univ. of Chicago Press, 1977).

56. On the date of composition of *England's Treasure,* see B. E. Supple, "Thomas Mun and the Commercial Crisis, 1623," *Bulletin of the Institute of Historical Research* 27 (1954): 91–94, and two articles by J. D. Gould, "The Trade Crisis of the Early 1620's and English Economic Thought" and "The Date of *England's Treasure by Forraign Trade,*" both in *Journal of Economic*

History 15 (1955): 121–33 and 160–61. In the final chapter of her *Cultural Aesthetics: Renaissance Literature and the Practice of Social Ornament* (Chicago: Univ. of Chicago Press, 1991), Patricia Fumerton discusses Mun's treatise in the context of the specific economic crisis that prompted it.

57. Thomas Mun, *Englands Treasure by Forraign Trade* (1664; facs. rpt. Oxford: Economic History Society, 1928), p. 88.

58. Mun, *Englands Treasure*, p. 3 (Mun's italics). Quint (pp. 195–96) finds similar sentiments expressed still more openly in Lewis Roberts' *Treasure of Traffic* (1641): "It is not our conquests, but our commerce; it is not our swords, but our sails, that first spread the English name in Barbary, and thence came into Turkey, Armenia, Moscovia, Arabia, Persia, India, China, and indeed over and about the world." Quint comments: "Insisting that the true heroes of exploration are merchants, Roberts provides an alternative"— an alternative, we might add, that Hakluyt had a large share in making available—"to an aristocratic ideology which interprets the discoveries in terms of imperial conquest."

59. The phrase *world system* alludes to Immanuel Wallerstein's three-volume work, *The Modern World-System* (New York: Academic Press, 1974, 1980, and 1990). These volumes provide an excellent introduction to the origins and consolidation of what Wallerstein calls "the European world-economy."

60. Mickle, *The Lusiad*, p. cxlvii.

Chapter Five

1. Identification of quotations from Shakespeare will normally be found in the text and correspond to the act, scene, and line divisions of *The Riverside Shakespeare*, edited by G. Blakemore Evans (Boston: Houghton Mifflin, 1974). I have, however, checked the quotations themselves against the quarto and folio texts and have sometimes made editorial and modernizing choices that differ from those in *The Riverside Shakespeare*.

2. On the date of *2 Henry VI*, the play the quarto edition calls *The First Part of the Contention betwixt the Two Famous Houses of York and Lancaster* and that I abbreviate as *The Contention*, and its chronological relation to *Henry VI, parts 1* and *3*, see Stanley Wells and Gary Taylor, *William Shakespeare: A Textual Companion* (Oxford: Clarendon Press, 1987), pp. 111–12. Wells and Taylor's view of the ordering of the three Henry VI plays—that *2* and *3 Henry VI* preceded *1 Henry VI*—is widely, though not universally, shared. For an argument that *1 Henry VI* was the first written and first produced, see Hanspeter Born, "The Date of *2, 3 Henry VI*," *Shakespeare Quarterly* 25 (1974): 323–34. Nothing in my argument depends on the priority of *The Contention*, though the story I tell develops more neatly that way.

3. I am thinking here of Queen Katherine's intervention on behalf of the overtaxed commons in the second scene of *Henry VIII* and, with some

prompting from my colleague Lee Bliss, of Cranmer's prophecy in the play's concluding scene.

4. Geoffrey Bullough, ed., *Narrative and Dramatic Sources of Shakespeare,* 8 vols. (London: Routledge, 1957–75), 3.90.

5. Here and throughout this chapter, I use the terms *commoner, commons,* and *common people* to stand for craftsmen and countrymen—that is, for those groups that had little or no claim to gentility. On the varied and sometimes conflicting meanings of the word *common,* see Raymond Williams, *Keywords* (1976; rev. ed. London: Fontana, 1983), pp. 70–72.

6. See Leah S. Marcus's *Puzzling Shakespeare* (Berkeley: University of California Press, 1988), pp. 1–50, for a discussion of the way in which the 1623 folio presents Shakespeare as an author independent of the conditions under which his plays were first written and produced.

7. E. K. Chambers, *The Elizabethan Stage,* 4 vols. (Oxford: Clarendon Press, 1951), 4.224, 269, and 216. Cited hereafter in the text as *ES.*

8. Ann Jennalie Cook, *The Privileged Playgoers of Shakespeare's London* (Princeton: Princeton Univ. Press, 1981). Cook's arguments have been rebutted by Martin Butler in *Theatre and Crisis 1632–1642* (Cambridge: Cambridge Univ. Press, 1984), pp. 293–306.

9. For a recent discussion of Shakespeare's audience, see Andrew Gurr, *Playgoing in Shakespeare's London* (Cambridge: Cambridge Univ. Press, 1987).

10. Robert Wilson, *The Cobler's Prophecy 1594,* edited by A. C. Wood (Oxford: Malone Society, 1914), p. vi.

11. Alfred Harbage, *Shakespeare and the Rival Traditions* (1952; rpt. New York: Barnes and Noble, 1968), pp. 3 and 277.

12. Robert Weimann, *Shakespeare and the Popular Tradition in the Theater: Studies in the Social Dimension of Dramatic Form and Function* (Baltimore: Johns Hopkins Univ. Press, 1978), and Walter Cohen, *Drama of a Nation: Public Theater in Renaissance England and Spain* (Ithaca, New York: Cornell Univ. Press, 1985).

13. C. L. Barber, *Shakespeare's Festive Comedy: A Study of Dramatic Form in Relation to Social Custom* (Princeton: Princeton Univ. Press, 1959), and Michael D. Bristol, *Carnival and Theater: Plebeian Culture and the Structure of Authority in Renaissance England* (New York: Methuen, 1985).

14. For an important recent attempt to account for the shift in genres, see Leonard Tennenhouse, *Power on Display: The Politics of Shakespeare's Genres* (New York: Methuen, 1986).

15. Christopher Marlowe, *Tamburlaine the Great,* edited by J. S. Cunningham (Manchester: Manchester Univ. Press, 1981), pp. 113 and 111.

16. *The Works of Thomas Nashe,* edited by Ronald B. McKerrow and F. P. Wilson, 5 vols. (Oxford: Blackwell, 1958), 3.323–24, and *The Life and Complete Works of Robert Greene,* edited by Alexander B. Grosart, 15 vols. (1881–83; rpt. New York: Russell, 1964), 8.132. See also Greene, *Complete Works,* 12.130ff.

17. Greene, *Complete Works*, 12.144. Compare Nashe's earlier attack on those "mechanical mate[s]" who "think to outbrave better pens with the swelling bombast of a bragging blank verse" (*Works*, 3.311).

18. Peter Stallybrass and Allon White, *The Politics and Poetics of Transgression* (Ithaca, New York: Cornell Univ. Press, 1986), p. 3.

19. Sir Philip Sidney, *An Apology for Poetry*, edited by Geoffrey Shepherd (Manchester: Manchester Univ. Press, 1965), p. 135; George Whetstone, *ES* 202; and Joseph Hall, *Virgidimiarum*, 1.3.39–40, in *The Collected Poems*, edited by A. Davenport (Liverpool: Liverpool Univ. Press, 1949), p. 15.

20. Over the last few years, several important essays have discussed the subversive implications of the theater's staging of monarchy: Franco Moretti, "'A Huge Eclipse': Tragic Form and the Deconsecration of Sovereignty," and Stephen Orgel, "Making Greatness Familiar," both in *Genre* 15 (1982): 7–48, and David Scott Kastan, "Proud Majesty Made a Subject: Shakespeare and the Spectacle of Rule," *Shakespeare Quarterly* 37 (1986): 459–75.

21. *The Three Parnassus Plays (1598–1601)*, edited by J. B. Leishman (London: Ivor Nicholson, 1949), pp. 343–45.

22. Walter Cohen discusses the "artisanal" character of the Elizabethan theater in *Drama of a Nation*, pp. 136–85.

23. "Go they never so brave," wrote Philip Stubbes in 1583, "yet are they counted and taken but for beggars. . . . Are they not taken by the laws of the realm for rogues and vagabonds?" To this rhetorical question the London authorities would have given an unequivocal "yes." The players, they wrote to the privy council, "if they were not her majesty's servants, should by their profession be rogues" (*ES* 4.224 and 301).

24. I owe this suggestion to Andrew Gurr, *The Shakespearean Stage, 1574–1642* (2nd ed. Cambridge: Cambridge Univ. Press, 1980), p. 81. Though the allusion is likely enough—certainly Jonson alluded elsewhere to Shakespeare in equally unflattering ways—it is complicated here by Thomas Nashe's earlier use of the phrase "not without mustard" in *Pierce Penilesse his Supplication to the Divell* (*Works* 1.171). See also the discussion of Shakespeare's coat of arms in S. Schoenbaum, *William Shakespeare: A Documentary Life* (New York: Oxford Univ. Press, 1975), pp. 166–73. In addition to the "not without mustard" slur, which he discusses briefly, Schoenbaum cites Jonson's sneer in *Poetaster* "at common players who aspire to heraldic distinctions": "They forget they are i' the statute, the rascals; they are blazoned there; there they are tricked, they and their pedigrees. They need no other herald, I wiss" (p. 167).

25. Depending on the date assigned *The Contention*, it might also be preceded by *The Reign of Edward III* (1590), *The Life and Death of Jack Straw* (1591), *The True Tragedy of Richard III* (1591), and/or *The Troublesome Reign of King John* (1591).

26. Thomas Nashe furnishes an early example of this struggle in his *Pierce Penilesse his Supplication to the Divell* (1592) where he celebrates the history play both for its inclusiveness, bringing together thousands in the "open" theater to witness "our forefathers' valiant acts," and for its exclusiveness,

banishing the familiar theatrical figures of pantaloon, whore, and zany from the stage in favor of "emperors, kings, and princes" and banishing unpatriotic apprentices and their burgher masters from the audience in favor of courtiers, students, and soldiers—gentlemen all. See *Works*, 1.211–15.

27. See, for example, Robin Headlam Wells, "The Fortunes of Tillyard: Twentieth-Century Critical Debate on Shakespeare's History Plays," *English Studies* 66 (1985): 391–403.

28. See Frank Whigham, *Ambition and Privilege: The Social Tropes of Elizabethan Courtesy Theory* (Berkeley: Univ. of California Press, 1984).

29. Phyllis Rackin has recently made a similar observation with regard to the likeness in status between the two rebels and the actors who first played them. See her *Stages of History: Shakespeare's English Chronicles* (Ithaca, New York: Cornell Univ. Press, 1990), pp. 205 and 221. Rackin's fine and subtly argued book, which reached me after my text was already in the hands of its publisher, contains a chapter on "Historical Kings/Theatrical Clowns" that shares many of the issues and much of the evidence of this chapter. Our conclusions do, however, differ significantly. Rackin blames "the aristocratic bias" of Shakespeare's first tetralogy on chronicle sources and dramatic convention (p. 218), and she sees Shakespeare achieving greater, though still sharply limited, freedom from these baneful influences in his second tetralogy. I disagree on both counts. As I attempt to show in later sections of this chapter, other dramatists working in the same genre with the same sources and conventions managed nevertheless to grant commoners far greater dignity and significance than did Shakespeare, while the aristocratic bias of the first tetralogy, which I would rather call a fixation on monarchic power, is repeated and enforced in the second.

30. Annabel Patterson, "The Very Name of the Game: Theories of Order and Disorder," *SAQ* 86 (1987): 529. Patterson's argument has recently been expanded to take in the whole Shakespeare canon in *Shakespeare and the Popular Voice* (Oxford: Blackwell, 1989). Both the agreement and the disagreement I express with regard to Patterson's *SAQ* article apply equally to the book. Shakespeare does give expression to the popular voice, but that, I am convinced, is not the side his plays represented most compellingly. As I will argue, the popular voice could be heard much more distinctly in plays produced at the theaters Henslowe controlled.

31. *The Dramatic Works of Thomas Heywood,* edited by J. Payne Collier, 4 vols. (London: Shakespeare Society, 1851), 1.9.

32. *The Book of Sir Thomas More,* edited by W. W. Greg (London: Malone Society, 1911), p. 2. The date and circumstances of this play, to which Shakespeare may or may not have contributed some 148 lines, have recently been examined by Scott McMillin, *The Elizabethan Theater and* The Book of Sir Thomas More (Ithaca, New York: Cornell Univ. Press, 1987) and by McMillin and others in *Shakespeare and* Sir Thomas More*: Essays on the Play and Its Shakespearean Interest,* edited by T. H. Howard-Hill (Cambridge: Cambridge Univ. Press, 1989).

33. Edmund Tilney had been master of the revels since 1581 and had been charged with the censoring of plays since 1589. Yet, so far as we know, the Ill May Day episode in *Sir Thomas More* was the first and only insurrection he kept from being staged. Such matter could be dangerous, but he seems usually not to have thought it was. As for the mayor and aldermen, they objected to everything the players did. In their view, scenes of popular revolt were no worse than the usual theatrical run of "profane fables, lascivious matters, cozening devices, and other unseemly and scurrilous behaviors" (*ES* 4.318)—none of which were bearers of a peasant ideology.

34. David Bevington, *Tudor Drama and Politics: A Critical Approach to Topical Meaning* (Cambridge, Mass.: Harvard Univ. Press, 1968), pp. 230–59. The quotation from Heywood is on p. 241. In fairness it should be noted that though Bevington classes these plays together as all contributing to an "orthodox reply," he sees marked differences between their representations of popular political action.

35. Comparing Shakespeare's rebel leader to his prototype in Hall's chronicle, which is usually identified as Shakespeare's main source for *The Contention,* Richard Wilson writes: "Cade, whom Hall respects as 'a young man of goodly stature and pregnant wit,' 'a subtle captain,' 'sober in communication' and 'wise in disputing,' whose advisers were 'schoolmasters' and 'teachers,' is metamorphosed into a cruel, barbaric lout, whose slogan is 'kill and knock down,' and whose story as 'the archetype of disorder' is one long orgy of clownish arson and homicide fueled by an infantile hatred of literacy and law" ("'A Mingled Yarn': Shakespeare and the Cloth Workers," *Literature and History* 12 [1986]: 167). Wilson's article, uses much of the same evidence I present to arrive at a similar but nevertheless significantly different set of conclusions. Wilson sees Shakespeare and his theater as unequivocally exclusionist from the beginning. That, it seems to me, requires ignoring much evidence to the contrary and choosing in a very carefully selective way among arguments where the evidence is doubtful—as, for example, with regard to the date (1592) and location (the Rose) of the first productions of *The Contention* and to the composition of Shakespeare's audience in the early 1590s (exclusively privileged). Still, Wilson's one-sided argument provides a much needed corrective to the more familiar celebration of Shakespeare's universal and disinterested inclusiveness.

36. Annabel Patterson supplies several examples from the mid-seventeenth century of this guilt by association. Sir John Colepepper linked John Pym to Jack Cade and Wat Tyler; an anonymous royalist pamphleteer wrote of *The Just Reward of Rebels, or the Life and Death of Jack Straw and Wat Tyler;* and another royalist, John Cleveland, published *The Idol of the Clowns, or Insurrection of Wat the Tyler with his Fellow Kings of the Commons.* See Patterson, "Name of the Game," pp. 527–30. Patterson produces no example of anyone deliberately taking on the mantle of the fourteenth-century rebels, though later rebels did express similar grievances. Tyler, Ball, and their fol-

lowers had been too thoroughly discredited for their names to be used in a positive way, even by those who might have agreed with them.

37. In *The Populace in Shakespeare* (New York: Columbia Univ. Press, 1949), Brents Stirling argued that the fear of Anabaptists was the principal inspiration for the Elizabethan theater's hostility to popular political action. While this argument now appears considerably overstated, Stirling's book does supply an impressive body of evidence demonstrating the Elizabethan linkage of Anabaptism and popular revolt, including the revolts of Jack Straw and Jack Cade. See especially pp. 97–181.

38. See note 26 above.

39. Patterson, "Name of the Game," p. 540. As an example of this ideological confusion, Patterson cites the accusation Cade directs at Lord Say: "Thou hast put [poor men] in prison, and because they could not read, thou hast hanged them" (4.7.43–44). This points to a real injustice that was still prevalent in Elizabethan England, where by proving he could read a convicted felon might escape hanging.

40. I am again adopting here the commonplace notion that *The First Part of the Contention (2 Henry VI)* and *The True Tragedy (3 Henry VI)* were written and produced before *1 Henry VI* (see note 2 above). Were this not the case, the word *subsequent* in the sentence to which this note is attached would have to be replaced by *other,* a change that would upset the linear order of my argument but would not trouble its central claims.

41. David Wiles, *Shakespeare's Clown: Actor and Text in the Elizabethan Playhouse* (Cambridge: Cambridge Univ. Press, 1987), p. 44.

42. John Davies, *Wits Bedlam* (1617), quoted in E. Nungezer, *A Dictionary of Actors* (New Haven: Yale Univ. Press, 1929), p. 362.

43. *Tarlton's Jests and News Out of Purgatory,* edited by James Orchard Halliwell (London: Shakespeare Society, 1844), p. 5.

44. *Include* in its various verbal and nominal forms is one of the key words in Barber's study. His book is, in effect, a celebration of inclusion. Typical in this regard is the opening sentence of his chapter on *Henry IV:* "The two parts of *Henry IV* . . . are an astonishing development of the drama in the direction of inclusiveness, a development possible because of the range of traditional culture and the popular theater, but realized only because Shakespeare's genius for construction matched his receptivity" (p. 192). From this point of view, the conclusion of *2 Henry IV* can only seem a failure, which is what Barber calls it. I would not want to deny the inclusiveness, but rather to insist that it is in constant competition with an at least equally powerful inclination toward exclusion. The failure of one is the triumph of the other. To place "genius" or "art" or "humanity" on one side or the other is to adopt a highly charged ideological position.

45. *The Life and Death of Jack Straw, 1594,* edited by Kenneth Muir and F. P. Wilson (Oxford: Malone Society, 1957), sig. A3^v.

46. Much work has been done on the historical connection of rebellion and

carnival in early modern Europe. See Natalie Zemon Davis, "The Reasons of Misrule" and "The Rites of Violence" in *Society and Culture in Early Modern France* (Stanford: Stanford Univ. Press, 1975), pp. 152–87; Yves-Marie Bercé, *Fête et Révolte: Des mentalités populaires du xvie et xviie siècles* (Paris: Hachette, 1976); Emmanuel Le Roy Ladurie, *Carnival in Romans,* translated by Mary Feeney (New York: George Braziller, 1979); and, for England, Thomas Pettitt, "'Here Comes I, Jack Straw': English Folk Drama and Social Revolt," *Folklore* 95 (1984): 3–20. Nothing in my argument is meant to deny the fact of this connection. I claim rather that the connection was reproduced for ideological reasons in the theater even when chronicle sources did not authorize it.

47. Carol A. Chillington, "Playwrights at Work: Henslowe's, Not Shakespeare's, *Book of Sir Thomas More,*" *English Literary Renaissance* 10 (1980): 471.

48. Wiles, *Shakespeare's Clown,* p. 81. I have made a small correction in Wiles's quotation of the clown's speech to bring it into agreement with the Malone Society reprint (p. 69).

49. In making this argument, I am accepting the contention that Tilney's orders for excision predate the most substantial revisions, including the addition of the clown's role. See McMillin's discussion of these matters in *The Elizabethan Theater,* pp. 53–95.

50. See *2 Henry IV,* 4.4.67–78. Two important essays have explored the workings of this process in *Henry IV* and in Elizabethan culture generally: Stephen Greenblatt, "Invisible Bullets: Renaissance Authority and Its Subversion," *Glyph* 8 (1981): 40–61, and Steven Mullaney, "Strange Things, Gross Terms, Curious Customs: The Rehearsal of Cultures in the Late Renaissance," *Representations* 3 (1983): 40–67. An expanded version of Greenblatt's essay appears in his *Shakespearean Negotiations: The Circulation of Social Energy in Renaissance England* (Berkeley: Univ. of California Press, 1988), pp. 21–65. Mullaney's has been reprinted in *The Place of the Stage: License, Play, and Power in Renaissance England* (Chicago: Univ. of Chicago Press, 1988), pp. 60–87.

51. Susanne Wofford in an unpublished essay entitled "Theater and the Politics of Carnival in Shakespeare's *Henry IV*" provides the fullest recent examination of Falstaff and his rejection in these terms. I thank Professor Wofford for allowing me to read her very interesting paper in manuscript.

52. Joseph Allen Bryant, Jr., "Shakespeare's Falstaff and the Mantle of Dick Tarlton," *Studies in Philology* 51 (1954): 149–62. For the characterization of Falstaff as "an immortalized Tarlton," see p. 151. The identification of Will Kemp as the player who took the part of Falstaff dates back at least as far as H. D. Gray's "The Roles of Will Kemp," *Modern Language Review* 25 (1930): 265–66, and has often been reasserted since then, most recently by David Wiles in *Shakespeare's Clown,* pp. 116–35.

53. The longevity of this dispute is suggested by G. K. Hunter, "Shakespeare's Politics and the Rejection of Falstaff," *Critical Quarterly* 1 (1959): 229–36.

54. William Kemp, *Nine Daies Wonder,* edited by G. B. Harrison (1922; rpt. New York: Barnes and Noble, 1966), p. 3.

55. The "conflict of interests between the comedian who played 'clown' or 'Vice' and the Elizabethan dramatist who wanted scope and recognition for his own talents as a writer" (p. 43) is one of the principal concerns of David Wiles in *Shakespeare's Clown.* Throughout this section, I am much indebted to Wiles's important book.

56. Weimann, *Shakespeare and the Popular Tradition,* esp. pp. 73–85 and 208–52.

57. As part of a concerted effort to gain control over the contents of plays, the London common council in 1574 ordered that no one with the responsibility for the staging of plays "shall suffer to be interlaced, added, mingled, or uttered in any such play, interlude, comedy, tragedy, or show any other matter than such as shall be first perused and allowed" (*ES,* 4.274–75). A similar prohibition is implicit in the later privy-council regulations establishing governmental censorship of plays.

58. Quoted in the appendix to *Tarlton's Jests,* edited by Halliwell, p. 107.

59. Charles Read Baskervill, *The Elizabethan Jig and Related Song Drama* (Chicago: Univ. of Chicago Press, 1929), pp. 107–8. I have taken Kemp's name from a marginal note—"Kemp's"—in the Stationers' Register and included it in the title of the *Pleasant New Jig of the Broomman.*

60. With the exception of the line from *Julius Caesar,* these examples are all taken from Baskervill, *Elizabethan Jig,* pp. 109–11.

61. The evidence here is negative and indirect. As Baskervill points out, "among the public theaters it is noticeable that the only houses mentioned by name in connection with the jig are those to the north of the city—the Curtain, the Fortune, and the Red Bull" (p. 115). This silence concerning the Globe extends to the "fool" who played there in the first years of that theater's existence, Robert Armin. Unlike Tarlton and Kemp, Armin was never associated with the jig.

62. On the issues discussed in this paragraph, see Wiles, *Shakespeare's Clown,* pp. 47–48.

63. David Scott Kastan, "'Clownes shoulde speake disorderlye': Mongrel Tragicomedy and the Unitary State," paper read at a meeting of the Shakespeare Association of America (1989). My thanks to David Kastan for sending me a copy of his paper.

64. In an article brought to my attention by Steven Mullaney only after the completion of this chapter, Colin McCabe links the banishment of Falstaff, the departure of Kemp, the move to the Globe, the repudiation of the jig, and the development of a less participatory theatrical style with the construction of that élite culture of which Shakespeare has since become "the major named guarantor." Though I am disappointed to have struggled up this heap of evidence only to find McCabe already at the top, I am nevertheless pleased at the support his company gives me. See Colin McCabe, "Abusing Self and Others: Puritan Accounts of the Shakespearean Stage," *Critical Quarterly* 30 (1988): 3–17.

65. William Kemp, *Nine Daies Wonder 1600,* printed with Henry Chettle, *Kind-Hartes Dreame 1592,* in the Elizabethan and Jacobean Quartos, edited by G. B. Harrison (1922–26; rpt. New York: Barnes & Noble, 1966), p. 5.

66. Quoted in Wiles, *Shakespeare's Clown,* p. 37.

67. *A Critical Edition of* I Sir John Oldcastle, edited by Jonathan Rittenhouse (New York: Garland, 1984), pp. 104–5.

68. Anne Barton, "The King Disguised: Shakespeare's *Henry V* and the Comical History," in *The Triple Bond: Plays, Mainly Shakespearean, in Performance,* edited by Joseph G. Price (University Park, Pa.: Pennsylvania State Univ. Press, 1975), pp. 92–117.

69. Barton also includes two other anonymous plays, *Fair Em* (1590) and *The True Chronicle History of King Leir* (1590). These, however, seem to me to have only a tangential relation to the type, since in neither does the disguised king meet his own subjects.

70. Sir John of Wrotham clearly resembles Sir John Falstaff, but, as Barton remarks, his attitude toward his illegal profession is quite unlike that of his Shakespearean model. Unlike Falstaff, he is "'an honest thief,' concerned to 'take where it may be spared.'" "It is," Barton suggests, "in the outlaw ballads of the late middle ages, particularly those centered upon Robin Hood, that the source of this Sir John's attitude may be found. What the *Oldcastle* authors have done is to reach back through Falstaff to resurrect the far older figure of Friar Tuck" (p. 112).

71. For a description of many of these ballads and versions of several, see Francis James Child, *The English and Scottish Popular Ballads,* 5 vols. (1882–94; rpt. New York: Dover, 1965), 5.67–87. E. K. Chambers also discusses the type in *English Literature at the Close of the Middle Ages* (Oxford: Clarendon Press, 1947), pp. 128–29.

72. Shakespeare's name is not mentioned in Henslowe's *Diary,* but the *Diary* does list fifteen performances of a "harey the vj," usually identified as Shakespeare's *1 Henry VI.* The other six "Shakespearean" titles in Henslowe's *Diary*—"titus & ondronicus," "kinge leare," "hamlet," "the tamynge of A shrowe," "harey the v," and "Troyeles & creasse"—are generally thought either not to be the plays Shakespeare wrote under these titles or not to have been originally written for a Henslowe company. See *Henslowe's Diary,* edited by R. A. Foakes and R. T. Rickert (Cambridge: Cambridge Univ. Press, 1961), pp. 16–22, 33, and 106, and Neil Carson, *A Companion to Henslowe's* Diary (Cambridge: Cambridge Univ. Press, 1988), p. 68. If Hand D in *The Book of Sir Thomas More* is Shakespeare, a second connection to the Henslowe companies would be established. A probable date for Hand D's addition is 1592, though dates as much as ten years later have been proposed. See *Shakespeare and* Sir Thomas More, edited by Howard-Hill, p. 8.

73. In the last speech of the second scene of *Part One,* Hal promises that, despite his apparent prodigality, he will one day "be himself" (1.2.200). Scene three opens with King Henry assuring Northumberland, Worcester, and Hotspur that "I will from henceforth . . . be myself" (1.3.5). Their similarity

to one another goes, of course, much further than such verbal likenesses. Throughout both plays, Hal manipulates appearances in precisely the politic way that Henry says he used in gaining the crown.

74. For the ballads of Jane and Matthew Shore, see *The Roxburghe Ballads,* edited by W. M. Chappell and J. Wodfall Ebsworth, 8 vols. (1869–1901; rpt. New York: AMS Press, 1966), 1.479–92. "King Edward IV and the Tanner of Tamworth" can also be found in *The Roxburghe Ballads,* 1.529–37.

75. These four ballads can be found in *The Euing Collection of English Broadside Ballads,* edited by John Holloway (Glasgow: University of Glasgow Publications, 1971), pp. 314–19.

76. The phrase "people's history of England" comes from W. M. Chappell, *The Roxburghe Ballads,* 1.181. Maurice Keen interprets the Robin Hood poems as songs of lower-class protest in *The Outlaws of Medieval Legend* (Toronto: Univ. of Toronto Press, 1961).

77. Stephen Greenblatt makes much of Shakespeare's use of Iden in "Murdering Peasants: Status, Genre, and the Representation of Rebellion," *Representations* 1 (1983): 1–29. What Greenblatt regards as a brilliantly original, if ideologically loaded, solution to the problem that he finds in the courtly narratives of Sidney and Spenser—namely, how to represent the brutal defeat of lower-class rebellion—is in fact quite conventional on stage.

78. George Peele, *King Edward the First 1593,* edited by W. W. Greg (Oxford: Malone Society, 1911), sig. B2.

79. *Heywood's Dramatic Works,* edited by Collier, 1.46. It is worth noting that "York, York, for my money" comes from the refrain of an Elizabethan ballad that had nothing to do with the War of the Roses. Heywood's Hobs is a ballad character who speaks in ballads. See *The Roxburghe Ballads,* 1.1–9.

80. This fascination with the dynamics of power is writ large in the most recent critical movement to appropriate Shakespeare and Elizabethan literature generally. The leading new historicists have, almost without exception, devoted the major part of their critical energy to exploring the representational workings of the early modern English monarchy. The books of Stephen Greenblatt, Jonathan Goldberg, Leah Marcus, Louis Montrose, Stephen Orgel, and Leonard Tennenhouse listed in my introduction (note 9) provide striking evidence of this inclination, an inclination I have sometimes shared. What the Henslowe history plays have helped me see is that such a focus is powerfully exclusionary. In adopting it, we replicate, even as we sometimes attempt to repudiate, a particular ideology of power.

81. Something of this sort is assumed by Robert Boies Sharpe in the most systematic study we have of the differences between the repertories of Shakespeare's company and its chief rival, *The Real War of the Theaters: Shakespeare's Fellows in Rivalry with the Admiral's Men, 1594–1603* (1935; rpt. New York: Klaus, 1966). Of the history play in particular, Sharpe writes, "In general, the Admiral's Men aimed at the groundlings and the citizens through folklore and legendary romance; Shakespeare's company, at a cavalier audience through stirring dramatization of actual history which was still very

much alive to their hearers through the intensely genealogical social and political issues of Elizabethan England" (p. 85).

82. Richard Brome, *The Antipodes*, edited by Ann Haaker (Lincoln: Univ. of Nebraska Press, 1966), p. 40.

83. Peter Burke, *Popular Culture in Early Modern Europe* (New York: Harper Torchbooks, 1978), pp. 270–72.

84. Marston, *Plays*, edited by Wood, 3.273–74.

85. For discussions of Shakespeare's ideological function in modern Britain, see Tom Nairn, *The Enchanted Glass: Britain and Its Monarchy* (London: Hutchinson Radius, 1988), esp. pp. 125–26, and Alan Sinfield, "Royal Shakespeare: Theatre and the Making of Ideology," in *Political Shakespeare: New Essays in Cultural Materialism*, edited by Jonathan Dollimore and Alan Sinfield (Ithaca, New York: Cornell Univ. Press, 1985), pp. 158–81.

86. Louis Adrian Montrose, "The Purpose of Playing: Reflections on a Shakespearean Anthropology," *Helios*, new series 7 (1980): 71 and 66.

Chapter Six

1. John Foxe, *The Acts and Monuments*, edited by Josiah Pratt, 8 vols. (4th ed.; London: Religious Tract Society, 1877), 3.320. This edition, first brought out in 1841 by Stephen Reed Cattley and then revised by Pratt without changing page numbers, remains the only complete version of *Acts and Monuments* available in most university libraries. It is not, however, a dependable edition. I have thus cited its volume and page numbers but have checked all quotations against the editions of 1563 and 1583, the first and last published in Foxe's lifetime, and have retained the Cattley/Pratt reading only when it corrected an obvious printer's error. For the passages cited later in this paragraph concerning Oldcastle's martyrdom, see 3.541.

2. See *2 Henry VI* 4.2.16 and *1 Henry IV* 1.2.105.

3. Brents Stirling, *The Populace in Shakespeare* (New York: Columbia Univ. Press, 1949), p. 151. Other quotations in this paragraph come from Stirling, pp. 134 and 113.

4. In later editions of the *Acts and Monuments*, Foxe spends more pages (3.348–402) rebutting this charge than he did telling Oldcastle's story in the first place.

5. On Spenser's use of apocalyptic literature, see Frank Kermode, *Shakespeare, Spenser, Donne: Renaissance Essays* (London: Routledge, 1971), pp. 40–49; Michael O'Connell, *Mirror and Veil: The Historical Dimension of Spenser's* Faerie Queene (Chapel Hill: Univ. of North Carolina Press, 1977), pp. 38–68; and Florence Sandler, "*The Faerie Queene:* An Elizabethan Apocalypse," in *The Apocalypse in English Renaissance Thought and Literature*, edited by C. A. Patrides and Joseph Wittreich (Ithaca, New York: Cornell Univ. Press, 1984), pp. 148–74.

6. *A Catalogue of the Library of Sir Edward Coke,* edited by W. O. Hassall (New Haven, Conn.: Yale Univ. Press, 1950).

7. Conrad Russell, "The 1620s and the English Civil War: Predictors of Allegiance," paper read to the Pacific Coast Conference on British Studies (Huntington Library, March 1990). My thanks to Sears McGee for refreshing my memory of this talk.

8. For a discussion of these plays and their political implications, see Judith Doolin Spikes, "The Jacobean History Play and the Myth of the Elect Nation," *Renaissance Drama* 8 (1977): 117–49. Two other Foxian plays mentioned by Spikes show that neither Shakespeare nor his company wholly escaped the martyrologist's influence. The anonymous *Thomas, Lord Cromwell* (1600), which, according to the title pages of its two editions, was played by both the Chamberlain's and the King's Men, and Shakespeare's *Henry VIII* (1613) are both heavily dependent on Foxe. Both are, however, very unlike the English history plays Shakespeare wrote in the 1590s, when the pressure to differentiate himself and his company from the rival Admiral's Men was greatest. Two other plays serve to illustrate the more characteristic antipathy between Shakespearean history and the Foxian sort: the anonymous *Troublesome Reign of John, King of England* (1591) and Shakespeare's *King John* (1591). Though the two plays closely resemble one another, Shakespeare's is as unsympathetic to the Foxian view of John as antipapal martyr as his Henriad is to the Foxian view of Oldcastle. *The Troublesome Reign* is governed by the Foxian view of John.

9. Throughout this chapter, I will be using *apocalyptic* and *apologetic* as nouns to designate particular discursive modes. There is ample precedent for this in the case of *apologetic,* where the term *apology* is also available. In the case of *apocalyptic,* where there is no precedent (or at least none listed in the *OED*), I have resorted to this nominal appropriation of an adjectival form to avoid constant repetition of the cumbersome *apocalyptic discourse.*

10. The one obvious exception to this claim is Sir Francis Bacon. But Bacon's legal writings, which I discussed in chapter two, are largely incidental to his reputation as a thinker, and the work on which that reputation is based has little to do with any discourse of Elizabethan nationhood.

11. Such disobedience to kings and magistrates is precisely the fault Foxe blames in papists. Pope Gregory's humiliation of the emperor at Canossa, Thomas à Becket's rebellious defense of the church against King Henry II, Pope Innocent III's subjection of King John are conspicuous markers in the rise of Antichrist. To those who call Protestants "disturbers . . . of peace and public authority," Foxe answers: "What doctrine did ever attribute so much to public authority of magistrates as do the Protestants? Or who ever attributed less to magistrates, or deposed more dukes, kings, and emperors, than the papists? He that saith that the bishop of Rome is no more than the bishop of Rome and ought to wear no crown is not by and by a rebel against his king and magistrates, but rather a maintainer of their authority" (5.603).

12. John Bale, *The Image of Bothe Churches* (1548; facs. rpt. Amsterdam: Theatrum Orbis Terrarum, 1973), sig. Avi.

13. Richard Bauckham, *Tudor Apocalypse* (Oxford: Sutton Courtenay Press, 1978), pp. 62–63.

14. See Revelation 18.4: "And I heard another voice from heaven say, Go out of her, my people, that ye be not partakers in her sins and that ye receive not of her plagues." The title on this page of the Geneva Bible (1560) reads "To flee from Babylon."

15. As Bauckham shows (pp. 54–67), tracing the true church back to Abel, the first martyr, and the false church back to Cain, the first persecutor, was one of the commonplaces of apocalyptic literature. In explaining why God allows "his own people and faithful servants" to suffer such terrible persecutions in this world, Foxe evokes the familiar divided lineage: "We ought not to be moved with this iniquity of things, to see the wicked to prevail against the body. Forsomuch as in the beginning of the world we see Abel the just to be killed of wicked Cain, and afterward Jacob being thrust out, Esau to reign in his father's house. In like case, the Egyptians with brick and tile afflicted the sons of Israel. Yea, and the lord himself, was he not crucified of the Jews, Barabbas the thief being let go?" (1.288).

16. Foxe objected to the burnings of Joan of Kent and George the German under Edward VI and to the executions of Anabaptists and papists under Elizabeth. "To burn up with fiery flame, blazing with pitch and sulphur, the living bodies of wretched men," he wrote the queen in a futile attempt to rescue several Flemish Anabaptists, "is a hard thing and belongs more to the example of Rome than to the spirit of the gospel." And if the godly government of Elizabeth could be made to seem ungodly by such an action, so the brave deaths of the Anabaptists would make their false belief seem true: "When men of false doctrine are killed, their error is not killed; nay, it is all the more strengthened, the more constantly they die" (J. F. Mozley, *John Foxe and His Books* [New York: Macmillan, 1940], p. 87).

17. On Foxe's opposition to the execution of heretics, see Mozley, *John Foxe*, pp. 35–36, 80, and 86–91, and V. Norskov Olsen, *John Foxe and the Elizabethan Church* (Berkeley: Univ. of California Press, 1973), pp. 197–219.

18. "What papist," Foxe asked his Catholic detractors in a preface to the 1570 edition of *Acts and Monuments*, "have you seen in all this land to lose either life or limb for papistry during all these twelve years hitherto since this queen's reign?" (1.525).

19. John N. King discusses this image in *Tudor Royal Iconography: Literature and Art in an Age of Religious Crisis* (Princeton: Princeton Univ. Press, 1989), pp. 154–9. See also the important earlier discussion of the image and its relation to the imperial tradition in Frances A. Yates, *Astraea: The Imperial Theme in the Sixteenth Century* (London: Routledge, 1975), pp. 42–44.

20. According to Foxe's calculation, the precise dates of Satan's captivity were 324 to 1324. He arrived at this conclusion by multiplying the forty-two months of Antichrist's power (Rev. 13.5) by seven ("a sabbath of years"). This

gives 294, to which he adds 30 for the year of Christ's passion. See *Acts and Monuments* 1.288–92 and 2.724–6.

21. William Haller, *The Elect Nation: The Meaning and Relevance of Foxe's* Book of Martyrs (New York: Harper, 1963).

22. Katherine R. Firth, *The Apocalyptic Tradition in Reformation Britain, 1530–1645* (Oxford: Oxford Univ. Press, 1979), pp. 106 and 108. See also Olsen, *John Foxe*, pp. 36–37, 42–47, and 77–78, and Bauckham, *Tudor Apocalypse*, pp. 12–13. Without reviving Haller's thesis in its original form, Warren W. Wooden supplies a succinct and convincing demonstration of the historical importance Foxe attributed to England in his *John Foxe* (Boston: Twayne, 1983), pp. 34–36.

23. Milton quoted by Haller, *Elect Nation*, p. 241.

24. In a chapter that takes much of its evidence from Foxe, Stephen Greenblatt brilliantly describes the power of the English Bible in the decades immediately following its initial printing. See "The Word of God in the Age of Mechanical Reproduction" in *Renaissance Self-Fashioning: From More to Shakespeare* (Chicago: Univ. of Chicago Press, 1980), pp. 74–114.

25. Greenblatt compares this statement of Tyndale's to the passage in Erasmus from which it probably derives: "What Erasmus is willing to express as a wish, Tyndale puts as his personal mission" (*Renaissance Self-Fashioning*, p. 106).

26. Asked why he did not believe in "the sacrament of the altar" by one Dr. Parker, an officer of the diocesan court of Norwich, John Fortune, a blacksmith, responded, "Because it is not written in God's book." The examination, as Fortune himself recorded it, continued as follows: "Then said he, 'You will not believe unwritten verities.' And I said, 'I will believe that those unwritten verities that agree with the written verities be true. But those unwritten verities that be of your own making and invented of your own brain I do not believe'" (8.161). Such assertions are frequent in *Acts and Monuments* and testify powerfully to the extraordinary confidence possession of God's word in English gave men and women like John Fortune, Alice Driver, and Rawlins White.

27. Quoted in Mozley, *John Foxe*, p. 177.

28. Of Alice Driver, Parsons writes, "A man may easily guess"—notice that a man is doing the guessing, and doing it with no other evidence than his *a priori* sense of what is possible—"how light a gospeling sister she was, yet does Foxe make such account of her and of her rare learning in the scriptures as of no one sister more in all his history, setting down two large disputations which she had with Doctor Spenser, chancellor to the bishop of Norwich, and other doctors that assisted him, all which she brought to be dumb and mute by her wise oppositions, answers, and alleging of scriptures, if you will believe Foxe, who playeth also the notorious reynard and fraudulent companion in this, as in many other things." Quoted by Leslie Mahin Oliver, "The *Acts and Monuments* of John Foxe: Studies in the Growth and Influence of a Book," Ph.D. diss. (Harvard, 1945), p. 396.

29. We may still find Foxe's articulate commoners difficult to credit. In describing the interrogations in Foxe to friends, I have several times encountered the almost automatic presumption that Foxe was just making it up, that Shakespeare's bumbling commoners must be closer to reality—and this despite the fact that there is considerable documentary evidence in support of Foxe's representations and none at all in support of Shakespeare's.

30. Benedict Anderson, *Imagined Communities: Reflections on the Origins and Spread of Nationalism* (London: Verso, 1983).

31. Alice Driver was not alone in insisting on the separation of the sacramental sign from the thing signified. This was, on the contrary, a fundamental element in the Protestant attack on the Catholic establishment. See, for example, Edmund Grindal's "Dialogue between Custom and Verity" in Foxe (6.336–49). What is remarkable is that someone like Alice Driver should have been so fully apprised of these issues and have been able to present her views with such skill and sophistication.

32. Mozley, *John Foxe*, p. 147.

33. As evidence of that identification, one might cite the similar role providence plays in both. Introducing the "notable story" of the avenging bull, Foxe remarks that it was "brought to [his] hands" just as he was finishing his account of the reign of Henry VII, a coincidence that he takes to be a sign of "God's holy will and providence" (4.127). A similar providence is responsible for the delivery of many of the other stories he prints, as it is for the invention of printing itself. "What man soever was the instrument" of this invention, "without all doubt God himself was the ordainer and disposer thereof" (3.719). And of course providence also guided the bull to the destruction of Dr. Whittington.

34. Wooden, *John Foxe*, pp. 44–48.

35. The persistence of apocalyptic tradition is suggested by the way Latimer's words echo those spoken by a voice from heaven to the ancient martyr Polycarp as he entered the Roman stadium: "Be of good cheer, Polycarpus, and play the man" (1.133).

36. *The Works of Richard Hooker*, edited by W. Speed Hill, 4 vols. (Cambridge, Mass.: Harvard Univ. Press, 1977–82), 1.65–66.

37. E. M. W. Tillyard, *The Elizabethan World Picture* (1943; rpt. New York: Vintage Books, 1961), pp. 9–17; *The Norton Anthology of English Literature*, edited by M. H. Abrams et al., 2 vols. (rev. ed. New York: Norton, 1968), 1.421–51.

38. *The Works of John Whitgift*, edited by John Ayre, Parker Society, 3 vols. (Cambridge: Cambridge Univ. Press, 1851–53), 2.334–35.

39. Henry Barrow, *Writings, 1587–1591*, edited by Leland Carlson, English Nonconformist Texts (London: Allen and Unwin, 1962), p. 188. Oldcastle tells his interrogators that they and the pope "together maketh whole the great Antichrist, of whom he is the great head; you bishops, priests, prelates, and monks are the body; and the begging friars are the tail" (3.334).

Ridley addresses Bishop Bonner as a "whorish bawd of Babylon," a "wicked limb of Antichrist" (7.559).

40. C. J. Sisson, *The Judicious Marriage of Mr. Hooker and the Birth of The Laws of Ecclesiastical Polity* (Cambridge: Cambridge Univ. Press, 1940); Hardin Craig, "Of the Laws of Ecclesiastical Polity—First Form," *Journal of the History of Ideas* 5 (1944): 91–104; and W. Speed Hill, "The Evolution of Hooker's *Laws of Ecclesiastical Polity*," in *Studies in Richard Hooker: Essays Preliminary to an Edition of his Works,* edited by W. Speed Hill (Cleveland, Ohio: Case Western Reserve, 1972), pp. 117–58.

41. See Hill, "Evolution," pp. 145–47.

42. This testimony comes from Hooker's friend and literary executor, John Spenser. It is quoted in *Works,* 1.xiv. The information in the next two paragraphs concerning the publishing history of Hooker's *Laws* comes from Georges Edelen and W. Speed Hill's introduction to volume 1 of the Folger *Works* (pp. xiii–xxvii). William Haller summarizes the publishing history of Foxe's *Acts* in *The Elect Nation,* p. 9.

43. Debora Kuller Shuger, *Habits of Thought in the English Renaissance: Religion, Politics, and the Dominant Culture* (Berkeley: Univ. of California Press, 1990), pp. 32–33. The italics are Shuger's. On Hooker's historicism, see also Arthur B. Ferguson, "The Historical Perspective of Richard Hooker: A Renaissance Paradox," *Journal of Medieval and Renaissance Studies* 3 (1973): 17–49.

44. Peter Lake discusses Hooker's "sacrament-centered" religion, contrasting it to the "word-centered" religion of his Puritan opponents, in *Anglicans and Puritans?: Presbyterianism and English Conformist Thought from Whitgift to Hooker* (London: Unwin Hyman, 1988), pp. 162–82.

45. Brian Vickers, "Authority and Coercion in Elizabethan Thought," *Queen's Quarterly* 87 (1980): 114.

46. E. T. Davies, *The Political Ideas of Richard Hooker* (London: Society for Promoting Christian Knowledge, 1946); F. J. Shirley, *Richard Hooker and Contemporary Political Ideas* (London: Society for Promoting Christian Knowledge, 1949); Peter Munz, *The Place of Hooker in the History of Thought* (London: Routledge, 1952); Alexander Passerin d'Entrèves, *The Medieval Contribution to Political Thought: Thomas Aquinas, Marsilius of Padua, Richard Hooker* (1939; rpt. New York: Humanities Press, 1959); Gunnar Hillerdal, *Reason and Revelation in Richard Hooker* (Lund: C. W. K. Gleerup, 1962); and Gottfried Michaelis, *Richard Hooker als Politischer Denker* (Berlin: Verlag dr. Emil Ebering, 1933).

47. On Hooker's debt to his apologetic precursors, see W. D. J. Cargill Thompson, "The Philosopher of the 'Politic Society': Richard Hooker as a Political Thinker," in *Studies in Hooker,* edited by Hill, pp. 13–16.

48. Izaak Walton, *Lives* (London: Nelson, n.d.), p. 191.

49. Alfred Pollard's expression of this commonplace perception of Hooker's accomplishment is typical. Hooker, writes Pollard, goes "beyond

the bickering world of wrangling about ecclesiastical power and scriptural interpretation into the majestic realm of eternal verity." Quoted by Rudolph Almasy, "The Purpose of Richard Hooker's Polemic," *Journal of the History of Ideas* 39 (1978): 251. Almasy argues against this position but with a sense of how prevalent it is.

50. Walton, *Lives,* pp. 191–92.

51. The fullest expression of this longing comes in Hooker's first sermon, "Of the Certainty and Perpetuity of Faith in the Elect," reprinted in *The Works of that Learned and Judicious Divine, Mr. Richard Hooker,* edited by John Keble, 3 vols. (7th ed. Oxford: Clarendon Press, 1888), pp. 468–81. See Debora Shuger's fine discussion of this sermon and of the more general problem of reason and certainty in *Habits of Thought,* pp. 17–45, 69–90, and 128–41.

52. Henry King in a letter to Izaak Walton, quoted by David Novarr, *The Making of Walton's* Lives (Ithaca, New York: Cornell Univ. Press, 1958), p. 234. My account of the Restoration response to Hooker's *Laws* comes from Novarr (pp. 226–80).

53. The most pointed questioning of consistency has come from H. F. Kearney, "Richard Hooker: A Reconstruction," *Cambridge Journal* 5 (1952): 300–311, and Peter Munz, *The Place of Hooker in the History of Thought.*

54. W. D. J. Cargill Thompson, "The Philosopher of the 'Politic Society,'" p. 66. See also Arthur S. McGrade, "The Coherence of Hooker's Polity: The Books of Power," *Journal of the History of Ideas* 24 (1963): 163–82.

55. In the space marked by my ellipsis, Hooker introduces two qualifications: "and not either by express commission immediately and personally received from God or else by authority derived at the first from their consent upon whose persons they impose laws . . . " Neither of these qualifying conditions applied, in Hooker's view, to England. On the relation of Hooker's political thought to that of English common lawyers, see Lawrence Manley, *Convention, 1500–1750* (Cambridge, Mass.: Harvard Univ. Press, 1980), pp. 90–106.

56. Oliver, "The *Acts and Monuments,*" p. 400.

57. Lake, *Anglicans and Puritans,* pp. 229–30.

58. Izaak Walton, *The Compleat Angler* (London: Dent, 1970), p. 6. The subtitle of *Grace Abounding* is *A Brief and Faithful Relation of the Exceeding Mercy of God in Christ to his Poor Servant John Bunyan.*

59. See B. D. Greenslade, "*The Compleat Angler* and the Sequestered Clergy," *Review of English Studies* 5 (1954): 361–66.

60. "Devotion," begins the poem's last stanza, "will add life unto the letter: / And why should not / That, which authority / Prescribes, esteemed be / Advantage got?" (p. 99). In celebrating the *Book of Common Prayer,* Walton also celebrates the royal and episcopal power that authorized it. The phrase "our good old service-book" occurs earlier in *The Complete Angler,* on p. 39.

61. *Fox's Book of Martyrs,* edited by William Byron Forbush (Philadelphia, Pa.: Winston, 1926), p. 328.

62. J. H. Plumb, *The Death of the Past* (Boston: Houghton Mifflin, 1970), p. 84. I am indebted to Everett Zimmerman for drawing my attention to this passage. Concerning Foxe's influence on Bunyan, see Oliver, "The *Acts and Monuments,*" pp. 466–85, and Christopher Hill, *A Turbulent, Seditious, and Factious People: John Bunyan and His Church, 1628–1688* (Oxford: Clarendon Press, 1988), pp. 109 and 157–58.

63. John Bunyan, *A Relation of the Imprisonment of Mr. John Bunyan* in *Grace Abounding to the Chief of Sinners,* edited by Roger Sharrock (Oxford: Clarendon Press, 1962), pp. 124, 105, 111, 106, 114, and 120.

64. On this long-distance separation and the apocalyptic interpretation applied to it, see Stephen J. Stein, "Transatlantic Extensions: Apocalyptic in Early New England," in *The Apocalypse,* edited by Patrides and Wittreich, pp. 266–98.

65. See, for example, Walton's tale of the beggars who, like "pertinacious schismatic[s]," debated "whether it was easiest to rip a cloak or to unrip a cloak" (pp. 102–3)—a fairly obvious reference to the commonplace association of the official state-church with the undivided cloak of Christ rent by puritanical rebels.

66. Job 40.21 (Geneva translation).

67. See, for example, F. J. Shirley, *Richard Hooker,* pp. 209–13, and Alexander Passerin d'Entrèves, *The Medieval Contribution,* pp. 140–41.

68. J. G. A. Pocock, "Time, History and Eschatology in the Thought of Thomas Hobbes," in *Politics, Language and Time: Essays on Political Thought and History* (New York: Atheneum, 1971), pp. 148–201. The specific quotations in this paragraph occur on pp. 166 and 183. For a broader discussion of apocalyptic in relation to European political thought, see Pocock, *The Machiavellian Moment: Florentine Political Thought and the Atlantic Republican Tradition* (Princeton: Princeton Univ. Press, 1975).

69. Thomas Hobbes, *Behemoth: The History of the Causes of the Civil Wars of England,* edited by William Molesworth (New York: Burt Franklin, 1963), p. 28.

70. Thomas Hobbes, *Leviathan, or the Matter, Forme & Power of a Commonwealth, Ecclesiasticall and Civill,* edited by A. R. Waller (Cambridge: Cambridge Univ. Press, 1935), p. xiv.

71. In *Leviathan,* Hobbes writes, "consisteth the essence of the commonwealth, which (to define it) is one person, of whose acts a great multitude by mutual covenants one with another have made themselves every one the author, to the end he may use the strength and means of them all, as he shall think expedient, for their peace and common defense" (p. 119).

72. Margery Corbett and Ronald Lightbown, *The Comely Frontispiece: The Emblematic Title-Page in England, 1550–1660* (London: Routledge, 1979), pp. 229–30.

Afterword

1. Sir John Davies, *Le Primer Report des Cases . . . en Ireland* (1615), sig. *2ᵛ, and Samuel Daniel, *The Complete Works in Verse and Prose,* edited by Alexander B. Grosart, 5 vols. (London: Spenser Society, 1885–96), 4.77.

2. Eugen Weber in the *Times Literary Supplement* (October 26–November 1, 1990), p. 1149. The book Weber reviews, E. J. Hobsbawm's *Nations and Nationalism Since 1780: Programme, Myth, Reality* (Cambridge: Cambridge Univ. Press, 1990), develops this argument at some length. My thanks to Paul Hernadi for drawing my attention to Weber's review.

3. George Chapman, *De Guiana,* in Richard Hakluyt, *The Principal Navigations Voyages Traffiques and Discoveries of the English Nation,* 12 vols. (Glasgow: MacLehose, 1903–5), 10.448.

4. Gabriel Harvey in *The Works of Edmund Spenser: A Variorum Edition,* edited by Edwin Greenlaw et al., 11 vols. (Baltimore: Johns Hopkins Press, 1932–57), 10.474, and William Fulbecke, *A Parallele or Conference of the Civill Law, the Canon Law, and the Common Law of this Realme of England* (1601), sig. 丞咅 iᵛ.

5. There are many important exceptions to this pattern in *The Faeric Queene,* most notably Britomart, Spenser's lady knight. *The Faerie Queene* not only upsets the categories that control most of the other major textual representations of England to emerge from Spenser's generation, it also upsets its own categories.

6. *The Political Works of James I,* edited by Charles Howard McIlwain (1918; rpt. New York: Russell, 1965), p. 272.

7. Elizabeth's androgynous self-presentation is discussed by Leah Marcus in *Puzzling Shakespeare: Local Reading and Its Discontents* (Berkeley: Univ. of California Press, 1988), pp. 51–105, and by Louis Montrose in a number of important articles. See especially his "'Shaping Fantasies': Figurations of Gender and Power in Elizabethan Culture," in *Representing the English Renaissance,* edited by Stephen Greenblatt (Berkeley: Univ. of California Press, 1988), pp. 31–64, and "The Elizabethan Subject and the Spenserian Text," in *Literary Theory/Renaissance Texts,* edited by Patricia Parker and David Quint (Baltimore: Johns Hopkins Univ. Press, 1986), pp. 303–40. The quotation from Elizabeth's speech to her troops at Tilbury in 1588 can be found in Marcus, *Puzzling Shakespeare,* p. 54.

8. This sentence closely paraphrases a sentence in the preface to my *Elizabethan Prodigals* (Berkeley: Univ. of California Press, 1976), p. ix. Though my concern in that book with a particular *literary* generation expands here to take in the generational cohort at large, my starting point remains a sense of the unique and momentous significance of the Elizabethan accomplishment in literature as in other fields.

Index

Abbott, L. W., 317 n. 30
Absolutism. *See* Monarchic power
Acton, Lord, 21–23
Acts and Monuments (Foxe): Antichrist and martyrdom in, 254–68, 297; Hooker's *Laws* contrasted with, 254–55, 269–82; influence of, 283–94; martyrdom of Oldcastle in, 249–54; other references, 6, 195–96, 296, 300
Adams, Clement, 179–80, 331 n. 50
Adams, John, 320 n. 60
Adams, Robert P., 309 n. 33
Addison, Joseph, 42, 309 n. 30
Admiral's Men, 199, 224, 234, 244
Admonition to the People of England (Cooper), 251
Aeneid (Virgil), 4, 30, 155, 160
African nationalism, 17
Akerman, James R., 326 n. 58
"Allegory of the Poem, The" (Tasso), 47, 48
Allerton, Ralph, 267
Alleyn, Edward, 202
Almasy, Rudolph, 348 n. 49
Alpers, Svetlana, 326 n. 57
America, colonization of, 183, 185–86
Amidigi (Tasso), 44
Anabaptists, 250, 258, 277, 344 n. 16
Analysis of the Law (Hale), 102
Anatomy of Wit (Lyly), 33
Ancient-medieval dichotomy, 21–62; Acton on, 21–22; chivalric romance vs. classicism, 40–59; and Drayton, 140–41; and Milton, 59–62; rime vs. quantitative verse, 25–40
Anderson, Benedict, 266, 305 n. 17, 346 n. 30
Andrewes, Lancelot, 303 n. 1
Andrews, Kenneth R., 178, 180, 330 n. 38, 331 n. 46
Annals (Camden), 129

Antichrist. *See* Apocalyptic discourse
Antipodes, The (Brome), 240–41
Antiquaries, Society of, 15, 127–28, 300
Antiquities of Warwickshire (Dugdale), 138
Apocalypse of St. John. *See* Revelation, Book of
Apocalypsis Apocalypseos (Brightman), 263
Apocalyptic discourse, 253–54; apologetic discourse contrasted with, 270–83; of Foxe, 254–68; of Foxe's successors, 283–94; other references, 7, 11
Apologetic discourse, 253–54; of Hooker, 269–83; of Hooker's successors, 283–94; other references, 7, 11, 16
Apologia Ecclesiae Anglicanae (Jewel), 253
Apology for Actors (Heywood), 212
Aquinas, St. Thomas, 281
Arcadia (Sidney), 39, 50
Archer, Simon, 135
Areopagus, 14–15, 30, 107
Argumentis Scientiarum, De (Bacon), 74
Ariosto, Lodovico, 44, 48, 50, 54, 160
Aristocracy: in Camões, 155, 160–62; in English history plays, 193–245, 297; in Hakluyt, 168–81; in Mun, 188; and poetry, 43–44, 56–59; other references, 10, 11. *See also* Gentlemen; Monarchic power
Aristotelians, Italian, 61
Aristotle, 49, 52, 59
Armin, Robert, 198, 223, 339 n. 61
Arthur, King, 49–50, 55
Art of English Poetry (Puttenham), 31
Ascham, Roger: on chivalric romance, 42–44; *Schoolmaster*, 28–34, 65, 70; other references, 39, 40, 53, 65, 70, 139, 242, 306 n. 5
Astrophel and Stella (Sidney), 31, 39
As You Like It (Shakespeare), 220

351

Attridge, Derek, 307 n. 8, 308 n. 24
Augustine, St., 274
Azo (Azzone dei Porci), 96

Bacon, Sir Francis: *De Argumentis Scientiarum,* 74; *Instauratio Magna,* 78, 79, 84; law theories and relations with Coke, 82–84, 87, 88, 90, 93, 102; other references, 9, 12, 51, 303 n. 1, 343 n. 10
Bacon, Leonard, 328 n. 8
Baker, J. H., 67–68, 97, 314 nn. 5, 7, 8, 317 nn. 31, 37, 318 n. 40, 319 n. 53
Bale, John, 258–59, 267, 278
Ball, John, 209, 211, 336 n. 36
Ballad, 231–32, 237, 240, 241, 252
Barbarism: of chivalric romance, 40–59; in law, 65–104; of rime, 25–40, 60; theater and purgation from, 240–45
Barber, C. L., 198, 220, 333 n. 13, 337 n. 44
Barrow, Henry, 271, 277, 287
Bartolomeu, Dom Frei, 159
Bartolus de Saxoferrato, 96
Barton, Anne, 231–33, 237, 240, 324 n. 30, 340 nn. 68–70
Baskervill, Charles Read, 224, 339 nn. 59, 61
Bauckham, Richard, 344 nn. 13, 15, 345 n. 22
Beaton, David, 255, 256
Behemoth (Hobbes), 291
Bell, Aubrey F. G., 329 n. 29
Bell, H. E., 313 n. 4
Benveniste, Emile, 22, 306 n. 3
Bercé, Yves-Marie, 338 n. 46
Bernard, John, 265
Bevington, David, 212, 336 n. 34
Bevis (actor), 207–8, 212
Bible: and Bunyan, 287, 288; Geneva, 259, 262, 278; and Hobbes, 290, 291; Hooker on, 273, 274; Revelation, Book of, 258–60, 262, 263, 267, 271; vernacular, 264–67; other references, 253, 276
Blackfriars, 226, 230, 241, 242
Blackmore, Sir Richard, 42
Blackstone, Sir William, 97, 102, 103, 319 n. 55

Blunderville, Thomas, 322 n. 12
Boiardo, Matteo Maria, 48
Book of Common Prayer, 275, 276, 286, 288
Book of Entries (Coke), 70
Book of Homilies, 270
Book of Martyrs (Foxe). See *Acts and Monuments* (Foxe)
Book of Revelation. *See* Revelation, Book of
Book of Sir Thomas More (Munday *et al.*). See *Sir Thomas More* (Munday *et al.*)
Boon, James, 327 n. 5
Born, Hanspeter, 332 n. 2
Bowen, Catherine Drinker, 317 n. 28, 318 nn. 39, 43
Bowra, C. M., 159, 328 n. 16, 329 n. 25
Bracton, Henry de, 65, 82, 87, 97, 99, 282
Bridge, John, 253
Brightman, Thomas, 263
Bristol, Michael D., 198, 222, 333 n. 13
Britannia (Camden): authority symbols in, 114–17; author's attribution, 109; Camden's authorship, 126–27; Hakluyt's work compared with, 151, 152; other references, 1, 5–6, 15, 105, 131, 138, 142, 143, 146, 147, 196, 243
Britannia's Pastorals (Browne), 130–31
Britton (law book), 97
Brome, Richard, 240–41, 342 n. 82
Brooks, Christopher W., 314 n. 12, 315 n. 13
Browne, William, 129–31
Brut, 140
Bryant, Joseph Allen, Jr., 338 n. 52
Bryant, L. A., 222
Buckhurst, Baron (Thomas Sackville), 36
Buisseret, David, 326 n. 58
Bullough, Geoffrey, 333 n. 4
Bunyan, John, 287–90; *Grace Abounding,* 285, 287, 288; *The Holy War,* 287; *Life and Death of Mr. Badman,* 281; *Pilgrim's Progress,* 287, 288; *Relation of the Imprisonment of Mr. John Bunyan,* 287–88; other references, 285, 300
Burbage, Richard, 202, 203
Burghley, Lord. *See* Cecil, William

Burke, Peter, 10, 11, 241–42, 304 n. 12, 342 n. 83
Burton, William, 126, 132, 325 n. 50
Butler, Charles, 96
Butler, Martin, 333 n. 8
Butterfield, Herbert, 306 n. 1

Cabot, John, 151
Cabot, Sebastian, 180
Cade, Jack: rebellion of, 207–10, 212–15, 249–51; other references, 205, 216, 220, 224, 229–30, 238
Cain, Thomas H., 311 n. 57
Cairns, John W., 315 n. 16, 321 n. 65
Calvin, John, 274
Calvinists, 273–75, 277, 281
Cambridge University, 66
Camden, William: *Annals,* 129; *Britannia,* see *Britannia* (Camden); discursive community of, 15; on English classes, 172; Hakluyt contrasted with, 151, 152; on his ambition, 127; on Littleton, 92; name for England, 8; and Society of Antiquaries, 127–28; as transitional man, 13; other references, 9, 12, 16, 17, 132, 135, 139, 140, 144–45, 147, 244, 279, 298, 300, 303 n. 1
Camden Society, 16
Camões, Luís de, 155–63; Hakluyt contrasted with, 154, 163–76, 180; Mickle's translation of, 189–90; other references, 7, 9, 180, 182, 296
Campion, Thomas: *Observations on the Art of English Poesy,* 36; and quantitative verse, 26, 31, 36–40
Carew, Richard, 126, 132–36, 143, 151
Carnival, 215–29, 241, 244
Carson, Neil, 340 n. 72
Cartography. *See* Chorography and cartography
Cartwright, Thomas, 271, 277, 283
Catiline (Jonson), 225
Cato the Elder, 27, 33
Cattley, Stephen Reed, 342 n. 1
Cecil, Sir Robert, 53, 73
Cecil, Sir William, 53, 57, 125, 322 n. 11
Certain Small Works (Daniel), 37
Cervantes, Miguel de, 160
Chamberlain's Men, 199, 223, 226, 245.

See also King's Men
Chambers, E. K., 333 n. 7, 340 n. 71
Chancellor, Richard, 151, 180, 182
Chapman, George: *De Guiana, Carmen Epicum,* 173; other references, 49, 175, 179, 181, 198, 243, 297, 303 n. 1
Chappell, W. M., 341 n. 76
Charles I, king of England: Jonson on, 32; and law, 71, 89, 91, 300; Milton on, 61; other references, 281, 285
Charles V, Emperor, 183–84
Chaucer, Geoffrey, 299, 306 n. 5
Chettle, Henry, 197, 233, 234, 237–38
Child, Francis James, 340 n. 71
Chillington, Carol A., 221, 338 n. 47
Chivalric romance: and Camões, 160; Milton on, 60; politics of, 40–59; and rime, 34; theater compared with, 204; other references, 2, 6, 7, 16, 251, 294
Chorographical Description or Survey of the County of Devon (Risdon), 131
Chorography and cartography, 107–47, 294; authority symbols on maps, 108–24; global ambitions due to, 185; ideology of place and particularity, 131–39; and poetry, 139–47; shift away from court sponsorship, 125–31; theater compared with, 204, 243; written voyages contrasted with, 151–53; other references, 5–7, 9, 10, 16, 18, 295–96, 300
Christianson, Paul, 314 n. 6
Christus Triumphans (Foxe), 256
Chronicle (Grafton), 12, 195–96
Chronicle history: chorography contrasted with, 132–33, 140; development of, 11–12; Foxe's *Acts* compared with, 260; other references, 7, 295
Chronicles (Holinshed), 108–9, 132–33
Church of England: and development of national identity, 249–94; other references, 4, 299. *See also* Religion
Cinthio, Giraldi, 44
Civil wars, English, 108, 286, 290
Civil Wars (Daniel), 42, 184–85
Class: and humanism, 43–44, 56–57; in national self-representation, 10–11, 297. *See also* Aristocracy; Commoners; Gentlemen; Merchants

Classicism. *See* Ancient-medieval dichotomy
Clement VIII, Pope, 279
Cleveland, John, 336 n. 36
Clown, 215–28, 237, 241, 244, 245. *See also* Kemp, Will; Tarlton, Richard
Cobb, Samuel, 42, 309 n. 30
Cobbler's Prophecy, The (Wilson), 218–19
Cohen, Walter, 198, 333 n. 12, 334 n. 22
Coke, Sir Edward, 70–104; Bacon, rivalry and disagreement with, 73–79; *Book of Entries,* 70; discursive community of, 15; Hooker compared with, 279, 282; *Institutes,* see *Institutes of the Laws of England* (Coke); and religion, 251; *Reports,* see *Reports* (Coke); as transitional man, 14; other references, 9, 12, 40, 120, 154, 243, 244, 298, 300, 303 n. 1, 308 n. 22
Coke on Littleton (Coke), 88–102. See also *Institutes of the Laws of England* (Coke)
Coker, John, 132, 135
Colepepper, Sir John, 336 n. 36
Columbus, Christopher, 151, 161, 185, 191
Comedy, 214, 220, 232–34
Commendams, Case of, 88
Commentaries (Blackstone), 102
Commoners: in Foxe, 252, 264–66; in Henslowe playwrights, 210, 231, 233–40; in Hooker, 273; and poetry, 43–44, 56–57, 59; popular revolt, 204–15; in Shakespeare, 193–245, 249–50; other references, 10, 11, 297–98
Common law. *See* Law
Complete Angler (Walton), 285–90
Constantine I, emperor of Rome, 258, 260, 263, 268
Contention, The (Shakespeare): carnival and clown in, 215–16, 220, 221; popular element in, 195–200, 238, 240; popular revolt in, 204–15; and religion, 249–51; other references, 203, 227, 229, 234
Cook, Ann Jennalie, 333 n. 8
Cooper, Thomas, 251
Coquillette, Daniel R., 314 n. 8, 316 n. 22

Corbett, Margery, 349 n. 72
Corpus Juris Civilis (Justinian), 7, 70, 75, 78, 299
Corrigan, Philip, 304 n. 10
Cortés, Hernando, 161
Cortesão, Armando, 328 n. 18
Council, Norman, 309 n. 34
Counter-Reformation, 46, 52
Cowell, John, 318 n. 49; *Interpreter,* 76, 78–79; other references, 82, 87, 90, 93, 303 n. 1
Craig, Hardin, 272
Cranmer, Thomas, 234
Cromwell, Oliver, 108, 112
Cromwell, Thomas, 70
Crone, G. R., 326 n. 56

Da Gama, Vasco, 151, 154–61, 173, 189
Danes, 81, 122
Daniel, Samuel: on British history, 122, 305 n. 16; *Certain Small Works,* 37; *Civil Wars,* 42, 184–85; Coke compared with, 103–4; *Defense of Rime,* 36–39, 41, 42, 59–60, 70, 243; on English-Spanish rivalry, 184–85; *Faerie Queene* contrasted with, 41; Milton compared with, 59–62; Spenser, criticism of, 42; on verse form and politics, 35–40; other references, 12, 132, 244, 296, 300, 303 n. 1, 306 n. 5
Davies, E. T., 347 n. 46
Davies, Sir John, 86–87, 93–96, 295
Davis, Natalie Zemon, 338 n. 46
De Bry, Theodore, 152, 331 n. 54
Decades of the New World (Eden), 151, 179, 182
Decades (Peter Martyr), 173, 183
Dee, John, 322 n. 12
Defense of Poesy (Sidney), 34
Defense of Rime (Daniel), 36–39, 41, 42, 59–60, 70, 243
Defense of the Answer to the Admonition (Whitgift), 253
Defense of the Apology (Jewel), 253
Defense of the Government Established (Bridge), 253
Defert, Daniel, 155, 327 n. 7
Dekker, Thomas, 198, 233, 234, 252
Deloney, Thomas, 178

Dennis, John, 42, 309 n. 30
Description of Britain (Harrison), 108–9, 131–32, 142
"Description of Florida" (Laudonnière), 186–87
Descriptions, 131. *See also* Chorography and cartography
Devon, Collections Towards a Description of (Pole), 135
Dialogue between Pole and Lupset (Starkey), 65–66, 69–70
Diary (Henslowe), 340 n. 72
Discourse of English Poetry (Webbe), 30–31
"Discourse of the Commodity of the Taking of the Strait of Magellan" (Hakluyt), 163–66, 171, 180, 183, 185
Discourse of the Invention of Ships (Raleigh), 181
Discourse Touching the Reformation of the Laws of England (Morison), 70
Discursive communities, 12–16
Divers Voyages (Hakluyt), 167
Doctor and Student (St. Germain), 86
Dodderidge, Sir John, 76, 78
Dodsworth, Roger, 135
Dolce, Lodovico, 44
Domesday Book, 97
Donne, John, 286
Dorchester, Viscount (Dudley Carlton), 91
Dorotheus, 90
Dorsetshire, A Survey of (Coker), 135
Dorsten, Jan van, 53
Drake, Sir Francis, 16–17, 151, 164, 165, 184, 186
Drama of a Nation (Cohen), 198
Drant, Thomas, 26
Drayton, Michael: alienation from court, 128–31; discursive community of, 15; Hakluyt compared with, 152; on lack of English national identity, 14; name for England, 8; *Pastorals,* 129; *Poly-Olbion,* see *Poly-Olbion* (Drayton); *Robert, Duke of Normandy,* 129; *The Shepherd's Sirena,* 129; as transitional man, 14; other references, 12, 16, 17, 147, 244, 303 n. 1
Driver, Alice, 264–66, 284
Dryden, John, 42
Dudley, Guilford, 234, 237

Dugdale, Sir William, 138, 325 n. 45, 326 n. 51
Dumont, Louis, 331 n. 55
Dunham, W. H., 314 n. 4
Dyer, Sir Edward, 15, 25–26, 30
Dyer, Sir James, 80, 84, 85
Dying Pellicane (Spenser), 26

E. K., 49
East India Company, 172
Eccles, Mark, 311 n. 52
Eclogues (Virgil), 4, 77
Edelen, Georges, 324 n. 34, 347 n. 42
Eden, Richard, 151, 179, 182
Edward I (Peele), 231–34, 237, 238, 252–53
Edward III (play), 334 n. 25
Edward IV (Heywood), 209–13, 221, 228, 231, 233–35, 237–39, 252–53
Edward VI, king of England, 182, 258, 344 n. 16
Egerton, Thomas, 84–89
Eikonoklastes (Milton), 61
Elizabeth I, queen of England: and chivalry, 50–53; and chorography, 107, 109–16, 120, 125–31, 139, 145; and Drake, 16; and *Faerie Queene,* 49, 52, 55–59; and law, 71, 73, 75, 77, 82, 88; and monarchy, concept of, 298–99; and national identity, 9, 15–16; and religion, 252, 253, 258–60, 266–68, 272, 344 n. 16; and theater, 197, 198, 201, 210, 219–20; on trade, pursuit of, 185; other references, 26, 28, 36, 43, 182, 234, 237, 316 n. 17
Elizabethan World Picture (Tillyard), 270
Elton, G. R., 4, 303 n. 7, 313 nn. 2, 4, 314 n. 11
England's Treasure by Foreign Trade (Mun), 188
English history plays. *See* Henslowe, Philip; Shakespeare, William; Theater
English Law and the Renaissance (Maitland), 66–69
English Voyages (Hakluyt). *See Principal Navigations of the English Nation* (Hakluyt)
Enterprise and Empire (Rabb), 172, 178, 180

Epic: Camões' *Lusiads* as, 154–56, 161, 190; *Faerie Queene* as, 41, 48; in Milton, 60–61; in Tasso, 45–48; other references, 7, 296, 297
Epithalamion Thameses (Spenser), 142
Erasmus, Desiderius, 23, 42, 44, 61
Erdeswicke, Simon, 132, 143
Esler, Anthony, 310 nn. 46, 48
Esquival, Pedro de, 146, 326 n. 58
Essex, earl of (Robert Devereux), 51–54, 57–59, 237
Essex (Jekyll), 135
Euphues and His England (Lyly), 33
European Community, 68
Eusebius of Caesaria, 260
Evans, Ifor M., 322 n. 10
Ewell, Barbara C., 325 n. 46

Faerie Queene, The (Spenser): as chivalric romance, 48–59; Drayton's *Poly-Olbion* contrasted with, 140–43; prosody of, 26, 27, 31; religion in, 251; other references, 1, 4, 5, 14, 19, 154, 196, 296, 298–99
Fair Em (play), 340 n. 69
Faith, Rosemond, 209
Falstaff, Sir John (fictional character), 220, 222–24, 227–30, 232, 236, 249–53, 265
Famous Victories of Henry V (play), 203
Fanshawe, Sir Richard, 158
Ferguson, Arthur B., 309 n. 35, 310 nn. 45, 46, 48, 347 n. 43
Finch, Heneage. *See* Nottingham, earl of
Finch, Henry, 75–79, 82, 87, 90, 99, 102, 303 n. 1
Firth, Katherine R., 345 n. 22
Fleta (law book), 97
Fletcher, Angus, 325 n. 46
Fortescue, Sir John, 59, 69, 86
Fortune, John, 265, 266, 284, 345 n. 26
Foxe, John: *Acts and Monuments,* see *Acts and Monuments* (Foxe); *Christus Triumphans,* 256; other references, 6, 9, 195–96
Foxford, Dr., 255, 256
France: chorography in, 146; poetic form in, 39; and Roman law, 67, 69; other references, 165, 299

Franciscus Accursius, 96
Fraunce, Abraham, 31, 76, 78
Frith, John, 259
Frobisher, Martin, 151, 167
Froude, J. A., 175, 190, 191
Frye, Northrop, 49
Fulbecke, William, 76, 78–79, 297, 307 n. 9
Fumerton, Patricia, 303 n. 5, 332 n. 56

Gaius, 90
Gardiner, Stephen, 255, 256
Gavelkind, 137
Gellner, Ernest, 10, 11, 304 nn. 11, 13
Gendering of state and nation, 11, 297–99
General History of the Indes (Oviedo), 154
Geneva, of Calvin, 274–75, 277
Geneva Bible, 259, 262, 278
Gentlemen: Hakluyt on, 168–81; and theater, 197, 200–202, 208, 209, 213, 241–45. *See also* Aristocracy; Merchants
George a Greene, the Pinner of Wakefield (play), 231–34, 237–38, 252–53
George the German, 344 n. 16
German law, 67
Gerusalemme Conquistata (Tasso), 47
Gerusalemme Liberata (Tasso): *Faerie Queene* contrasted with, 44–48, 50, 52, 54, 57, 59, 61; other references, 7, 9, 154
Giddens, Anthony, 304 n. 13
Gilbert, Sir Humphrey, 151, 167, 171, 173, 175
Gildas, 132
Girouard, Mark, 306 n. 2
Glanville, Ranulf de, 87
Globe Theater, 198, 223, 226–30, 241, 242
Goldberg, Jonathan, 304 n. 9, 308 n. 25, 323 n. 19, 341 n. 80
Gorboduc (Sackville and Norton), 36
Gorla, Gino, 314 n. 8
Gosson, Stephen, 201, 202
Gothic. *See* Ancient-medieval dichotomy; Barbarism
Gould, J. D., 331 n. 56
Grace Abounding (Bunyan), 285, 287, 288
Grafton, Richard, 12, 195–96

Gray, Charles, 320 n. 59
Gray, H. D., 338 n. 52
"Great dualism." *See* Ancient-medieval dichotomy
Greece, ancient: and ancient-medieval dichotomy, 21, 33; law of, 87, 103, 104; reform of language, 29–30; Spenser on "language kingdom" of, 1, 3, 14, 22, 25, 69; and theater, 243; other references, 1, 159. *See also* Ancient-medieval dichotomy
Greek, ancient, 29–30
Greenblatt, Stephen, 304 n. 9, 305 n. 19, 323 n. 18, 338 n. 50, 341 nn. 77, 80, 345 nn. 24, 25
Greene, Robert, 31, 197, 200–204, 218, 333 n. 16
Greenslade, B. D., 348 n. 59
Greenwood, John, 271
Greville, Sir Fulke (Lord Brooke), 15, 31, 129, 300, 303 n. 1
Grey, Lady Jane, 234, 237, 238, 297
Gridley, Jeremiah, 320 n. 60
Grindal, Edmund, 346 n. 31
Groatsworth of Wit (Greene), 201
Grundy, Joan, 324 n. 29, 326 n. 53
Guarini, Giovanni Battista, 35
Guiana, Carmen Epicum, De (Chapman), 173
Guilpin, Everard, 225
Gurr, Andrew, 333 n. 9, 334 n. 24

Habington, Thomas, 126, 132, 134
Hakluyt, Richard, the elder, 166, 168, 171
Hakluyt, Richard, the younger, 151–55, 163–91; "Discourse of the Commodity of the Taking of the Strait of Magellan," 163–66, 171, 180, 183, 185; discursive community of, 15; *Divers Voyages,* 167; influence on later writers, 187–91; *Principal Navigations of the English Nation,* see *Principal Navigations of the English Nation* (Hakluyt); and religion, 251; and Spain, tyranny of, 182–87; as transitional man, 13; other references, 9, 12, 16, 17, 244, 303 n. 1
Hakluyt Society, 16, 175, 187

Hakluytus Posthumus, or Purchas His Pilgrims (Purchas), 152, 187
Hale, J. R., 108, 322 n. 5
Hale, Sir Matthew, 96, 102
Hall, Edward, 12, 132
Hall, John, 283–84
Hall, Joseph, 201, 334 n. 19
Haller, William, 23, 263, 345 nn. 21, 347 n. 42
Hamlet (Shakespeare), 223, 225
Harbage, Alfred, 197–98, 333 n. 11
Hardin, Richard F., 324 n. 30
Hargrave, Francis, 96
Hariot, Thomas, 327 n. 2
Harley, J. B., 322 n. 5
Harrison, William, 108–9, 131–33, 142, 171–72, 201
Harvey, Gabriel: and quantitative verse, 26–28, 33, 37; Spenser criticized by, 41, 42; Spenser's correspondence with, 1, 14–15, 25, 30–31, 38; other references, 53, 59, 295, 297, 350 n. 4
Hasler, P. W., 325 n. 41
Hassall, W. O., 317 nn. 26–28, 319 n. 52
Hawkins, Sir John, 151, 186
Hayward, Sir John, 12, 76, 81, 303 n. 1
Hazeltine, H. D., 314 n. 10
Helgerson, Richard, 304 n. 8, 312 n. 60, 313 n. 69, 350 n. 8
Henri IV, king of France, 146
Henry IV, Pts. 1 and 2 (Shakespeare), 114, 220, 222–23, 226–30, 232, 235, 236, 249–53
Henry V, king of England, 249
Henry V (Shakespeare), 201, 223, 231–32, 235–36, 240–41, 252
Henry VI, king of England, 238
Henry VI, Pt. 1 (Shakespeare), 214, 332 n. 2
Henry VI, Pt. 2 (Shakespeare). See *Contention, The* (Shakespeare)
Henry VI, Pt. 3 (Shakespeare), 214, 332 n. 2
Henry VII, king of England, 254
Henry VIII, king of England, 4, 65–66, 185, 258, 267, 299
Henry VIII (Shakespeare), 332 n. 3, 343 n. 8
Henry, Prince, 43, 128

Henry the Navigator, Prince, 190

Henslowe, Philip: *Diary,* 340 n. 72; and Oldcastle, martyrdom of, 249, 252; popular tradition in dramatists of, 231–40; other references, 6–7, 9, 197, 210, 296, 297

Herbert, George, 286

Hernadi, Paul, 350 n. 2

Heroic verse, 60–61

Hexter, J. H., 309 n. 36

Heywood, Thomas: *Apology for Actors,* 212; *Edward IV,* 209–13, 221, 228, 231, 233–35, 238, 239, 252–53; *If You Know Not Me, You Know Nobody,* 234, 252; *The Royal King and the Loyal Subject,* 230, 234, 239; *Sir Thomas More* revisions, 221–22

Higden, Ranulf, 132, 133

Hildebrand, Pope, 262

Hill, Christopher, 327 n. 61, 331 n. 48, 349 n. 62

Hill, W. Speed, 272, 347 nn. 40-42

Hillerdal, Gunnar, 347 n. 46

History, chronicle. *See* Chronicle history

History of Great Britain (Speed), 132

History of the Indes (Oviedo), 183–84

History plays. *See* Henslowe, Philip; Shakespeare, William; Theater

Histriomastix (Marston), 203, 211–12, 243

Hobbes, Thomas, 290–96; on Coke, 98; Drayton contrasted with, 297, 298, 300–301; *Leviathan,* 290–96

Hobsbawm, E. J., 350 n. 2

Holdsworth, W. S., 75, 313 n. 4, 316 n. 18

Holinshed, Raphael, 12, 108–9, 132–33, 140

Holland, 17, 67, 162, 181–82

Holland, John, 207–8, 212

Holland, Lord (Henry Rich), 91

Holy War, The (Bunyan), 287

Homer, 29, 49, 60, 161, 173

Hooker, John, 132

Hooker, Richard: discursive community of, 15; *Of the Laws of Ecclesiastical Polity,* see *Of the Laws of Ecclesiastical Polity* (Hooker); as transitional man, 13; other references, 9, 12, 16, 303 n. 1

Horace, 29

Hotman, François, 318 n. 49

Howard, Charles (earl of Nottingham), 178

Huddy, John, 321 n. 1

Hughes, John, 40–42, 54

Humanism: and ancient-medieval dichotomy, 23; of Camões, 159–60; and chivalric romance, 41–44, 50, 57–59; and law, 69, 72, 74, 80, 81, 96, 101, 103; of Milton, 60–61; other references, 5, 242, 245

Humphrey, duke of Gloucester, 195, 196, 207, 214, 234

Hunter, G. K., 33, 308 n. 15, 338 n. 53

Hurd, Richard, 41, 42, 44, 48, 50, 54, 310 n. 40

If You Know Not Me, You Know Nobody (Heywood), 234, 252

Ill May Day, 210–11

Image of Both Churches (Bale), 258–59

Imagined communities, 266

Improvisation, in theater, 223–24

Inclusion and exclusion: class and gender in, 297; in history plays, 193–245, 249; principle of, 9, 11; in written voyages, 154, 160. *See also* Class

Industrialism, 10

Innocent III (pope), 262

Instauratio Magna (Bacon), 78, 79, 84

Institute of the Laws of England (Wood), 102

Institutes, in law, 7, 16, 75, 88–104

Institutes (Gaius), 90

Institutes (Justinian), 75–76, 84, 90–93, 96

Institutes of English Law (Cowell), 76, 78, 79

Institutes of the Laws of England (Coke), 70–71, 88–101; influence of, 101–4; other references, 1, 5, 17, 63, 74, 196, 294

Interpreter, The (Cowell), 76, 78–79

Invective against Tarlton's News out of Purgatory, An, 224

Irish Reports (Davies), 86–87, 93–96

Italia Liberata dai Goti (Trissino), 47

Italy: and chivalric romance, 43–44; humanism of, 23; poetic form in, 35, 39; other references, 67, 159, 299

Jack Straw (play). See *Life and Death of Jack Straw*

James, Mervyn, 47, 52, 310 nn. 41, 46, 311 n. 59, 311 nn. 48, 51, 312 n. 62

James I, king of England: and chorography, 111, 114, 124, 125, 127–30, 135, 145; and Daniel, 37–38, 40, 59; and law, 71, 74–85, 88–89, 93, 98–100, 103; monarchy, concept of, 298–99; *True Law of Free Monarchies,* 77; other references, 8, 9, 43, 279, 281, 282, 303 n. 4, 308 n. 22, 316 n. 17

Javitch, Daniel, 308 n. 15

Jefferson, Thomas, 101–3

Jekyll, Thomas, 135

Jenkins, Dafydd, 314 n. 4

Jewel, John, 253, 278, 279

Jig, 224–27, 241

Joan of Arc, 214–15

Joan of Kent, 344 n. 16

John, St., 258, 262. *See also* Revelation, Book of

Joint-stock companies, 169

Jones, Howard Mumford, 329 n. 20

Jones, Richard Foster, 303 n. 6

Jonson, Ben: *Catiline,* 225; on chivalric romance, 43, 44; "Ode to Himself," 32; *Prince Henry's Barriers,* 43; on quantitative verse and rime, 39–40; on Shakespeare, 203; other references, 198, 243

Julius Caesar (Shakespeare), 225

Jung, C. G., 49

Jurisprudence, 67. *See also* Law

Justinian I: *Corpus Juris Civilis,* 7, 70, 75, 78, 299; *Institutes,* 75–76, 84, 90–93, 96; other references, 9, 65, 68, 70, 72, 75–77, 97, 99, 100, 102, 103, 154

Kastan, David Scott, 226–27, 334 n. 20, 339 n. 63

Kearney, H. F., 348 n. 53

Keen, Maurice, 341 n. 76

Kelley, Donald R., 314 n. 12

Kemp, Will, 198, 215–16, 218, 222–31, 241

Kemp's Nine-Days' Wonder (Kemp), 228–29

Kennedy, Duncan, 321 n. 65

Kermode, Frank, 342 n. 5

King, Henry, 348 n. 52

King, John N., 344 n. 19

King, power of the. *See* Monarchic power

"King Disguised, The" (Barton), 231–33, 237, 240

King John (Shakespeare), 8, 343 n. 8

King Lear (Shakespeare), 114

King Leir (play), 340 n. 69

King's Men, 240. *See also* Chamberlain's Men

Knafla, Louis A., 317 n. 35, 318 n. 40

Kostić, Veselin, 309 n. 37

Krueger, Robert, 328 n. 14

Kyd, Thomas, 197

Ladurie, Emmanuel Le Roy, 338 n. 46

Lake, Peter, 284, 347 n. 44, 348 n. 57

Lambarde, William, 132, 133, 136–38, 143, 151, 152

Landino, Cristoforo, 49

Languet, Hubert, 58

Larsen, Neil, 328 n. 14

Las Casas, Bartolomé de, 183

Latimer, Hugh, 269, 284

Latin, 29–30, 65, 70

Laud, William, 284

Laudibus Legum Angliae, De (Fortesque), 69, 86

Laudonnière, René, 186–87, 327 n. 2

Law, 65–104; ancient-medieval dichotomy, 23–24; English vs. continental experience, 65–72; Hooker on religion and, 253, 276–78, 280; influence of Coke, 101–4; and *Institutes* of Coke, 88–101; and *Reports* of Coke, 73–88; theater compared with, 204; other references, 5, 6, 15, 18, 299. *See also* Coke, Sir Edward

Law, or a Discourse Thereof (Finch). See *Nomotechnia* (Finch)

Lawrence, Heather, 322 n. 10

Lawson, F. H., 315 n. 16

Leicester, earl of (Robert Dudley), 14–15, 53–59

Leland, John, 126, 132, 133

Leonard, Irving A., 329 n. 20

Leslie, Michael, 311 n. 55

Lestringant, Frank, 327 n. 7

Letters on Chivalry and Romance (Hurd), 41
Levack, Brian P., 316 n. 22
Leviathan (Hobbes), 290–94, 295–96
Levy, F. J., 12, 305 n. 14, 323 n. 23
Lewis, A. D. E., 315 n. 16
Lhuyd, Humphrey, 133, 136, 321 n. 1
Libelle of English Policy, 188–89
Life and Death of Jack Straw (play), 209–13, 221, 237, 334 n. 25
Life and Death of Mr. Badman, The (Bunyan), 281
Life of Sir Philip Sidney (Greville), 300
Lightbown, Ronald, 349 n. 72
Lily, George, 321 n. 1
Littleton, Sir Thomas, 89–99
Lives (Walton), 286, 289
Lloyd, Lodowick, 76
Lodge, Thomas, 31
Lollards, 256, 292. *See also* Oldcastle, Sir John
Louis XIV, king of France, 146
Love's Labor Lost (Shakespeare), 220
Luig, Klaus, 315 n. 16
Lusiads (Camões), 7, 155–63; Hakluyt's writings contrasted with, 163–76, 180; Mickle's translation of, 189–90; other references, 7, 180, 182
Lycurgus, 85
Lyly, John, 33, 303 n. 1

McCabe, Colin, 339 n. 64
McCoy, Richard C., 50–51, 310 nn. 46–48
McGee, Sears, 343 n. 7
McGrade, Arthur S., 348 n. 54
McKisack, May, 323 n. 23
Maclean, Gerald M., 308 n. 20
McMillan, Scott, 335 n. 32, 338 n. 49
Macrobius, 49
Madison, James, 101
Magalhães-Godinho, Vitorino, 159, 328 n. 17, 329 n. 23
Magellan, Ferdinand, 151
Magna Carta, 97, 98
Maitland, Frederic William, 66–69, 309 n. 27, 313 n. 3, 314 n. 10
Maltby, William S., 331 n. 52
Manley, Lawrence, 348 n. 55

Mannheim, Karl, 303 n. 8
Maps. *See* Chorography and cartography
Marcus, Leah S., 304 n. 9, 312 n. 61, 333 n. 6, 341 n. 80, 350 n. 7
Marlowe, Christopher: on jig, 225; *Tamburlaine,* 199–200; other references, 197, 204, 242, 243, 303 n. 1
Marprelate controversy, 250–51, 271
Marsilius of Padua, 281
Marston, John, 198, 203, 204, 211–12, 243
Martyr, Peter. *See* Peter Martyr
Martyrdom: in Foxe, 249–69, 284, 294, 297; in Walton, 286. *See also* Apocalyptic discourse
Marx, Karl, 175
Mary I, queen of England: and religion, 255, 256, 258–60, 267, 271; and Spanish rule, 182; other references, 234, 238
Mary, Queen of Scots, 182
Mary Tudor. *See* Mary I, queen of England
Massinger, Philip, 225–26
Medievalism. *See* Ancient-medieval dichotomy
Merchant Adventurers, 180, 181
Merchant of Venice, The (Shakespeare), 220
Merchants: in Hakluyt, 163–81; in Mun, 188; and Spain, imperialism of, 181–87; and theater, 241–42; and trade in Camões, 156–63
Michaelis, Gottfried, 347 n. 46
Mickle, William Julius, 189–91
Middleton, Thomas, 198
Midsummer Night's Dream, A (Shakespeare), 220
Milton, John, 60–62; *Eikonoklastes,* 61; *Paradise Lost,* 60–61, 156; on Russia, 331 n. 50; other references, 263, 283
Minturno, Antonio, 44, 52
Moccia, Luigi, 314 n. 8
Monarchic power: in Bunyan, 288; in Camões, 160; and chorography, 107–46; and chronicle history, 12; in Coke, 74–78, 82–85, 88–90, 92, 93, 98–100, 103; in English tradition, 69; in Foxe, 253, 258–64, 268; in Hakluyt,

152–53, 165; in Henslowe playwrights, 234–40; in Hobbes, 292–94; in Hooker, 253, 275, 281–82, 285; in Justinian, 90; in Milton, 60, 61; relation between nationhood concept and, 1–4, 9–10, 296–300; in Shakespeare, 195–245; in Spenser, 48, 55–60; in Tasso, 45–46

Montalboddo, Fracanzano da, 152

Montrose, Louis Adrian, 304 n. 9, 312 n. 61, 341 n. 80, 342 n. 86, 350 n. 7

More, Sir Thomas, 42, 44, 61, 234, 238, 239

Moretti, Franco, 334 n. 20

Morgan, Edmund S., 327 n. 6

Morgan, Victor, 321 n. 4, 323 n. 12, 324 n. 26

Morison, Richard, 70–72, 87, 90

Morris dancing, 215–16, 228–29

Moser, Gerald M., 329 n. 26

Mozley, J. F., 344 nn. 16, 17, 345 n. 27, 346 n. 32

Mukerji, Chandra, 326 n. 59

Mulcaster, Richard, 172

Mullaney, Steven, 338 n. 50, 339 n. 64

Mun, Thomas, 188

Munday, Anthony, 197, 233, 234, 237–38

Munz, Peter, 347 n. 46, 348 n. 53

Nairn, Tom, 342 n. 85

Nashe, Thomas, 31, 200, 204, 212, 213, 334 nn. 24, 26

Navigatione, De (Parmenius), 173

Navigazioni e Viaggi (Ramusio), 152

Neale, J. E., 326 n. 55

Newbery, John, 174–75, 177, 179

Newdigate, Bernard H., 324 n. 27

New Inn (Jonson), 32

New Institute of the Imperial or Civil Law (Wood), 102

"New Navigation and Discovery of the Kingdom of Moscovia, The" (Adams), 179–80

Nobility. *See* Aristocracy

Nohrnberg, James, 49, 310 n. 44

Nomotechnia (Finch), 75–79, 82, 87, 90, 99, 102

Norbrook, David, 324 n. 29

Norden, John: *Preparative to his Speculum Britanniae,* 125; *Speculum Britanniae,* 125; other references, 108, 114, 117, 128, 131, 133, 147, 303 n. 1

Normans, 81, 103–4, 122, 124

North, Francis (Baron Guilford), 97

Northamptonshire, Visitation of (Vincent), 135

Northumberland, duke of (John Dudley), 182

Norton, Thomas, 36

Norton Anthology of English Literature, 270

Nottingham, earl of (Heneage Finch), 96

Nowell, Laurence, 321 n. 1

Observations on the Art of English Poesy (Campion), 36

Observations on the Faerie Queen (Warton), 54–55

O'Connell, Michael, 311 n. 58, 342 n. 5

"Ode to Himself" (Jonson), 32

Officio Regis, De (Wycliffe), 69

Of the Laws of Ecclesiastical Polity (Hooker): as apologetic discourse, 253–54, 269–83; influence of, 283–94; other references, 1, 5, 6, 17, 247, 296, 297, 300

Oldcastle, Sir John (Lord Cobham), 230–40, 249–51, 249–53, 265, 271, 284

Oliveira Marques, A. H. de, 160, 329 n. 21

Oliver, Leslie Mahin, 345 n. 28, 348 n. 56, 349 n. 62

Olsen, V. Norskov, 344 n. 17, 345 n. 22

Orbe Novo, De (Peter Martyr), 154

Orgel, Stephen, 304 n. 9, 334 n. 20, 341 n. 80

Orlando Furioso (Ariosto), 44, 50, 160

Ortelius, Abraham, 6, 107–9, 112, 126

Oviedo, Fernández de, 154, 183–84

Owen, George, 126, 132, 136

Oxford University, 66, 70

Paesi Novamente Ritrovati (Montalboddo), 152

Paradise Lost (Milton), 60–61, 156

Parallels (Fulbecke), 78–79
Parker, John, 327 n. 1
Parker, Matthew, 16
Parks, George Bruner, 327 n. 2, 330 n. 32, 331 n. 46
Parmenius, Stephan, 173, 179
Parry, J. H., 329 n. 27
Parsons, Robert, 265
Passerin d'Entrèves, Alexander, 347 n. 46
Pastorals (Drayton), 129
Patterson, Annabel, 208–9, 211, 213, 227, 324 n. 31, 335 n. 30, 336 n. 36, 337 n. 39
Peasant ideology, 209, 227
Peasants' Revolt, 208–9, 213
Peckham, Sir George, 172, 179, 183, 185
Peele, George, 197, 231–34, 237, 238, 303 n. 1
Pembroke, countess of (Mary Sidney), 31
Pennington, L. E., 176, 189, 330 n. 44
Pernoud, Georges, 326 n. 56
Pernoud, Régine, 326 n. 56
Peter Martyr, 154, 173, 183
Petrarch, 306 n. 5
Pettitt, Thomas, 338 n. 46
Philip II, king of Spain, 146, 162, 163, 182
Pigman, G. W., 317 n. 24
Pigna, Giovanni Battista, 44
Pilgrim's Progress, The (Bunyan), 287, 288
Pires, Tomé, 159
Pizarro, Francisco, 161
Plays Confuted (Gosson), 202
Plowden, Edmund, 80, 85, 86
Plucknett, Theodore F. T., 317 nn. 30, 37
Plumb, J. H., 287
Pocklington, John, 284
Pocock, J. G. A., 71, 290, 314 n. 12, 318 n. 37, 323 n. 15, 349 n. 68
Poetry: ancient-medieval dichotomy, 23–62; chorography's relation to, 139–47; tension between national needs and, 1–2; other references, 5, 15, 18, 242, 299, 300. *See also* Ancient-medieval dichotomy; Chivalric romance; Quantitative verse; Rime; Spenser, Edmund
Pole, Sir William, 132, 135

Pollard, Alfred, 347 n. 49
Poly-Olbion (Drayton): additions by other writers, 128–30; authority symbols in, 117–24, 133; Hobbes contrasted with, 297, 298, 300–301; as poem, 139–47; other references, 1, 5, 9, 126, 131–32, 154, 196
Poore, Leonard, 174
Portugal: Camões on, 154–63, 182; Hakluyt on, 163, 165, 167–68, 180; other references, 17, 67, 164, 181–82
Power, 8, 107, 297. *See also* Monarchic power
Pratt, Joseph, 342 n. 1
Preparative to his Speculum Britanniae (Norden), 125
Presbyterians, 250, 271, 277
Preservation of Henry VII (play), 31
Prest, Wilfred, 316 n. 19
Preston, Thomas, 26
Prince Henry's Barriers (Jonson), 43
Principal Navigations of the English Nation (Hakluyt), 152–54, 165–71; and class relations, 171–81; economic orientation of, 163–71; influence on later writings, 187–91; and religion, 251; and Spain, tyranny of, 182, 185, 186; other references, 1, 5, 6, 15, 196, 296, 298
Printing, invention of, 264, 267–68, 284
"Prothalamion" (Spenser), 53
Ptolemy, 152
Purchas, Samuel, 152, 187, 330 n. 36
Puritans: and Hooker, 270, 272, 274, 275, 278–80; other references, 202, 213, 249, 250
Puttenham, George, 26, 31, 34
Pye, Christopher, 326 n. 55
Pym, John, 336 n. 36
Pyrard de Laval, François, 329 n. 23

Quantitative verse: and Milton, 60; and rime, 25–40; other references, 7, 70
Quartermaster's Map, 108, 112, 114
Queen, power of the. *See* Monarchic power
Quinn, David B., 175, 176, 189, 330 nn. 31, 43
Quint, David, 328 nn. 11, 15, 332 n. 58

Rabb, Theodore K., 172, 178, 180, 330 nn. 40, 41, 331 nn. 45, 47

Rackin, Phyllis, 335 n. 29

Raleigh, Sir Walter: *Discourse of the Invention of Ships,* 181; Hakluyt on, 173; on Spain's ambition, 184; Tarlton on, 218–19; on trade and English classes, 181; other references, 15, 48, 58, 151, 171, 303 n. 1

Ramusio, Giovanni Battista, 152

Read, Conyers, 311 n. 53

Reason, in law, 97–100, 280–82, 286

Relación de la Destruyción del las Indias (las Casas), 183

Relation of the Imprisonment of Mr. John Bunyan (Bunyan), 287–88

Religion, 249–94; and apocalyptic of Foxe, 254–68; and apologetic of Hooker, 269–83; in Hobbes's *Leviathan,* 290–94; importance to Elizabethans, 251–53; Walton and Bunyan contrasted, 285–90; other references, 5, 6, 16, 18, 299–301. *See also* Apocalyptic discourse; Apologetic discourse; Foxe, John; Hooker, Richard

Renaissance, 21, 22, 103, 122, 155

Reports, in law, 7, 16, 79–81. See also *Reports* (Coke)

Reports (Coke), 5, 78–88; attack on, 89–90; Davies, influence on, 86–88; other references, 70, 74

Republica Anglorum, De (Smith), 86

Revelation, Book of, 258–60, 262, 263, 267, 271

Revolt, popular. *See* Commoners

Reynolds, John, 129–30

Richard II, king of England, 235, 236, 238, 256

Richard II (Shakespeare), 235–36

Richard III, king of England, 235

Richard III (Shakespeare), 235–36

Ridley, Nicholas, 269, 271

Ridley, Sir Thomas, 76, 78–79

Rime: common law compared with, 65, 70, 103–4; Milton on, 60; and quantitative verse, 25–40; other references, 6, 7, 41, 59

Rimes against Martin Marprelate, 250–51

Risdon, Tristram, 126, 131, 132

Robert, Duke of Normandy (Drayton), 129

Robert, Earl of Huntington (Munday and Chettle), 234, 237–39, 252–53

Roberts, Lewis, 332 n. 58

Robin Hood, 231–32, 234, 237–38

Robin Hood (Munday and Chettle). See *Robert, Earl of Huntington* (Munday and Chettle)

Roman Actor (Massinger), 225–26

Roman Catholic Church: Foxe on, 253, 255, 258, 261–62, 267; Hooker on, 71, 253, 273, 275, 278; and martyrdom of Oldcastle, 249; other references, 4, 251, 289. *See also* Religion

Romance, chivalric. *See* Chivalric romance

Rome, ancient: civil law of, and English common law, 65–104, 297; epic of, and Camões, 159, 160; imperialism of, 186–87; religion of, 258; and theater, 243; other references, 3, 22, 33, 122

Rose, The, 196–98, 242

Rowley, Samuel, 234, 252

Rowse, A. L., 323 n. 18

Royal King and the Loyal Subject, The (Heywood), 230, 234, 239

Rudd, John, 321 n. 1

Russell, Conrad, 251–52, 289–90, 343 n. 7

Russia, 164, 331 n. 50

Rymer, Thomas, 42, 309 n. 30

Sacheverell Riots, 208

Sackville, Thomas. *See* Buckhurst, Baron

St. Germain, Christopher, 86

Sanderson, Robert, 286

Sandler, Florence, 342 n. 5

Sandys, Edwin, 272–73, 283, 288, 300, 303 n. 1

Sannazaro, Jacopo, 42

Saxons, 81, 122, 140

Saxton, Christopher: influence on later mapmakers, 107–26; other references, 5, 9, 131, 133, 135, 139, 144, 146, 147, 151

Sayer, Derek, 304 n. 10

Scaliger, Julius Caesar, 49, 52

Schama, Simon, 309 n. 36

Schoenbaum, S., 334 n. 24

Schoolmaster (Ascham), 28–34, 65, 70
Scott, William Robert, 330 n. 34
Scottish law, 67
Sebastião, king of Portugal, 162
Seckford, Thomas, 108–12, 126
Second Part of the Return from Parnassus (play), 201–2
Selden, John, 16, 67–68, 90, 128, 130–31, 300
Self-alienation: ancient-medieval dichotomy, 22, 24; and Hobbes, 294; and national self-representation, 16–17; and theater, 243. *See also* Barbarism
Separatists, 271
Servius, 49
Shakespeare, William, 162, 193–245; *As You Like It*, 220; authorship question, 111; carnival and clown in, 215–228; *Contention, see Contention, The* (Shakespeare); discursive community of, 15; Foxe contrasted with, 265–66; *Hamlet*, 223, 225; *Henry IV, Pts. 1 and 2*, 114, 220, 222–23, 226–30, 232, 235, 236, 249–53; *Henry V*, 201, 223, 231–32, 235–36, 240–41, 252; *Henry VI, Pt. 1*, 214, 332 n. 2; *Henry VI, Pt. 2, see Contention, The* (Shakespeare); *Henry VI, Pt. 3*, 214, 332 n. 2; *Henry VIII*, 332 n. 3, 343 n. 8; Hooker compared with, 270, 273, 279; *Julius Caesar*, 225; *King John*, 8, 343 n. 8; *King Lear*, 114; *Love's Labor Lost*, 220; maps, use of, 114; *Merchant of Venice*, 220; *Midsummer Night's Dream*, 220; popular revolt in, 204–15; and religious reform, 249–54; *Richard II*, 235–36; *Richard III*, 235–36; sonnets, 203; as transitional man, 13; *Troilus and Cressida*, 203; *Twelfth Night*, 220; other references, 1, 5–7, 9, 12, 296, 297, 303 n. 1, 305 n. 19
Shakespeare and the Popular Tradition in the Theater (Weimann), 198
Shakespeare and the Rival Traditions (Harbage), 197–98
Shakespeare's Festive Comedy (Barber), 198, 220
Shakespeare Society, 16
Sharpe, Kevin, 127, 314 n. 12, 323 nn. 22, 23, 324 n. 28

Sharpe, Robert Boies, 341 n. 81
Sharswood, George, 101–2
Shepheardes Calender (Spenser), 4, 26, 33, 42, 49
Shepherd's Sirena (Drayton), 129
Shirley, F. J., 347 n. 46, 349 n. 67
Shore, Jane, 233–35, 237, 239, 297
Shore, Matthew, 233–35, 237–39, 297
Short Treatise of Scottish Poetry (James I), 37–38
Shuger, Debora Kuller, 18, 274, 306 n. 25, 347 n. 43, 348 n. 51
Sidney, Sir Henry, 180
Sidney, Sir Philip: *Arcadia*, 39, 50; *Astrophel and Stella*, 31, 39; chorographers compared with, 107, 129, 137; *Defense of Poesy*, 34; Hakluyt's letter to, 167, 168; and quantitative verse, 25–26, 30–36, 39, 40; on Spenser's language, 42; on theater, decorum in, 201; other references, 1, 15, 51, 58–60, 70, 303 n. 1
Simpson, A. W. B., 315 n. 16
Sinfield, Alan, 342 n. 85
Singer, John, 216, 218
Sir John Oldcastle (play), 230–40, 249, 252
Sir Thomas More (Munday *et al.*), 210, 212, 221–22, 234, 237–39, 252, 335 n. 32, 340 n. 72
Sir Thomas Wyatt (Dekker and Webster), 230, 234, 238–40, 252–53
Sisson, C. J., 272, 347 n. 40
Skelton, R. A., 321 n. 3, 322 nn. 6–9, 11, 324 n. 36
Slomber (Spenser), 26
Smith, Adam, 189, 190
Smith, Anthony D., 305 n. 17
Smith, Sir Thomas, 86, 172
Smith, William, 133, 136
Sommerville, J. P., 316 n. 20, 318 n. 37, 327 n. 61
Sonnet, 39
Sonnets (Shakespeare), 203
Spain: chorography in, 146; England and imperialism of, 181–87; Hakluyt on, 167–68, 180; Portugal, relations with, 160–64, 181; other references, 17, 67, 165, 271, 299
Speculum Britanniae (Norden), 125

Speed, John: discursive community of, 15; *History of Great Britain,* 132; name for England, 8; *Theater of the Empire of Great Britain,* see *Theater of the Empire of Great Britain* (Speed); as transitional man, 13–14; other references, 9, 12, 17, 128, 129, 133, 139, 303 n. 1
Spelman, Sir Henry, 324 n. 25
Spenser, Edmund, 25–62; and chivalric romance, 40–45, 48–59; chorographers compared with, 107, 129–30, 139, 140–43; Coke compared with, 104; comedies, 26, 27, 42; discursive community of, 14–15; *Dying Pellicane,* 26; *Epithalamion Thameses,* 142; *Faerie Queene,* see *Faerie Queene, The* (Spenser); name for England, 8; on need for kingdom of English language, 1–3, 11, 14, 16, 22, 25, 69, 242; and prosodic form of English verse, 24–39; "Prothalamion," 53; *Shepheardes Calender,* 4, 26, 33, 42, 49; *Slomber,* 26; as transitional man, 13; other references, 7, 9, 12–13, 16, 17, 70, 154, 196, 244, 279, 294, 295, 303 n. 1, 305 n. 19
Spenser, John, 347 n. 42
Spenser Society, 16
Spikes, Judith Doolin, 343 n. 8
Stallybrass, Peter, 200, 334 n. 18
Stanyhurst, Richard, 26, 30, 31
Starkey, Thomas: *Dialogue between Pole and Lupset,* 65–66, 69–70; other references, 71, 72, 74, 76, 81, 87, 90, 96
State and nation, relation between, 295–301
Stein, Peter G., 315 n. 16, 317 n. 29
Stein, Stephen J., 349 n. 64
Stephens, Sir James, 97
Stevenson, Laura Caroline, 169, 170, 176–78, 330 nn. 33, 39
Still, John, 26
Stirling, Brents, 250, 337 n. 37, 342 n. 3
Stone, Lawrence, 327 n. 61
Stow, John, 12, 126, 131–32, 147
Strange's Men, 196, 216
Straw, Jack, 210, 213, 250. See also *Life and Death of Jack Straw* (play)
Strong, Roy C., 15, 53, 306 n. 21, 309

n. 34, 310 n. 46, 311 n. 54
Stubbes, Philip, 334 n. 23
Supple, B. E., 331 n. 56
Survey of Cornwall (Carew), 133–36, 143
Survey of Worcester (Habington), 134
Surveys, 131. See also Chorography and cartography

Tamburlaine (Marlowe), 199–200
Tarlton, Richard, 199, 203, 222, 224, 228, 241
Tasso, Bernardo, 44
Tasso, Torquato: "Allegory of the Poem," 47, 48; *Gerusalemme Conquistata,* 47; *Gerusalemme Liberata,* see *Gerusalemme Liberata* (Tasso); other references, 154–55, 296
Taylor, E. G. R., 327 n. 1
Taylor, Gary, 332 n. 2
Tenancy, in law, 92–93
Tennenhouse, Leonard, 304 n. 9, 333 n. 14, 341 n. 80
Tenures (Littleton), 89–99
Theater, 193–245; carnivals and clowns in, 215–28; decline of popular element, 195–204, 228–40; popular revolt representations in, 204–15; purgation from barbarism, 240–45; other references, 5, 6, 11, 16, 18, 296, 297, 299, 300. See also Henslowe, Philip; Shakespeare, William
Theater, The, 196, 197, 241, 242
Theater and Carnival (Bristol), 198
Theater of the Empire of Great Britain (Speed): authority symbols in, 116–17, 120–22; other references, 1, 126, 131, 132, 145–47
Theatrum Orbis Terrarum (Ortelius), 107, 112
Theocritus, 42
Theophilus, 90
Thomas, J. H., 102, 103, 321 n. 65
Thomas, Lord Cromwell (play), 343 n. 8
Thomas of Woodstock (play), 234–35, 237–38
Thompson, W. D. J. Cargill, 281–82, 347 n. 47, 348 n. 54
Thorne, Robert, 185, 329 n. 21
Thorne, S. E., 314 nn. 4, 11

Tillotson, K., 324 n. 32
Tillyard, E. M. W., 270, 346 n. 37
Tilney, Edmund, 210
Trade. *See* Merchants
Transitional men, 13
Travel accounts. *See* Voyages, written
Travers, Walter, 272, 277
Treatise of the New India (Eden), 151
Tribonian, 75, 84, 90
Trissino, Gian Giorgio, 44, 47
Troilus and Cressida (Shakespeare), 203
Troublesome Reign of John, King of England (play), 334 n. 25, 343 n. 8
True Law of Free Monarchies (James I), 77
"True Report of the Newfound Lands" (Peckham), 179, 183, 185
True Tragedy of Richard Duke of York (Shakespeare). See *Henry VI, Pt. 3* (Shakespeare)
True Tragedy of Richard III, The (play), 334 n. 25
Turner, Frank M., 306 n. 2
Twelfth Night (Shakespeare), 220
Tyacke, Sarah, 321 n. 1
Tyler, Wat, 209–11, 250, 336 n. 36
Tyndale, William, 265, 284

United States, law in, 17, 101–2
University wits, 199, 200, 204, 213, 218, 242
Usher, Roland G., 320 n. 58

Van Dorsten, J. A., 311 n. 54
Van Norden, Linda, 323 n. 23, 324 n. 25
Vespucci, Amerigo, 151
Vickers, Brian, 278, 347 n. 45
Victoria I, queen of England, 15
View of the Civil and Ecclesiastical Law (Ridley), 76, 78–79
Vilar, Pierre, 329 n. 24
Villiers, Sir John, 89
Vincent, Augustine, 135
Virgil: *Aeneid*, 4, 30, 155, 160; *Eclogues*, 4, 77; other references, 29, 41–42, 60, 161
Virginia Company, 172
Vives, Juan Luis, 42
Voltaire, 155
Voyages, written, 151–91; after Hakluyt,

198–91; of Camões, 155–63; chorography contrasted with, 151–53; of Hakluyt, 163–81; theater compared with, 204; other references, 5–7, 15, 18, 299. *See also* Hakluyt, Richard, the younger
Voyages (de Bry), 152

Wallerstein, Immanuel, 332 n. 59
Walsingham, Sir Francis, 201
Walton, Isaak, 285–92; *Complete Angler*, 285–90; and Hooker, 278–79, 281, 300; *Lives*, 286, 289
Warner, William, 303 n. 1
Warton, Thomas, 54–55
Warwick (Archer), 135
Waterman, Julian S., 321 n. 62
Watson, Alan, 315 n. 16, 316 n. 19
Wayne, Don E., 308 n. 26
Wealth of Nations (Smith), 189
Webb, William, 136
Webbe, William, 26, 30–31
Weber, Eugen, 350 n. 2
Webster, John, 243, 252
Weimann, Robert, 198, 223, 333 n. 12, 339 n. 56
Wells, Robin Headlam, 311 n. 57, 335 n. 27
Wells, Stanley, 332 n. 2
Westcote, Thomas, 132, 134–35, 325 n. 37, 326 n. 51
When You See Me, You Know Me (Rowley), 234, 252
Whetstone, George, 201, 334 n. 19
Whiggery, 101–2, 146
Whigham, Frank, 335 n. 28
White, Allon, 200, 334 n. 18
White, Rawlins, 265
Whitgift, John, 253, 271, 272, 278, 279, 283
Whittington, Dr., 254–56, 268
Whore of Babylon (Dekker), 252
Wiles, David, 221, 230, 231, 337 n. 41, 338 n. 48, 339 nn. 55, 62, 340 n. 66
Williams, Raymond, 333 n. 5
Willoughby, Sir Hugh, 151, 180, 182
Wilson, Richard, 336 n. 35
Wilson, Robert, 197, 199, 218, 224, 333 n. 10

Wither, George, 129–30
Wofford, Susanne, 338 n. 51
Women. *See* Gendering of state and nation
Wood, Thomas, 102
Wooden, Warren W., 345 n. 22, 346 n. 34
Woodstock (play). See *Thomas of Wood-stock* (play)
Woolf, D. R., 324 n. 30
Worcester's Men, 230, 234, 244
Wotton, Sir Henry, 286
Wyatt, Sir Thomas, 234, 237–40

Wycliffe, John, 69, 258, 263–64, 284, 288

Yates, Frances A., 310 n. 46, 344 n. 19
Yorkshire Church Notes (Dodsworth), 135
Young, Alan, 310 n. 46

Zagorin, Perez, 326 n. 61
Zamorin, 157–58, 160
Zatti, Sergio, 309 n. 39, 311 n. 50
Zimmerman, Everett, 349 n. 62